Warfare State

This book challenges the central theme of the existing histories of twentieth-century Britain, that the British state was a welfare state. It argues that it was also a warfare state, which supported a powerful armaments industry. This insight implies major revisions to our understanding of twentieth-century British history, from appeasement to wartime industrial and economic policy, and the place of science and technology in government. David Edgerton also shows how British intellectuals came to think of the state in terms of welfare and decline, and includes a devastating analysis of C. P. Snow's 'two cultures'. This groundbreaking book offers a new, post-welfarist and post-declinist, account of Britain, and an original analysis of the relations of science, technology, industry and the military. It will be essential reading for those working on the history and historiography of twentieth-century Britain, the historical sociology of war and the history of science and technology.

DAVID EDGERTON is Hans Rausing Professor at the Centre for the History of Science, Technology and Medicine at the Imperial College London. His previous publications include *England and the aeroplane: an essay on a militant and technological nation* (1991) and *Science, technology and the British industrial 'decline', 1870–1970* (1996).

Warfare State

Britain, 1920–1970

by

David Edgerton

Imperial College London

CAMBRIDGE
UNIVERSITY PRESS

CAMBRIDGE UNIVERSITY PRESS
Cambridge, New York, Melbourne, Madrid, Cape Town, Singapore, São Paulo, Delhi

Cambridge University Press
The Edinburgh Building, Cambridge CB2 8RU, UK

Published in the United States of America by Cambridge University Press, New York

www.cambridge.org
Information on this title: www.cambridge.org/9780521672313

First published 2006
Reprinted 2008

Printed in the United Kingdom at the University Press, Cambridge

A catalog record for this publication is available from the British Library

ISBN 978-0-521-85636-2 hardback
ISBN 978-0-521-67231-3 paperback

For Claire, Francesca and Lucía

Contents

Figures

Tables

Acknowledgements

I began the work that led to this book in the early 1980s, arguing that accounts of the British state in war and peace (wrongly) generalised from its civil functions only. The implications of that insight have taken a long time to work through. It has led me, for example, to reconsider the seminal work of both my supervisor, Gary Werskey, and my external examiner, Keith Middlemas. I have also had the privilege of being attacked, supported and otherwise engaged with by a number of scholars, who have seen the point of my insistence on the warfare state, even if they did not like it. At a seminar nearly fifteen years ago Charles Webster, the historian of the National Health Service, noted the damage my account did to the standard labourist historiographies; Bill Barnett responded as vigorously as one would expect to my criticisms and we have had many pleasurable encounters since. Among the economic historians and economists I am particularly indebted to Martin Daunton, Leslie Hannah, Kirsty Hughes, Frankie Lynch, Alan Milward, Deirdre McCloskey, George Peden, Jim Tomlinson and Jonathan Zeitlin. The military historians, John Ferris, David French, Sir Michael Howard, Paul Kennedy and Hew Strachan, have been kind enough to give me the confidence to stray into military history a little. Among the political scientists I am particularly grateful to David Coates, Paul Heywood, Simon Lee and Brendan O'Leary, and among the historians of science, technology and medicine to Roger Cooter, Paul Forman, John Krige, Eduardo Ortiz, Dominique Pestre, John Pickstone and Steve Sturdy.

I have had the pleasure of presenting papers associated with this book in many different departments: Security Studies at Yale; Government in Manchester, the PIPES international relations seminar at Chicago, Politics in Nottingham, Economic History in Bristol, Cambridge and Paris; the Business History Unit at the London School of Economics; a number of summer schools in British contemporary history organised by the Institute of Contemporary British History; the Socialist History Society, the European University Institute, seven different seminars at the Institute of Historical Research in London, and history of science and technology seminars at seminars at Manchester, Cambridge, Oxford, Cornell, the Smithsonian Institution, Centre d'Histoire des Sciences et des Techniques, La Villette, in Paris, Delaware, Pennsylvania and Harvard. The material on C. P. Snow was first given at the 1997 meeting of the British Association for the Advancement of Science; that on P. M. S. Blackett at a conference on Blackett held at Imperial College in 1998. Gillian Sutherland's invitation to give a paper at a conference on the history of women in higher education led me to notice the masculinisation of British science around the Second World War. Philip Gummett and Robert Bud's invitation to speak at a conference on the history of defence research laboratories stimulated my thinking on scientific civil servants. I am grateful too to organisers of conferences on a wide range of subjects, from the history of public ownership to the history of science in the twentieth century, which stimulated my thinking on many broader issues, among them Helen Mercer, Jim Tomlinson and Neil Rollings, Kirsty Hughes, Robert Millward and John Singleton, Paul Forman and José Manuel Sánchez-Ron, and John Krige and Dominique Pestre. I am particularly grateful to Dominique Pestre and the Ecole des Hautes Etudes en Sciences Sociales in Paris for the opportunity to present four seminars based on this book. The last chapter has benefited from having been given in an earlier form as a Hans Rausing Lecture in the History of Technology at the University of Cambridge.

Many other people have contributed to this project over the years. I am grateful to Richard Coopey and James Small, research fellows on the Ministry of Technology and Defence R&D project I directed at the University of Manchester (ESRC Award no. Y307 25 3002). Over the years I have benefited greatly from supervising the work of masters and doctoral students on related topics; references to some of their work will be found in the notes. Russell Potts and Colin Hughes, both former students and both former civil servants associated with the warfare state, gave me invaluable insights. Several undergraduate students undertook projects connected with this book through the Imperial College Undergraduate Research Opportunities scheme, notably Weerawan Sutthisripok, Surangsee Dechjarern and Neilesh Patel (of Johns Hopkins University). Thanks also to Admiral Peter Middleton of the 1851 Commission, David Davies of the trade union Prospect and Alison McGregor of the Ministry of Defence. Many friends and colleagues have sent me papers, suggestions, theses, films and so on I would have missed including John Bradley, Bill Brock, John Brooks, Hannah Gay, Takehiko Hashimoto, Paul Heywood, David Horner, Kurt Jacobsen, Ann King-Hall, Jonathan Harwood, Frankie Lynch, Roy MacLeod, Anna Mayer, Emily Mayhew, Alan Milward, Chris Mitchell,

Bill Moore, Carlo Morelli, Mary Morgan, Andrew Nahum, Brendan O'Leary, Guy Ortolano, Russell Potts, Dominic Power, Lisbet Rausing, Marelene and Geoffrey Rayner-Canham, Bernhard Rieger, Ralph Schroeder and Nick Tiratsoo. I am most grateful to a group of doctoral students from Imperial and elsewhere who commented on an early draft, among them Daniela Bleichmar, Sabine Clarke, Clive Cohen, Guy Ortolano and Jessica Reinisch. John Brooks saved me from some errors in naval history and very kindly passed on calculations of warship production which appear in ch. 1. Andrew Mendelsohn helped sharpen my arguments in a number of places. Martin Daunton, Kurt Jacobsen, Emily Mayhew, Russell Potts, Jim Rennie, Andrew Warwick and Waqar Zaidi read the manuscript at various stages, and I am most grateful to them for their criticisms. Martin Daunton and Emily Mayhew, and also Kurt Jacobsen, gave me quite invaluable advice on the structure of the book, which has improved the final version very significantly. My thanks. I am grateful too to referees for their comments.

I am grateful to the Royal Society for a small grant in the history of science, to the ESRC for funding of the Ministry of Technology and Defence R&D project; to Tony Benn for access to his papers; to Noble Frankland for permission to use the Tizard Papers at the Imperial War Museum; to the Blackett family for permission to use the P.M.S. Blackett Papers at the Royal Society and to Anne Barrett of Imperial College archives and to various other archives which are referred to in footnotes.

Most of this book was written while I was head of department at the Centre for the History of Science, Technology and Medicine at Imperial College, and I am grateful to my colleagues in the Centre, especially Andrew Warwick, as well as to Magda Czigany, Dorothy Wedderburn, Sir Eric Ash, Lord Oxburgh, John Archer and Bill Wakeham for their support over the last decade.

Abbreviations

AEA	Atomic Energy Authority, sometimes UKAEA
AEI	Associated Electrical Industries
AGR	Advanced Gas Cooled Reactor (nuclear reactor)
ARE	Armament Research Establishment (formerly, Research Department, Woolwich)
AScW	Association of Scientific Workers
BAC	British Aircraft Corporation
BP	British Petroleum Company
BSA	Birmingham Small Arms
CND	Campaign for Nuclear Disarmament
Comintern	Communist International (the Third International)
DNB	Dictionary of National Biography (old)
DNC	Director of Naval Construction
DSR	Director of Scientific Research
DSIR	Department of Scientific and Industrial Research
EE	English Electric
ELDO	European Space Vehicle Launcher Development Organisation
ESC	English Steel Corporation
FRS	Fellow of the Royal Society
FSSU	Federated Superannuation Scheme for Universities
GDP	Gross Domestic Product
GEC	General Electric Company
GNP	Gross National Product
FBI	Federation of British Industries
HMS	His/Her Majesty's Ship
ICI	Imperial Chemical Industries
IPCS	Institution of Professional Civil Servants
IWM	Imperial War Museum
LMS	London Midland and Scottish Railway
MAP	Ministry of Aircraft Production
Mintech	Ministry of Technology

MoS	Ministry of Supply
NATO	North Atlantic Treaty Organisation
NHS	National Health Service
NPL	National Physical Laboratory
NRDC	National Research Development Corporation
OECD	Organisation for Economic Cooperation and Development
PEP	Political and Economic Planning
PP	Parliamentary Papers
PPS	parliamentary private secretary
PRO	Public Record Office (now National Archives)
R&D	Research and development
RAE	Royal Aircraft Establishment
RAF	Royal Air Force
SBAC	Society of British Aircraft Constructors
TUC	Trades Union Congress
UKAEA	United Kingdom Atomic Energy Authority

Introduction

This book gives an alternative account of the development of one of the greatest states of the twentieth century. In the first decades of the century this state created and commanded a military-industrial-scientific complex which was, in the phrase of the time, 'second to none'. For some decades after the Second World War it held a sharply differentiated third place in a bipolar world. It was the pioneer of modern, technologically focused warfare; its naval and air forces long led the world. It was for a very long time the leading exporter of arms. It had a state machine operated not just by bureaucrats but also by technicians. It had intimate links with business, and indeed it successfully intervened in the economy, transforming its industrial structure. It saw itself as a global, liberal power, as a world political-economic policeman, an arbiter of the fate of nations. Those familiar with histories of international relations, twentieth-century warfare and twentieth-century states will, or should, find it hard to believe that that state was the British state. For the standard histories of the great powers and the relations between them associate modern military power first with Germany and then with the United States. Britain is the 'weary titan', an effete declining power, which disarmed in the interwar years and then appeased a resurgent Germany. This supposed failure to be warlike enough in the past still has enormous ideological resonance. In Britain the claim is made, to this day, as the last argument in favour of high armaments expenditure and interventions abroad; this warning from history has been deployed before every post-war conflict from the invasion of Suez in 1956 to that of Iraq in 2003. This image of Britain was also important in post-war United States politics, and indeed in US academic writing on the history of relations between nations.[1] It is not surprising then that in accounts of the twentieth-century state the British state appears, if at all, as one which became a Keynesian-welfare state which was singularly unsuccessful in

---

[1] Kevin Narizny, 'The political economy of alignment: Great Britain's commitments to Europe, 1905–1939', *International Security* 27 (2003), 184–219.

transforming the economy. In this alternative account there is a British warfare state of some importance to both world history and British history.

For those familiar with the historiography of twentieth-century Britain, and the British state, as it stood even a decade ago, the arguments presented here will seem particularly odd. Indeed their very oddity is a measure of the significance of putting the warfare state into the history of twentieth-century Britain. Most histories saw Britain as a 'welfare state', an assumption to be found in nearly all economic histories, social histories, labour histories and even the most recent cultural histories. Most histories of British armed force relied on the idea that as a liberal nation Britain was anti-militaristic. Accounts of science, technology and industry associated with its armed forces were saturated with the powerful declinist assumptions of so much Anglo-American writing on the history of the British elite, and of the British economy, industry, science and technology. Those assumptions have been challenged for some time, by many historians, but do retain a good deal of influence.

This book builds on and expands the scope and depth of the arguments presented in my *England and the aeroplane* and associated papers on Britain's 'liberal militarism' and the technocratic and militaristic critiques of twentieth-century Britain.[2] I have taken the argument in new and more radical directions than I could put forward a decade ago, partly in response to reactions to the earlier work.[3] The empirical and conceptual bases of the argument are also much wider and deeper. The book covers the period 1920 to 1970, and discusses three main areas. First, it deals with the arms industry and state policies and practices in relation to this industry, and the economy more generally. Chapter 1 provides a new account of defence expenditure and of the arms industry in the interwar years, particularly naval armaments. It also reflects on the relations

[2] *England and the aeroplane: an essay on a militant and technological nation* (London: Macmillan, 1991); 'Liberal militarism and the British state', *New Left Review*, 185 (1991), 138–69; 'The prophet militant and industrial: the peculiarities of Correlli Barnett', *Twentieth Century British History* 2 (1991), 360–79; *Science, technology and the British industrial 'decline', 1870–1970* (Cambridge: Cambridge University Press, 1996).

[3] For example, George Peden, in *Business History* 34 (1992), 104; John Ferris in *International History Review* 15 (1993), 580–3; Maurice Kirby, 'British culture and the development of high technology sectors' in Andrew Godley and Oliver Westfall (eds.), *Business history and business culture* (Manchester University Press, 1996), pp. 190–221; David Coates, *The question of UK decline: the economy, state and society* (London: Harvester Wheatsheaf, 1994), esp. pp. 181, 195–201; Kevin Theakston, *The Civil Service since 1945* (Oxford: Blackwell, 1995), pp. 191–2; Andrew Cox, Simon Lee and Joe Sanderson, *The political economy of modern Britain* (Cheltenham: Edward Elgar, 1997) and Andrew Gamble, *Britain in decline*, 4th edn (London: Macmillan, 1994).

between political economy and appeasement.[4] Chapter 2 looks at the development of the warfare state between 1939 and 1955, relating this to a more general nationalisation and scientisation of Britain in the middle of the century.[5] It gives a new account of the control of the war economy, of the wartime arms industry and of public ownership and industrial policy, defence production and the search for national technological security. Chapter 6 looks at the declining warfare state of the late 1950s and 1960s, and in particular its relationship to the 'white heat' of the 1960s, and to the Ministry of Technology in particular.[6]

Secondly, the book is concerned with the nature of the British state elite and in particular the higher reaches of the civil service. In chs. 3 and 4 a new account is provided of the civil service and of science–state relations in both peace and war. The administrators and scientific officers are compared, and the supposed conflict between them is re-examined; the first reasonably complete picture of the controllers of armament production is given, showing the continued importance in war of technical civil servants, businessmen (particularly from the arms industry) and servicemen. Chapter 4 also links the history of the expansion of the largely military scientific civil service to the history of the technical middle class and the masculinisation and scientisation of the university in mid-century.

The third element of the book is a study of interpretations and conceptualisations of the British state, and of British militarism and technocracy. Chapter 5 looks at the emergence in the late 1950s and 1960s of new technocratic ideologies which were and are central to 'declinism'. Taking C. P. Snow and the physicist P. M. S. Blackett as exemplary and influential figures, it shows how they wrote expertise out of their accounts of the British state and British warfare; how they created an influential anti-history of British technocracy, especially in relation to war. The chapter also sheds new light on the seminal 1960s' debate between Perry

---

[4] The account differs significantly from some of the most recent highly specialised work on these topics. See Elizabeth Kier, *Imagining war: French and British military doctrines between the wars* (Princeton: Princeton University Press, 1997); Cecelia Lynch, *Beyond appeasement: interpreting interwar peace movements in world politics* (Ithaca, NY: Cornell University Press, 1999); Martin Ceadel, *Semi-detached idealists: the British peace movement and international relations* (Oxford: Oxford University Press, 2000).

[5] Chapter 2 has some material from 'Whatever happened to the British warfare state? The Ministry of Supply, 1945–1951' in Helen Mercer, Neil Rollings and Jim Tomlinson (eds.), *Labour governments and private industry: the experience of 1945–1951* (Edinburgh: Edinburgh University Press, 1992), pp. 91–116 and my 'Public ownership and the British arms industry, 1920–1950' in Robert Millward and John Singleton (eds.), *The political economy of nationalisation, 1920–1950* (Cambridge: Cambridge University Press, 1995), pp. 164–88.

[6] This chapter is an expanded and revised version of 'The "white heat" revisited: British government and technology in the 1960s', *Twentieth Century British History* 7 (1996), 53–82.

Anderson and E. P. Thompson, showing how Anderson reproduced standard technocratic declinist analyses while Thompson already showed an anti-declinist streak, and was expressing a concern that the British military-industrial complex was ignored by declinist analysts such as Anderson.

Chapter 7 looks at how intellectuals (including particularly political economists and historians) dealt with the key issue of the relationship of Britain to militarism, and how the welfare state, rather than the welfare *and* warfare states, became central to the historiography of modern Britain. It does so by examining how a standard image of Germany shifted from being a means to celebrate Britishness to a critique of Britishness, and how a militaristic critique of Britain became central to understanding Britain's relationship to the armed services. It also looks at how social democratic historians linked war to the rise of the welfare state and made this the central theme of the historiography of twentieth-century Britain. It also examines the return, from the late 1970s, of the techno-declinism that had been so important a part of British culture in the late 1950s and early 1960s. Chapter 8 examines how the existing literature on industry, technology and science in modern war (including the important literature focused on the USA) systematically takes out the military and/or treats it in very specific ways. It proposes a new framework for thinking about the relations between science, technology, industry and war in the twentieth century.[7] It explores what is called historiography from below as, among other things, a means of understanding the crucial hidden assumptions made in the existing academic and non-academic literatures on these topics.

Putting the British warfare state into the twentieth-century history of Britain is to rewrite some of the most important passages of its political, military, economic and cultural history. The revisions to standard accounts are at least as great as those brought about by highlighting the 'fiscal-military state' of the eighteenth century.[8] Many of the most

---

[7] This chapter has some material which first appeared in David Edgerton, 'British scientific intellectuals and the relations of science, technology and war' in Paul Forman and J. M. Sánchez Ron (eds.), *National military establishments and the advancement of science: studies in twentieth century history* (Dordrecht: Kluwer, 1996), pp. 1–35.

[8] See John Brewer, *The sinews of power: war, money and the English state 1688–1783* (London: Unwin Hyman, 1989). Of course, Edwardian militarism has long been the subject of revisionist thinking. See Anne Summers, 'Militarism in Britain before the Great War', *History Workshop Journal* 2 (1976), 104–23; David French, *British economic and strategic planning, 1905–1915* (London: Allen & Unwin, 1982); Bernard Semmel, *Liberalism and naval strategy: ideology, interest and seapower during the Pax Britannica* (London: Allen & Unwin, 1986); J. T. Sumida, *In defence of naval supremacy* (London: Unwin Hyman, 1989); Avner Offer, *The First World War: an agrarian interpretation* (Oxford: Clarendon Press, 1989); J. M. Hobson, 'The military-extraction gap and the weary titan: the

common images in the historiography of twentieth-century Britain will now need explaining instead of being parts of explanations. For example, rather than 'disarming' in the interwar years Britain kept arms spending high and focused on the most modern military technologies. Rather than leading to 'appeasement', liberal internationalism, which had a strong political-economic core, was not only anti-Nazi but militantly so. The development of the welfare state around the Second World War changed the structure of the central state much less than the quickly expanding warfare state. The already strong warfare state had expanded its scope and power, militarising and nationalising Britain. From the mid-1930s to the late 1940s warlike spending went up much more than welfare spending, and the 'welfareness' of British state spending did not return to early 1930s levels until 1970. The pre-war state was expert and the post-war state was even more expert, despite the image of dominance by non-expert administrators. C. P. Snow's notion of the 'two cultures', so influential in understanding the British elite, including the state elite, was garbled and wrong-headed, but for all that typical, technocratic, declinist, anti-history of Britain. The 1964–70 Labour government, far from trying, and failing, to inject technocracy into the British *ancien régime*, instead cut back on techno-nationalist projects and ceased to believe that Britain suffered from a lack of innovation. A great modernisation project brought into being alongside the creation of declinism provided the context in which key theses of declinism were refuted.

The last decade and a half has seen the beginnings of a transformation in the study of twentieth-century Britain. Breaking away from 'inverted Whiggism' and 'declinist' accounts, and the 'decline debate' more generally, has been of central importance in rethinking the broad contours of twentieth-century British history.[9] For declinism was never confined to economic history, nor was it just an interpretative framework: it painted very particular pictures of Britain, its elite, its businesses, its armed forces, its culture, which have proved very influential.[10] Not surprisingly, anti-declinism has gone along with a powerful sense of the historical stories

---

fiscal-sociology of British defence policy 1870–1913', *Journal of European Economic History* 22 (1993), 461–506; Niall Ferguson, 'Public finance and national security: the domestic origins of the First World War revisited', *Past and Present* no. 142 (1994), 141–68 and *The pity of war* (London: Allen Lane, 1998); Nicolas Lambert, *Sir John Fisher's naval revolution* (Columbia, SC: South Carolina University Press, 1999).

[9] See my 'Science and technology in British business history', *Business History* 29 (1987), 84, 'Barnett's audit of war: an audit', *Contemporary Record* 4 (1990), 37–9 and *England and the aeroplane.*

[10] See for examples of broad analyses of the issue and its general ideological significance: D. N. McCloskey, 'The politics of stories in historical economics' in *If you're so smart* (Chicago: Chicago University Press, 1990), pp. 40–55; Edgerton 'The prophet militant and industrial'; W. D. Rubinstein, *Capitalism, culture and economic decline in Britain,*

about twentieth-century Britain being seriously inadequate. One historian observes that there is a sort of history of Britain which 'explains an outcome which never happened ... by a cause that is equally imagined'.[11] He only half-jokingly suggested that in reading comparative business histories

a helpful rule of thumb is to assume that (at least after World War I) what they say about Germany applies to the United Kingdom, that what they say about the United Kingdom applies to Italy; and that neither can be assumed to have anything whatsoever to do with competitive advantage or economic performance.[12]

Another historian notes in a review of literature on the Royal Air Force (RAF) that some recent works 'begin by invoking causes which do not exist, continue with arguments based on imagination instead of evidence, and end by describing events which did not happen'.[13] Another asked whether the opposite to what is stated in much literature on British science and technology might be closer to an adequate historical picture than that put forward.[14] It is little wonder then that a recent textbook on British economic history is animated by a 'mood of growing disenchantment with the level of debate'.[15]

Welfarism has been at least as important as declinism, probably more so, in shaping the historiography of twentieth-century Britain. It remains central to the understanding of the British state, at least after 1914. Yet here too great changes are under way in understanding the place of the military in the state, and in society more generally. A key indicator is that the term 'militarism' is now being used by British historians in studies of twentieth-century Britain. For example a military historian writes that if militarism is 'interpreted as a veneration of military values and

1750–1990 (London: Routledge, 1993); Barry Supple, 'Fear of failing: economic history and the decline of Britain', *Economic History Review* 47 (1994), 441–58; Jim Tomlinson, 'Inventing "decline": the falling behind of the British economy in the post-war years', *Economic History Review* 49 (1996), 731–57, and *The politics of decline* (London: Arnold, 2000); P. Mandler, 'Against "Englishness": English culture and the limits to rural nostalgia, 1850–1940', *Transactions of the Royal Historical Society*, 6th series, 7 (1997), 155–75; Peter Mandler, *The fall and rise of the stately home* (London: Yale University Press, 1997); David Matless, *Landscape and Englishness* (London: Reaktion Books, 1998); P. Mandler, 'The consciousness of modernity? Liberalism and the English national character, 1870–1940' in M. Daunton and B. Rieger (eds.), *Meanings of modernity: Britain from the late-Victorian era to World War II* (Oxford: Berg, 2001), pp. 119–44.

[11] Leslie Hannah, 'Afterthoughts', *Business and Economic History* 24 (1995), 248.

[12] Leslie Hannah, 'The American miracle, 1875–1950, and after: a view in the European mirror', *Business and Economic History* 24 (1995), 204–5.

[13] John R. Ferris, 'The Air Force brats' view of history: recent writing and the Royal Air Force, 1918–1960', *International History Review* 20 (1998), 120.

[14] Edgerton, *Science, technology and the British industrial 'decline'*, p. 69.

[15] Alan Booth, *The British economy in the twentieth century* (London: Palgrave, 2001), p. ix.

appearances in excess of what is strictly necessary for effective defence, then it is not as inapplicable to Britain as the orthodoxy allows'.[16]

This book challenges the welfarist interpretation of the history of the twentieth-century British state. It also seeks to understand it, and indeed its close relationship with declinism. The book looks at the history of the warfare/welfare and the decline/growth dichotomies and other binary oppositions which have been central in understanding the British state. Among them are the opposition between the military and the civilian, which turns out to be hugely important to our understanding of industry, science, technology and war in the twentieth century; that between liberalism and militarism, which is central to the understanding of British militarism; that between 'specialists' and 'generalists' or 'amateurs' and 'professionals' in the civil service, the core issue in its historiography; and the overarching 'two cultures' opposition between science and arts, a dichotomy central to the study of the intellectual elite and much else besides. This book shows how these particular oppositions emerged from particular understandings of Britain and the British state and were forged in particular contests about reforming the state. More generally this is an invitation to see how important particular critiques of the state have been in its formation and understanding. British intellectuals, and politicians, have thought of the state in very distinctive ways, using distinctive language – that of political economy, welfare and technocratic and militaristic critiques among others. Particular social-scientific understandings were also, I show, crucial to forming the contemporary understanding of the state, and historians' understandings too, in ways which we need to appreciate more. We need to recognise the structures of analysis embodied in concepts like the welfare state, Keynesianism and nationalisation, all standard terms in analyses of the development of the twentieth-century state.

The history of the state, the book argues, has been understood in very particular ways, focusing on one side of each of the dichotomies. In many accounts the British state is all welfare, administrators, civilians, arts graduates, Keynesianism and nationalisation. The overall argument of this book is not that the state should be seen as all warfare, specialists, military men, scientists and engineers and technocratic intervention, that it was a warfare state *rather* than a welfare state or a nation becoming more powerful rather than declining. The book does not invert the usual dichotomies, it subverts them. It tells a different story about the state and about the conceptualisation of the state than those that can be told from within the standard conceptualisations. The post-declinist and

---

[16] Hew Strachan, *The politics of the British army* (Oxford: Clarendon Press, 1997), pp. 264–5.

post-welfarist historiography it calls for will not come from ignoring declinism or welfarism, or writing histories that merely challenge such accounts, which we might call anti-welfarist and anti-declinist histories. On the contrary, it must understand the significance of welfarism and declinism to the history and the historiography of twentieth-century Britain. In arguing for a new history of the British state the book will have fully succeeded only if it succeeds in this second task as well. Indeed, I hope the book will help open up the history of welfare and of *relative* economic decline to new questions, as much as the history of the warfare state and of British economic development.

My argument thus does not rest on existing historiography or on a critique of existing historiography but rather on a series of crucially important re-understandings of our accounts of the British state, and the histories of twentieth-century science, technology, industry and war. For this reason it cannot deal with existing literature in the conventional way. Academic historians usually fill lacunae in the literature; we revisit (empirically and/or theoretically) well-established debates, challenge well-developed authoritative original positions, claiming original contributions, and/or synthesise specialist literatures. We also contextualise particular cases within wider existing historiographies. None of these strategies has been usable in this case. The problem is not a lack of writing on the themes covered here but the particular ways in which we know what we know.[17] What this book is arguing against and across, what it stands instead of, is by the very nature of the project not easily – or profitably – discussible in terms of existing accounts. For example, declinism and welfarism interacted in very particular and complex ways with seemingly neutral specialised accounts of, say, the civil service or the armed forces or the universities. These specialised histories are already contextualised within particular histories of Britain. It is difficult to untangle one from another, and thus the crucially important reconfigurations of arguments at many levels which putting the warfare state in involves are not easily described. I deliberately do not set out to attack a

---

[17] The usual academic response to a situation in which there was no great academic tradition would be that we should start from scratch – it is not beyond the capacity of academics to convince ourselves, and others, that we know less than we really do, thereby increasing the stock of collective ignorance. It would be going too far to engage only with the private knowledge of the informed, though the public can be more challenging to argue with than the academy. This was brought home to me by discovering that things I have written against particular academic positions caused no surprise to lay people; for those working in the aircraft industry it was too obvious for comment that the industry was essentially military; for those like me who read about it, this was a surprise. It would be amusing to tally the claims to ignorance now exaggeratedly made in the academic literature of the 'surprisingly little is known about' kind.

particular historical literature. Instead I write about a wide range of historical and non-historical literatures, from many different periods, as part of a wider story about the state and how it was understood. One aim is to demonstrate the pervasiveness of (and changes in) the understandings I am criticising as partial accounts. I want to avoid any suggestion that I am attacking straw men, or outdated conceptions, or particular recent ones, or that I am engaged in a debate on decline. I also want to avoid the danger that in convincing readers of the significance of the warfare state, I undermine the idea that the welfare state was indeed central to the conceptualisation of the British state. The aim is to understand how and why welfarism and declinism became so significant, and how and why the warfare state has not registered in the elite British imagination. Part of the way this is done is by exploring the intellectual traffic between practitioners and specialist historians, by studying the assumptions of specialist historians, by examining, historically, the thinking of practitioners.

The British warfare state has been surrounded by near impregnable thickets of historical accounts and other accounts which camouflage it. A title/keyword search on militarism in any large library catalogue will show that there is a substantial literature on German, Japanese, Soviet and many 'third world' species of militarism, but virtually none associating the concept with Britain. Furthermore, in all the vast commentary on the British state, there is hardly even an allusion to the 'military-industrial complex' or the 'military-scientific complex', ideas which are central to the discussion of militarism in the United States. In post-war Britain both the left and right, for different reasons, were to complain of the weakness of the state. In Britain, it seems, there was apparently no close engagement with industry and the state, or interpenetration of state and science.

Admitting the existence of a modern and modernising warfare state, in peace or war, would have entailed profound changes in the analysis of the state, and of the place of expertise, science and technology in the life of the state and the nation. It would have discomfited the post-war right, which complained of a lack of militarism, particularly but not only in the interwar years, to keep arms spending up. But it would also upset the arguments of the left which asserted that the state was incapable of modernising intervention and that it was hostile to expertise. Indeed a catalogue search would suggest not only that Britain has had no militarism but no technocrats either. A large literature supports the idea that this has been a central problem for British economic and military performance.[18] British

---

[18] Andrew Massey, *Technocrats and nuclear policy: the influence of professional experts in policy-making* (Aldershot: Avesbury, 1988), is the only book on Britain I know which uses the term in a title.

technocrats, of left and right, consistently complained of the supposed anti-scientific and anti-technological character of the British state and industry and sought to advance their positions through such critiques. Particularly long-standing and influential has been the technocratic critique of the higher civil service, which is seen as being made up of men trained in the classics and at best, history, rather than the scientists and engineers that a modern society was felt to need as state administrators.

The militaristic and technocratic critiques of twentieth-century Britain have proved very influential, particularly but not only in declinist writing.[19] They were often themselves historical in the sense of drawing on past cases, but they were often anti-histories in that, paradoxically, they removed the military or technocratic from British history. Instead, they often provided elaborate historical explanations for what they took to be a weak commitment to the armed forces and to science and technology. I turn these critiques around in a very particular way. I take the very ubiquity in the post-war years of the claim that Britain was an anti-militarist and anti-technological society (which I demonstrate) as evidence not of the theory put forward, but of the success (and power of) the militaristic and technocratic strands in British culture.

Such a move implies a very different account of British cultural and intellectual history, for this too is dominated by assumptions linked to declinism and welfarism. Much discussion of 'Englishness' or the 'English ideology' has long been a site for the reproduction of declinist theses, rather than a re-examination of 'Englishness' and how it has changed.[20] Furthermore, it is focused on humanistic/literary intellectuals, just like the technocratic critique.[21] It is thus hardly surprising

[19] Edgerton, 'The prophet militant and industrial'.

[20] For examples see Patrick Wright, *On living in an old country: the national past in contemporary Britain* (London: Verso, 1985); Tom Nairn, *The enchanted glass* (London: Radius, 1988); Angus Calder, *The myth of the Blitz* (London: Cape, 1991); David Morgan and Mary Evans, *The battle for Britain: citizenship and ideology in the Second World War* (London: Routledge, 1993); Meredith Veldman, *Fantasy, the bomb, and the greening of Britain: romantic protest, 1945–1980* (Cambridge: Cambridge University Press, 1994); and many chapters in A. K. Mayer and C. J. Lawrence (eds.), *Regenerating England: science, medicine and culture in interwar Britain* (Amsterdam: Rodopi, 2000). For an argument making explicit the connection between declinism and the question of national identity see R. English and Michael Kenny, 'British decline or the politics of declinism?', *British Journal of Politics and International Relations* 1 (1999), 252–66, and 'Public intellectuals and the question of British decline', *British Journal of Politics and International Relations* 3 (2001), 259–83.

[21] Studies of scientific and technical intellectuals are rare. Among the exceptions are Bill Luckin, *Questions of power* (Manchester: Manchester University Press, 1990), my own *England and the aeroplane*; Patrick Wright, *The village that died for England: the strange case of Tyneham* (London: Cape, 1995) and his *Tank: the progress of a monstrous war machine* (London: Faber, 2000) and Mayer and Lawrence, *Regenerating England*.

that it is only recently that the significance of declinism on British cultural history and cultural historians has been appreciated.[22] Welfarism too remains central to cultural and intellectual history. Even the newer literature focused on 'national identity', centrally concerned with gender, race, empire and nation, is best seen as a rereading of the conventional welfarist accounts rather than as a challenge to them.[23] Post-declinist and post-welfarist cultural histories will incorporate political economy, militarism and technocracy and, of course, declinism itself, in their accounts, rather than being carriers of their implicit assumptions.

Long ago E. P. Thompson argued for the centrality of political economy and science to English ideology.[24] It was a vital element in Britain's self-understanding, and in particular, it turns out, Britain's understanding of militarism and of how to wage war. Political economy was, I show, the language of preference for the critical discussion of international relations, war, militarism and the state in Britain in the interwar years and beyond, as well as, and more obviously, economic performance. Scientists, engineers and their propagandists also derived much of their language and imagery from political economy: science and political economy both saw war in civilian terms for example. It is also vital to understand the significance of critiques of liberal political economy for our conceptualisation of the British state and British liberalism. For welfarism, declinism and the militaristic and technocratic critiques are all critiques of a particular liberal political-economic conception of the state. All correlated well with economic nationalism, hostility to *laissez-faire*, and celebration of the continental European (and particularly the German) way of doing things.[25] The militaristic critique saw liberalism as a pacific, even pacifist, doctrine, which was associated with vacuous moralising and a flawed analysis of the real world. Britain, as a liberal nation in this sense, was seen as being reluctant to invest in armed force

[22] See Marcus Collins, 'The fall of the English gentleman: the national character in decline, c. 1918–1970', *Historical Research* 75 (2002), 90–111, for a splendid account of how declinism did for the gentleman.
[23] See, for example, Richard Weight and Abigail Beach (eds.), *The right to belong: citizenship and national identity in Britain* (London: I. B. Tauris, 1998); Kevin Davey, *English imaginaries: studies in Anglo-British modernity* (London: Lawrence & Wishart, 1999); Richard Weight, *Patriots: national identity in Britain, 1940–2000* (London: Macmillan, 2002); Robert Colls, *Identity of England* (Oxford: Oxford University Press, 2002).
[24] E. P. Thompson, 'The peculiarities of the English' (1965), reprinted in *The poverty of theory* (London: Merlin, 1978), p. 57. The other two points were that Anderson and Nairn, the butts of this analysis, ignored the Protestant and bourgeois democratic inheritance and confused the British empirical idiom with an empiricist ideology.
[25] See Peter Clarke and Clive Trebilcock (eds.), *Understanding decline* (Cambridge, Cambridge University Press, 1997) and my review in *The Historical Journal* 42 (1999), 313–14.

and especially armies; governments, backed by liberal public opinion, kept the forces on short rations through the power of the ultra-liberal Treasury. In this account only war broke the complacent consensus – mass armies were sent to Europe in two world wars. In other words Britain became European. The technocratic critique saw the elite as amateur and old fashioned, as financial and commercial, committed to *laissez-faire*, which all had disastrous consequences for economic and military performance. Again, only in war did the genuinely creative new men rise temporarily from despised marginality to centrality: war was as crucial for the technocrats as for the militarists. The welfarist, social democratic accounts focusing on the welfare state were also profoundly critical of liberal Britain for its lack of commitment to welfare and a strong state: they also saw war as providing the opportunity for labour to create, or have created for it, a welfare state. More than that, success in modern war was a matter of creating a welfare state which could mobilise the citizenry. The standard post-war view was that the elite remained too economically liberal, to a lesser extent too pacifist, too committed to a weak state, and that only welfarism became newly significant. Of course, it also supposedly remained hostile to European integration. We need to appreciate, I suggest, the dramatic but largely unrecognised change in Britain between the interwar and post-war periods. For all the insistence on the importance of the war as a turning point, it is not sufficiently recognised that Britain was no longer as liberal – economically, politically, intellectually – as many supposed it remained. Britain changed radically, in many more ways than are captured by ideas of the rise of the welfare state or social democracy. Welfarism was crucially important, but so were technocracy, militarism and declinism, though these are invisible to themselves (another reason why the term anti-history is useful in relation to them).

One major difficulty in thinking about the military-industrial-scientific complex in the British case has been that the relations between modernity and militarism have been understood in very particular ways. Although it is now a commonplace to put the state and the military back into history, for example in the new historical sociologies that have followed Theda Skocpol's pioneering work, the history of science, technology and industry, even in relation to the military, continues to be treated differently.[26]

---

[26] See the key work: Theda Skocpol, *States and social revolutions* (Cambridge: Cambridge University Press, 1979). On expertise see Theda Skocpol and Kenneth Finegold, 'State capacity, economic intervention and the early New Deal', *Political Science Quarterly* 97 (1982), 255–78, and for a rare questioning of the usual stories about technology in historical sociology, Randall Collins, *Weberian sociological theory* (Cambridge: Cambridge University Press, 1986).

Science, technology and industry have routinely and systematically been seen, without need of argument or evidence, as products of civil society. In the standard arguments this civilian industry, science, technology has transformed modern war. This was the dominant view of political economists, scientific intellectuals and some military intellectuals too, from say Norman Angell to C. P. Snow and on to Mary Kaldor, and it has become enshrined in the work of historians, most eloquently perhaps in William H. McNeill's *The pursuit of power*.[27] As a result we have a historiography of war economies in which the military and military agencies hardly figure; histories of science and technology and the military, which are histories only of civilian science and technology applied to war; and histories of the relations of industry, technology, science and war which see the transformation of war in the twentieth century as the civilianisation of war. 'Civilian' and 'liberal' are very useful modifiers to describe modern 'militarism', but we need to take care not to identify modern science, technology and industry only with the modifiers.[28] This book suggests that we have had a very particular and very partial account of modern warfare which has systematically downplayed, without this being evident, the role of the military, and it puts the history of war and the military into the history of industry, science and technology in new ways.

Militarism has been scientifically, technically and industrially creative in ways we have barely begun to understand. Specifically military/state sciences and technologies and industries have been crucial for the development of twentieth-century science and technology and also warfare. They tend to be left out of the history of twentieth-century science, which focuses on academic particle physics and biology. The state, specifically its military branches, will appear here as one of the creators of a new research-oriented science, and modern armed forces, long before the Second World War, and not as a late, reluctant, respondent to a new scientific revolution. My account also stresses the need to distinguish between science or technology, on the one hand, and 'research' on the other, and indeed to distinguish between the advisory and other roles scientists and engineers have played. This latter distinction is central to overturning the standard stories of science at war. In my account important state and industrial military laboratories, design centres and

---

[27] Oxford: Blackwell, 1982.

[28] Michael Sherry, *In the shadow of war: the United States since the 1930s* (New Haven: Yale University Press, 1995), pp. 80–1. See also Edgerton, 'Liberal militarism', where I argued that 'liberal militarism' was a civilian-controlled and inspired form of militarism directed at the civilians and industry of enemy nations.

workshops were responsible for most of the major innovations in military technology of the Second World War. I shift, and show the significance of so doing, from what I show is the existing unacknowledged emphasis on the work of (some) civilian academic scientists to the history of military research and development in peace and war. More generally I argue that histories of science and technology must take on the full scope of the twentieth-century scientific and technical enterprises, and not merely parts of them.[29]

This book also re-examines more generally the relations between national innovative capacity and both military and economic power. First, it gives a rather different account of national innovative capacities than the usual overly academic-centred ones, by taking full account of industry and the military. Secondly, it rejects, and shows the importance of so doing, the deeply rooted assumption that national rates of economic growth correlate positively with national investments in innovation, for Britain, or for any other country. This key assumption of techno-nationalism, which is also central to most global accounts of the place of science and technology in economic growth, does not hold.

[29] 'De l'innovation aux usages. Dix thèses éclectiques sur l'histoire des techniques', *Annales Histoires, Sciences, Sociales*, nos. 4–5 (1998), 815–37; the English version, 'From innovation to use: ten (eclectic) theses on the history of technology', is in *History and Technology* 16 (1999), 1–26.

1 The military-industrial complex in the interwar years

The 1935 Defence White Paper, the very first in a continuing series of annual reviews of defence policy, regretted that 'our desire to lead the world towards disarmament by our example of unilateral disarmament has not succeeded'.[1] For decades afterwards there reigned a 'consensus of historical opinion ... that by 1932 retrenchment had reduced Britain's defence services and armaments industry to a dangerously low level'.[2] Even that is rather an understatement: there seemed to be a competition among historians to find new ways of evoking for the reader the full horror of the cutbacks without making the point specific enough to make it easily verifiable or refutable. In the 1960s the social democratic historian A. J. P. Taylor accepted that in the very early 1930s the National government was 'almost as reluctant to spend money on armaments as on the unemployed'.[3] In the 1970s the naval historian Paul Kennedy pronounced with assurance that 'governmental concern to balance the budget by cutting down armaments expenditure' had the distressing consequence that

when the decision for *rearmament* was made in the more threatening circumstances of the 1930s, industry itself could not adequately respond ... The productive capacity of the country as a whole, and those of specialized armament firms in particular, were too run-down to be reversed without major investment in factories and machine-tools.[4]

In the 1980s the military historian Brian Bond repeated a similar refrain:

Britain demobilised her huge, conscript armies with remarkable speed after 1918 and at the same time largely dismantled her defence industries. Swingeing

---

[1] *Statement on the Defence Estimates*, Cmd 4827, March 1935.
[2] George Peden, *British rearmament and the Treasury* (Edinburgh: Edinburgh University Press, 1979), p. 8.
[3] A. J. P. Taylor, *English history, 1914–1945* (Harmondsworth: Penguin, 1975), p. 450 (first published 1965).
[4] Paul Kennedy, *The realities behind diplomacy* (London: Fontana, 1981), p. 230; emphasis in the original.

reductions were made in the budget of all three services [after 1921] and in the disturbed economic conditions of the next decade further cuts were made every year.[5]

More recently some historians have been even more categorical. Donald Cameron Watt wrote of a near hopeless situation for Britain:

During the 1920s her three services had barely existed on budgets cut to the bone. In 1931 and 1932 all kinds of normal current expenditure on her armed forces had been postponed ... In 1933, for the third year running, the Chiefs of Staff warned that the level of Britain's armed forces and their state of preparedness was not adequate to defend Britain or her overseas dominions and possessions against foreign attack.[6]

Examples of such bleak assessments could easily be multiplied, despite the glaring fact that, as George Peden had pointed out in 1979, 'one would be hard put to argue that Britain was in a worse position than Germany in 1932'.[7] Or indeed, as we shall see, than any other power. Britain may not have spent enough according to historians writing with a very particular form of hindsight; but that is a very different proposition from claiming that it spent less than its competitors or allies.

Specialist inquiries into each armed service and the arms industry have habitually presented detailed accounts and explanations to match the gloomy conclusions of the general accounts.[8] For example, the official historian of factories and plant in the Second World War wrote of the interwar years that the 'armament industry reached the verge of extinction' and complained that there 'was a general lack of foreign orders' for

---

[5] Brian Bond, *War and society in Europe, 1870–1970* (London: Fontana, 1984), p. 146.

[6] D. C. Watt, *How war came* (London: Mandarin, 1990), p. 20 (first published 1989).

[7] Peden, *British rearmament*, p. 8.

[8] A. J. Grant, *Steel and ships: the history of John Brown* (London: Michael Joseph, 1950); M. M. Postan, *British war production* (London: HMSO, 1952); W. Hornby, *Factories and plant* (London: HMSO, 1958); J. D. Scott, *Vickers: a history* (London: Weidenfeld and Nicolson, 1962); O. F. G. Hogg, *The Royal Arsenal: its background, origins and subsequent history*, 2 vols. (London: Oxford University Press, 1963); M. M. Postan, D. Hay and J. D. Scott, *Design and development of weapons* (London, HMSO, 1964); R. P. T. Davenport Hines, 'The British armaments industry during disarmament', unpublished doctoral thesis, University of Cambridge (1979); M. S. Moss and J. R. Hume, *Beardmore: the history of a Scottish industrial giant* (London: Heinemann, 1979); Eric Mensforth, *Family engineers* (London: Ward Lock, 1981); R. P. T. Davenport Hines, *Dudley Docker: the life and times of a trade warrior* (Cambridge: Cambridge University Press, 1984); Hugh B. Peebles, *Warshipbuilding on the Clyde: naval orders and the prosperity of the Clyde shipbuilding industry, 1889–1939* (Edinburgh: John Donald, 1987); G. A. H. Gordon, *British seapower and procurement between the wars: a re-appraisal of rearmament* (London: Macmillan, 1988); Kenneth Warren, *Armstrongs of Elswick: growth in engineering and armaments to the merger with Vickers* (London: Macmillan, 1989); Kenneth Warren, *Steel, ships and men: Cammell Laird, 1824–1993* (Liverpool: Liverpool University Press, 1998).

British armaments.[9] Paul Kennedy complained that in the 'years of decay' the most powerful navy that the world had ever seen, the Royal Navy of 1918, was dragged down by an 'ailing economy' and the 'unprecedented public demand for defence cuts'.[10] He described the warship building industry thus:

The long lean years of virtually no construction, the lack of incentive for technological innovation, the unwillingness to invest capital in what had been regarded as unprofitable fields and, above all, that steady, cancerous decay of the country's industrial sinews, were now [in the mid-1930s] showing their fruit. The drastic reduction in the [war]shipbuilding industry – in 1914 it was building 111 warships, in 1924 only twenty-five – was the chief cause of the delays in the Admiralty's rearmament schemes.[11]

M. M. Postan's official history, *British war production*, published in 1952, is a key source for a similar argument about the supposedly struggling interwar aircraft industry:

the re-equipment of the 20s and early 30s was little more than nominal. In the early 1930s the bulk of the Air Force was still made up of types dating to the war of 1914–18. The types available for replacement, though more recent, were not only few in number, but as a rule were below the technical and operational standards of the day. As late as 1935 the principal 'new' fighter coming into service was the Gloster-Gauntlet with a speed of 230 mph and the 'new' bombers were the Hind and the Hendon ... The general impression is that throughout these years the quality of RAF equipment was falling below the standards which in the early thirties were being established in foreign countries, such as Italy and the United States ... the Air Ministry had great difficulty in maintaining its industrial reserves. The aircraft firms, including the principal engine firms, found themselves in a position of chronic penury and sometimes on the very verge of bankruptcy.

The 'diet' of orders, he went on, 'though just sufficient to keep the bulk of the firms alive, was too meagre to enable them to keep pace with the aircraft industry abroad, especially in the United States, and to acquire the equipment and technique for quantity production'.[12] This potent image of deficiency was reproduced again and again.[13] As we shall see, nearly

---

[9] Where this means armaments other than shipbuilding and aircraft: Hornby, *Factories and plant*, p. 25.

[10] Paul Kennedy, *The rise and fall of British naval mastery* (London: Macmillan, 1983) p. 316 (first published 1976).

[11] Ibid., p. 339.   [12] Postan, *British war production*, p. 5.

[13] 'On the eve of major rearmament in 1936 ... the British aircraft industry remained a cottage industry with obsolescent products; sleepy firms with facilities little more than experimental workshops employed hand-work methods and centred on their design departments', said Correlli Barnett, *Audit of war: the illusion and reality of Britain as a great nation* (London: Macmillan, 1986), p. 130. According to Malcolm Smith, '[c]hief among' the difficulties faced during rearmament 'was the shallow base of aircraft

every element of these arguments about interwar defence spending, the specialised arms industry and the shipbuilding and aircraft industries is either straightforwardly wrong or in need of serious reconsideration.

As is evident from the continuing prevalence of the analysis reported above, revisionist accounts have been slow in coming and patchy in impact. George Peden's study of the Treasury and rearmament showed, crucially, that the Treasury did not hinder rearmament but helped direct it towards the build up of the air force and the navy rather than the army.[14] For the 1920s, John Ferris has stressed the high level of defence spending, the strength of the Royal Navy and the RAF, and dismissed the hoary myth of the ten-year rule which, needless to say, still appears regularly. He suggested that British foreign and defence policy should be labelled 'liberal realist'.[15] Dick Richardson, in the first serious historical challenge to the myth of disarmament, has shown that in the late 1920s of Britain's leaders only one, Viscount Cecil, believed in disarmament and the remainder were largely actively hostile: 'the philosophical propensities of the Cabinet and the foreign policy making elite of the country were sceptical of, if not outrightly opposed to, the whole movement for arms limitation'.[16] He concluded that the 'allegation – supported

production in Britain' (*British air strategy between the wars* (Oxford: Clarendon Press, 1984), p. 247). See also Peter King, *Knights of the air* (London: Constable, 1989), chs. 11–14; Keith Hayward, *The British aircraft industry* (Manchester: Manchester University Press, 1989); Peter Fearon 'The British airframe industry and the state, 1918–35', *Economic History Review* 27 (1974), 236–51; Peter Fearon, 'The vicissitudes of a British aircraft company: Handley Page Limited between the wars', *Business History* 20 (1978), 63–86; Peter Fearon, 'Aircraft manufacturing' in N. K. Buxton and D. H. Aldcroft (eds.), *British industry between the wars* (London: Scolar Press, 1979), pp. 216–40; Peter Fearon, 'The growth of aviation in Britain', *Journal of Contemporary History* 20 (1985), 21–40. See also A. J. Robertson, 'The British airframe industry and the state in the interwar period: a comment', *Economic History Review* 28 (1975), 648–57 to which Fearon replied in 'The British airframe industry and the state in the interwar period: a reply', *Economic History Review* 28 (1975), 658–62. In 1940 Britain produced more aircraft than any country in the world, and 50 per cent more than the Germans. Malcolm Smith suggests that the strengths of the RAF and the Luftwaffe on 1 September 1939 were about equal in terms of numbers of bombers and interceptor fighters (Smith, *British air strategy*, table XI, p. 338). As far as quality is concerned the consensus is that the best on each side in 1939/40 were about equal, especially in the case of fighters; for bombers one study noted that the 'He 111s, Do 17s and Ju 88s were marginally better than the Wellingtons, Hampdens and Whitleys of RAF Bomber Command' (Matthew Cooper, *The German air force, 1933–1945: an anatomy of failure* (London: Jane's, 1981), p. 87). See also Erik Lund, 'The industrial history of strategy: reevaluating the wartime record of the British aviation industry in comparative perspective, 1919–1945', *Journal of Military History* 62 (1998), 75–99.

[14] Peden, *British rearmament*.

[15] John Ferris, *The evolution of British strategic policy 1919–1926* (London: Macmillan, 1989).

[16] Dick Richardson, *The evolution of British disarmament policy in the 1920s* (London: Pinter, 1989), p. 27.

by a number of historians – that Britain disarmed while other powers did not, is far from the truth'.[17] Some new work on interwar peace movements has also shown the shallowness, and indeed lack of substance, of the claim that they sought or caused unilateral disarmament and appeasement.[18] A second set of reassessments, starting in the early 1990s, has come from a historiography which has been overtly critical of the declinism that has so pervaded the historiography of British power.[19] In the case of the aircraft industry, contrary to the standard wisdom the British industry was at least one of the largest in the world and was far from being on the verge of bankruptcy.[20] However, many RAF histories still hold to the familiar older images.[21] In the case of the army, Paul Harris has neatly inverted the picture presented by critics, notably Sir Basil Liddell Hart and Major-General J. F. C. Fuller, by stressing the importance, indeed perhaps the exaggerated importance, of tanks to the interwar army.[22] The standing and authority of these two key 'military intellectuals', who contributed so much to the image of technically deficient and backward interwar forces, have been drastically revised.[23] In the case of the navy and the naval-industrial complex, the revisionist arguments have been much weaker (hence the

[17] Richardson, *British disarmament policy*, p. 98. See also Gregory C. Kennedy, 'Britain's policy-making elite, the naval disarmament puzzle, and public opinion, 1927–1932', *Albion* 26 (1994), 623–43.

[18] James Hinton, *Protests and visions* (London: Radius, 1989), and especially Cecelia Lynch, *Beyond appeasement: interpreting interwar peace movements in world politics* (Ithaca, NY: Cornell University Press, 1999).

[19] See the special issue of the *International History Review* on 'The decline of Great Britain' 13 (4) (1991) and in particular the contributions by Ferris, McKercher and Nielson, and my *England and the aeroplane: an essay on a militant and technological nation* (London: Macmillan, 1991) and 'Liberal militarism and the British state', *New Left Review* 185 (1991), 138–69. See also Sebastian Ritchie, *Industry and air power: the expansion of British aircraft production, 1935–1941* (London: Cass, 1996). William R. Thompson mounts a chapter-long attack on the contributions to the 1991 special issue of *International History Review* (ignoring the wider attacks on declinist historiography). He claims to have rebutted the claims of what he calls this 'anti-structuralist' school, and thus to have re-affirmed the 'structural' school which includes both himself and Paul Kennedy. See his *The emergence of global political economy* (London: Routledge, 2000), ch. 9.

[20] See my *England and the aeroplane*, Ritchie, *Industry and air power* and Lund, 'The industrial history of strategy'.

[21] John R. Ferris, 'The Air Force brats' view of history: recent writing and the Royal Air Force, 1918–1960', *International History Review* 20 (1998), 119–43.

[22] J. P. Harris, *Men, ideas and tanks: British military thought and armoured forces, 1903–1939* (Manchester: Manchester University Press, 1995).

[23] John J. Mearsheimer, *Liddell Hart and the weight of history* (Ithaca, NY: Cornell University Press, 1988); Harris, *Men, ideas and tanks*. See also Patrick Wright, *The village that died for England: the strange case of Tyneham* (London: Cape, 1995) and David French, 'The mechanisation of the British cavalry between the wars', *War in History* 10 (2003), 296–320.

discussion of naval strength and the naval industrial complex which follows). Still, one historian writes that the peace movement did not 'affect the Royal Navy in any measurable degree'[24] while another has argued that no 'doubt exists that the British Navy was the strongest in the world when the Second World War broke out in 1939'.[25] Yet that is far from the image of a penurious, conservative navy one still gets from standard naval histories.

The differences between the older accounts and some of the newer ones reported and to be developed on here are stark. How could historians come to such different conclusions? The answer is twofold. First, to make the still dominant case for weakness historians repeated very particular comparisons over time and across countries, made very particular definitions of armaments and selected very particular technical characteristics of weapons. For example Paul Kennedy, as cited above, implicitly wanted a navy kept at 1918 levels, with 1914 levels of shipbuilding, rather than one adjusted to a peacetime standard devised in comparison with other navies. Furthermore he elides defence expenditure as a whole and naval spending, though both changed differently and with different consequences from those suggested. He also makes strong, unwarranted, assumptions about the decline of the 'nation's industrial sinews' and their relationship to warship building. For Postan the British aircraft industry is to be compared to the US industry in particular, and also the Italian – industries which seemed to encapsulate the state of the art in aviation. Oddly he did not use the most obvious comparators, Germany and France. As we will see as we explore the interwar arms industries, all sorts of definitional issues will come into play which centre on what constituted the arms industry, a topic we shall return to in ch. 8. There is also a deeper issue. Historians implicitly wanted more of everything: more battleships, more bombers, more soldiers, more tanks. They have tended not to ask questions about effectiveness and how this might affect such a historical judgement (for such historians are seeking to judge): even historians critical of battleships and bombers implicitly wanted more battleships and more bombers to have been built in the interwar years.[26] Finally, there are very particular assessments being made about the nature of the British economy, and its place in the world, and the world

---

[24] Kennedy, 'Britain's policy-making elite', 644. By the late 1930s, the Admiralty pursued a two-power standard, ahead of government policy (Peden, *British rearmament*, pp. 113–21, 160–7).

[25] B. McKercher, 'The greatest power on earth: Britain in the 1920s', *International History Review* 13 (1991), 753.

[26] See John Terraine's fine *The right of the line: the Royal Air Force in the European war, 1939–1945* (London: Hodder & Stoughton, 1985), p. 28.

view of British intellectuals and the British state, which themselves are open to challenge.

A new look at interwar armaments

The Great War had demanded armaments on a vast scale, not simply because of the size of the forces deployed but because of the huge expenditure of munitions. So too would the Second World War. It is hardly surprising that in the 1920s and 1930s the production of armaments was, by comparison, at a trivial level. This variability in production, involving changes in output unparalleled in scale and rate in the civilian economy, suggests that the economists' rule of thumb that one should compare peak to peak and trough to trough ought to apply with particular force. In a well-known book on public expenditure published in 1961, the economists Peacock and Wiseman produced an index for defence expenditure in the first half of the century corrected for price changes. Their figures suggested that interwar defence expenditure was significantly higher than in the 1890s, and only just below the figures for 1905 and 1910. Their figures also suggested stability in defence expenditure between 1924 and 1934.[27] That expenditure was broadly at the same level just before the Great War, and from the early 1920s to the mid-1930s is confirmed in figs. 1.1 and 1.2. For our purposes we need to go into a little more detail, and consider total expenditures and procurement expenditures by service. In the Edwardian years naval expenditure accounted for more than half of defence expenditure, but significantly less in the interwar period. The pre-war navy dominated procurement but its relative position became much weaker in the interwar years (table 1.1). In other words, the navy declined relative to the forces as a whole, and the naval-industrial complex declined faster relative to the arms industry as a whole. This is another way of saying that a new, procurement-intensive force, the RAF, was growing at the expense of the navy and the naval-industrial complex. Otherwise the naval procurement budget for new ships of the 1920s could have been doubled.

Controlled comparisons with other countries are equally revelatory. Excepting the United States and Weimar Germany, the other Great Powers had more men under arms than Great Britain in the interwar years. However, defence expenditure gives a different picture. John Ferris

---

[27] Alan T. Peacock and Jack Wiseman, *The growth of public expenditure in the United Kingdom* (London: Oxford University Press, 1961), table A–8, p. 170. For the population figure to correct this see table A–1, p. 151. For defence as a percentage of gross national product (GNP) see A–17, pp. 190–91.

Table 1.1 *Expenditure on armaments and warlike stores, 1923–33 (£ million)[a]*

	RAF	Army	Navy	
Year			Total	New ships
1923/4	4.9	2.6	11.8	5.0
1924/5	6.9	2.6	13.0	6.0
1925/6	7.6	2.2	14.1	5.4
1926/7	7.4	1.8	16.0	8.3
1927/8	7.6	1.8	16.3	9.0
1928/9	7.1	2.0	15.0	8.5
1929/30	7.9	2.2	14.7	7.7
1930/1	8.9	1.5	10.7	5.0
1931/2	8.7	1.8	10.3	4.8
1932/3	7.8	1.6	10.7	6.0

Note:
[a] Not corrected for deflation.

Source: M. M. Postan, *British war production* (London: HMSO, 1952), table 1, p. 2.

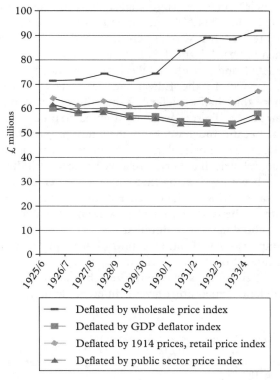

Figure 1.1 British defence expenditure in constant 1913 prices (£ million)

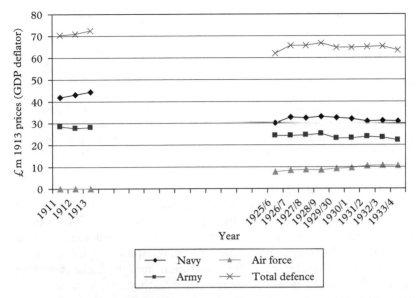

Figure 1.2 British defence expenditure by service 1911–35 in 1913 constant prices (£ million)

has argued that in the 1920s the United Kingdom had the highest warlike expenditure in the world in absolute terms, and that that of the empire as a whole was even higher.[28] That conclusion is supported by contemporary League of Nations figures.[29] By the early 1930s, the picture is rather different. In 1932 Britain, France and the USA were spending about the same in absolute terms, with Britain at the bottom of this list. The USSR, set on a course of forced industrialisation, was, on these figures, the largest spender. But by 1934 Germany was easily the largest spender, with France and Japan also showing substantial rises. The relative British position had slipped since the 1920s, but this was due to expenditure increases in other countries not British 'cuts'.[30]

Some contemporaries would not have been in the least surprised by the picture of a well-funded military presented above. Political economists noted that interwar British warlike expenditure was high by historical

[28] John Ferris, 'Treasury control: the ten year rule and British service policies, 1919–1924', *Historical Journal* 30 (1987), 865.

[29] Reproduced in Philip Noel-Baker, *The arms race* (London: Calder, 1960), p. 45. See also the figures produced by Paul Kennedy, *The rise and fall of the Great Powers* (London: Fontana, 1989), table 27, p. 382, and the cautionary footnote.

[30] A. J. Brown, *Applied economics* (London: Allen & Unwin, 1948), p. 41.

standards. For example, that great Liberal party plan of 1928, *Britain's industrial future* (the *Yellow Book*) noted that:

There is no automatic standard of reasonableness in the connection [arms expenditure]; but we may find comparatively firm ground if we regard our expenditure on defence as an insurance premium incurred to enable us to live our own lives in peace and consider what rate of premium we have paid for this privilege in the past. During the last quarter of the nineteenth century we were in no imminent danger of war … Our defence expenditure was £25 m – a premium of 2 per cent. In 1913 … the premium had jumped to 3½ percent. Today it is still 3 per cent, though we see no reason for regarding this country as in greater peril than in the last quarter of the nineteenth century.[31]

In 1934 F. W. Hirst, a former editor of *The Economist*, wrote that 'Despite the unparalleled burdens of growing taxation, the British Government, like other Governments, though participating in a Disarmament Conference, is increasing or maintaining enormous armaments for land, sea and air.'[32] Hirst, quoting from the main speech in favour of the Oxford Union's scandalising 1933 resolution (that the house would not fight for King and Country) argued with irony that:

The War, according to Mr. Lloyd George, was to make England 'a land fit for heroes to live in'; but it had produced a mass of unemployment previously unknown. It had also been described as 'a war to end war', with the result that 'we are now spending forty millions more than in 1913 in preparations for the next war'.[33]

Correction for inflation was not an immediate reflex, but it would have got rid of most of the increase Hirst mentioned.

Yet allowing for price changes had different effects on analyses of defence expenditure changes in the interwar years. For, while prices inflated during and after the Great War, they deflated in the 1920s and early 1930s. Noting this, H. N. Brailsford, another veteran political economist concerned with war, observed in 1934 that Britain was spending more in real terms on defence in the early 1930s than it had been in the late 1920s.[34] A 1937 Sheffield Peace Council pamphlet, comparing defence expenditures from the 1920s into the 1930s with the wholesale price index, noted that the 'apparent decrease in expenditure between 1924–5 and

[31] Liberal Industrial Enquiry, *Britain's industrial future* (London: Ernest Benn, 1928) (known as the *Yellow Book*), p. 428. Quoted in Robert Skidelsky, *John Maynard Keynes*, Vol. II: *The economist as saviour 1920–1937* (London: Macmillan, 1992), p. 269. Skidelsky argues that it is plausible to attribute the point to Keynes.

[32] Francis W. Hirst, *The consequences of the war to Great Britain* (London: Oxford University Press, 1934), p. 96.

[33] Ibid., pp. 97–8. Hirst also noted that Britain was the largest exporter of arms.

[34] H. N. Brailsford, *Property or peace?* (London: Gollancz, 1934), p. 177.

1932–3 is not a real one, since prices during that period fell by nearly half'.[35] The interwar critics were certainly right to correct for deflation, just as they should have corrected for the earlier inflation, thus avoiding needless alarm about supposedly rising defence expenditure.

A political-economic conception of warfare was influential not just in highlighting the raw level of defence expenditure, but the significance of the arms industry. There was much more criticism in this literature, and more generally, of the armaments industry than of Britain's armed forces. Indeed the greatest campaign waged by the interwar peace movement was against the private arms industry and the international arms trade. The campaign succeeded in establishing a Royal Commission on the Private Manufacture of and Trading in Arms – it sat from 1935 into 1936 and generated a great deal of evidence on the industry.[36] A leading campaigner, and another political economist, Philip Noel-Baker, followed up his own evidence with a book, *The private manufacture of armaments*, which, like most of the evidence, drew much of its material from the pre-war era, focused on the arms trade (in the sense of traffic), the degree of monopoly of arms firms, the links between these firms and the military through directorships and the international nature of the firms involved.[37] The campaigners, like their pre-war predecessors, called for the nationalisation of the arms firms and the arms trade.[38]

There were definite limits to this activist agenda, particularly with respect to British arms firms. Although a good deal of telling detail can be gleaned on the contemporary British arms industry and arms lobbies, the campaigners did not produce an adequate overall description of the interwar British military-industrial complex on the world stage or in British politics.[39] For example Noel-Baker's account, easily the most serious, did little more than lament that the British Navy League and the Air League were consistent opponents of the League of Nations and

---

[35] *Sheffield and rearmament: an exposure of the 'defence' programme* (Sheffield Peace Council, March 1937), p. 2. The pamphlet was written by the Council's secretary, E. L. (Bill) Moore, to whom I am indebted for sending me a copy.

[36] D. E. H. Edgerton, 'Technical innovation, industrial capacity and efficiency: public ownership and the British military aircraft industry, 1935–1948', *Business History* 26 (1984), 247–79 and David G. Anderson, "British rearmament and the "merchants of death": the 1935–6 Royal Commission on the Private Manufacture of and Trading in Arms', *Journal of Contemporary History* 29 (1994), 5–37.

[37] For example, Fenner Brockway, *The bloody traffic* (London: Gollancz, 1933).

[38] H. N. Brailsford, *War of steel and gold*, 8th edn (London: Bell, 1917), pp. 268–9.

[39] See for example Union for Democratic Control, *Secret international* (1932), and *Patriotism Ltd: an exposure of the war machine* (1933); Winifred Holtby, 'Apology for armourers', in Philip Noel-Baker et al, *Challenge to death* (London: Constable, 1934); W. H. Williams, *Who's who in arms* (Labour Research Department, 1935), ch. 6.

of disarmament.[40] Only the Communist party consistently, though never comprehensively, pointed to the strength and connections of the British arms industry and to the size of the British arms trade (as we shall see). Through the 1930s the party publicised the rising share prices of armourers, a movement which had started even before rearmament got under way;[41] the coincidence of pro-Nazi and pro-rearmament senti- ment, as in the cases of the *Daily Mail* and the *Aeroplane*;[42] and the politics of the leadership of the service leagues.[43] Critical analysis of the British arms industry, never especially strong, abruptly ended in the late 1930s and was not to revive until the 1970s.[44]

The strength of the British fleet

Despite the laments of the historians, interwar Britain was without doubt a great naval power. The core of the Royal Navy, as of all the major interwar navies, was its fleet of battleships. These extraordinary things were, apart from the greatest of passenger liners, the largest ships afloat. Their engines – usually steam turbines fed by oil-fired boilers – were as powerful as many electric power stations: British battleships were driven by between 30 and 100 megawatts of power. The main guns could fire a broadside many times heavier than the bomb load of an interwar bomber, and do so again and again; the mountings could adjust the position of the gun with such accuracy that shells could hit targets many miles away; analogue computing devices (fire-control gear) allowed the shells fired from one moving ship to hit another moving ship; the armour plating could protect against repeated hits from shells weighing hundreds of kilogrammes. In the 1930s there were fewer than fifty of these leviathans in existence, and a majority were British or US. But this strength turned out to be largely irrelevant. Battleship– battleship encounters were very rare in the Second World War: indeed, only one British battleship was sunk by another battleship. HMS *Hood* was sunk in 1941 by the *Bismarck*, which was itself sunk by the combined action of

---

40 Philip Noel-Baker, *The private manufacture of armaments* (London: Gollancz, 1936), pp. 290–345.

41 R. Palme Dutt, *World politics, 1918–1936* (London: Gollancz, 1936), p. 114. See also Patricia Cockburn, *The years of the week* (London: Comedia, 1985) (first published, 1968).

42 Palme Dutt, *World politics*, pp. 305–7.

43 Simon Haxey noted a striking point which he did not dwell on: the Air League in contrast to the Army League, and to a lesser extent the Navy League, did not contain a single dissident conservative on its council in 1938–9. Simon Haxey, *Tory MP* (Gollancz, 1939), p. 227. On the politics of aviation see my *England and the aeroplane*.

44 Fenner Brockway and Frederick Mullally, *Death pays a dividend* (London: Gollancz, 1944) added little to Brockway, *The bloody traffic*.

British naval air power and two British battleships. This raises the interesting counterfactual point that Britain might have been better off had it not invested in battleships in the interwar years. As it happens the primary intention of the naval treaties so lambasted by historians for reducing British seapower was to reduce battleship numbers, types regarded as obsolete even by naval historians who bitterly complain about the treaties.[45]

Battleships were clearly not regarded as finished in the interwar years. But estimating their fighting power against other battleships, other ships and against aircraft was and is no easy task, and all navies were aware of this. We should therefore be wary of computations of battleship numbers, even of battleship qualities, so characteristic of the pre-1914 naval race. But playing the numbers game can be instructive, even without getting too deep into the complications. In 1935 the British navy had, as a result of multilateral disarmament, fifteen battleships to the USA's fifteen and Japan's ten. One Japanese ship, the *Kongo*, had been built by the British armourer Vickers. The *Nelson* and the *Rodney*, both British and both completed in 1927, were the newest in the world and the most modern-looking; they seem to disappear from our image of interwar British sea power. Emphasis is placed on the age of the remainder of the British fleet, though it was not in fact much older than other fleets.[46] In any case, the age of a battleship was an unreliable guide to performance, both because British battleships of the Great War era were reckoned superior to others, certainly by the British[47] who felt that their greater design skills gave British ships better overall fighting power.[48] Just as importantly, battleships were often reconstructed. They were mobile fortifications of great power, which like land installations could have a very long life and be radically overhauled and remodelled. In 1939 each of these major fleets had the same battleships they had in 1935 but some had by then been radically changed.

Every one of the fifteen British battleships of the 1930s had at least a large refit in the interwar years costing at least £240,000 (see fig. 1.3).[49] Five

---

[45] I owe this point to Robert O'Connell, *Arms and men* (New York: Oxford University Press, 1989), p. 272.

[46] Britain had one battleship completed between 1920 and 1925; the USA five and Japan two; from the war years Britain had eleven, the USA seven and Japan six; from the pre-war period Britain had one, the USA three and Japan two.

[47] Joseph A. Maiolo, *The Royal Navy and Nazi Germany, 1933–39: a study in appeasement and the origins of the Second World War* (London: Macmillan, 1998), p. 96.

[48] Ibid., pp. 95–7.

[49] The account here, based on the research of Neilesh Patel, who used *Ship's Covers* and the *Naval Estimates*. The figures differs in some respects from the best survey published thus far: D. K. Brown, *From Nelson to Vanguard: warship design and development, 1923–1945* (London: Chatham, 2000), pp. 150–55. See also D. K. Brown, *A century of naval construction: the history of the Royal Corps of Naval Constructors 1883–1983* (London: Conway Maritime, 1983), p. 146.

Battleships and battlecruisers

Warspite	1913 … .(24–26) … … … … … … [34–37] … … … …
Queen Elizabeth	1913 … … (26–27) … … … … … … …[37–40] … …
Malaya	1915 … … … (27–29) … … … (34–36) … … … …
Valiant	1914 … … … … … (29–30) … … … …[37–39] … …
Barham	1914 … … … … … … … (30–33) … … … … …
Ramillies	1916 … … … … … … … (33–4) … … … … …
Resolution	1915 … …..(26–28) … … … … … … … … …
Revenge	1915 … … … (27–28) … … … … … … … …
Royal Oak	1914 … … … … … … … (33–36) … … … …
Royal Sovereign	1914 … … … … … … (31–32) … … … … …
Renown	1916 … .(23–26) … … … … … … … [36–9] … ….
Repulse	1916 … … … … … … ….. (33–36) … … … …
Hood	1920 … … … … … (29–31) … … … … … …
Nelson	1925 … … … … … …(36–7) … … … … …
Rodney	1925 … … … … … …(37–39) … … … …
King George V	1939 … …
Prince of Wales	1939 … …
Anson	1940 … …
Duke of York	1940 … …
Howe	1940 … …

Aircraft carriers

Argus	1917 … … … ….. (25–26) … … … … … … …
Furious	[18]..[21–24] … … … … … … … … … … …
Hermes	1919 … … … … … … … … … … … … …
Eagle	[20–24] … … … … … … … … … … … … …
Courageous	[24–28] … … … … … … … … … … … … …
Glorious	[24–30] … … … … … … … … … … … … …
Ark Royal	1937 … …
Illustrious	1939 … …
Formidable	1939 … …
Victorious	1939 … …
Indomitable	1940 … …

Figure 1.3 British capital ships of the 1930s
Notes:
1916 – date of launching; (34–36) – date of refit costing at least £240,000; [37–40] – date of conversion or reconstruction; reconstruction means new machinery and many other changes costing at least £2 million. *Vindictive* was completed as an aircraft carrier in 1918 but reconverted to a cruiser in 1923–4. There were more battleships in service before 1930.

Sources: E. H. H. Archibald, *The fighting ships of the Royal Navy*, 1897–1984 (New York: Military Press, 1987) and work by Neilesh Patel based on *Naval Estimates,* and Ships' Covers (National Maritime Museum).

battleships had refits costing between £1 million and £1.5 million – *Barham*, *Malaya*, *Royal Oak*, *Renown* and *Repulse*. Four, *Queen Elizabeth*, *Warspite*, *Valiant* and *Renown* were 'reconstructed' in the mid-1930s on top of earlier large refits. They were given new engines, they had their gun-mountings modified to increase range and were given new fire-control gear – at total costs of £2–3 million each. These costs approached half what it would have cost to build a battleship from scratch. Japan reconstructed its eight 14-inch-gunned battleships mainly in the mid-1930s. Their re-engining gave the Japanese ten ships matching the eight high-engine-power British ships. The refit/reconstruction effort in the United States appears to have been largely over by 1931. US navy battleships remained low powered by design.[50] Where all navies were similar was in realising that new fire-control gear made greater ranges possible, and in many reconstructions gun elevations were extended, increasing ranges dramatically. Here the Royal Navy did fall behind the US and Japanese navies by the mid-1930s, but by the end of 1941 all three navies had a rough parity in ships with long-range guns.[51]

In 1939 the British fleet confronted as its primary foe neither the large Japanese or US fleets, but rather (with France) the German fleet. Not only was the German fleet small, smaller indeed than the French fleet, it was below the strength permitted under the 1935 naval agreement with Britain.[52] As Winston Churchill, the First Lord of the Admiralty, put it in September 1939: 'the Germans have only seven ships worth considering, to wit: the two 26,000 tons battle cruisers *Scharnhorst* and *Gneisenau*; the three so-called pocket battleships, which are really ill-constructed heavy cruisers, and two excellent 10,000 ton 8 inch cruisers'.[53] What a contrast to 1914! More threatening was the Italian fleet which came into the war against Britain in 1940: it had seven battleships. It was not until the very end of 1941 that the Royal Navy confronted a major naval power: Japan. By then the Imperial Japanese Navy had eleven battleships, but the Royal Navy would have had no fewer than eighteen battleships had it not been for

---

[50] US ships had total horsepower of no more than 40,000 shaft horsepower (shp). The lowest powered of the British ships (the five *Royal Sovereign*-class battleships and the *Nelson* and *Rodney* had 45,000 shp, five had around 75,000, and three had more than 120,000. After reconstruction, and only then, the Japanese fleet had around six ships with around 75,000 shp and four around 130,000.

[51] I owe this crucial point to John Brooks, personal communication. I am most grateful to him for sharing preliminary results of his research with me.

[52] S. Roskill, *The war at sea*, 3 vols. (London: HMSO, 1954–1964), I, p. 52.

[53] 'Report of the First Lord of the Admiralty to the War Cabinet, No. 1', in Martin Gilbert (ed.), *The Churchill war papers*. Vol. I: *At the Admiralty, September 1939 to May 1940* (New York: Norton, 1993), p. 107. The 'pocket-battleships' were 'pocket' in the sense that they were about one-third the size of a contemporary battleship, and 'battleships' in that they carried 11-inch guns, like the *Scharnhorst* and *Gneisenau*. These were however small compared to the 14-, 15- and 16-inch guns of British, Japanese and US battleships.

the losses of *Royal Oak*, *Hood* and *Barham*. Even with these losses the British had fifteen battleships; only with the sinking of the *Repulse* and the *Prince of Wales* by the Japanese in early 1942 did the battleship ratio narrow to 13:11. It was warfare, not policy or disarmament treaties, which reduced the Royal Navy to rough battleship parity with the Imperial Japanese Navy.[54] Given these relatively straightforward numbers, the case for British weakness is quite hard to make, but naval historians, among them the great luminaries like Roskill, Marder and Kennedy, have managed it.[55]

Historians of the navy often imply that the Royal Navy was irrationally committed to battleships and thus failed to develop new classes of warship. On the contrary, the Royal Navy was strong across the board, including in what turned out to be the new 'capital' ships, aircraft carriers.

[54] In terms of ships with long-range guns, the Royal Navy had ten to the Imperial Japanese Navy's eleven in late 1941. Of the war losses only *Hood* had long-range guns, reducing the navy's actual total to nine by the beginning of the war against Japan (thanks to John Brooks for this point).

[55] Paul Kennedy described the British empire fleet at the outbreak of war in 1939 as consisting of 'only' twelve battleships and battlecruisers, and six aircraft carriers (some ships were still in reconstruction), with more to be added to the fleet by 1941; while Japan had (in late 1941) ten battleships and ten aircraft carriers. He does not compare what the fleets were/would have been in late 1941 (Kennedy, *British naval mastery*, pp. 346–7). Kennedy also suggests backwardness by noting that the new British battleships had 14-inch guns, while those of other nations had 15- or 16-inch guns, or in the Japanese case some 18-inch guns (Kennedy, *British naval mastery*, p. 340). In fact Germany had only two 15-inch battleships, its two battlecruisers had 11-inch guns; of its three modern capital ships France had two with 13-inch guns; Italy's four old battleships had 12.6-inch guns, the two newer ones 15-inch guns. Japan had but one recently built battleship, and this had 18-inch guns. Of the ten old battleships only two had 16-inch guns, the remainder made do with 14-inch. All but three of the older US battleships had 14-inch or smaller guns; the new ones completed in 1941 had 16-inch. By contrast all the older British battleships had 15-inch guns; the *Nelson* and *Rodney* had 16-inch guns. In guns size was not everything in any case: the 14-inch guns being lighter allowed the British battleships to carry an unprecedented 42 per cent of their displacement in armour (Gordon, *British seapower and procurement*, p. 173). The new battleships were 'the best of those of her contemporaries whose displacement bore any resemblance' to 35,000 tons. Further, they 'had the thickest armour, a fine torpedo protection, guns adequate to pierce the armour of her enemies, and speed as good as most' (Brown, *A century of naval construction*, p. 160). Arthur Marder too made an unfavourable comparison between Britain and Japan, claiming that in 1941 Britain did not have ten old battleships which could match the ten old, though modernised, Japanese battleships (A. J. Marder, *Old friends, new enemies* (Oxford: Clarendon Press, 1981), p. 299) which ignores the point that Britain had more 'old' battleships than did Japan, and more newer ones. For another example see Stephen Roskill, *The navy at war, 1939–1945* (London: Collins, 1960), pp. 24–5, or Julian Thompson, *The Imperial War Museum book of the war at sea: the Royal Navy in the Second World War* (London: Sidgwick & Jackson/Imperial War Museum, 1996). Historians complain about the naval treaties as if they affected only Britain: but other navies complained too. See William M. McBride, 'The unstable dynamics of a strategic technology: disarmament, unemployment and the interwar battleship', *Technology and Culture* 38 (1997), 386–423.

Table 1.2 *Tonnage of ships in service and building, 1937, standard displacement*

	UK	USA	Japan
Battleships and battlecruisers	544,750	438,200	272,070
Cruisers	482,700	332,925	249,005
Aircraft carriers	149,050[a]	146,500	129,470

Note:
[a] Excluding two being built.

Source: Brassey's naval annual, 1937.

In 1935 the navy had six aircraft carriers to four each for Japan and the USA, while in 1939 it had seven and the others six each. Neither Germany nor Italy completed an aircraft carrier. By the end of 1941, had it not been for the losses of *Courageous, Glorious* and *Ark Royal*, Britain would have had eleven carriers to the Japanese eight (and the USA's seven). In terms of tonnage, the Royal Navy would have continued to have had a clear lead (tables 1.2 and 1.3). Indeed the only index by which the British fleet can be shown to be inferior is that it appears to have carried fewer aircraft.[56] Yet one would not guess from the work of naval historians that Britain was anything except seriously backward in carriers. They have constructed elaborate accounts of failure (details are best left to a footnote).[57] In

[56] *Conway's all the world's fighting ships, 1922–1946* (London: Conway, 1980) is my source. Norman Friedman, *British carrier aviation: the evolution of ships and their aircraft* (London: Conway, 1988), explains this phenomenon – essentially the Royal Navy chose to have all aircraft stowable below decks. Unusually, many British carriers had armoured decks.

[57] One particularly risible and very recent bit of hyper-declinism gives us an elaborate, even judicious, explanation of the backwardness of the British carrier fleet but does not establish that it was inferior. The only comparative data presented, and that not clearly, concern numbers of aircraft carried (p. 202). See Geoffrey Till, 'Adopting the aircraft carrier: the British, American and Japanese case studies' in Williamson Murray and Allan R. Millett (eds.), *Military innovation in the interwar period* (Cambridge: Cambridge University Press, 1996), pp. 191–226. Paul Kennedy's condemnation of the aircraft carrier fleet consists in pointing out that the only 'designed' fleet carrier in the British fleet in 1939 was the *Ark Royal*, though there was the small *Hermes*. The remaining ships were 'four converted warships' (Kennedy, *Naval mastery*, p. 340). Unfortunately for this argument nearly all the early carriers were conversions. The USA completed the *Langley*, a converted collier, in 1922 (in 1937 the *Langley* was converted to a seaplane tender); *Lexington* and *Saratoga*, both very large carriers completed in 1927, were converted battlecruisers (H. H. Archibald, *Fighting ships*, p. 265). The first fully designed US carrier, the *Ranger*, was completed in 1934. Japan's first three carriers, *Hosho* (completed 1922), *Akagi* (completed 1927) and *Kaga* (completed 1928) were all conversions; the first fully designed carrier *Ryujo* was completed in 1933. The first British fully designed carrier, the *Hermes*, a small vessel, was completed in 1923; the large carriers *Eagle* (1924),

Table 1.3 *Totals of aircraft carriers and cruisers completed, 1918–41*

	No.	Displacement		Aircraft
		Standard	Full load	
Aircraft carriers				
Royal Navy	11	228,480	281,835	397
Imperial Japanese Navy	10	199,846	244,360	542
United States Navy	8	176,562	214,405	614
Cruisers				
Royal Navy	45	366,360	476,330	–
United States Navy	28	268,854	335,763	–
Imperial Japanese Navy	18	164,230	227,116	–

Source: personal communication, John Brooks.

cruisers the British lead was even stronger than in battleships or aircraft carriers: in both 1930 and 1936 Britain had a cruiser tonnage some 50 per cent higher than the USA's; in 1939 Britain had twice the number of cruisers as did the US and many more than any other country.[58]

Implicit in the above story is an important point that needs to be made explicit. The Royal Navy out-built all other navies in nearly all periods of the interwar years and in nearly all classes of warship. In terms of overall tonnage of warships completed between 1928 and 1941 the Royal Navy achieved, in round figures, 1 million tons while the United States managed 700,000 tons and the Japanese 600,000 tons.[59] After 1941 the US Navy out-built the Royal Navy by a huge margin but was the only navy to do so. Let us start by considering battleships. France responded to the German 'pocket battleships' by laying down much more serious battleships in 1932, 1934 and 1935; Italy responded with two battleships in 1934; Germany with two each in 1935 and 1936. In 1937 Britain trumped all the others by announcing the laying down of no fewer than five battleships in just one year.[60] Japan

---

Furious (1925), *Courageous* (1928) and *Glorious* (1930) were all conversions from battle-cruisers or in the case of *Eagle*, a battleship. *Argus*, the remaining small carrier, was also a conversion. The *Ark Royal* was the first modern British carrier to be designed from scratch; she was completed in 1938. Friedman, *British carrier aviation*, is an exception to the general denigration, but he does not fully set out British strength.

[58] McKercher, 'The greatest power on earth', 765, 766.

[59] Personal communication, John Brooks.

[60] As early as March 1936 the Admiralty had reserved space for a battleship at John Browns and permission to start work was given in November, but this was to be kept quiet until April 1937 (Peebles, *Warshipbuilding on the Clyde*, p. 146). Although there is a case to be made that the USA started the 1930s' naval race under Roosevelt, the battleship arms race started with Europe's weaker naval powers: McBride, 'Disarmament, unemployment and the interwar battleship'.

responded with one huge battleship in 1937, and thereafter all the powers except Germany laid down additional units. By the end of 1941 Germany completed its two battlecruisers with 11-inch guns (the two battlecruisers Churchill referred to) and two battleships with 15-inch guns; France completed its three battleships (two 13-inch and one 15-inch) and Italy two (15-inch), Japan completed one very large battleship (with 18-inch guns); the mighty USA completed two (with 16-inch guns). Britain, although the last to start, completed three battleships: *Duke of York*, *Prince of Wales* and *George V* (all with 14-inch guns). In addition the British reconstructed four battleships from the mid-1930s, the Japanese six, the USA none. Nor was Britain behind in other classes of warship. Between 1931 and 1941 Britain completed five aircraft carriers, as did the USA and Japan, the only countries to complete any at all. In cruisers, the British performance was spectacular. Between 1922 and the end of 1941 Britain had built fifty cruisers (all 1928 or later); the USA managed twenty-seven; Japan twenty-five; France nineteen; Italy nineteen; Germany twelve (including three 'pocket battleships'); the USSR seven; and Holland five.[61] In destroyers too the Royal Navy led the interwar construction effort. Only in submarines was it not first but second, but to Japan and not, as might be supposed, Germany.

The naval-industrial complex

What exactly the armament industry consisted of is rarely very clear in the literature. Indeed the definitions used can sometimes be extremely narrow and at other times very broad. For example the official historian of war production distinguished the specialised armament industry from both the aircraft and shipbuilding industries and other arms-related industries.[62] The Royal Commission on the Private Manufacture of and Trading in Arms was interested mainly in this specialised armament industry, rather than the aircraft and shipbuilding industries. It demanded detailed information from six private firms,[63] while aircraft firms, other than Vickers, did not give detailed firm-level evidence, though the aircraft industry trade association did. Warship builders, excepting Vickers, were not involved at all. In general in the interwar years arms and armament had very restricted meanings in official documents.

Who built the navy's ships in the interwar years is a deceptively simple question. The simple answer is that they were built in royal dockyards and private warship yards. The royal dockyards at Devonport, Portsmouth and

---

[61] *Conway's all the world's fighting ships.*   [62] Hornby, *Factories and plant*, pp. 30–1.
[63] Vickers, Beardmore, Hadfield, Birmingham Small Arms (BSA), Firth-Brown and ICI (Imperial Chemical Industries).

Chatham were the single largest builder: they launched nineteen cruisers between 1920 and 1940, were responsible for the early conversions of battlecruisers and other ships to aircraft carriers and the refitting and reconstruction of battleships.[64] The private shipyards of the north of England, Scotland and Northern Ireland built more warships overall, but fewer individually. *Nelson* and *Rodney* were built by Armstrong-Whitworth on the Tyne and Cammell-Laird on the Mersey; both yards would build battleships in the late 1930s, along with John Brown and Fairfield (both on the Clyde) and Swan Hunter (a merchant yard on the Tyne). Cruisers were built by all these yards plus Beardmore, Scotts and Stephen on the Clyde; Hawthorn Leslie and Palmers on the Tyne; Harland and Wolff in Belfast; and Vickers at Barrow. Such information is easy to come by but warships were only in part the product of the warship building industry. Some 40 per cent of all the costs of battleships was accounted for by guns, gun-mountings and armour plate.[65] In *Nelson* and *Rodney* the cost of the guns and turret armour alone came to £3 million out of a total cost of around £7.5 million.[66] The armaments alone of the 1937 battleships cost £2.9 million per ship:[67] the quadruple mountings for their 14-inch guns weighed 1,550 tons, were 60 feet deep and were 'comparable in bulk to a four-storey house' made up of the 'most delicate and at the same time immensely strong machinery, machined to thousandths of an inch'. These were 'the bases upon which British sea power revolved'.[68] Armour, guns, mountings and much else besides were products of the specialist 'armament industry'. This industry was far from being coterminous with the war shipyards, although its main market was the navy, not the army. The royal dockyards, and most private warship yards, did not make armour plate, guns or gun-mountings. Many of the private shipyards, like the royal dockyards, could not even make engines. Only a minority of the firms that built warships could make an entire warship.

[64] Portsmouth built 7 cruisers and 4 destroyers in the interwar years, Devonport built 9 cruisers, 1 minelayer and 7 sloops, and Chatham built 17 submarines, 3 cruisers and 3 sloops (Brown, *A century of naval construction*, pp. 260–1). They were also responsible for the conversion in the 1920s of ships such as *Courageous* (Devonport), *Glorious* (Devonport) and *Furious* (Devonport) to aircraft carriers. The refitting of battleships, and the extensive modernisations to four battleships in the mid-1930s, was also a dockyard job.

[65] *Financial News*, 19 December 1935.

[66] *Jane's fighting ships of World War II* (London: Studio Editions, 1989), p. 24.

[67] Ibid., p. 22.

[68] Scott, *Vickers*, p. 222. The only detailed history of guns and mountings I have seen is Peter Hodges, *The big gun: battleship main armament, 1860–1945* (Greenwich: Conway Maritime, 1981). Unfortunately it gives nearly no information on gun and mounting manufacture. I have not been able to find a copy of John Campbell, *Naval weapons of World War II* (Greenwich: Conway Maritime, 1985).

Before the Great War the major private armament companies were large, growing and technically innovative integrated steel/armament/ shipbuilding firms. Steel, armour and armament were their core businesses. The Sheffield steel and armour plate makers Vickers, John Brown and Cammell expanded into warship building from the 1890s: Vickers at Barrow-in-Furness from 1897, John Brown on the Clyde from 1899, Cammell on the Mersey from 1903 (forming Cammell-Laird). The Scottish steelmaker Beardmore built a huge naval yard and gun and mountings plant on the Clyde after 1900. On the Tyne Armstrong expanded rapidly in this period, merging with the Manchester armourer Whitworth in 1897: Armstrong-Whitworth's Scotswood works dated from around 1900; the huge new Walker naval yard from 1913.[69] Around 1900 Armstrong-Whitworth and Vickers were the only two firms which could produce complete heavy warships. They were joined before the Great War by two more groupings with facilities on the Clyde, never before a centre for gun or mounting manufacture. Beardmore (50 per cent owned by Vickers), produced heavy guns from 1908 and mountings from 1910. John Brown and Cammell-Laird joined with Clyde shipbuilder Fairfield to make guns and mountings through the Coventry Ordnance works. Coventry Ordnance is a somewhat misleading name, since its mounting plant was in Glasgow, between the John Brown and Fairfield yards. It was a newcomer to large naval guns and mountings, had great difficulty acquiring orders before the war (as did Beardmore) and it started the notorious scaremongering scandal named after its managing director, Mulliner.[70] As suppliers to an expanding navy and new export markets the industry had grown rapidly before the war, to such an extent that 'the resources of the heavy armament industry in 1914 were a good deal larger than they had been in 1905'.[71]

How did this already powerful naval-industrial complex fare in the interwar years? There is no doubt that the demand for warships was lower in the 1920s and early 1930s than immediately before the Great

---

[69] The best sources for the industry before 1914 are Scott, *Vickers*; Clive Trebilcock, *The Vickers Brothers: armaments and enterprise 1854–1914* (London: Europa, 1977); Warren, *Armstrongs of Elswick*; and G. Tweedale, *Steel city: entrepreneurship, strategy and technology in Sheffield 1743–1993* (Oxford: Clarendon Press, 1995). Trebilcock and Tweedale stress the importance of technical advance and commitment to such advance in the main firms.

[70] Peebles, *Warshipbuilding*, ch. 5. See also Warren, *Steel, ships and men*, ch. 9. Coventry Ordnance was encouraged by the Admiralty to force more competition on Vickers and Armstrong: Trebilcock, *Vickers*, p. 93.

[71] Hornby, *Factories and plant*, p. 8

War. But even recently historians have grossly overstated the change in demand. Gordon states that 'warship tonnage under construction in 1930 was a seventh of the 1913 level'.[72] Perhaps, but 1913 was not typical, and nor was 1930: in the decade 1900–10 warship tonnage ordered averaged about 100,000 tons; in the 1920s and early 1930s it was about half this figure. Engine horsepower built was greater in the later period.[73] A recent estimate that expenditure on warship building fell from around £25 million pre-war to £5 million in the 1930s is exaggerated.[74] Demand for armour plate, gun-mountings and guns fell, but to claim, as Gordon has, that most 'armament corporations disappeared or disintegrated, although some of the pieces were to be picked up by Vickers', is to give quite the wrong impression.[75] Historians have particularly mentioned Beardmore, Coventry Ordnance and Palmers as the great casualties of interwar retrenchment. Yet Beardmore and Coventry Ordnance were, as we have seen, new entrants to the industry in the Edwardian boom. Furthermore, Beardmore remained a producer of armour and guns, though not a warship builder, after 1930; Palmers, of the symbolic town of Jarrow, was a shipbuilder and marine engineer only, with no armour, gun or mounting capability at all.[76] Coventry Ordnance had been a minor player in guns and mountings only. They were nothing like as important as the two major integrated armourers, Armstrong-Whitworth and Vickers, which between them employed 48,000 people in 1907.

How far these giants retrenched is not a question historians have asked themselves. We can make a very rough estimate. Vickers-Armstrong, which was formed by merging most, but not all, the armament business of these two firms,[77] employed between 15,000 and 24,000 workers in the early

[72] Gordon, *British seapower and procurement*, pp. 77–9.

[73] However, these figures take no account of the early to mid-1920s, which saw orders for two battleships, and a large number of cruisers. Nevertheless a halving of output overall is a reasonable estimate. See Peebles, *Warshipbuilding*, appendix D, p. 169.

[74] David K. Brown, *Nelson to Vanguard: warship development 1923–1945* (London: Chatham, 2000), pp. 17–18. Brown correctly corrects for inflation, concluding that naval expenditure in the early 1930s was about the same as just before the war, which is probably too high (see above). However, he certainly underestimates early 1930s' procurement expenditure.

[75] Gordon, *British seapower and procurement*, pp. 77–9.

[76] On Palmers see Ellen Wilkinson, *The town that was murdered: the life-story of Jarrow* (London: Gollancz, 1939).

[77] Since some parts of each company stayed out of Vickers-Armstrong (for example, the Armstrong Scotswood works) and because the steel-making parts of both Vickers and Armstrong went to the ESC. Furthermore, various other activities of the pre-war companies, for example aviation, motor-cars and much else besides did not go into Vickers-Armstrong.

1930s, more than 80 per cent of whom worked on armaments.[78] Vickers (which controlled Vickers-Armstrong) was now the only company which could make an entire battleship by itself.[79] The *Financial News* estimated that it would get over 50 per cent of the orders for naval armament (including armour).[80] Indeed for the five new *King George V*-class battleships, the Vickers subsidiary the English Steel Corporation (ESC) produced all the gun forgings, the guns were completed by Vickers, Beardmore and Woolwich and Vickers-Armstrong made all the mountings.[81] In 1935, before rearmament, Vickers, some 50 per cent of whose turnover was in armaments, was the third largest manufacturing employer in Britain after Unilever and ICI.[82] We do not know what proportion of the work of the pre-war companies was civilian, but making the assumption that nearly all their output was armaments (which is unlikely), it seems that employment on arms did not fall by much more than one-half between the Edwardian arms boom and the early 1930s.[83] The private armament industry defined more broadly to include the aircraft industry and the private warship builders employed at least 38,000 workers making armaments even before rearmament got under way. Including the public sector, there were more than 80,000 workers involved in what was an energetic research-conscious industry (see tables 1.4 and 1.5). This was not an industry near extinction.

That is not to say that Vickers and the other firms were working at full stretch, but their shops were hardly empty. In 1934 the gun-mounting department at Barrow (ex-Vickers) was two-thirds full; that at Elswick (ex-Armstrong) half full.[84] In other sectors and firms the story was similar. In armour plate, the five main pre-war suppliers had been Vickers, Armstrong-Whitworth, John Brown, Cammell-Laird and Beardmore, and their combined capacity at the end of the Great War stood at 60,000 tons. In the early 1930s the Admiralty subsidised the ESC (a 1929 merger of the steel plants of Vickers, Armstrong and Cammell-Laird),[85] Firth-Brown (a rationalisation of Firth and

---

[78] Of its output 54 per cent was for the British government; 30 per cent was armaments for foreign governments, leaving only 16 per cent for civilian work (*Financial News*, 30 January 1936).

[79] *Financial News*, 18 December 1935.   [80] *Financial News*, 2 January 1936.

[81] Gordon, *British seapower and procurement*, p. 193; Scott, *Vickers*, p. 222.

[82] David Jeremy 'The hundred largest employers in the United Kingdom in manufacturing and non-manufacturing industries in 1907, 1935 and 1955', *Business History* 33 (1991), 93–111.

[83] Vickers appears to have been overwhelmingly an arms firm before 1914. Trebilcock, *Vickers*, pp. 20–1.

[84] Scott, *Vickers*, p. 220.

[85] Duncan Burn, *The economic history of steelmaking, 1867–1939* (Cambridge: Cambridge University Press, 1961), pp. 438–9; J. C. Carr and W. Taplin, *History of the British steel industry* (Oxford: Blackwell, 1962), pp. 439–50.

Table 1.4 *The largest armament firms, ranked by total employment in 1907 and 1935*

	1907	1918		1935	1934 (arms)
Royal dockyards	25,580	na	Vickers	44,162	18,030[a]
Armstrong-Whitworth	25,000	78,000	Royal dockyards	31,680	31,680
Vickers	22,500	107,000	Royal Ordnance	14,231	14,231
John Brown	20,000	na	Hawker-Siddeley	13,800	10,000[b]
Ordnance factories	15,651	80,000 +	John Brown	11,513	767[a] (steel only)
Palmers	7,500	na	Beardmore	8,000	592[a] (steel only)
Fairfield	6,000	na	Rolls-Royce	6,900	5,000[b]
Scotts	5,000	na	De Havilland[c]	5,191	na
Beardmore	4,500	42,000	Scotts	5,000	na
BSA	4,190	na	Cammell-Laird	5,000	na
			BSA	4,907	169[a]
			Bristol Aeroplane	4,200	3,000[b]
			Hadfield	4,052	616[a]
Total	135,921	–		158,636	84,085

Notes:

[a] These figures were derived from the *Royal Commission on the Private Manufacture of and Trading in Arms, 1935/6, Minutes of evidence* (London, 1935–6).

[b] These are my estimates; 1918 estimates are from Kenneth Warren, *Armstrongs of Elswick: growth in engineering and armaments to the merger with Vickers* (London: Macmillan, 1989), pp. 192, 195.

[c] 1937.

Sources: David Jeremy, 'The hundred largest employers in the United Kingdom in manufacturing and non-manufacturing Industries in 1907, 1935 and 1955', *Business History* 33 (1991), 93–111, Lewis Johnman, 'The large manufacturing companies of 1935', *Business History* 28 (1986), 226–45 and as in notes above.

John Brown[86]) and Beardmore (now independent of Vickers) to maintain nearly one-third of this capacity.[87] The ESC and Firth-Brown not only dominated armour plate production, together with Hadfield (a specialist in shells), they were the largest of the Sheffield steel firms. All had substantial armament turnovers in the early 1930s: Hadfield 17 per cent, the ESC 20 per cent and Firth-Brown 10 per cent.[88] All were

[86] *Financial News*, 8 January 1935. John Brown had long controlled Firth.
[87] Between 1903 and 1911 Vickers had produced 26,263 tons of armour plate or 2,918 tons per annum (Scott, *Vickers*, p. 59). In 1914 its output had been 13,637 tons, and in 1915 11,078 tons; in the rest of the war it was only 2–3,000 tons (Scott, *Vickers* 112). The ESC accounted for half the total interwar reserve capacity. Hornby, *Factories and Plant*, p. 58; Gordon, *British seapower and procurement*, pp. 82–5.
[88] Tweedale, *Steel city*, pp. 298–300.

Table 1.5 *Armament employment in selected private firms, 1930–4*[a]

	1930	1931	1932	1933	1934
Vickers-Armstrong[b]	13,331	11,089	11,747	12,724	13,583
Vickers (Aviation) Ltd[b]	1049	1195	1450	1529	1729
ICI	765	485	850	1412	613
Supermarine[b]	751	711	687	722	732
Thos. Firth and J. Brown (steel only)	677	599	555	701	767
ESC[b]	600	950	600	1050	1100
Hadfield	564	582	501	567	616
Whitehead Torpedo Co. Ltd[b]	519	475	411	401	709
Beardmore (Parkhead steel works only)	433	434	3314	495	592
Cooke, Troughton and Simms[b]	239	160	111	76	85
BSA	208	270	158	198	169
Darlington Forge[b]	100	150	75	–	–
Thames Ammunition Works[b]	73	59	60	101	92
Vickers total	16,662	14,789	15,141	16,603	18,030
Total	19,309				

Notes:
[a] Exludes all shipyards except Vickers-Armstrong, and all aircraft makers except the two Vickers firms.
[b] Owned or controlled by Vickers Ltd.

Source: Royal Commission on the Private Manufacture of and Trading in Arms, 1935/6, Minutes of evidence (London, 1935–6).

technical leaders in the steel industry.[89] Unfortunately we do not have a comparison for the proportion of armament work before 1914, except for Hadfield, where it was 18 per cent.[90] Total employment in these firms was less than in the predecessor companies in 1914 but not hugely so (see table 1.6).

Another key indicator of strength of the naval-industrial complex armament industry was that relatively little investment was required to prepare it for war. Between April 1936 and April 1939 the Admiralty spent over £12 million on new plant for private contractors, Admiralty factories and dockyards.[91] Between 1936 and 1945 the figure was just under £90 million (divided about equally between the dockyards and the private sector). Although this was a large sum, it was less than 10 per cent

[89] Ibid., pp. 122–9, 133–5, 188–93, 239–56, 297–313.   [90] Ibid., p. 128.
[91] Gordon, *British seapower and procurement*, p. 233.

Table 1.6 *Employment in Sheffield and district by the largest steel firms in Sheffield, 1914–34*

	1914	1918	1934	1934 arms employment
Vickers	6,000	11,000[a]	na	na
Cammell-Laird	4,894	6,067	na	na
ESC	na	na	6,660[b]	1,100
Hadfield[c]	5,690	13,000	4,052	616
John Brown	3,200	3,500[a]	na	na
Firth	3,100	6,868	na	na
Firth-Brown	na	na	5,188	767

Notes:

[a] 1916;

[b] 1932; includes employment outside Sheffield.

[c] Hadfield's plant finally closed in the early 1980s, while in 1982 the ESC and Johnson and Firth-Brown merged to form Sheffield Forgemasters, makers of the Iraqi supergun. In 1993 the company employed 2,000 (Tweedale, *Steel city, passim*).

Sources: G. Tweedale, *Steel city: entrepreneurship, strategy and technology in Sheffield 1743–1993* (Oxford: Clarendon Press, 1995), *passim*; and *Royal Commission on the Private Manufacture of and Trading in Arms, 1935/6, Minutes of evidence* (London, 1935–6), *Passim*.

of total state investment for war production.[92] Indeed much of the Great War capacity that had been taken out of naval production by the early 1930s was reactivated.[93] The Coventry Ordnance works gun-mounting plant at Scotstoun, which had been bought by Harland and Wolff in 1919/20, was making small naval gun-mountings from the late 1930s.[94] Beardmore, as we have seen, remained in some aspects of armaments production. Its Dalmuir naval ordnance and shipbuilding works, given up in 1930, was brought back into military production as a Royal Ordnance factory in 1940, and was later managed by Beardmore once more.[95] Palmers was bought by Vickers in 1934 and reconditioned for repair and conversion work.[96] And yet, new capacity was needed for the great battleship programme: for example a doubling of capacity for heavy gun-mountings.[97] The Barrow gun-mounting pits were not large enough for the new 14-inch and 16-inch gun mountings

[92] W. Ashworth, *Contracts and finance* (London: HMSO, 1952), p. 252.

[93] Hornby, *Factories and plant*, pp. 147–54.

[94] M. Moss and J. R. Hume, *Shipbuilders to the world: one hundred years of Harland and Wolff, Belfast 1861–1986* (Belfast: Blackstaff Press, 1986), pp. 221–2; Gordon, *British seapower and procurement*, pp. 203–4, 212; Hornby, *Factories and plant*, pp. 59–60.

[95] Hornby, *Factories and plant*, p. 164.   [96] Scott, *Vickers*, pp. 218–19, 294.

[97] Hornby, *Factories and plant*, p. 59.

(the latter were for a new class of battleships which were in fact not completed), and from 1935 discussions were under way about building three new pits, plus an additional one on the Tyne. Vickers invested £0.5 million, and in return was given the supply of all the heavy mountings for all the battleships ordered. The rearmament programme also required additional armour plate, at peak 60,000 tons per annum; nearly £3 million was provided by the Admiralty for plant for armour plate between 1936 and 1939.[98] The official historian – the same one who wrote of near extinction – stated that the specialist armament firms

whatever might have been the external estimate of their technical capacity in 1935 ... were capable of undertaking the planning and establishment of a volume of production at least equal to that which they had undertaken at the height of war production in 1917.[99]

Indeed Vickers-Armstrong, Beardmore, ICI and BSA produced more than their predecessor companies had done in the Great War. More than this, weapons of the type produced in the Great War were made on a similar scale in the Second World War.[100] Battleships were a great exception: production plans were cut back, and the war saw the end of this extraordinary product of the British naval-industrial complex.[101]

While it is undoubtedly the case that the new private arms industry had displaced much nineteenth-century state arms production, as many histories of arms production rightly insist, the state factories remained huge and of continuing importance, before, during and after the Great War. True, in key areas like engine building, armour and heavy mountings there was no state production. Yet in the interwar years the dockyards were still huge employers (on both new build and repair), as were the Ordnance factories, the most important of which was the Woolwich Arsenal. This was larger than any armament firm with the sole exception of Vickers-Armstrong: it employed some 7,000 workers in the interwar years. Enfield, making small arms, usually employed fewer than 1,000 and Waltham Abbey, making propellants and explosives, a few hundred.[102] But they were to multiply themselves many times over in the form of Royal Ordnance factories in the Second World War, spreading out from their historic base in the London area to the rest of the country. Indeed, not only were they expanded, they expanded relative to arms production as a whole. Furthermore, the Ordnance factory model was to be applied to new technologies, including tanks and later nuclear weapons.

[98] Ibid., pp. 59, 317.   [99] Ibid., p. 150.   [100] Ibid., pp. 150–2.
[101] Scott, *Vickers*, p. 297.   [102] Hornby, *Factories and plant*, p. 83.

The aircraft and tank industries

One of the great oddities of the story of armaments is that while interwar commentators thought of the specialised arms industry primarily in relation to Vickers, Hadfield, BSA, Beardmore, Firth-Brown and sometimes Imperial Chemical Industries (ICI), it was the aircraft industry which was the most dependent on arms. While the Sheffield steel firms devoted around 20 per cent of turnover to arms, and Vickers as a whole 50 per cent, for the aircraft firms the proportion was closer to 80 per cent.[103] It was a military industry, created by nation states in competition with each other.[104] That the aircraft industry was basically an arms industry was no British peculiarity: every significant aircraft industry depended on air forces. The army and the navy accounted for at least 50 per cent of sales of the supposedly civilian-oriented US industry between 1927 and 1933, rising to at least two-thirds in 1936. US aircraft exports rose from under 10 per cent of US production in the 1920s to over 40 per cent in the late 1930s, largely because of sales of military types.[105] US aero-engines, like aero-engines everywhere, were typically first designed for military use and then introduced into civil service with only minor modifications.[106]

Furthermore, the aircraft industry was, long before rearmament, a very significant part of the arms industry. Already by 1935 aircraft firms were clearly in the list of major armourers. By that year five firms – Hawker-Siddeley, Vickers, Rolls-Royce, Bristol and De Havilland – accounted for 66 per cent of aircraft industry employment.[107] Hawker-Siddeley, formed in 1935, employed over 13,000 workers, putting it in the top thirty British manufacturing employers. Vickers employed about 3,500 on aircraft production in November 1935.[108] From 1935 the aircraft industry continued

---

[103] In Britain in 1934 the market for aircraft was dominated by the Air Ministry with £6 million; exports, mostly of military types, came to £1.5 million; while home civil sales were a mere £0.5 million. Union of Democratic Control Memorandum, *Royal Commission on the Private Manufacture of and Trading In arms, 1935/36, Minutes of evidence*, Cmd 5292 (London, 1935–6), p. 195.

[104] This was a key argument in my *England and the aeroplane*.

[105] Elsbeth E. Freudenthal, 'The aviation business in the 1930s' in G. R. Simonson (ed.), *The history of the American aircraft industry: an anthology* (Cambridge, MA: MIT Press, 1968). Between 1927 and 1933 US army and navy production and design contracts accounted for 68 per cent of the output of eleven major aircraft manufacturers; the proportion of warlike output was higher still since many of the export sales were of military types. Jacob Vander Meulen, *The politics of aircraft: building an American military industry* (Lawrence, KA: University Press of Kansas, 1991), table 3.4, p. 57.

[106] R. Schlaifer and R. D. Heron, *The development of aircraft engines and aviation fuels* (Boston, MA: Harvard University Graduate School of Business Administration, 1950), p. 48.

[107] S. Ritchie, *Industry and air power* (London: Cass, 1996), p. 21.

[108] *Royal Commission, Minutes of evidence*, p. 434.

its relative expansion. In an advertisement issued in November 1938 Hawker-Siddeley called itself 'the leading aircraft organisation in the world'.[109] By 1939 Vickers was selling nearly as much in the form of aircraft as naval arms: it sold £8.3 million of aircraft, £5.1 million land armaments, £7.1 million naval armaments and £2.9 million of warships.[110]

There is no doubt either that the interwar rise of the British aircraft industry was due directly to the RAF. There was no aircraft industry in 1905, but in the interwar years aviation was without a doubt seen as the key new military technology and was supported accordingly. RAF procurement expenditure increased between 1924 and 1932, from £6.9 to £8.7 million, while in the same period naval and army procurement expenditures had decreased. Although the RAF was the smallest of the services in terms of total expenditure in this period (it overtook the army by 1937 and the navy by 1938), its procurement was considerably above that of the army. It spent less than the navy, though in the 1920s air force procurement expenditures were about the same as new warship building, and in the early 1930s were ahead of this. As we can see from table 1.7 the idea that Britain was somehow using Great War aircraft in the early 1930s or that the types were similar (as suggested so influentially by Postan) is balderdash. The RAF re-equipped itself more than once in the 1920s and 1930s, including in the early 1930s.

The aircraft industry also did not fit into the implicit models of the historians in another way: for all its association with modernity it was not a mass production industry. In the interwar years it was a craft-based, small-scale industry. Even Ford produced aircraft (briefly) on a small scale; Fiat of Italy was the only significant car producer and airframe maker.[111] Even in the Second World War, US attempts to truly mass produce aircraft ended in failure.[112] Aircraft orders were usually relatively small and spread over many types and firms. One of the most successful aircraft of the period was the French Potez 25, of which 7,000 were made, 3,000 under licence. There is no evidence to suggest that British aircraft makers were losing out to others by having fewer aircraft to produce or smaller production runs. Between 1918 and 1935 some twenty types of aircraft were ordered for the RAF in quantities greater than 100 copies. Eight were ordered in numbers greater than 300. Orders of this size were fully comparable with those placed by the US army and navy.[113] The number of designing and producing firms was

---

[109] *The Aeroplane*, 16 November 1938.   [110] Scott, *Vickers*, p. 264.

[111] Vander Meulen, *Politics of aircraft*, pp. 47–52.

[112] I. B. Holley, 'A Detroit dream of mass-produced fighter aircraft: the XP-75 fiasco', *Technology and Culture* 28 (1987), 578–93.

[113] Vander Meulen, *Politics of aircraft*, apps. 2 and 3.

Table 1.7 *Aircraft of the RAF produced in numbers more than 100 after 1918, and in service before 1935*

Type	In service
Trainers	
Avro 504N[a]	1927–
Avro Tutor[a]	1931–
Fighters	
Gloster Grebe	1923–9
AW Siskin[a]	1927–32
Bristol Bulldog[a]	1929–36
Hawker Fury I	1931–
Hawker Demon	1933–9
Gloster Gauntlet	1935–
Army cooperation	
Bristol Fighter	1920–7
AW Atlas[a]	1927–
Hawker Audax[a]	1932–7
General purpose	
Fairey IIID	Early 1920s mostly naval seaplane
Fairey IIIF[a]	1927–33 (also FAA)
Fairey Gordon	1931–8
Bombers	
DeH D9A[a]	Early 1920s
Hawker Horsley	1927–34 (also torpedo)
Westland Wapiti[a]	Ca. 1930–
Hawker Hart[a]	1930–6
Vickers Vildebeest	1933– (torpedo bomber)
Heavy bombers	
Vickers Virginia	1924–37
HP Heyford	1933–

Note:
[a] More than 300.

Source: Extracted from O. Thetford, *Aircraft of the Royal Air Force since 1918* (London: Putnam, 1968); O. Tapper, *Armstrong Whitworth aircraft since 1913* (London: Putnam, 1973); F. K. Mason, *Hawker aircraft since 1920* (London: Putnam, 1961); Gerald Howson, *Aircraft of the Spanish Civil War* (London: Putnam, 1990).

similar in all the great producing nations. Between 1926 and 1933 the US navy alone placed contracts worth over a total of $1 million with eight firms.[114] There were nineteen French airframe designing units in 1936.[115] In Britain the number of units was very similar. Only in countries with

---

[114] Ibid., app. 3.
[115] Emmanuel Chadeau, *L'industrie aeronautique en France, 1900–1950* (Paris: Fayard, 1987), p. 485.

much lower aircraft production were there fewer firms, for example Italy, Spain and Poland. There is little doubt about the comparative strength of the British aircraft industry in the interwar years.

Where Britain was weak was in the small size of its army. However, recent work has shown how important the tank was to this small army.[116] During and after the war, the British army had a very effective tank lobby which made Britain the leading tank power of the 1920s. Not only were tank officers enthusiasts for their machines, but most interwar heads of the British army were highly sympathetic. Vickers was the principal designer and builder of tanks. The Vickers medium tank dominated the British army's tank forces from the mid-1920s to the late 1930s.[117] So influential was the idea of tank warfare in the British army that Harris suggests that by the late 1930s and the early part of the war Britain had tank formations which over-rated the power of the tank and under-played the importance of supporting formations. In this context it is not surprising that the British army produced two 'military intellectuals' who were pioneering theorists of armoured warfare, Major-General J. F. C. Fuller and Captain Sir Basil Liddell Hart. What is surprising is that they themselves influentially peddled a very different picture as propagandists for armour and as historians of British armour.[118] In their accounts the British military were stupidly resistant to the tank, right into the Second World War. As we shall see this kind of inversion was to become a standard feature of the technocratic and militaristic critiques of British institutions.

---

[116] Harris demonstrates that Ernest Swinton, later professor of military history at Oxford, wrongly but influentially claimed to be the originator of the tank.

[117] The Carden-Loyd company designed some very light tanks which were bought by the British army in the very late 1920s. In 1928 the company was taken over by Vickers, and Sir John Carden became the key Vickers tank designer. Vickers produced many new light tanks which were adopted in the early 1930s. In the medium tanks, the late 1920s and early 1930s were a period of new design rather than new production. Vickers designed the A6 'sixteen ton', the A8, the Medium C and the Medium Mark III; Woolwich designed the A7. In the 1920s Vickers built a 32-ton 'Independent' tank which was used for experimental purposes by the army. From 1934 design started on a new generation of cruiser and infantry tanks. Vickers designed nearly all of them: the A9 Cruiser Mk I (125 built); A10 Cruiser Mk II (175 built); the A11 Infantry Mk I (Matilda I 139 built). Vickers also designed as a private venture the Mark III infantry tank (Valentine), and designed and supplied through the 1930s all but one of the light tanks (the exception being the RO Mark III). In the mid–late 1930s new firms were brought in: Nuffield Mechanisation designed the A13 cruiser with the new Christie suspension, and many of the subsequent developments; the other designing firms were Vulcan Foundry, Vauxhall and Leyland.

[118] Harris, *Men, ideas and tanks*. See also the fine book by Harold R. Winton, *To change an army: General Sir John Burnett-Stuart and British armoured doctrine* (Lawrence, KA: University Press of Kansas, 1988).

The export of armaments

The trade in armaments became an international *cause célèbre* in the early 1930s. Surprising as it may seem, in most of the evidence and discussion before the Royal Commission on the Private Manufacture of and Trading in Arms, the British role in the world arms trade was ignored. Only the Communist party made a clear assessment of its scale.[119] It started its evidence with the claim that the UK was 'the largest world exporter of armaments' and was therefore 'the main pillar of the world arms traffic, the evils of which have been universally condemned'.[120] This argument was based on League of Nations data for the years 1928–32, and covered armaments in the narrow sense, excluding warships and military aircraft. Sir Maurice Hankey, secretary of the British Cabinet and of the Committee of Imperial Defence, went to great lengths to challenge this conclusion and to play down British strength. By looking at later years, and only at exports outside imperial territories, he showed that in 1934 Britain had 11.1 per cent of the trade, well behind France and Czechoslovakia (which had the key arms plants of the former Austro-Hungarian empire). However, by the same criteria, Hankey handily omitted to mention, Britain was the largest exporter in 1929, 1930 and 1931, with shares ranging from 19 per cent to 28.1 per cent. For the years 1932 and 1933 Britain was behind France, but between them they shared almost half the world market.[121] The communists were right. There is no doubt that Britain was a major arms exporter, whose main competitor was France.[122]

If a broader definition of armaments had been adopted the British and French shares would probably have been larger. For the export of warships and aircraft were indeed very important, especially for Britain, and indeed France (see tables 1.8 and 1.9). Though British warship exports

---

[119] Interestingly the claim was not made by either the Union for Democratic Control or Philip Noel-Baker.

[120] Memorandum submitted on behalf of the Communist party of Great Britain, *Royal Commission, Minutes of evidence*, p. 71.

[121] First Memorandum by Sir Maurice Hankey, appendix E, table C, *Royal Commission, Minutes of evidence*. Anthony Sampson makes the point that Britain was the largest exporter of arms in the world before 1932, based on this data, noting the omission of empire. He does not however point to the fact that these figures exclude warships and aircraft (Anthony Sampson, *The arms bazaar* (London: Coronet, 1978), p. 74 (original edition, 1977)).

[122] For example Robert Harkavy, *The arms trade and international systems* (Cambridge, MA: Ballinger, 1975); Sampson, *Arms bazaar*; Keith Krause, *Arms and the state: patterns of military production and trade* (Cambridge: Cambridge University Press, 1992), ch. 3 (though on p. 73 this work wrongly states that by 1930 Vickers-Armstrong was out of the export trade save for warships).

Table 1.8 *British arms exports, 1925–33 (£)*

	New warships[a]	Aeroplanes Engines and spares[b]	Armaments[c]	Ammunition[c]	Vickers-Armstrong[d]
1925	14,345	1,146,000			
1926	19,300	1,119,000			
1927	45,388	1,085,000	996,100	2,169,500	
1928	5,143,150	1,327,000	1,246,800	2,861,800	
1929	3,820,250	2,159,000	1,840,000	2,078,500	
1930	707,400	2,050,000	1,429,100	1,558,100	2,013,634
1931	600,000	1,860,000	1,389,800		1,684,515
1932	525,000	1,742,000			1,303,547
1933	254,928	1,466,000			1,472,937
1934					2,555,973

Notes:

[a] Exports of new warships from the United Kingdom, including machinery and armament.
[b] Includes civil aircraft (*Annual Report of the Director of Civil Aviation, 1933*, cited in Noel-Baker, Memorandum).
[c] League of Nations data, cited in Noel-Baker, Memorandum.
[d] Vickers-Armstrong (i.e. excluding other Vickers companies including aircraft, sales outside the British empire only. (*Royal Commission, Minutes of evidence*, p. 420).

Source: Brassey's Naval Annual 1935, p. 347, cited in Philip Noel-Baker, Memorandum, *Royal Commission on the Private Manufacture of and Trading in Arms, 1935/6, Minutes of evidence* (London, 1935–6).

were low (except in 1928 and 1929 when they reached many millions of pounds), aircraft exports were usually larger than 'armament' exports. In the late 1920s and early 1930s British arms exports in this wider sense were worth around £6 million. About £2 million of this was military aircraft, engines and spares.[123] Until the mid-1930s Britain was probably the largest exporter of aircraft of them all.[124] Foreign orders may have been hard to come by, but Britain got a lot of them, and across the board.

[123] Noel-Baker Memorandum, *Royal Commission, Minutes of evidence*, p. 280.
[124] The *Aeroplane* claimed in 1936 that Britain had been in aggregate the largest exporter of aircraft in the world: 11 November 1936, p. 588. Spain, one of the largest third markets in the world, provides an interesting case of British strength. First, most aircraft were Spanish built – by CASA and Hispano-Suiza (HASA), and engines by Elizalde and Hispano-Suiza – but most of the designs were foreign; indeed all the major suppliers were represented. By the late 1920s the standard aircraft were the CASA-Breguet 19, the Hispano-Nieuport 52, the CASA-Vickers Vildebeest; de Havilland DH9s and Avro 504s were extensively used as trainers. In 1934–5 a major re-equipment programme, largely annulled by the civil war, was based on Spanish-built (American) Martin twin-engined bombers and Hawker Fury fighters. Gerald Howson, *Aircraft of the Spanish Civil War* (London: Putnam, 1990), pp. 5–10.

Table 1.9 *Percentage shares of export markets for armaments (by number of units)*

	1930–4	1935–40
Combat aircraft		
(excluding transport and trainer)		
France	26.1	11.3
UK	24.6	14.2
USA	17.3	25.0
Italy	14.7	11.8
Germany	4.5	11.5
Tanks		
France	38.8	21.6
UK	34.0	21.4
USA	21.7	10.6
Italy	2.2	15.9
Germany	0	6.5
Warships (excluding submarines and patrol craft)		
UK	42.7	46.6
Italy	19.5	8.0
France	2.4	12.5
USA	0	3.4
Germany	0	0

Source: Robert Harkavy, *The arms trade and international systems* (Cambridge, MA: Ballinger, 1975).

Reflections on political economy and appeasement

In a well-known essay Paul Kennedy suggested that Britain's particular political-economic position, its relative decline and its political culture led to a preference for 'appeasement' from the late nineteenth century. 'Appeasement' was a natural strategy for a state in such a condition, and furthermore the left and 'idealists', including Lord Cecil, Norman Angell and Gilbert Murray, were particularly hostile to any foreign intervention by Britain.[125] This account, which draws on others, is an interesting summary of many strands of thinking about appeasement. But this analysis needs challenging at many different levels. This can be done by looking at a key but neglected aspect of the language of discussion of international relations in interwar Britain: political economy. Most accounts of international relations in interwar Britain ignore its crucial

[125] Paul Kennedy, 'The tradition of appeasement in British foreign policy, 1865–1939' in *Strategy and diplomacy* (London: Fontana, 1984), pp. 15–39.

political-economic aspects, both in relation to actual political-economic relations, but also to the political-economic mode of thinking about international relations. Writings about peace movements provide a good example. For example James Hinton, in one of the richest and most acute analyses, treats the interwar peace movement as primarily political, while stressing the political-economic aspects of the pre-1914 movement. Yet many of the protagonists, as well as the arguments, were the same.[126] More recently Cecelia Lynch treats the interwar peace movements as 'social movements' with essentially political understandings and ambitions.[127] Nor is there a hint of the centrality of political economy in the relevant chapters of Martin Ceadel's recent book, despite the fact that it sets out to

interpret peace movements above all as ideological protagonists driven by the conviction that they have achieved fundamental insights into international relations. This is to see them as genuinely concerned with the moral, ethical, and analytical problems posed by war ...[128]

Although some historians have noticed some of the continuing significance of political economy,[129] its full importance in the interwar years has clearly not been appreciated; it has been seen as at best a curiosity.[130] Yet

---

[126] Hinton, *Protests and visions.*   [127] Lynch, *Beyond appeasement.*

[128] *Semi-detached idealists: the British peace movement and international relations* (Oxford: Oxford University Press, 2000), p. 6.

[129] Alan Milward contrasts an interwar political-economic view of war, which was liberal and internationalist and took a negative view of the effects of war, with a post-Second World War view which not only rated the effects of war as positive, but also shifted its focus to the national and social. Alan Milward, *The economic effects of the two world wars on Britain*, 2nd edn (London: Macmillan, 1984). In a powerful recent re-examination of interwar thinking on international relations, Long and Wilson noted, almost in passing, that 'economics constituted one of the main disciplinary contributors to international relations despite its apparent exclusion from IR (international relations) scholarship after 1945': David Long, 'Conclusion' to David Long and Peter Wilson (eds.), *Thinkers of the twenty years' crisis: interwar idealism reassessed* (Oxford: Clarendon Press, 1995), p. 307. Unfortunately, the book as a whole, despite including chapters on Hobson, Keynes and Noel-Baker, does not reflect this centrality. This is all the more surprising given the importance of the critique of classical political economy in Carr's *Twenty years' crisis*, the critique being reassessed. Andrew Williams, *Failed imagination? New world orders of the twentieth century* (Manchester: Manchester University Press, 1998) notes the centrality of liberal political economies to schemes for new world orders, and devotes an interesting chapter to it; but the book is centred on a political understanding.

[130] Post-war international relations academics without training in political economy and the disappearance of political economy from the new academic discipline of international relations after the Second World War meant that the founders of the discipline are seen in the same disciplinary light. Recent historians of economics have also wondered why the economics of war is so underdeveloped: see Craufurd D. Goodwin, 'Introduction' *Economics and national security: a history of their interaction* (Durham, NC: Duke University Press, 1991). See also the historical introduction to Gavin Kennedy,

it was central, as we have already seen in the importance attached to the arms industry and defence spending.

Being sensitive to the political-economic language of both peace movements and other interests in international relations is important in understanding what they were arguing. We can be easily misled by the highly abstract, theoretical and universalistic approach in to thinking that it lacks what we take to be the essential gritty details of the foreign and defence policies of 'realist' nations, reflected in the analyses of 'realist' historians of international relations. It does not follow that such thinking was utopian, in the pejorative international relations sense of the term, that it did not recognise even stark dangers to peace. On the contrary it often did, and with more clarity than the 'realists'. Furthermore, political-economic thinking was to be remarkably sanguine about Britain's capacity to wage war successfully against Germany, on the basis of Britain's inherent economic strength. It did not recognise a British 'decline', but rather a distinct superiority of Britain over Germany. Interwar political economists thus challenged Kennedy's subsequent political-economic arguments.

The very terms 'idealist' and 'utopian', labels subsequently used by students of international relations to describe interwar peace activists and students of international relations, do a grave disservice to those so labelled. 'Idealists' and 'utopians' had a sharp eye for the enemies of international equilibrium, as is clear once we understand their language and its resonances, and its own particular code words and phrases: they hated nationalism, economic and ideological, and militarism and saw them as profoundly dangerous. For example, Viscount Cecil – a key 'utopian' and former Minister of Blockade – warned in the early 1930s that there was 'scarcely a European country which does not furnish some ground for anxiety' as a threat to peace. 'Especially disquieting' was that 'all over the civilised world there has been a growth of bitter nationalism', a recrudescence of a pre-war school of thought which had been 'most vocal and perverse in Germany'.[131] A year later, commenting on the

---

Defence economics (London: Duckworth, 1975), which concentrates on famous economists and what they said about war. See A. C. Pigou, *The political economy of war* (London: Macmillan, 1921 and 1940); Arthur Bowley, *Some economic consequences of the Great War* (London: Butterworth, 1930); E. F. M. Durbin, *How to pay for the war* (London: Routledge, 1939); Lionel Robbins, *The economic causes of war* (London: Cape, 1939); J. M. Keynes, *How to pay for the war* (London: Macmillan, 1940); J. E. Meade, *The economic basis of a durable peace* (London: Allen & Unwin, 1940); J. Keith Horsefield, *The real cost of the war* (Harmondsworth: Penguin, 1940); R. W. B. Clarke, *The economic effort of war* (London: Allen & Unwin, 1940); A. J. Brown, *Applied economics: aspects of the world economy in war and peace* (London: Allen & Unwin, 1948).

[131] Viscount Cecil, foreword to Noel-Baker et al., *Challenge to death*, pp. vii–ix.

Peace Ballot, Cecil made it very clear that there was an enemy to be confronted: 'a militarist nation' – Japan was the case he had in mind – had shaken the whole 'system of organised peace'; in Europe dictatorships 'openly preached force as the right method for settling international relations'; economic nationalism had helped revive 'isolation', 'racialism' and 'tribalism' in Europe. For The Next Five Years group (which included Gilbert Murray and Norman Angell) dangers arose from a lack of confidence, generated in part by the private manufacture of arms, but in particular from 'nationalistic militarism' and 'anarchic economic nationalism':

Nor can confidence thrive when anarchic economic nationalism is prevalent as now, and when the nations struggle to master profitable markets for their exports while simultaneously imposing recklessly injurious restrictions upon their imports. Whether we assign a first place or a secondary place to economic anarchy as a cause of war, we must in any case recognize that it is among the chief contributions to political anarchy and to the creation of conditions favourable to war. For these and other reasons, we are compelled to recognize that the danger of war within the next decade or so may become extremely grave.[132]

These classic liberal arguments, echoing the versions eloquently put forward in the nineteenth century by Cobden and Bright were, to be sure, losing their authority by the 1930s, but even in 1939 the academic economist Lionel Robbins argued that 'A world of national socialist states is analytically on all fours with the world of primitive times when the rival hordes owned and had "sovereignty" over the lands which they roved'; 'National ownership of the means of production is not conducive either to international union or to international peace'.[133] The key problem was sovereign nation states which were subject to the policies of restrictionism.[134]

Already in the 1930s important ideological transformations were taking place within the political economy of war and peace.[135] For liberals like Norman Angell and Lionel Robbins free-trade capitalism remained

---

[132] *The next five years: an essay in political agreement* (London: Macmillan, 1935), pp. 220–1.

[133] Robbins, *The economic causes of war*, p. 98.

[134] Robbins suggested, in September 1939, the creation of a 'United States of Europe' (Robbins, *The economic causes of war*, p. 98 and *passim*). In the years before the war the idea of a 'federal union' of the United States, the White Dominions and the democratic countries of western Europe, put forward by the American Clarence K. Streit, proved very popular. See for example W. B. Curry *The case for federal union* (Harmondsworth: Penguin Special, 1939).

[135] Trentman is certainly right to argue for the end of the liberal consensus: Frank Trentman, 'The strange death of free trade: the erosion of "liberal consensus" in Great Britain, c. 1903–1932', in Eugenio Biagini (ed.), *Citizenship and community: liberals, radicals and collective identities in the British Isles, 1865–1931* (Cambridge: Cambridge University Press, 1996), pp. 219–50.

pacific.[136] But John Hobson and H. N. Brailsford argued that a section of capitalists benefited from imperialism, which was necessarily connected to militarism, and from militarism itself. Political economy was also central to the new 'Anglo-Marxist' tradition represented by R. Palme Dutt and John Strachey.[137] A central argument of these Marxists was that Britain was a very strong imperialist power. Dutt described as the 'theory of the apologists of British imperialism' the view that because Britain was 'satiated' it was 'pacific'.[138] He warned innocents against swallowing the 'illusion of the tiger turned pacifist'.[139] John Strachey shared a similar understanding: the British empire was threatened and it would fight: in Britain one simultaneously found 'specious pacifism' and 'hurried preparations for war'.[140]

E. H. Carr's later critique of interwar thinking about international relations has become much more famous, and it too was political-economic and ideological. Carr's critique of what he called 'utopianism' drew explicitly on Marxian notions of ideology, and Mannheim's sociology of knowledge, arguing that utopianism represented a pre-scientific understanding of the world based on ideological visionary projects.[141] For Carr the outstanding achievement of modern realism was the sociology of knowledge which enabled utopianism to be seen as the product 'of circumstances and interests and weapons framed for the furtherance of interests'.[142] For example, economic sanctions were the weapon of

---

[136] Robbins, *The economic causes of war*, preface dated 16 September 1939.
[137] See Edwin A Roberts, *The anglo-marxists: a study in ideology and culture* (Lanham, MD: Rowman and Littlefield, 1997), especially ch. 3.
[138] Palme Dutt, *World politics*, p. 183.   [139] Ibid., p. 184.
[140] John Strachey, *The theory and practice of socialism* (London: Gollancz, 1936), pp. 248–9.
[141] It is nice to note that Carr's book is seen as bringing about a 'Kuhnian' paradigm shift in thinking about international relations; a case then where the sociology of knowledge is used to make the change and then to analyse it! See also Charles Jones, 'Carr, Mannheim, and a post-positivist science of international relations', *Political Studies* 45 (1997), 232–46. For a discussion of continental sociology of knowledge in the interwar years see: David Frisby, *The alienated mind: the sociology of knowledge in Germany, 1918–1933*, 2nd edn (London: Routledge, 1992). It is a notable feature of ideological transformations that they involve a conscious consideration of the nature of knowledge (usually other people's). Other pertinent examples in this book are the Marxist political economists and scientists of the 1930s; the 'Austrian' reconsideration of planning in relation to philosophies of knowledge (Hayek, Polanyi) and Perry Anderson's 'sociology of ignorance' deployed in his critique of the English national culture. Perry Anderson, 'Components of the national culture'(1968) reprinted in Perry Anderson, *English questions* (London: Verso, 1992), pp. 48–104: 'Mannheim proposed a sociology of knowledge: what is called for here is a sociology of ignorance' (p. 56). In this influential paper Anderson made much of the empirical tradition in British sociology, and the 'White emigration', particularly from the former Austro-Hungarian empire, which included both Mannheim and Popper (and Michael Polanyi).
[142] E. H. Carr, *The twenty years' crisis, 1919–1939*, 2nd edn (London: Papermac, 1995), p. 65 (first published 1939, 2nd edn 1946).

the powerful.[143] The assumptions of nineteenth-century liberalism, including particularly its political-economic assumptions on which inter-war utopianism was based, were 'in fact untenable' and it was therefore no surprise that they had no impact on reality.[144] For Carr, the 'inner meaning of the modern international crisis is the collapse of the whole structure of utopianism based on the concept of the harmony of interests'.[145]

Carr's critique became the foundational text for the transformed disci-pline of international relations after the war, a discipline created by 'utopians'. Carr's attacks on the interwar 'utopians' – renamed 'idealists' – meant that they were summarily dismissed from the canon of post-war academic international relations. The contrast between a caricatured 'ideal-ist' and the 'realists', who were to be heeded, was the key theme of introductory courses on international relations.[146] The meaning of 'realism' also changed: it no longer meant the sociology of knowledge and a usable political economy – it meant geopolitical cynicism. The utopians or idealists were no longer seen as apologists for British imperialism, or bearers of the ideology of the powerful, but rather poor, deluded, woolly-minded pacifists and appeasers. In view of the odium which has become attached since the war to 'idealists' for supposedly encouraging appeasement, it is important to note that in the late 1930s it was Carr, and not the utopians, who was for appeasement. Norman Angell, clearly a butt of Carr's analysis, reviewed the *Twenty years' crisis* in 1940, pointing out the link between Carr's realism and the appeasement that had by then failed; and the adoption by the British government of a 'utopian' policy of war.[147] In 1940 Angell saw Carr's book as an example of a general critique of liberalism which he saw as fashionable but extremely dangerous for Britain's internal and external policy – a view shared by other liberals, including for example William Beveridge.[148]

---

[143] Ibid., pp. 115–20.   [144] Ibid., p. 39.   [145] Ibid., p. 58.

[146] Even before Carr's book was published the language was in the air:

> whether our foreign policy is dictated by what is called 'realism', which means a short-sighted, narrow selfishness willing to exchange honour for expediency and to pander and cringe to might and money; or whether it is dictated by what is called 'idealism', which means the support of international law and justice ... and the belief ... whatever our foreign policy, it must be influenced by the relative strength of ourselves, of other nations who share our democratic views, and of dictator nations whose views differ from ours (Hugh Wansey Bayly, *Air challenge and the locusts* (London: John Lane the Bodley Head, 1939) (preface dated December 1938), p. 3).

> The author was a Harley Street medical man, who believed in air power and rearmament.

[147] See J. D. B. Miller, 'Norman Angell and rationality in international relations', in Long and Wilson, *Thinkers*, pp. 114–16.

[148] Norman Angell, *Why freedom matters* (Harmondsworth: Penguin, 1940), ch. 3, 'Hitler's intellectual allies in Britain'. See also William Beveridge, *The price of peace* (London: Pilot Press, 1945), pp. 41–2.

Though much comment insinuates that interwar liberal internationalists were appeasers opposed to rearmament, evidence for this is very hard to
find. For example the League of Nations Union, one of the key liberal
internationalist bodies, was for rearmament.[149] The famous Peace Ballot it
organised, in which over 11 million people voted, is still often misleadingly
treated as an endorsement of pacifism. Yet there were clear majorities for
the use of economic and military measures against aggressor nations and
only minorities against the use of military force (25.8 per cent of definite
answers).[150] The right-wing press baron Lord Beaverbrook called it a
Blood Ballot, and with some justification.[151] Liberal political-economic
thinkers on war did not reject the use of force: it was not only necessary but
indeed beneficial in certain circumstances. For Norman Angell force 'used
to secure completer co-operation between the parts, to facilitate exchange,
makes for advance'.[152] Angell felt that this was the way Britain used force: it
had an 'industrial type' empire rather than a 'military empire'.[153] This was
not merely pre-Great War innocence or Great War propaganda: in 1947
Angell approvingly argued that for nearly four hundred years it had been
British policy to use force to hold back powers less enlightened than the
'English-speaking type'.[154] Already before 1914, Angell wrote in *The great
illusion*, 'So long as current political philosophy in Europe remains what it
is, I would not urge the reduction of our war budget by a single sovereign'.[155] Contrary to the image of Angell as a pacifist he not only supported
rearmament but was a member of the 'Focus' group of Churchill supporters (with Lord Cecil and Gilbert Murray). Indeed Churchill was at this
time an enthusiast for the liberal state and the righteous use of force.[156]

[149] Donald S. Birn, *The League of Nations Union, 1918–1945* (Oxford: Clarendon Press,
1981) makes this clear.

[150] Cecil however took a very particular view: the Ballot clearly showed that it was 'a slander on
our people' to suggest that 'the British people would not be ready to fulfil their obligations
under the Covenant; that they would never be ready to risk their money, and still less their
lives, in the repression of lawless breaches of international peace'. Viscount Cecil,
'Conclusion' to Dame Adelaide Livingstone, *The peace ballot: the official history* (London:
Gollancz, 1935), pp. 61–2. That it was not a pacifist result was also stressed in 1945 by Sir
William Beveridge, another confirmed liberal: Beveridge, *The price of peace*, p. 28.

[151] Stephen Koss, *The rise and fall of the political press in Britain* (London: Fontana, 1990),
p. 976 (first published, 1981).

[152] Norman Angell, *The great illusion: a study of the relation of military power in nations to their
economic and social advantage*, 3rd edn (London: Heinemann, 1911), p. 217.

[153] Ibid., p. 219.

[154] Norman Angell, *The steep places* (London: Hamish Hamilton, 1947), p. 8.

[155] Angell, *Great illusion*, p. 278, quoting 1909 version.

[156] Victor Feske, *From Belloc to Churchill: private scholars, public culture and the crisis of British
liberalism, 1900–1939* (Chapel Hill, NC: University of North Carolina Press, 1996),
pp. 208, 214, 227.

Angell republished the bulk of *The great illusion* as a Penguin special in 1938 as an anti-Nazi book, which of course it was.[157]

The Edwardian tradition of thinking about warlike strategy in political-economic terms was also very evident in the 1930s.[158] Basil Liddell Hart's notion of the 'the British way in warfare' summarised what he took to be a British principle of minimising resources devoted to warfare and of economy in the use of force. The British limited their liability by profiting from the defence given by the English Channel and by using sea power to exert economic pressure.[159] Liddell Hart was a strong supporter of the League of Nations; he saw the 'British way in warfare' and collective security as complementary.[160] Blockade, so important in the Great War, appeared as economic sanctions in the 1930s and as a central plank of British strategy in 1939 – Britain had a Ministry of Economic Warfare. The use of air power was envisaged in the same terms. In other words a liberal

----

[157] *The great illusion – now* (Harmondsworth, 1938). Angell's very strong anti-fascism is evident in his introduction to 'Vigilantes' (the pseudonym of Konni Zilliacus) *Between 2 wars* (Harmondsworth: Penguin 1939).

[158] Thus A. J. Balfour in 1912:

another point which, obvious as it may seem, is too little considered by those who are interested in problems of defence – I mean the question of money. Now whatever money is required for our security must be found, at whatever sacrifice. But the burden of armaments is already enormous, and if we increase it, we are bound to increase it in a manner which will give us what we want at the least possible cost ... would not ... money be much better spent, from the point of view of national security, upon increasing the Navy? ... Remember that a sufficient Navy not only secures your shores, but secures your commerce. A sufficient Army only secures your shores.

Quoted in Blanche Dugdale, *Arthur James Balfour, earl of Balfour*, 2 vols. (London: Hutchinson, 1936), II, p. 58. Indeed the greatest advocate of sea power in the late nineteenth century, Admiral Mahan, was an American. He saw Britain and the United States as 'insular democracies', which eschewed mass armies, preferring a navy: 'the mass of citizens are paying a body of men to do their fighting for them' (quoted in B. Semmel, *Liberalism and naval strategy: ideology, interest, and sea power during the Pax Britannica* (London: Allen & Unwin, 1986), p. 179).

[159] There were two supplementary weapons: subsidies and provisions to allies, and small expeditionary forces. Basil Liddell Hart, *The defence of Britain* (London: Faber and Faber, 1939), p. 44. Mearsheimer is wrong to suggest that Liddell Hart gave up the idea of the British way after 1933 (Mearsheimer, *Liddell Hart and the weight of history*, p. 93).

[160] Liddell Hart, *Defence of Britain*, pp. 45–6. The 'British way' was contrasted with in effect a continental way:

The theory of human mass dominated the military mind from Waterloo to the World War. This monster was the child of the French Revolution by Napoleon. The midwife who brought it into the military world was the Prussian philosopher of war, Clausewitz, cloudily profound ...

He went on to argue 'The consequences were, the threefold consequences, were: to make war more difficult to avoid, more difficult to conduct successfully, and more difficult to terminate save by sheer exhaustion' (pp. 27–8).

political-economic understanding of war and the causes of war also suggested political-economic means of waging war, which limited the negative consequences of militarism. Britain in important respects was developing a strategy of 'liberal militarism' alongside its liberal internationalism.[161]

A particularly interesting case is that of Alfred Zimmern, the Montague Burton Professor of International Relations at Oxford, clearly another target of Carr's attack on idealists. Welfare states, he claimed in a lecture in 1934 were, despite appearances, gaining over continental power states: 'science has reduced them to a subordinate political position' since in an industrialised world modern armaments depended on key metals and materials which were unevenly distributed in the world, making sea-power critical. He claimed the 'welfare states enjoy an overwhelming preponderance of power, confirmed and increased by their command of all the oceans, except, for the time being, the Western Pacific'.[162] These welfare states, the British Commonwealth, European states bordering the Atlantic (including France) and only two landlocked nations, Switzerland and Czechoslovakia, could without difficulty take on the totalitarian power states, even though Britain could no longer do so alone.

Although some historians have stressed the debilitating effect of supposed economic decline on British strategy, as Kennedy did, and others have pointed to the sense of economic vulnerability felt by the British government on the eve of war, there was a good deal of political-economic writing on war in 1939/40 which was remarkably sanguine.[163] Some very clearly expressed the view that what mattered for war was general, and thus essentially civilian, economic capacity, a point we will return to in subsequent chapters. That, surprisingly from the perspective of post-war declinist historiography, gave them confidence in a British victory. Geoffrey Crowther, editor of *The Economist*, estimated the total national income of the British empire to be higher, by a substantial margin, than that of Germany and occupied Europe combined. He was writing just after the fall of France in 1940. Indeed Britain and the white dominions alone had an income of £40 million (arbitrary) units while the whole of Nazi Europe had £55 million.[164] This meant that Britain and the dominions could devote the same amount to warlike expenses in absolute terms as Germany and the continent, while maintaining a higher standard of living. The British could acquire food and raw materials more cheaply

[161] Edgerton, 'Liberal militarism and the British state'.
[162] Alfred Zimmern, *Quo Vadimus? A public lecture delivered on 5 February 1934* (London: Oxford University Press, 1934), pp. 35, 36.
[163] Keynes, *How to pay for the war*; Clarke, *The economic effort of war*; Durbin, *How to pay for the war*; G. Crowther, *Ways and means of war* (Oxford: Oxford University Press, 1940).
[164] Crowther, *Ways and means of war*, ch. 2.

in terms of manpower, thus putting a higher proportion of population into the field and into arms production. About industrial capacity too Crowther was optimistic: British and dominion car production added up to 700,000 per annum; that of Germany and France to only 538,000. Crowther felt that there were 'no fatal weaknesses in our economic strength-in-war'.[165] He argued that it was worthwhile to fight against Hitlerism, and that the economic damage would not be very great, based on the experience of the Great War. R. W. B. Clarke, also in 1940, similarly made much of the fact that Britain's income per head was higher than Germany's and that this was crucial to fighting capacity.[166] A similar analysis is found in the official history of the war economy, published in 1949. Sir Keith Hancock and Margaret Gowing noted that

Taking full advantage of the international division of labour, the United Kingdom was enabled in large measure to rectify her numerical inferiority by mobilising in the immediate war zone a much higher proportion of her much smaller population.[167]

Britain could import food from high productivity temperate areas; it could import oil rather than waste resources on synthetic oil; it could also import manufactures. If Britain had had to become economically self-sufficient, it 'could neither have made effective war nor even maintained [its] civilian population'.[168] In a striking formulation they suggested that Great Britain depended on 'the international economic order' while Germany depended on and was creating a 'new order'.[169] Even in war then the economics of trade were seen as crucial. But it is important to note that the main argument was not the now often implicit view that economic nationalism was necessary to the successful fighting of war, or that liberal internationalism was intrinsically hostile to war, or that a trading nation was incapable of fighting. It was rather that Britain had the good fortune to be able to fight a war in a particularly effective way because of its economic strength and its connections to the global economy.

---

[165] Ibid., p. 167. The importance of the level of development (income per head) has recently been stressed in Mark Harrison, 'The economics of World War II: an overview', in Mark Harrison (ed.), *The economics of World War II: six Great Powers in international comparison* (Cambridge: Cambridge University Press, 1998), pp. 1–42. It would be clear to a student of the Soviet war economy like Harrison; specialists on Britain have ignored the point.

[166] Clarke, *The economic effort of war*, pp. 221–50.

[167] H. K. Hancock and M. M. Gowing, *British war economy* (London: HMSO, 1949), p. 101.

[168] Ibid., p. 103.   [169] Ibid.

Conclusion

The idea that Britain had unilaterally disarmed in the 1920s and 1930s, so assiduously repeated and ingeniously defended, is clearly untenable. The peacemongers of the 1930s were more right than wrong. In absolute terms Britain spent at least as much as any other country on warfare, and about the same as it had spent in the Edwardian years. Furthermore, its expenditure was concentrated on the two technological arms, the navy and the air force, both of which were among the very strongest in the world. Its armament industry, it may be safely surmised, was at least as large as any other in the world. Britain was not a military-technological superpower in the interwar years for there was then no such thing; but it could claim to be the most powerful of the great powers. It had certainly lost its pre-eminent place as a naval power to non-European powers, but it was still the strongest. In air armament it was as strong as any other country, and its competitors before rearmament were France and the USA; in land arms, though weaker, it showed a strong predilection for technological means. As we shall see in a subsequent chapter the British armed services had a technical infrastructure and research and development (R&D) laboratories of huge size by the standards of the period.

The second crucial point to take forward is that standard explanations of the supposed disarmament of the interwar years, and in part of appeasement too, do not work. They mischaracterise the views of liberal internationalist intellectuals. Although weakened in many respects British liberalism still felt it had a global mission, and a globally based capacity, to intervene in Europe to make the world safe for multinational capitalism. And it would do so, and in the process Britain would change very dramatically. Indeed it would change so significantly that it would see the interwar years in very different terms from those in which contemporaries saw them.

2   The warfare state and the nationalisation of Britain, 1939–55

'"this time" things are going to be "different". Militarization is not going to mean militarization. Colonel Blimp is no longer Colonel Blimp.'

George Orwell, September 1939[1]

This is the hour
When death is rationed out,
When iron eggs, fruits of some monstrous coupling in Hell
Are hatched in blood.
This is the hour when cities rise up
Shrieking in the night
And lamentations sound from iron throats
This is destruction's hour.   Ewan McColl, *Uranium 235.*[2]

The term 'welfare state', so central to the analysis of the British state, appears to have been coined by an expert not in social policy, but in international relations. That expert was Sir Alfred Zimmern, Montague Burton Professor of International Relations at the University of Oxford between 1930 and 1944. Zimmern's notion of the 'welfare state' was powerfully attacked by E. H. Carr in his famous 1939 attack on 'utopian' thinking in international relations; Zimmern was for Carr an exemplary case of a utopian. Carr noted that Zimmern distinguished between 'welfare' and 'power' states, but objected to Zimmern's contention that the 'welfare states' had more power than the 'power states'.[3] As far as Carr was concerned the relations of power and welfare had changed: he insisted that before 1933, satisfied with its power, Britain was a 'welfare' state; after that, as its power was threatened, it became a

---

[1] George Orwell, 'Democracy in the British army', *Left Forum* September 1939, reprinted in *The collected essays, journalism and letters of George Orwell.* Vol. I: *An age like this, 1920–1940* (Harmondsworth: Penguin, 1970), p. 444.

[2] Ewan MacColl, *Uranium 235: a documentary play in eleven episodes* (Glasgow: William MacLellan, 1948), p. 11.

[3] The *Oxford English Dictionary* claims that the term 'welfare state' does not appear in Zimmern's published writings. But Peter Hennessy, *Never again: Britain 1945–1951* (London: Cape, 1992), p. 121, shows that it appears in Alfred Zimmern, *Quo Vadimus? A public lecture delivered on 5 February 1934* (London: Oxford University Press, 1934).

'power' state.[4] Carr's rich analytical point was not taken up, then or since. The *Oxford English Dictionary* attributes the first published usage of 'welfare state' to Archbishop (of York and then Canterbury) William Temple, who in wartime claimed that Britain was a welfare state and Nazi Germany a power state.[5] Clearly 'welfare state' was meant as a term of approbation. In fact it was rarely used until the 1950s, and when it *was* used it tended to be used critically. However, in the context of the cold war it quickly became well established as a positive term to describe both particular civil functions of the state and increasingly the state itself. 'Welfare state' became the term of art and indeed the central concept used to think about the post-war state, not just the British state. The meaning of the term had changed radically. For Zimmern it meant a state governed by law, rather than power; based on responsibility rather than force; which was constitutional rather than revolutionary; which was consensual rather than commanding; a state which diffused and shared power, rather than concentrated it; a state which was democratic rather than demagogic. It carried no implication of high public expenditure on welfare, rather the contrary. It was an image of a classic liberal democracy.[6] By contrast, after the war the term came to mean, in the British case, the provision of many services by the state, in a highly state-centred and centralised manner.

In accounts of Britain and the Second World War the rise of the 'welfare state' became the central motif in the work of historians. Even if they do not always use the term, though many do, 'the triumph of social democracy'[7] or the rise of the 'benign state' is central to accounts of Britain in and after the Second World War.[8] A recent text on the British state, one which takes seriously the fiscal-military state of the eighteenth century, gives Britain a 'social-service state' between 1880 and 1939, while the period 1939 to 1979 is covered in a chapter on 'total war and cradle-to-grave welfare'.[9] Although historians have challenged old accounts of how particular sectors benefited from the war, and in doing so cast doubt on the optimistic

---

[4] E. H. Carr, *The twenty years' crisis, 1919–1939*, 2nd edn (London: Papermac, 1995), p. 65 (first published 1939, 2nd edn 1946), p. 110.

[5] Citing William Temple, *Citizen and Churchman* (London: Eyre & Spottiswoode, 1941).

[6] Zimmerm, *Quo Vadimus?*, pp. 35, 36.

[7] James E. Cronin, *Labour and society in Britain, 1918–1979* (London: Batsford, 1984). Chapter 7 is entitled 'The triumph of social democracy, 1940–1948'.

[8] Martin Pugh, *State and society: a social and political history of Britain*, 2nd edn (London: Arnold, 1999) covers the war and post-war state under the rubric of the 'benign' state, and has the usual references to the welfare state and the Keynesian era.

[9] Philip Harling, *The modern British state: an historical introduction* (Cambridge: Polity, 2001).

picture, the rising 'welfare state' stubbornly remains the frame of reference for studies of wartime Britain.[10] Neither 'power state' nor anything like it was used with reference to Britain, despite Carr's suggestive formulations. Indeed 'power state' would have been a very apt term to describe Britain not only at war but also in the comparatively peaceful 1950s. Britain was both a power state, or a warfare state, and a welfare state, but the balance of these aspects changed over time, as Carr noted; but they have not always changed in the ways that have been supposed.

Carr was not alone in detecting an important change in the nature of the British state something more like a power state than a welfare state. Even in the early 1930s some analysts, relying on familiar arguments linking autarchy, nationalism and militarism, saw danger in Britain's move towards a general tariff and the system of imperial preferences: 'One begins by "buying British": one ends by shouting for a colossal air-fleet', lamented H. N. Brailsford.[11] The British right, let us recall, backed tariffs, imperialism and strong national armaments and loathed the League of Nations.[12] Elie Halevy, the great French student of British liberalism, was brutally frank in his defence of the true liberal political-economic faith, speculating in 1934 about where the ideological transformation he saw underway would end:

It is queer in England to observe how the free-trade spirit, with its pacifist implications, has survived the introduction of protection. But you have to recognise that you have become a protectionist nation, and, having become protectionist, you have become nationalistic at the same time. I know several socialist

---

[10] See for example, Harold Smith (ed.), *War and social change: Britain in the Second World War* (Manchester: Manchester University Press, 1986); Penny Summerfield, *Women workers in the Second World War: production and patriarchy in conflict* (London: Croom Helm, 1984) and *Reconstructing women's wartime lives: discourse and subjectivity in oral histories of the Second World War* (Manchester: Manchester University Press, 1998); José Harris, 'Society and the state in twentieth-century Britain' in F. M. L. Thompson, *Cambridge social history of Britain*. Vol. III: *Social agencies and institutions* (Cambridge: Cambridge University Press, 1990), pp. 63–118; Tom Ling, *The British state since 1945: an introduction* (Cambridge: Polity, 1998); Lawrence Black, et al., *Consensus or coercion: the state, the people and social cohesion in post-war Britain* (Cheltenham: New Clarion Press, 2001).

[11] H. N. Brailsford, *Property or peace?* (London: Gollancz, 1934), p. 229.

[12] Just as left and liberal attitudes to the rise of Nazi Germany were mixed, so were the attitudes of the right, despite their enthusiasm for armaments. On the extreme right one can make some generalisations as to attitudes: imperial isolationists were often indifferent to what happened on the continent until the British empire was threatened (e.g. Leo Amery and Lords Wolmer and Lloyd). Militarist pro-Nazis (Francis Yeats-Brown, Anthony Ludovici, Arnold Leese and William Joyce) remained appeasers (G. C. Webber, *The ideology of the British right 1918–1939* (London: Croom Helm, 1986), pp. 113–15) as did people linked with two sorts of 'right-wing supra-nationalism', one Catholic, the other pro-Nazi (Webber, *Ideology*, pp. 122–7).

intellectuals who profess to be at the same time radical protectionists and radical pacifists. I do not understand how you can be both at the same time ... As soon as you have begun to accept protectionism, you are bound to accept something like nationalism, and can you have nationalism without something like militarism? I was struck last winter in reading a speech made at a public meeting by Sir Stafford Cripps in which he declared that he was not 'an out and out pacifist'. I know that just now he is delivering highly pacifist speeches in Canada, but I cannot forget how struck I was by this former declaration of his. I am making a bold, perhaps an absurd forecast. But who knows? Sir Stafford Cripps' father, after being a Conservative, went over to Labour because he was a pacifist. Who knows whether Sir Stafford Cripps himself will not find himself going over to patriotism and perhaps something like militarism because he is a socialist? ... [Herbert Spencer argued that] the world was evolving towards what he called new toryism – protective, socialistic and militaristic ... who knows whether the prophecy is not going to be true?[13]

Was Halevy right? Only a decade or so later, and for years afterward, Britain had a highly protected economy, it was socialistic and had very high defence spending and conscription. This is not to say that this was by conscious choice, much less that it was the product of overt campaigns to bring it about. But the fact that we hardly remark on these differences, or see them in a negative light as Halevy did, is a measure of the profound change in thinking that has taken place in the interval.

These ideological changes did not just concern political economy. As Halevy had suggested, attitudes to war changed quickly and unexpectedly too. Yet as the historian Donald Cameron Watt has argued the political dimensions of the decisions to go to war in the late 1930s have been given insufficient attention.[14] Contemporary ideologically informed comment was clear enough. In 1940 the former Comintern agent Franz Borkenau 'witnessed in the two years preceding the war the strange emergence of pacifist Conservatives and violently bellicose Socialists'.[15] This peculiar conjunction made war politically possible, hinted Borkenau, since 'An ideological war of the Popular Front type advocated by the Communists would have set the Conservative section against the war. A war of conquest would have been unacceptable to Socialists and Progressives.'[16] These new arrangements of forces also broke up conventional sets of arguments about the economy and about armed force, creating what to Halevy would

---

[13] E. Halevy, 'Socialism and the problem of democratic parliamentarism', address at Chatham House 24 April 1934, reproduced in *The era of tyrannies: essays on socialism and war* (London: Allen Lane, 1967), p. 201.

[14] D. C. Watt, *Too serious a business: European armed forces and the approach to the Second World War* (London: Norton, 1992) (first published 1975), pp. 9, 13.

[15] Franz Borkenau, *The totalitarian enemy* (London: Faber and Faber, 1940), p. 13.

[16] Ibid., p. 14.

have seemed like preposterous, even oxymoronic hybrids. The post-war intellectuals did not have the straightforward language of the pre-war liberal to describe the rise of protection, preferences and military expenditure. Indeed such themes were hardly discussed at all. Instead the state was described as a welfare state, and its economic policies described in the language of Keynesian economics and labour politics – demand management, inflation, deflation, nationalisation, with a dash of planning and industrial policy. These concepts were, however, woefully inadequate for describing some of the key underlying changes in wartime and post-war Britain. Historians of the post-war years, themselves writing in a world of protection, nationalism and high defence spending, without fully grasping the import of these changes, relied on the new conceptual language in which the warfare state was nearly invisible.

Economic historians and war economies: the disappearing war economy

It is a testimony to the importance attributed by the British government to the economy in war that a large number of historians, including many economic historians, were employed to study the war economy in operation. These 'narrators' wrote up 'narratives', which were turned into pioneering works of contemporary history by historians already or soon to be distinguished. They appeared from 1949 onwards under the general title: *History of the Second World War: United Kingdom Civil Series*. In their preface to the first, general volume, W. K. Hancock and M. M. Gowing state: 'the positive employment of resources in the field of war is an immense subject. It is handled in the companion volume which Professor Postan is writing [*British War Production*]. The present volume shows, therefore, a distinct leaning towards the civilian side', a statement worth remarking on in a book called, as it was, *British war economy*.[17] The book would pay keen attention to 'manpower budgets', the means by which the War Cabinet shaped the overall production policy: 'If it be remembered that manpower signifies not merely a scarce factor of production but also the men and women of Britain, the accent will be put still more heavily on these chapters.'

They stress that their view is that from the War Cabinet, and for a period from the Lord President's Committee, the committee that oversaw the 'home front', and that it is not a full account of the war economy.[18] Yet the book was surely influential in creating the impression that

[17] W. K. Hancock and M. M. Gowing, *British war economy* (London: HMSO, 1949), p. xv.
[18] Ibid., p. xvi.

because the manpower budget became more important than the financial budget, power passed from the Treasury to the Ministry of Labour, and to Minister of Labour, the trade unionist Ernest Bevin, in particular. A second much cited source was Norman Chester's collection of articles by economists, *Lessons of the war economy* published in 1951, which had a similar focus. Thus Chester's own chapter, 'The central machinery of economic policy', which concentrated on the Lord President's Committee, could be read as meaning that it was responsible for the war economy, when in fact, as the author makes clear, it was not concerned with defence supply.[19] *British war economy* and *Lessons of the war economy* were thus studies of the civil economy in wartime, but ones which would be treated as studies of the war economy, and as such set a pattern for subsequent work. Thus a recent survey by Broadberry and Howlett of the war economy is the economy as seen by economists concerned with central economic balancing.[20] The broader literature is well summarised in a textbook on industrial modernisation: the chapter on the period 1940 to 1951 covers the rise of Keynesianism, the importance of Labour and Ernest Bevin, the 'key' new ministries, Supply, Fuel and Power, Food, and 'most crucial of all' the Ministry of Production, and then reconstruction, which is discussed largely in macroeconomic terms.[21] The war and the warfare state are curiously missing.

More specialised and more detailed work also neglects the warfare state. The history of wartime industrial policy affords a glaring example: it is very largely a history of planning for after the war, by purely civilian agencies, for future civil industry only.[22] The warfare state, which dominated industry in wartime, does not appear and indeed appears not to

[19] A. E. G. Robinson's chapter on 'The overall allocation of resources', though concerned with the role of the Ministry of Production in allocation, gives a better picture of the war economy as a whole. D. N. Chester (ed.), *Lessons of the British war economy* (Cambridge: Cambridge University Press, 1951).

[20] S. Broadberry and P. Howlett, 'The United Kingdom: "victory at all costs"', in Mark Harrison (ed.), *The economics of World War II: six great Powers in international comparison*, (Cambridge: Cambridge University Press, 1998), pp. 43–80. See also the survey in K. Jeffreys, *The Churchill coalition and wartime politics, 1940–1945* (Manchester: Manchester University Press, 1991), ch. 3.

[21] S. Newton and G. Porter, *Modernisation frustrated: the politics of industrial decline in Britain since 1900* (London: Unwin Hyman, 1988).

[22] F. H. Longstreth, 'State economic planning in a capitalist society: the political sociology of economic policy in Britain, 1940–1979', unpublished doctoral thesis, London School of Economics (1983) and F. Longstreth, 'The City, industry and trade' in Colin Crouch (ed.), *State and economy in contemporary capitalism* (London: Croom Helm, 1979); Keith Middlemas, *Power, competition and the state*. i: *Britain in search of balance, 1940–1961* (London: Macmillan, 1986); Corelli Barnett, *The audit of war* (London: Macmillan, 1986).

exist.[23] Another example concerns planning: the introduction to the Public Record Office (PRO) guide to papers on British economic planning between 1943 and 1951 tells the story as one starting with socialist intellectuals, moves on to reconstruction committees in wartime and then to the weak attempts at central planning by the post-war Labour government. The records selected exclude most of those concerned with the planning of the war and with defence procurement after it.[24] Certainly many of the wartime planners and administrators seemed to think that planning for the war was very different from planning in general.[25] But for historians the relations between different kinds of planning is, or rather should be, a matter for enquiry, not a matter of accepting the highly loaded definitions of economists.

Military expenditure and the development of the British state

There is much to be said for the notion that the British state was a 'welfare state' from well before the Second World War. From the interwar years welfare expenditures were already greater than warfare expenditures. There is, however, a poor correlation between historians' claims for the subsequent rise of the welfare state and changes in welfare spending. Increases are particularly associated with the Second World War and its immediate aftermath, but both the right and the left, each for its own purposes, have exaggerated their significance. Sidney Pollard cautioned long ago that 'In spite of a widespread belief to the contrary, Britain did not spend significantly more on the social services after 1948 than she did before 1939 apart from the retirement pension.'[26] Roger Middleton, another exception, has revised the picture in a different way, showing that the rise in welfare spending was much greater following the Great War than the Second World War, and that after around 1950 the rise in public spending was remarkably low, certainly lower than in the interwar

---

[23] I know of only two general texts in which an adequate overall picture of wartime economic administration is given: Alan Milward, *War, economy and society* (London: Allen Lane, 1977) and J. M. Lee, *The Churchill coalition* (London: Batsford, 1980).

[24] B. W. E. Alford, Rodney Lowe and Neil Rollings, *Economic planning 1943–1951: a guide to documents in the Public Record Office* (PRO Handbook no. 26) (London: HMSO, 1992).

[25] John Jewkes, *Ordeal by planning* (London: Macmillan, 1948) is about post-war planning by the Labour government not wartime planning. Oliver Franks, *Central planning and control in war and peace* (London: London School of Economics, 1947) draws the standard distinction between war and peace.

[26] Sidney Pollard, *The development of the British economy, 1914–1980* 3rd edn (London: Arnold, 1983), p. 272.

years.[27] A recent revised analysis of post-war poverty suggests, contrary to contemporary claims, that post-1936 welfare measures (excluding food subsidies) reduced the number of working class households below the poverty line by only 3.7 per cent.[28] The growth in welfare spending was hardly enormous, as fig. 2.1 shows. For health expenditure there are no real-terms cross-war estimates of expenditure – in itself interesting. Estimated total public and private health spending is £150 million in the mid-1930s (about 3 per cent of GNP).[29] That would have been worth around £300 million in the late 1940s, which suggests, since in the early years the National Health Service (NHS) was spending around £400 million, a hardly revolutionary increase of about 25 per cent over a decade. Remarkably, plans for the NHS during the war involved expenditure plans which were less (even without correction for inflation) than total 1930s' health expenditure, and the early plans appeared to envisage real-terms expenditure that was just as niggardly.[30]

The most significant change in public expenditure between the interwar years and the war and post-war years was in defence expenditure. This increased twentyfold from 1938/9 to its wartime peak, while conventional civil expenditure (that undertaken under the usual parliamentary procedure) hardly changed through the war (table 2.1). That is perhaps obvious; but less obvious is that from the interwar years to the post-war years warfare spending also grew a good deal more than welfare spending.[31] In relation to gross domestic product (GDP) as fig. 2.1 shows, defence expenditure was about twice as great in the late 1940s as in 1935 and three times greater in the early 1950s. In 1953 defence took over 30 per cent of public expenditure (net of debt interest), while health and social security took 26 per cent (see table 2.2). The 'warfareness' of the post-1914 peacetime state, the

---

[27] Roger Middleton, *Government and market: the growth of the public sector, economic management and British economic performance, c. 1890–1979* (Cheltenham: Elgar, 1996).

[28] T. J. Hatton and R. E. Bailey, 'Seebohm Rowntree and the postwar poverty puzzle', *Economic History Review* 53 (2000), 544–64.

[29] Charles Webster, *Health services since the War* (London: HMSO, 1988), I, pp. 12–13. Public expenditure on health was around 1.2 per cent of GNP. T. Cutler, 'Dangerous yardstick? Early cost estimates and the politics of financial management in the first decade of the National Health Service', *Medical History* 47 (2003), 217–38, does not do the trans-war comparison either.

[30] See Webster, *Health services*, pp. 133–4, though Webster does not appear to make the crucial correction for wartime inflation.

[31] A point surprisingly not made in Middleton's reassessment. Nor is the relationship between welfare and warfare spending explored in the interesting ch. 5 of Karen A. Rasler and William R. Thompson, *War and state making: the shaping of global powers* (London: Unwin Hyman, 1989), which notes the increases in both non-military and military expenditures comparing the post-great war periods in Britain, the USA and France.

Table 2.1 *Defence and civil expenditure by British central government*
(£ million)[a]

	1937/8	1938/9	1939/40	1940/1	1941/2	1942/3	1943/4	1944/5
Total supply services	605	696	1078	3637	4502	5295	5407	5625
Of which defence	197	254	626	3220	4085	4840	4950	5125
Of which civil votes	394	427	437	402	400	438	439	474

Note:
[a] this excludes civil expenditures on votes of credit.

Source: Statistical digest of the war (HMSO, 1951), table 173.

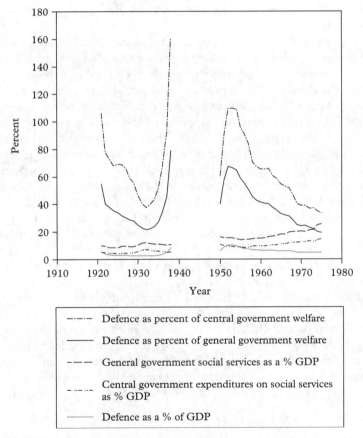

Figure 2.1 The warfareness and welfareness of British state
spending, 1921–75

Table 2.2 *Proportion of gross national income used by the state (percentage)*

	1938	1950	1952	1954/5
Health	1.2	3.4	3.0	
Education	1.9	2.1	2.3	
All social services	3.8	6.0	5.6	
Defence	5.9	5.9	9.3	11

Source: copied from *New Statesman and Nation*, 27 February 1954, giving *The Times* 17 July 1953 as source.

ratio of warfare to welfare spending, peaked in 1938 and 1952. Its inverse – 'welfareness' – peaked in 1932. Only in 1970 did the welfareness of the state return to this level.

It is clear from fig. 2.1 that there was a post-war pattern of a shift of government expenditure from warfare to welfare after both world wars. There were significant differences though: even if we date post-Second World War disarmament from the 1950s rather than 1945, it is worth noting not only that the welfare:warfare ratio stood at the same level as about 1920, but that welfareness increased more slowly after 1950 than after 1920. It is further worth noting that, in contrast to the interwar period, defence spending was falling as a proportion of GDP from the early 1950s. As a proportion of national income, peacetime defence spending was higher in 1928 than in 1890, it was considerably higher in 1937 than in 1912, and was very much higher in 1950 than in 1924. Even in 1979 it was twice the level it was in 1928, though lower than in 1950. Only in the late 1990s was defence consuming a similar proportion of national income as in the interwar and Edwardian years. The cold war was hugely important to the fiscal history of the British state, even though accounts of the state hardly take it into account.

Britain was not at all unusual among European states in being a 'welfare state'. As José Harris observed, the statistical sources consistently show that post-war Britain was a low spender on social services by comparison with European nations.[32] By contrast British defence expenditures, after the Second World War, were high by continental European standards. This is somewhat misleading as there was only one other post-war major power in Europe, and France was embroiled in colonial

[32] José Harris, 'Enterprise and welfare states: a comparative perspective', *Transactions of the Royal Historical Society* 40 (1990), 175–95; esp. 179–82.

struggles. Britain's post-war defence expenditure was about the same as a proportion of GDP as that of France, with a tendency to stay higher, while its welfare expenditure was larger, but only from the late 1950s. That British and French expenditures were broadly similar in the post-war years is notable in that before the war British defence expenditure was much smaller as a proportion of GDP than French: the British state became more like the French state by increasing defence expenditure.

It could be argued that even if the rise in welfare expenditures was not large, the transfer to the central state of many welfare and economic functions previously performed by the private sector and the local authorities was crucial in transforming the scale of the central state. Thus a 1950s' study of the British civil service claimed that 'The principal reason for the inability to slash the British Civil Service as drastically as the critics demand is the flood of new responsibilities which have fallen on public offices since the war. The welfare state requires huge staffs of officials.'[33] Yet the same book provides a table showing that between 1938 and 1954 the non-industrial civil service grew by 292,000, of which 100,000 was due to the now five defence departments, the service and supply ministries concerned with the armed forces, and supplying them with equipment. Only 42,000 went to social services of all sorts. Of the remainder, 56,000 went to the Post Office, and 40,000 to Trade, Industry and Transport, leaving 54,000 for all other departments.[34] The number of non-industrial civil servants in defence departments (which I will use as shorthand for service and supply departments) had been about 10,000 in 1914, 23,040 in 1935 and 135,270 in 1956.[35]

These figures in fact underestimate the growth of the warfare state because they exclude (and most figures on state employment do) the vast army of industrial civil servants. In 1929 there were 122,000 'industrial' workers in the civil service, a category which excluded the great majority of ('manipulative') postal workers.[36] In wartime the number peaked at 738,000 in 1943, with about 650,000 in defence departments.[37] During the war half of all civil servants were industrial workers. In 1957 there were a total of 418,300 industrial civil servants, of which 289,600 were in defence departments, a number which fell steadily to 154,200 by 1971.[38]

[33] G. A. Campbell, *The civil service in Britain* (Harmondsworth: Penguin, 1955), p. 95.

[34] Campbell, *Civil service*, p. 100.

[35] D. N. Chester and F. M. G. Willson, *The organisation of British central government*, 2nd edn (London: Allen & Unwin, 1968), table XVIII, p. 328.

[36] Royal Commission on the Civil Service, *Introductory factual memorandum relating to the civil service submitted by the Treasury*, 1930, Vol. x, Cmd 3909 (London: HMSO, 1931).

[37] Central Statistical Office, *Statistical digest of the war* (London: HMSO, 1951), table 32.

[38] F. M. G. Willson, 'Coping with administrative growth: super-departments and the ministerial cadre 1957–77' in David Butler and A. H. Halsey (eds.), *Policy and politics: essays in honour of Norman Chester* (London: Macmillan, 1978), p. 38.

By 1957 40 per cent of all civil servants were in defence departments compared with 20 per cent of non-industrial civil servants; in this year there were about the same number of civil servants in the defence departments (423,000) as in the whole British state in 1929 (434,000).[39] Here, again, the warfare state turns out to be by far the most significant area of growth of the civilian state.

And yet we have not mentioned that the most obvious manifestation of the warfare state was the increase in numbers of men and women in uniform. By 1945 there were 4.5 million men in the armed services and 0.4 million women.[40] After the war force levels fell to 689,000 in 1950, and were then pushed up to a peacetime peak of 872,00, before falling below 500,000 only in 1960. In the early 1930s the figure was around 320,000. These high levels were produced by conscription. Peacetime conscription had been introduced in 1939; after the war peacetime service remained, increasing from one year in 1947, to eighteen months from 1948 and to two years from 1950. No men were conscripted from the end of 1960 and the last conscripts left in 1963.[41] It was not for nothing that for the twenty years between 1939 and 1959 the Ministry of Labour was called the Ministry of Labour and National Service.

Controlling the war economy

Given the scale of the mobilisation of 'manpower' it is perhaps hardly surprising then that labour, and especially industrial labour, has such a prominent place in the historiography of Britain in the Second World War. As we have already seen, the economists and historians have placed great emphasis on 'manpower' as the limiting resource, on the 'manpower budget' becoming more important than the financial budget and on power passing from the Treasury to the Ministry of Labour and to Ernest Bevin. Keith Middlemas, for example, claims that from 1942 to the end of the war, the Ministry of Labour was 'the principal department of state' and that Bevin 'effectively ranked as Deputy Prime Minister'.[42] This is an extreme formulation, but one in keeping with the rest of the

---

[39] Calculated from Willson, 'Administrative growth', p. 38 and Royal Commission on the Civil Service, *Introductory factual memorandum*.

[40] *Statistical digest of the war*, table 9.

[41] On the internal politics of getting rid of conscription see Martin S. Navias, 'Terminating conscription? the British National Service controversy, 1955–1956', *Journal of Contemporary History* 24 (1989) 195–208. In the initial 1947 Bill conscription was set at eighteen months, but was reduced to one year.

[42] Middlemas, *Britain in search of balance*, pp. 20, 30. Compare N. Calder, *The people's war* (London: Cape, 1969), pp. 102 and 270. The crucial civil servant, in his later account of the Ministry of Labour and National Service, while stressing the importance of the manpower

literature. There is no denying that in conditions of over-full employment labour did gain significant concessions, nor of course that there was an enormous political shift which brought a Labour government to office in 1945. However, it is a different matter to suggest radical changes in the nature of the state of the sort implied by this picture or that war production was somehow controlled by the Ministry of Labour. We need to look in more detail at the control of the war economy and the key planning issues.

First, it is important to note that although manpower became the scarcest resource only from 1942 onwards, planning of war production was well under way already and the power of the Treasury was already much reduced.[43] Secondly, the key minister involved in deciding manpower allocations was not the trade unionist Ernest Bevin but Sir John Anderson, first as Lord President of the Council and later as Chancellor of the Exchequer (that is the head of the Treasury), though in his capacity of chairman of the Manpower Committee.[44] Thirdly, in war economies and centrally planned economies the overall allocation of the scarcest resource should not be confused with planning itself. It was a tool for enforcing priorities between ministries. The allocation of labour was not the plan for war production itself: it tells us nothing about what is planned and what for, nor does it reveal the huge complex of decision making, or the power relations involved, over a vast range of inputs and outputs (some scarce, some not) that planning required. The planning of military operations, of tank production or of aircraft production was the responsibility of specialist ministries not central planners.

A second theme of the literature is the sense of coming together of leading actors in running the war economy. There is a suggestion that decision making was at some level joint or corporatist – that government, industry and the unions, with Labour in the heart of government, all sat down and worked out the way forward. Clearly a political deal was done between state, capital and labour.[45] However, tripartism (or bipartism) had no part in war production planning. There were, as we shall see, tripartite and bipartite commissions and boards concerned with some

budget made clear the key control was with the war cabinet, and indeed that key wartime role of the ministry was confined to labour questions – Sir Geoffrey Ince, *The Ministry of Labour and National Service* (London: Allen & Unwin, 1960), p. 42. Ince was a mathematician.

[43] For the mechanisms for the allocation of steel, a crucial material whose supply hardly increased, see Peter Howlett, 'Resource allocation in wartime Britain: the case of steel, 1939–1945', *Journal of Contemporary History* 29 (1994), 523–44.

[44] Hancock and Gowing, *British war economy*, pp. 443, 450 especially. George Peden, *The treasury and British public policy, 1906–1959* (Oxford: Oxford University Press, 2000), p. 307.

[45] For a rare explicit statement of this usually implicit argument see Andrew Cox and Joe Sanderson, 'The political economy of Britain since 1939' in Andrew Cox, Simon Lee and Joe Sanderson, *The political economy of modern Britain* (Cheltenham: Elgar, 1997), pp. 13–14.

non-armament civilian industries, but they were certainly not used to direct war production nor indeed were they used in the armament ministries. Trade unionists are utterly absent from executive positions in arms production, which as we shall see in another chapter were dominated by men drawn from the military-industrial complex. The joint production committees were significant, but these operated only at plant level.

What then of a third factor often invoked, Keynesianism? As Robert Skidelsky has very usefully pointed out, Keynes's *How to pay for the war*, far from being a plan to plan the war economy was designed to avoid the need for physical planning: the price mechanism, Keynes hoped, could continue to work as 'an alternative to inflation as well as to physical planning'.[46] Keynes proposed compulsory working-class savings to remove private purchasing power from the economy to allow the slack to be taken up by armaments. During the war 'Keynesianism' did not provide economic tools to plan the economy, except in the important field of control of inflation. Less still did it suggest policies for the control of particular industries – indeed it had no distinctive industrial policy. Most professional economists were hostile to planning, especially perhaps those who were directly involved in industrial planning and programming.[47] In any case the economists in the supply departments were in no sense in directive positions. The small group of socialist economists who did argue for physical planning had little influence on wartime industrial control. Whatever the debate about 'planning' among the economists, and whatever the image of the self-mobilisation of labour to work with business and the state to produce armaments, the state's plans, actions and methods came from elsewhere.[48] High levels of arms production were the result of the realisation of the plans of the armed services. At the national level planning was the consequence, not the cause, of high arms production. It was a means of accommodation to the needs of the warfare state.

Perhaps the best measure of the impact of war was the rise in state consumption (government expenditure excepting transfers) – this rose from around 10 per cent of GDP in the interwar years to a wartime peak of 54 per cent, falling to 17 per cent in 1948, rising in rearmament to

---

[46] Robert Skidelsky, *John Maynard Keynes: fighting for Britain, 1937–1946* (London: Macmillan, 2000), p. 67.

[47] Thus Lionel Robbins was the head of the economic section of the Cabinet Office, a notable anti-planner. The successive directors general of planning in the MAP were Manchester liberals – John Jewkes and Ely Devons.

[48] On the socialist economists in the 1930s see Daniel Ritschel, *The politics of planning* (Oxford: Clarendon Press, 1997). On the lack of economists committed to planning in the 1940s see Jim Tomlinson, *Democratic socialism and economic policy: the Attlee years, 1945–1951* (Cambridge: Cambridge University Press, 1997), ch. 6.

22 per cent, and falling back further to 16.6 per cent in 1965.[49] In wartime most of this state demand was channelled through specialised ministries which supplied the forces with weapons and supplies. These supply ministries, as they will be called here, extended themselves deep into the national economy. The Ministry of Supply (MoS) took care of army supplies, raw material controls (a key aspect of the control of industry), and particular armament-related industries (including chemicals); the Ministry of Aircraft Production (MAP) took care of aircraft and related industries and also the emergent electronic industry. The Admiralty (which was also a service ministry) took over responsibility for the whole of shipbuilding. Around two-thirds of the output of wartime manufacturing industry was taken by these three ministries. The older historiography sees these ministries as expressions of the necessary victory of civilians over the military in matters of production, as civilian – industrial, academic, scientific – incursions on the military world rather than transmission belts for military demands on society.

In this the historiography followed contemporary arguments: through the rearmament period opposition forces claimed that the service ministries were incapable of organising industrial production for rearmament and war. They called in effect for a new Ministry of Munitions, a civilian ministry of armaments to be called the Ministry of Supply, to plan, to control the civilian economy and also to put civilians in charge of armament production. The government, the service ministries and Sir Maurice Hankey, the Cabinet secretary and secretary of the Committee of Imperial Defence, were hostile, even when the recommendation was made by a Royal Commission.[50] They pointed out that the services were capable of managing rearmament: as Lord Chatfield, the head of the navy, was to put it: 'The cry for a Ministry of Supply which eventually arose, was due to the War Office being unable to develop the Army's production needs, in the same way that Navy and Air Force has done, and were doing'.[51] The Air Ministry and the Admiralty – the two foci for rearmament – did manage the process well by any reasonable standard. Armament production expanded at a rate way beyond that of the fastest

[49] C. H. Feinstein, *National income, expenditure and output of the United Kingdom 1855–1965* (Cambridge: Cambridge University Press, 1972) table 19, public authorities' current expenditure on goods and services as percentage of GDP.

[50] See David G. Anderson, 'British rearmament and the "merchants of death": the 1935–6 Royal Commission on the private manufacture of and trading in arms', *Journal of Contemporary History* 29 (1994), 5–37.

[51] Lord Chatfield, *It might happen again.* Vol. II: *The navy and defence* (London: Heinemann, 1948), p. 34. G. A. H. Gordon, *British seapower and procurement between the wars: a reappraisal of rearmament* (London: Macmillan, 1988).

growing civilian industries. Between 1935 and 1939 aircraft structure weight produced increased fifteen-fold; between 1936/7 and 1939 the tonnage of major warships completed doubled. As we have seen, the British out-built all other navies in the rearmament period. Air rearmament gave the British the greatest aircraft production of any power in 1940.[52] At the same time the basis was deliberately and carefully laid for even larger future expansions by the creation of new plant. However, in early 1939, before war was declared, it was decided that the army was to be much larger in scale than hitherto planned. This led the Chamberlain government to create a Ministry of Supply which supplied only the army with weapons, but also provided general supplies for the forces, and prepared to operate raw material controls. The second supply ministry to be created, the MAP, has had much more political and historiographical resonance. Created in the dramatic month of May 1940, it put the dynamic newspaper magnate, and Churchill's close friend, Lord Beaverbrook in charge of aircraft production. Beaverbrook credited himself with transforming output, and he has been followed in this by others, including his acolytes the journalist and politician Michael Foot and the historian A. J. P. Taylor.[53] This picture of the energetic civilian ousting the complacent air marshals and putting production to the fore has long been doubted by historians.[54] Rightly so, since as we shall see in the next chapter there were also important continuities in personnel. Indeed it is important to note that these new ministries grew out of the service ministries. The new MoS of 1939 grew out of the Directorate-General of Munitions Production of the War Office; the MAP out of the Department of the Air Member for Development and Production. However, the retrospective case for separate ministries seemed compelling in the light of the standard picture of utterly inadequate inter-war armament production and rearmament.

---

[52] Gordon, *British seapower and procurement*, my *England and the aeroplane* (London: Macmillan, 1991) and Sebastian Ritchie, *Industry and air power: the expansion of British aircraft production, 1935–1941* (London: Cass, 1997).

[53] *Guilty men* (London: Gollancz, 1940) was the work of Beaverbrook journalists, among them Michael Foot editor of the *Evening Standard*. Taylor was to write Beaverbrook's biography: A. J. P. Taylor, *Beaverbrook* (London: Hamilton, 1972).

[54] A. J. Robertson, 'Lord Beaverbrook and the supply of aircraft, 1940–1941' in A. Slaven and D. H. Aldcroft (eds.), *Business, banking and urban history* (London: John Donald, 1982), pp. 80–100; D. E. H. Edgerton 'State intervention in British manufacturing industry, 1931–1951: a comparative study of policy for the military aircraft and cotton textile industries', unpublished doctoral thesis, university of London (1986); A. Cairncross, *Planning in wartime: aircraft production in Britain, Germany and the USA* (London: Macmillan, 1991).

The new arms industry

During the war, for every man and woman in uniform, there was an industrial worker producing goods for them. In 1943 for example there were almost exactly the same number (4.8 million) in the forces and in manufacturing industry supplying the forces. Together both groups amounted to around 45 per cent of the working population.[55] In March 1943 the largest group of workers in manufacturing supplying the forces directly were 4.02 million workers in engineering, metals (excluding iron and steel and related), explosives and chemicals, and shipbuilding. To these we need to add 270,000 in textiles, around 100,000 in clothing, boots and shoes, etc., another 100,000 in woodworking and furniture, another 60,000 or so in paper and publishing, and about 90,000 in leather, rubber, glass and pottery, and around 300,000 in construction.[56] These figures exclude the appropriate proportions of miners, steel workers, railway workers, agricultural and food workers, and so on that also supplied the forces directly and indirectly (see table 2.3).

Between June 1939 and June 1943 (the peak of war production) employment in manufacturing industry increased by only 13.7 per cent. The primary change brought about by the war was the increase in the proportion of workers making manufactures for the forces from 18 per cent to 66 per cent. This entailed very large falls in exports and in domestic civilian supply. The implicit image these figures, and many like them, convey is that particular firms in particular industries switched their factories from making export and civilian goods to making armaments. The image is of civilian industry producing for war as it produced for peace. Indeed there was, as we shall see, a powerful image that it was precisely from this move of civilian ingenuity, skill and organisational genius that victory in war came. There is a particular twist to this story that would later become important: the idea that British industry sacrificed itself not only in giving up its overseas markets but in eating up its capital stock. As the future Prime Minister Harold Wilson was to put it, there was a 'failure to make good the wear and tear of machinery overworked in war production';[57] indeed for Wilson there appeared to be no benefit whatever from war production.[58]

---

[55] *Statistical digest of the war*, table 9; H. M. D. Parker, *Manpower* (London, HMSO, 1957), table II, p. 483. By 1945 there were 10 million men in civil employment and 6 million women.

[56] *Statistical digest of the war*, tables 19–29. These figures include a suitable proportion of industrial civil servants. It is not clear from the industry tables, but it is in the note on p. 211 referring to tables 32–3 which deal with civil service employment.

[57] Harold Wilson, *Post-war economic policies in Britain* (London: Fabian Society, 1957), p. 2.

[58] Ibid., pp. 3–5.

Table 2.3 *Employment on the manufacture of arms at wartime peak (June 1943) by ministry and type of factory (thousands)*

	A[a]	B[b]	A+B	C[c]	A+B+C	Total manufacturing
Royal Ordnance factories	–	–	–	–	268[d]	–
Royal dockyards	–	–	–	–	37[d]	–
MAP agency	–	–	–	–	300[d]	–
MoS and Admiralty agency	–	–	–	–	210+[d]	–
Total of above (government factories)	500+[d]	–	–	250+[d]	c. 900[d]	–
MoS assistance	–	–	–	–	350[e]	
Admiralty assistance	–	–	–	–	76[e]	
MAP assistance	–	–	–	–	312[e]	
Total assistance	–	–	–	–	c.738[e]	
MoS total workers	–	–	1,100[f]	–	–	
MAP total workers	–	–	1,400[f]	–	–	
Admiralty total workers	–	–	650[f]	–	–	
Total all supply ministries	–	–	3,300[f]	500[f]	3,800[f]	
Total employment for civil use	556.9[g]	104.8[g]	–	166.5[g]	828.2[g]	2,625[h]
Total employment for the forces	3453.3[g]	167.5[g]	–	398.8[g]	4019.6[g]	5,121[h]
Total	4,010.2[g]	272.3[g]	–	565.3[g]	4847.8	7,746[h]

Notes:

[a] Engineering and allied (includes non-ferrous metals only).

[b] Shipbuilding and repairs

[c] Explosives, chemicals and ammunition.

[d] From W. Hornby, *Factories and plant* (London: HMSO, 1958) p. 383.

[e] My estimate calculated as follows: total spent on assistance to contractors by MoS to 1945 is £173.9 million, out of a total on buildings and plant of £460.4 million (Hornby, *Factories and plant*, p. 378). Up to 1945 £432.3 million was spent on government factories (government operation plus agency) (Hornby, *Factories and plant*, pp. 378–80). These factories employed c. 900,000, suggesting 2,000 workers per million pounds of capital. (The ratio is almost identical for aircraft agency factories only, and 1,500 for the Royal Ordnance factories). Assuming this figure of 2,000 gives 312,000 workers in government-funded extensions to firms by MAP, and 350,000 for MoS contractors, and 76,000 for the Admiralty (see the figure in Hornby, *Factories and plant*, p. 381). The figures may underestimate the number of workers working on government plant, since for the MoS and Admiralty the assistance to contractors was largely plant and not buildings (Hornby, *Factories and plant*, p. 381). In other words, in contrast to the government operations and agency factories (but not MAP assistance) existing buildings were used. The estimate assumes that the capital was used to set up complete operating units.

[f] From Hornby, *Factories and plant*, p. 30.

[g] From Central Statistical Office, *Statistical digest of the war* (London: HMSO, 1951).

[h] From H. M. D. Parker, *Manpower* (London: HMSO, 1947), p. 483.

Wilson was not alone – most commentators and historians imply that British industry was uniformly clapped out by the end of the war.[59]

The wartime story of manufacturing industry is better told another way: as a story of growth for some industries and firms and decline for others; of huge investments in some and running down in others. This is not at all obvious from the usual industrial statistics or indeed the official histories of war production. Many industries producing civilian consumer goods like textiles, clothing, furniture, jewellery were cut back, with plant and factories lying idle. Of course textiles, clothing and furniture were still needed in war, not least, as we have seen, for the forces, but the total requirement was pushed down and surplus workers used elsewhere. Some sectors, notably engineering and chemicals, saw their output increase. However, the statistical image of industrial 'sectors', and shifts between them, conceals one of the most extraordinary aspects of war production. A huge proportion, perhaps half, of all armaments were (in my estimate) produced not in existing facilities but in newly built, government-owned arms plants or on specialist machines supplied by government. The new armament industry, created with public money, has remained, with the partial exception of the Royal Ordnance factories, and shadow factories, invisible both because of its distribution across industrial 'sectors' but also because, as we shall see, it complicates the politically central story of British public ownership of industry. It even has a rather odd place in the macroeconomic statistics – it was subsumed not in investment figures but in current defence expenditure. Post-war statisticians had to make their own estimates as to how much should count as investment in industry, based in part on careful reading of the official histories of war production published in the 1950s.[60] The overall investment was enormous: between 1936 and 1945 the state invested around £1 billion in armament capacity. There was additional investment abroad.[61] Its comparative scale may be gauged from looking at the compensation paid for industries which were nationalised in the 1940s: £927 million for the railways, £392 million for the coal mines, and £246 million for the iron and steel industry.[62] Private investment in arms

---

[59] For example, A. Cairncross, *Years of recovery: British economic policy, 1945–1951* (London: Methuen, 1985, 1987), p. 13.

[60] Philip Redfern 'Net investment in fixed assets in the United Kingdom, 1938–1953', *Journal of the Royal Statistical Society* Series A 118 (1955), 10–182. Barna pointed out that Redfern had underestimated: T. Barna 'The replacement cost of fixed assets in British manufacturing industry in 1955', *Journal of the Royal Statistical Society* Series A 120 (1957).

[61] Keynes claimed that Britain spent $2.0 billion on building of arms plant in the USA before Lend-Lease; these plants were later 'sold' without payment. Skidelsky, *John Maynard Keynes*, p. 94.

[62] See Sir Norman Chester, *The nationalisation of British industry 1945–51* (London: HMSO, 1975), pp. 238, 257, 274, 315.

production was much smaller than public investment. In the wartime air-craft industry in 1944 some £60 million of privately owned capital was used, while the total value of assets used was at least £200 million.[63] In the case of the chemical giant ICI, three-quarters of all its investment between 1938 and 1944, which came to nearly £80 million, was provided by government.[64] One statistician estimated that much of the armament investment was of use to post-war industry – he thought some £680 million was so invested in chemicals, engineering, vehicles, shipbuilding and metal goods.[65] These investments had a huge, differential, effect on British industry. The same statistician found that in non-armament industries the proportion of plant existing in 1961 which had been installed between 1939 and 1947 was low: 8 per cent in food, drink and tobacco, 7 per cent in iron and steel, 8 per cent in textiles. By contrast it was no less than 40 per cent in metal-using and non-ferrous metals industries, where military demand and state investment was concentrated.[66] A. J. P. Taylor was partly right when in the penultimate paragraph of his *English History* he stated that:

the second war, unlike the first, stimulated or created new industries which could hold their own in peacetime. During the second World war [*sic*], and not before, Great Britain took the decisive step into the twentieth century. Before the war Great Britain was still trying to revive the old staples. After it, she relied on new developing industries. Electricity, motor cars, iron and steel, machine tools, nylons, and chemicals were all set for expansion, and in all of them output per head was steadily increasing. The very spirit of the nation had changed.[67]

This is a story confirmed by both production and export statistics.[68] What Taylor inevitably missed was the key role of (hidden) public investment in certain sectors.

That state investment would be required for most of the new armament capacity was clear from the 1930s. It was needed because of the temporal

[63] 'Financial development of the Main SBAC firms from the beginning of the rearmament period', AVIA 65/1731, PRO.

[64] It invested £58.5 million on behalf of the government and £20 million on its own account. W. J. Reader, *Imperial Chemical Industries: a history*, vol. II (London: Oxford University Press, 1975), p. 254.

[65] G. A. Dean 'The stock of fixed capital in the United Kingdom in 1961', *Journal of the Royal Statistical Society* Series A 127 (1964), 33–5.

[66] Dean 'Stock of fixed capital', table III, pp. 348–9.

[67] A. J. P. Taylor, *English history 1914–1945* (Oxford: Clarendon Press, 1965), p. 600. At a conference of the Institute for Contemporary British History in the early 1990s Eric Hobsbawm quoted this passage as an example of complacency about the state of British industry after the war.

[68] See for example Carl Glatt, 'Reparations and the transfer of scientific and industrial technology from Germany: a case study of the roots of British industrial policy and of aspects of British occupation policy in Germany between post-World War II reconstruction and the Korean War, 1943–1951', unpublished doctoral thesis, European University Institute, Florence, 3 vols.(1994), III, pp. 1068–79.

peculiarities of the demand for armaments, and because some capacity had no use other than for the production of armaments. Government accepted that it would have to finance the building of capacity which it was believed would become redundant either because war would not happen, or at the end of the war. In general it decided (not surprisingly) that such capacity would be state owned, but how it would be operated varied enormously between departments and cases. The Admiralty and MoS – the latter especially – expanded capacity they ran themselves in the form of royal dockyards, Admiralty factories and, most importantly of all, the Royal Ordnance factories. There was a massive expansion in the state's own industrial capacity largely using the manufacturing techniques already used in the state sector. The forty or so new Royal Ordnance factories – which grew out of the three historic ones – Woolwich, Enfield and Waltham Abbey – were a huge and very visible state effort. These factories made weapons, explosives and propellants and filled munitions. The 'filling factories' were particularly extraordinary places – series of small buildings surrounded by bunkers to create a weirdly cratered landscape. The staffs of these factories were industrial civil servants, just like the staff of the original factories. In the field of R&D there was also a good measure of hidden extension of public ownership. As we shall see in a following chapter, the laboratories of the military research corps were enormously expanded by the recruitment of (typically) young scientists and engineers from the civil world. Existing laboratories were expanded, older laboratories were relocated and new ones built. Indeed there was a push, as we will presently see, to extend the role of the state laboratories into areas which had been the prerogative of private industry.

Much less visible was the use of private firms to build and run state-owned capacity. The MAP, which ran no factories itself, and the MoS, through complicated 'agency' arrangements, and 'capital assistance' schemes, financed a vast expansion in capacity right across armament production. A crucial aspect was that while many important private firms managed new arms factories, and made arms in their own factories, there was a particular and unexpectedly large role for arms firms in running the new factories. The expansion of the pre-war aircraft firms was especially remarkable – for most airframe firms there was at the peak of war production about a tenfold increase in employment over 1936, and a six- to tenfold increase in floor space. At the same time the pre-war airframe firms employed no fewer than 225,000 people,[69] and the engine firms at least 120,000.[70] Vickers reached 53,000 in aircraft production alone; A. V. Roe, just one of the

[69] W. Hornby, *Factories and plant* (London: HMSO, 1958), pp. 240–2.
[70] Ibid., pp. 262–3.

Hawker-Siddeley companies, 35,000; three other firms employed between 17,000 and 20,000 workers. The largest outsider firms were smaller employers in airframes: the electrical engineers English Electric and the car maker Rootes employed only around 13,000 each, while the car maker Austin, London Aircraft Production (the name given to the London bus depots making aircraft) and the electrical engineers Metropolitan-Vickers came in at under 10,000. It had been expected that the car firms would have been more important – as exemplars of modern civilian industry they had been given shadow factories in the 1930s, but thereafter there was a marked trend for extra capacity to go to the aircraft firms. In one important case, the poor record of the car giant Nuffield in running the large Castle Bromwich Spitfire factory led to its being taken over by Vickers. In the case of aero-engines car firms would have a greater role, but it was found in the very late 1930s that 'very little of the existing plant' in motor car firms could in fact be used for aero-engines, so new capacity had to be provided. Motor firms did manage a large number of aero-engine plants, producing about 40 per cent of output.[71] At the end of the war two-thirds of Bristol engines came from car firms operating shadow factories and Rolls-Royce was producing around 60 per cent of its engines; the balance was made up by the Ford shadow factory in Manchester.[72] Ford employed over 16,000, the other four motor firms employed around 10,000 each on aero-engines.[73] By contrast, in 1943 Rolls-Royce employed 56,000 on aero-engines, Bristol 36,000 and Napier about 20,000, while others were well under 17,000.[74] In the case of the MoS more than half the agency factories (other than raw materials factories) were 'under the management of armament firms or other specialist firms. ... the agency system was used more to extend the use of the armament firms than to introduce outside firms to war production'.[75] Many of these agency factories were replica Ordnance factories where the firms provided the management of labour.

There was one area of arms production where neither Ordnance factories nor arms firms were dominant and that was tank production, and to a lesser extent tank design. Before the war, Vickers monopolised private design and production, while Woolwich made only a minor contribution. In the mid to late 1930s Vickers designed four tanks which went into production. From the late 1930s locomotive and railway workshops (Vulcan Foundry and London Midland and Scottish Railway (LMS)

[71] Ibid., p. 255.
[72] Ibid., pp. 256, 258. The Ford factory made Merlin engines on a huge scale.
[73] Ibid., p. 262. The figures are not entirely clear but the shadow firms employed about 30 per cent of total aero-engine labour – that is 70 per cent was with the traditional firms.
[74] Ibid., p. 262.   [75] Ibid., p. 154.

workshops) were brought into design, together with an arms offshoot of Nuffield Motors. Later the shipbuilders Harland and Wolff, the rolling stock makers Birmingham Railway Carriage and Wagon, and two lorry makers, Leyland Motors and Vauxhall, were brought in. Production of tanks was dominated by these outside firms.[76] But while the quality of the 1930s' Vickers tanks, but not quantities, were good, most of the other tanks proved very poor and British forces were to use very large numbers of US Grant and Sherman tanks. The state responded by very greatly strengthening in-house tank design, which resulted at the end of the war in a very successful tank, the Centurion, which significantly was built in an Ordnance factory.[77] As the official historian commented, 'the bulk manufacture of tanks of 40 tons or 50 tons was scarcely analogous with the peacetime pursuits of even heavy industry'.[78]

Just how big arms investment was in relation to wartime arms production has been implicitly and explicitly underestimated. The official historian of factories and plant sought to play up the continuity of industrial structure in wartime. He estimated that the workers in government factories and agency factories (900,000) employed only one-sixth of the total in the engineering, shipbuilding, and chemical and explosives industries.[79] He did not take a proportion of the total working for the forces, which would give a figure of about one-quarter. However, this calculation ignores the huge quantities of capital that went in other forms. I have estimated that an equivalent of some 1.6 million workers worked in state-owned (though not necessarily state-run) plant at the peak of war production. This is 43 per cent of the 3.8 million workers working in the key three sectors working for the supply ministries; 40 per cent of the 4 million workers in the key arms sectors working for the forces, 32 per cent of the 5 million workers in manufacturing supplying the forces; and 20 per cent of the 7.7 million workers in manufacturing. All these figures underestimate the significance of state investment for specialised arms production, since supply ministries bought a good deal of equipment that was identical to peacetime production. Out of 1.5 million workers working for the MoS, some 500,000 made commercial products or near commercial products for the ministry.[80]

---

[76] Ibid., pp. 183–90.
[77] Peter Beale, *Death by design: British tank development in the Second World War* (Stroud: Sutton, 1998), *passim*. M. M. Postan, D. Hay and J. D. Scott, *Design and development of weapons* (London: HMSO, 1964), ch. 13 and app. VII.
[78] Postan et al., *Design and development of weapons*, p. 352.
[79] Hornby, *Factories and plant*, p. 382.
[80] Ibid., p. 170. Of the remaining million, half were employed in arms firms (200,000) or Royal Ordnance factories (240,000), the other half in outside firms.

This astonishingly invisible industry of 1.6 million workers and nearly £1 billion of assets does not figure in accounts of public ownership, even those by writers aware of these investments. William Ashworth, one of the official historians of war production finance, argued in his later study of nationalised industries that 'the Second World War saw little change in the extension of state ownership to business undertakings' and cited only the cases of the aircraft firm Shorts, and the North of Scotland Hydro-Electric Board.[81] Although historians recognise that government departments operated industries themselves (for example the royal dockyards and Royal Ordnance factories), and indeed state-owned limited companies existed before 1939 (for example, British Petroleum (BP)), they assume as Ashworth did that 'when large new additions were made to public ownership of industry the form of institution used was always some sort of public corporation'.[82] This cannot be explained on the basis that historians were ignoring temporary wartime measures for, as we have seen, there were hugely increased numbers of state industrial workers after the war. Nor did the investment to be used by the private sector prove temporary. The state continued to add capacity to both the private and public sectors after the war. In the rearmament period state investment peaked at around £90 million in both 1952 and 1953, with about a third going on R&D facilities and another third on factories for private industry.[83] In another estimate between 1950 and 1954 some £150 million was spent on capital facilities for the arms industry, of which £106 million was for the aircraft industry and £21 million for a new tank factory run by Leyland.[84] Ely Devons reported in the late 1950s that for some aircraft firms, including some of the very largest, state-owned capital was equal to and in some cases greater than private capital.[85] Even in 1965 20 per cent of employment in the main aircraft firms was in seventeen government-owned plants.[86] We may indeed hazard that historians have tended to underestimate the role of state enterprise simply because

[81] W. Ashworth, *The state in business: 1945 to the mid-1980s* (London: Macmillan, 1991), pp. 17–18. It is also worth stressing that the official histories were misleading on the transfers to public ownership that did take place: see Edgerton 'State intervention', p. 145.

[82] Ashworth, *State in business*, p. 60.

[83] CSO, *National income and expenditure, 1946–1953* (August 1954), table 36.

[84] Peter Burnham, 'Rearming for the Korean War: the impact of government policy on Leyland motors and the British car industry', *Contemporary Record* 9 (1995), 361. Burnham argues that this investment had positive results, and should be included in assessments of the impact of rearmament.

[85] Ely Devons, 'The aircraft industry' in Duncan Burn (ed.), *The structure of British industry*, vol. II (Cambridge: Cambridge University Press, 1958), p. 80.

[86] Ministry of Aviation, *Report of committee of enquiry into the aircraft industry*, Cmnd 2853 (1965) (Plowden Committee), table IV.

the vast majority of studies of the state include tables which exclude 'industrial' civil servants. The fact that much of this state enterprise was military was enough to distance it from industrial questions in the minds of British intellectuals. It is no surprise then that when the issue of public ownership of the arms industry arose it did so as a result of concern with arms, rather than with industry, as in the 1930s. In the mid-1930s the public ownership of armaments production had been a major political issue, in Britain and elsewhere. But the key reason is that Ashworth, like most historians, equates public ownership with the transfer of privately owned, or local authority-owned, capital to nationalised public corporations. Naturally they see this as the product of Labour party thinking.

Labour and public ownership of the arms industry

The nationalisation of industry is rightly seen as the Labour party's distinctive, and indeed sometimes only, industrial policy. Nationalisation and Labour policy are so intimately tied in the historical imagination that non-Labour party sources of the drive to public ownership, and anything not resembling a Labour-government-style Morrisonian board (named after Herbert Morrison, a key Labour politician), tend to be discounted. The case above is exemplary. Indeed in this case Labour party policies, arguments and feelings are almost wholly irrelevant to this story, and partly because of this have been invisible in the historiography. Furthermore, Labour politicians, like Labour intellectuals, appear to have had little understanding of the huge role of the state in arms production. Perhaps most surprisingly of all, the Labour government of the late 1940s privatised (to use later terminology) arms plants and equipment.

The Labour party never clearly committed itself to nationalisation of the arms industry despite sometimes appearing to do so. In its 1934 programme For Socialism and Peace Labour called for the abolition of the private manufacture of armaments – not a particularly radical position in the mid-1930s: the Next Five Years group shared it.[87] The 1935 manifesto was highly circumspect:

Labour will propose to other nations the complete abolition of all national air forces, the effective international control of civil aviation and the creation of an international air police; large reductions by international agreement in naval

---

[87] The next five years: an essay in political agreement (London: Macmillan, 1935), p. 292.

and military forces; and the abolition of the private manufacture of, and trade in, arms.[88]

In an official statement of Labour's foreign policy Arthur Henderson stated that Labour would propose to the League of Nations a plan which would include the 'nationalisation and drastic international control of the manufacture of and trade in arms'.[89] In the very different context of rearmament the Labour party's Defence Sub-Committee considered whether state-owned companies, a public board or government manu-facture should be used for armaments, and suggested only very minimal changes to the government's plans.[90] It wanted to see public capacity extended and the 1939 party document *Labour and the Armed Forces* proposed that:

The Minister of Supply would be responsible for the existing state armament factories and under a Labour Government he would be under instructions to expand these factories or to set up new factories whenever possible, when an increase in industrial capacity was called for.[91]

That was a policy very different from taking the great armourers into public ownership, though it suggested – no more than that – a preference for state-run factories over 'agency' factories.

In the 1930s and 1940s official bodies and state officials were often keen to extend the role of the state, ahead of Labour party thinking. The Royal Commission on the Private Manufacture of and Trading in Arms had called for an extension of state design and manufacture to more types of armament, allowing it to build up a cadre of production experts to be deployed in production emergencies.[92] In the late 1930s Sir Henry Tizard, chairman of the Aeronautical Research Committee, called for the establishment of a corps of aircraft constructors;[93] Sir Wilfrid Freeman,

---

[88] F. W. S. Craig, *British general election manifestos 1900–1974* (London: Macmillan, 1975).

[89] Arthur Henderson, *Labour's way to peace* (London: Methuen, 1935), p. 45.

[90] Labour Party Defence Sub-Committee, 'Preliminary memorandum on public ownership and control of the arms industry', December 1937 (Labour Party Archives). However, this document is very general, highlights many difficulties, and asks for further research. See also 'Memorandum on Industrial Policy relating to defence: a plan for Labour', Defence Sub-Committee April 1938, which suggests only the taking over of shadow factories as 'National Assembly factories', and the paper on 'A Ministry of Supply' December 1938, which while well informed and long, suggests no drastic powers or innovations in ownership. All in Fabian Society Papers, J 36/3, LSE Archives.

[91] Labour party, *Labour and the armed forces* (London: Labour Party, 1939).

[92] *Report of the Royal Commission on the Private Manufacture of and Trading in Arms (1935–36)*, Cmd. 5292 (1936), paras. 127–30.

[93] Sir Henry Tizard to Sir Kingsley Wood (Secretary of State for Air), 11 October 1938, AVIA 10/306, PRO; see also Tizard to Air Vice Marshal Tedder, October 1938, quoted in R. W. Clark, *Tizard* (London: Methuen, 1965), p. 175.

the officer responsible for development and production in the Air Ministry, also wanted a measure of state design and manufacture of aircraft.[94] During the war, the MAP, under Sir Stafford Cripps, in its discussions on reconstruction advocated the setting up of a government aircraft design and manufacture organisation, a proposal which went to the Cabinet Reconstruction Committee at its first meeting.[95] Labour ministers argued that a larger part of the aircraft industry should come under state control.[96] These issues were not merely theoretical since the ministry nationalised two private firms: the well-known maker of flying-boats and heavy bombers, Short Brothers, and Frank Whittle's firm Power Jets, which was designing jet-engines.[97] However, Labour did not commit itself to public ownership of the arms industry in its 1945 manifesto. The only industry connected to arms nationalised by the post-war Labour government was iron and steel (which in fact included the ESC and the other armament steel makers).

After the war the party's position remained resolutely muddled. At the Labour party conference of 1945 there was a resolution demanding that arms production should become a government monopoly. None other than Philip Noel-Baker responded for the party's National Executive: 'Our Party has always stood for the abolition of the private trade and manufacture of arms. We stand for it today. We are pledged to the hilt, and our pledges will be carried through.' Noel-Baker was wise not to be specific as to what the pledges were. The resolution was referred back to the National Executive, that is to say buried.[98] A second question came up particularly among trades unionists: why should a socialist government not use the new government factories to make goods the community needed? Some engineering workers campaigned for the keeping of shadow factories in operation,[99] and at the 1945 Trades Union Congress (TUC), the Association of Scientific Workers (AScW) and the Amalgamated Engineering Union argued for keeping shadow and Ordnance factories in public ownership. The issue was referred to the TUC General Council which took the matter up with Stafford Cripps, to no effect.[100] In fact,

---

[94] Note of a meeting held on 25 January 1939, Air Ministry, AVIA 10/306, PRO.

[95] See the papers in AVIA 15/1915, PRO.

[96] Minutes of War Cabinet Reconstruction Committee, 20 December 1943, CAB 87/5, R(43)1st meeting, PRO.

[97] See D. E. H. Edgerton, 'Technological innovation, industrial capacity and efficiency: public ownership and the British military aircraft industry, 1935–1948', *Business History* 26 (1984), 247–79.

[98] Labour party, *Report of the 44th Annual Conference, 1945* (1945), pp. 149–50. The issue did not arise in 1946.

[99] R. Croucher, *Engineers at war* (London: Merlin, 1982), pp. 326–40.

[100] *TUC Report 1945* pp. 358, 360. *TUC Report 1946*, Report of the General Council.

some Royal Ordnance factories (which retained around 40,000 workers) were used for civil work, for example making watch parts, and parts for gas and electric cookers. However, the MoS was reluctant to use them in this way and there were confrontations with the unions on this.[101]

The issue of nationalisation did not go away. In the late 1940s the aircraft industry in particular did become a candidate in internal Labour party discussions. By now the whole issue was regarded as an administrative one in which questions of ownership of property were irrelevant. It was argued that government had all the power it needed, and in any case competition was essential, an argument used from at least the 1930s.[102] The industry did not make it on to any nationalisation shopping list, but a few radicals raised the issue at party conferences. In 1953 the response added another theme to anti-nationalisation arguments – that the British aircraft industry was a brilliant success under state control and thus should not be nationalised. George Strauss, formerly Minister of Supply, claimed that it was largely because of government 'control and direction that the aircraft industry today has proved itself supreme throughout the world and produced aeroplanes such as the Comet, the Canberra, the Valiant, and the Swift'.[103] For Morgan Philips, Labour party secretary, too the brilliant success of the British aircraft industry was a key argument against nationalisation – 'we have gained a lead in design and in development' he maintained.[104] The position in the party document *Challenge to Britain*, supported by Strauss and Philips, was that future Labour governments should take over failing firms. Strikingly, however, one key such example, the wartime nationalisation of Short Brothers (which remained in public ownership) did not figure in any of these discussions. Nor indeed, was there reference to the extraordinary story of Power Jets, or the selling off of arms plants under Labour.

For the 1945–51 Labour governments privatised large chunks of the arms industry. They sold many redundant arms plants and machine tools to the private sector[105] with the MoS realising some £61 million between 1946/7 and 1949/50.[106] Most of the aircraft firms appear to have bought

---

[101] Richard Williams-Thompson, *Was I really necessary? Reminiscences of a public relations officer* (London: World's Press News, 1951), pp. 86–95.

[102] 'The Aircraft Industry 1948', RD 182 Memorandum, Labour Party Archives. See also Sub-Committee on Industries for Nationalisation, Minutes, 8 November 1948, 8 December 1948. John Freeman MP, 'Memorandum on the aircraft industry', 26 October 1948, RD 181, Labour Party Archives.

[103] *Conference of the Labour Party, 1953*, pp. 125–6.

[104] '... I saw only a few weeks ago the excitement and interest occasioned by the landing of a Comet on the airfield at Calcutta'. *Conference of the Labour Party, 1953*, p. 127.

[105] *The Economist*, 6 October 1946; *British Industries*, 31, no. 9, p. 231.

[106] *Report to the Comptroller and Auditor General, civil appropriations account (Class IX) 1949/50*, p. vii, Parliamentary Papers (PP) 1950/51, vol. XXV.

some government-owned capacity. English Electric (EE), for example, bought all the extensions to its works: the tank plant at Trafford, the Napier extension in Liverpool, the aircraft extensions at Preston.[107] What price was paid for these factories and plants is not clear, but it seems unlikely that good prices were achieved: Cammell-Laird bought an Admiralty extension costing £374,000 for £140,000.[108] More remarkable still was what might be called the de-nationalisation of jet-engine design. Frank Whittle's firm Power Jets had been formed in 1936 with private funds, and designed Britain's first jet-engines. Production had been turned over to private firms who also started designing engines of their own. Whittle, then a socialist, wanted the whole jet-engine industry nationalised.[109] Cripps, however, took over only Whittle's firm and merged the ministry's own gas turbine research into it. Power Jets became a limited company owned by the state, which Cripps intended should continue to design jet-engines and to manufacture them on a small scale. However, the private firms objected and the MAP refused to let Power Jets design and manufacture new engines. Whittle hoped that the new Labour government would reverse this decision but, in early 1946, the government decided to convert Power Jets into the National Gas Turbine Establishment, a standard civil service research establishment. As Whittle himself put it, it was a 'striking paradox' that a 'Government company was virtually smothered to death while a Labour Government was in office'.[110] Whittle and his team resigned, never to design an aero-engine again.[111]

For all the confusions the role for state enterprise was very much larger after the war than before it. The key point, already suggested above, is not what was transferred from private industry but what was built up within the state sector. The withdrawal of the state, as in the case of the jet-engine, was exceptional. Generally the state took a greater direct role in the R&D, design and production of weapons than before the war. Seen from Vickers, for example, the state looked much more capable and willing to undertake design and to do it in new scientific research-minded ways.[112] The research establishments were stronger, more confident of

---

[107] R. Jones, and O. Marriott, *Anatomy of a merger* (London: Cape, 1970), p. 177.

[108] Kenneth Warren, *Steel, ships and men: Cammell Laird, 1824–1993* (Liverpool: Liverpool University Press, 1998), p. 273.

[109] Quoted in Sir Frank Whittle, *Jet: the story of a pioneer* (London: Mueller, 1953), p. 263.

[110] Whittle, *Jet*, p. 302.

[111] For a revisionist account which stresses the role of the existing aero-engine firms in the development of Whittle machines, and which thus downplays the significance of Power Jets, see Andrew Nahum, 'World war to cold war: formative episodes in the development of the British aircraft industry, 1943–1965', unpublished doctoral thesis, University of London (2002), ch. 3.

[112] J. D. Scott, *Vickers: a history* (London: Weidenfeld and Nicolson, 1962), p. 302.

getting the perfect weapon.[113] In tanks the design effort and production was, as we have seen, decisively shifted to the public sector. In new technologies such as radar the state had a commanding technical lead.[114] Although it was not always clear that industry would lose out – and indeed it did not in jet-engines – there was a shift toward the state. For example in the discussions on how to proceed with the development of atomic weapons there was a distinct possibility that the project would be handed over to ICI; indeed an ICI executive ran the project during the war and another had a crucial headquarters job after it. However, the project was run on the government establishment/Royal Ordnance factory model for the first few years. The Conservative government, pushed by Lord Cherwell, created a unique structure for the industry, but one still within the public sector. It converted part of a government department into a nationalised industry (a move repeated in the 1960s with the Post Office). The resulting United Kingdom Atomic Energy Authority (UKAEA or AEA) had research establishments, including the bomb design centre at Aldermaston, and factories producing fissile materials.[115]

Industrial policy

All these great wartime and post-war industrial developments had virtually nothing to do with the British state's historic ministry of industry and trade, the Board of Trade, or the new ministries born out of it like Labour (1917), Transport (1919), Food (1939) Shipping (1939), and Fuel and Power (1942). Although the Board of Trade had a role in the discussion of armaments issues in the interwar period, through the machinery of the Committee of Imperial Defence, it did not have a major role in the wartime mobilisation of industry. The function of the Board of Trade was an important but restricted one. In the very early years of the war it sought to promote exports to finance the war; an effort which became much less important with Lend–Lease. After that its main concerns were the 'concentration' of the consumer goods industries it looked after, and the operation of rationing and price control of such goods as textiles, and the related schemes for 'utility' products. In short, it sought to release labour and factory space, and to increase efficiency and cheapness of production

---

[113] Scott, *Vickers*, pp. 353, 358.

[114] S. R. Twigge, *The early development of guided weapons in the United Kingdom 1940–1960* (Amsterdam: Harwood Academic, 1993).

[115] Margaret Gowing, *Britain and atomic energy, 1939–1945* (London: Macmillan, 1964) and *Independence and deterrence: Britain and atomic energy 1945–1952*. Vol. I: *Policy making* (London: Macmillan, 1974).

of consumer goods.[116] The wartime Board of Trade did, however, think about post-war policy for industry as a whole. In the 1930s the ministry had moved towards greater intervention in industry, though of a very particular kind, in its moves to give legislative support to limited measures of 'industrial self-government', in for example, the shipbuilding and shipping, coal, iron and steel, and cotton industries. The most innovative such measure, the Cotton Industry Act 1939, never in fact came into operation. During the war, the ministry did set up many industry-wide bodies – export groups in 1940, and for example a Cotton Board – but only in some of the industries it was responsible for.[117]

The Labour politician Hugh Dalton (President of the Board of Trade, 1942–5) and his young 'post-warriors' deliberately set out to make the Board of Trade the key post-war industry ministry.[118] They proposed a new Industrial Commission which would have powers to prohibit inefficient firms from trading. This policy grew out of a critique of pre-war rationalisation schemes, which it was felt that it had been driven by financial rather than by technical considerations. The much watered-down Industrial Commission proposal found its way into the *Report of the Steering Committee on Post War Employment*,[119] but not into the subsequent, and famous, 1944 White Paper *Employment Policy*. This document had no specific industrial policy proposals, because this was too contentious an issue in the coalition government.[120] Historians have attached too much importance to this Board of Trade policy proposal

---

[116] See E. L. Hargreaves and M. M. Gowing, *Civil industry and trade* (London: HMSO, 1952). See also Ina Zweiniger-Bargielowska, *Austerity in Britain: rationing, controls and consumption, 1939–1955* (Oxford: Oxford University Press, 2000).

[117] Edgerton 'State intervention'; Marguerite Dupree (ed.), *Lancashire and Whitehall: the diary of Sir Raymond Streat 1931–1957*, 2 vols. (Manchester: Manchester University Press, 1987); 'The cotton industry, overseas trade policy and the cotton board 1940–1959', *Business History* 32 (1990) 106–28; 'The cotton industry: a middle way between nationalisation and self-government?' in Helen Mercer, Neil Rollings and Jim Tomlinson (eds.), *Labour governments and private industry: the experience of 1945–1951* (Edinburgh: Edinburgh University Press, 1992), pp. 137–61. The 1930s has been looked at afresh by Julian Greaves, 'Competition, collusion and confusion: the state and the reorganisation of the British cotton industry, 1931–1939', *Enterprise and Society* 3 (2002), 48–79.

[118] J. M. Lee, *Reviewing the machinery of government, 1942–1952: a study of the Anderson committee and its successors* (mimeo, 1977), p. 96. The impression has been given that the Board of Trade's policies were the only ones put forward for consideration. See Middlemas, *Power, competition and the state*; J. F. O. MacAllister, 'Civil science policy in British industrial reconstruction, 1942–1951', unpublished doctoral thesis, University of Oxford (1986); Barnett, *The audit of war*, ch. 13, 'Tinkering as industrial strategy'.

[119] 'Report of the steering committee on post war employment policy', paras. 280–9, CAB 87/7 R(44)6 11 January 1944, PRO.

[120] G. C. Peden, 'Sir Richard Hopkins and the "Keynesian revolution" in economic policy', *Economic History Review* 36 (1983), 281–96.

because they tend to have seen the Board of Trade as *the* industrial ministry. However, in the war and for decades afterwards, there many industry ministries and many policies. Thus Dalton's wartime proposals were strongly criticised by another wartime industrial minister, Sir Stafford Cripps, the Minister of Aircraft Production. Thinking about industrial policy in ways which reflected the experience of his ministry, he was very hostile towards the Industrial Commission proposal, which he thought would remove from ministers direct responsibility for industry and involve a return 'to a position in relation to the major industries not differing essentially from the *status quo ante-bellum*':

Industry is not an undifferentiated whole which can be brought to full employment merely by unselective measures designed to stimulate any and every trade ... the problems of the major industries are complex, both technically and financially; they involve questions of management and technical organisation; and if the cooperation of industry is to be secured they involve personal contact with the leading men. The Government has acquired through the Departments dealing with these industries the knowledge, the contact and the influence to secure the very varying degrees of assistance, guidance and of reorganisation which the industries if they are severally to contribute their quota to the policy of full employment, will be found to need. I cannot think that we should be wise, whilst committing ourselves to a full employment policy, to jettison the means by which full employment, industry by industry, can be achieved.[121]

Cripps's proposals were themselves attacked by the Minister of Works, Lord Portal, a businessman, who argued against a multiplication of industrial ministries, and for the building up instead of a strong Board of Trade; he was concerned that having ministries connected to particular industries would transfer competition from the market into government.[122] It is little wonder then, that no agreement was possible.

Another controversial issue during the war was the future of the supply ministries. The context for discussion here was a wartime review of the 'machinery of government'.[123] The Minister for Reconstruction, Lord Woolton, recalled that 'The Socialist members led by Sir Stafford Cripps, were eager to preserve the Ministry' of Supply.[124] Cripps was against returning to the pre-war practice of leaving supply to the service

---

[121] Memorandum by the Minister of Aircraft Production 'Government and the major industries' 8 March 1944, CAB 87/7 R(44)42, PRO.

[122] Memorandum by the Minister of Works, 'Government and the major industries', 22 March 1944. Cripps responded in Memorandum by the Minister of Aircraft Production 'Government and the major industries' 31 March 1944, CAB 87/7 R(44)59, PRO.

[123] Lee, *Machinery of government*, pp. 11–17.

[124] Lord Woolton [Frederick Marquis], *Memoirs of the Rt Hon. The Earl of Woolton* (London: Cassell, 1959), p. 169.

departments: as he put it '[t]he difference between an Industrial Department and a Service Department is a radical one'.[125] Cripps went further in arguing, as the Treasury official Sir Alan Barlow told the Chancellor of the Exchequer, for a unified supply ministry to be 'the tutelary deity of the engineering industry after the war'.[126] However, Andrew Duncan, the Minister of Supply, Oliver Lyttelton, the Minister of Production, and the three service ministries rejected the idea even of continuing to have a separate supply ministry in peacetime, let alone one with civil responsibilities.[127] No agreement could be reached by the coalition government on this topic either.[128]

The Labour government broke with the post-Great War precedent and retained a separate supply ministry and gave it very important civil responsibilities. The MAP and the MoS were brought together as a new MoS.[129] This was to be responsible primarily for the supply to the army and the RAF, to have a general responsibility for government purchases and it would also 'carry the primary Government responsibility for the field of engineering'. The combined ministry lost some responsibilities to the Board of Trade: non-engineering munitions industries, notably chemicals, and many, though not all, raw materials controls. The Board of Trade also got some of the responsibilities of the disbanded Ministry of Production, whose defence supply responsibilities went to the Ministry of Defence.[130] Although Cripps's wartime view carried the day, Cripps himself had already become President of the Board of Trade, and he saw his ministry as *the* ministry for private industry. Although this ambition was not to be realised in the Board of Trade, he told his civil servants in August 1945 that 'we shall be a sort of Civilian Supply Department and we must take as close and as intimate an interest in the production methods of industry as have the Supply Departments during the war'.[131] In fact the evolving tradition of the Board of Trade, rather than of the supply ministries, of establishing tripartite (employers, employees,

---

[125] Memorandum by the Minister of Aircraft Production 'The organisation of supply', 21 November 1944. ADM 1/17794 MG(44)28, PRO, quoted in P. Winston, 'The British government and defence production, 1943–1950', unpublished doctoral thesis, University of Cambridge (1982), p. 118.

[126] Quoted in Lee, *Machinery of government*, p. 109.

[127] *Memoirs of the Rt Hon. The Earl of Woolton*, p. 169.

[128] Memorandum by the Chairman of the Machinery of Government Committee, 'Organisation of supply', 20 December 1944, CAB 66/59 WP(44)713, PRO.

[129] CAB 129/2 CP(45)177, 178, 181, 197; CAB 128/1 CM(45)37 Conclusions 2 October 1945, PRO.

[130] Statement by Prime Minister, 29 October 1945, *House of Commons debates*, 1945–6, 415, cols. 35–8.

[131] Sir Richard Stafford Cripps, *Democracy alive: a selection of recent speeches* (London: Sidgwick & Jackson, 1946), p. 72.

independent) bodies with responsibilities in relation to particular industrial sectors was widely applied by the post-war Board of Trade. The
industrial 'working parties' were set up just after the war for the Board's
'concentrated' industries as a way of getting them back to normal production on a more efficient basis. The subsequent statutory development
councils (under the Industrial Organisation and Development Act 1947)
were set up in much the same spirit, though they were extendable to all
industry. In practice they tended to be in the same industries as the
working parties.[132]

The maintenance of a separate supply department, with very major
civil responsibilities, was an important step but one which was not easily
understood, even by those who took it. Despite a reputation for understanding the machinery of government, the Labour Prime Minister
Clement Attlee appeared to regard the MoS like the Post Office as a
'purely administrative' department, which should not be represented in
Cabinet.[133] This argument suggested that the ministry should not exist,
and that its functions should be returned to the service ministries.
However, it was to say the least odd that a purely administrative ministry
should be given responsibility for the engineering industry and for the
nationalisation of steel. Richard Williams-Thompson, the ministry's public relations officer, noted that Attlee's announcement of this policy in
October 1945 was 'complicated and not easily understood'; 'the Prime
Minister had created, although he probably did not realise it, the most
important Ministry in the country'.[134] *The Economist* welcomed a peacetime supply ministry and indeed regretted that the Admiralty was still
going its own way. It welcomed too the sponsorship of the engineering
industry by the MoS. Surprisingly it argued that the Board of Trade was
too large and should be split into a Board of Trade, concerned with
external trade, and a Ministry of Industry, as if a Ministry of Industry
did not already exist.[135] In 1947 the magazine *Future* noted the very great
importance of the MoS but was evidently unsure of the reasoning behind
its maintenance.[136] Richard Williams-Thompson regretted in 1951 that
'I imagine that many people do not know what the Ministry is or does,

---

[132] David Henderson 'Development councils: an industrial experiment' in G. D. N. Worswick
and D. H. Ady (eds.), *The British economy, 1945–1951* (Oxford: Clarendon Press, 1952),
pp. 455, 457.

[133] C. R. Attlee, *As it happened* (London: Heinemann, 1954), p. 154; Kenneth Harris, *Attlee*
(London: Weidenfeld & Nicolson, 1982) p. 402.

[134] Williams-Thompson, *Was I really necessary?*, p. 8.

[135] *The Economist*, 8 November 1945.

[136] 'Ministry of Supply', *Future* no. 3 (1947), 19. This article (pp. 17–25) is by far the most
detailed contemporary source on the ministry.

which is a fine testimonial to my three years' work!'[137] However, despite
the lack of clarity as to its role, and continued questioning of its reasons
for existence, and what its range of functions should be, something like
the post-war Ministry of Supply remained in existence for more than
twenty-five years of peace.

Attlee's view of the MoS as 'purely administrative' meant that it would
have no place in Cabinet and that it would have low-powered ministers.[138]
John Wilmot and George Strauss 'hardly counted politically   a really strong
political minister at Supply would have made it the most powerful Ministry
in the country'.[139] Both Wilmot and Strauss were very unusual among
Labour MPs in being businessmen. Wilmot, who had won the 1933 East
Fulham by-election, which will appear again in ch. 7, lost the seat in 1935,
returning for another London seat in 1939. A protégé of Hugh Dalton, he
became his parliamentary private secretary (PPS) during the war, and a
junior minister in the MoS. Strauss, another London MP, was Cripps's PPS
during the war. Wilmot was sacked in 1947 because he had 'failed to resolve
the division of opinion among his civil servants, and to stand up to the
steelmasters' over steel nationalisation. Dalton and Cripps, strong supporters of steel nationalisation, wanted Aneurin Bevan appointed to replace
him, but although Attlee offered him the job, he refused it.[140] However, it is
worth noting that from 1947 Cripps was in charge of economic matters, and
saw himself as having three lieutenants in this area: Harold Wilson at the
Board of Trade, and also in the Cabinet, Hugh Gaitskell at Fuel and Power,
and George Strauss at Supply: 'Supply had become largely a branch office
of Cripps – without decentralised powers'.[141]

However, the significance of the ministry, and especially of its civilian
role, was not lost on competitors; there was 'great rivalry' with the Board
of Trade.[142] Nor was it lost on those who were concerned to limit the
power of the state. The Conservative party opposed the very idea of a
separate supply ministry in peace, and was particularly opposed to such a
ministry having civil functions. Its 1950 manifesto promised to transfer
these to the Board of Trade.[143] Nevertheless, when Churchill returned to
office in October 1951 he kept the MoS, by then fully engaged in the
rearmament effort, and the new Minister of Supply, Duncan Sandys,

---

[137] Williams-Thompson, *Was I really necessary?*, p. 3.
[138] Ibid., p. 9.   [139] Ibid., p. 24.   [140] Harris, *Attlee*, pp. 342–4.
[141] Williams-Thompson, *Was I really necessary?*, p. 48. See also p. 166, and Ben Pimlott,
Harold Wilson (London: HarperCollins, 1992), pp. 104–5; Edwin Plowden, *An industrialist in the Treasury* (London: Deutsch, 1989), p. 22.
[142] Williams-Thompson, *Was I really necessary?*, p. 8.
[143] Craig, *British general election manifestos 1900–1974*. The 1951 Conservative Manifesto
was silent on the Ministry of Supply.

made it clear that engineering would stay in place.[144] It would go to the Board of Trade in 1955, at the end of the rearmament programme, and it was only from then on that the MoS was overwhelmingly military.[145]

Low political visibility and lack of understanding of its role by contemporaries has had important consequences: the ministry has been known to most historians only because of the controversy over steel.[146] In more specialised literature on government–industry relations and economic planning, its role as a 'production' or 'sponsoring' department is merely listed. The general view is that the Board of Trade was 'the leading production department'[147] or 'responsible for most sectors of industry';[148] in short, 'the key economic departments were the Treasury and the Board of Trade'.[149] Only texts centrally concerned with the organisation of British central government in the twentieth century cover it with any understanding of its functions.[150] It provides a nice illustration of the difference between state and political cultures, and of the dangers of understanding the state only through political culture. For even by purely civil criteria, the ministry should be reckoned as the leading industry department. It covered more industrial sectors than any other 'production department'.[151] In 1950 it had more non-industrial civil servants on civilian work (13,369) than did the Board of Trade (10,971), though fewer than the 36,993 at the Ministry of Food.[152] It was also very

[144] Minister of Supply, 'Some preliminary reactions to the Garrod Report' 1 February 1952, AVIA 54/1464, PRO. Within parts of government too there was clearly a desire to separate engineering from the MoS: DEFE 7/282, PRO; *Report by the Committee on the organisation and work of the scientific branches of the Ministry of Supply and Admiralty* (Chmn Air Chief Marshal Sir Guy Garrod), 20 April 1951, p. 14.

[145] Russell Potts, who joined the Ministry in mid-1956, recalls that he 'was never made aware that the Department had, or had had, an "industrial" role. One of the men I worked with had been involved with steel nationalisation but this was regarded as water under the bridge' (private communication).

[146] For example K. O. Morgan, *Labour in power* (Oxford: Clarendon Press, 1984).

[147] A. A. Rogow with P. Shore, *The Labour government and British industry, 1945–1951* (Oxford: Blackwell, 1955), p. 55. See also p. 52.

[148] J. Leruez, *Economic planning and politics in Britain* (London: Robertson, 1975), p. 37

[149] Cairncross, *Years of recovery*, p. 49.

[150] F. M. G. Willson, *The organisation of British central government, 1914–1964*, 2nd edn (London: Allen & Unwin, 1968). The first edition was published in 1957. See also Lee, *Machinery of government*.

[151] *Board of Trade Journal*, 26 August 1950, see also 8 September 1951. The *Board of Trade Journal* listed the Admiralty, Board of Trade and the Ministries of Agriculture and Fisheries, Food, Fuel and Power, Health, Supply, Transport and Works as 'production departments'.

[152] The MoS had a further 20,053 engaged on defence work. *Staffs employed in government departments*, February 1950, Cmd 7887, PP 1950 vol. XVI. The figures are for 1 October 1949. The suggestion made by Political and Economic Planning (PEP)

important in the field of industrial subsidies.[153] Through its control of the iron and steel industry it had a major tool for discriminatory policy, and indeed was itself allocated between 30 per cent and 40 per cent of steel output, much more than any other ministry.[154]

State–industry relations after the war

The account given so far of the war economy is very different from the conventional welfarist or macroeconomic accounts. The same is true of the following account of the post-war years. Indeed it is useful to think of the British economy in the post-war years as a low-key war economy which was very slowly liberalised.[155] There was something bigger and different going on in state–industry relations after the war than is captured by the usual meaning of 'nationalisation', or 'planning', or 'intervention' or 'industrial policy'. The term 'nationalisation' itself holds some clues to this bigger story. 'Nationalisation' in the public ownership sense had a vitally important, though often overlooked, 'national' dimension: nationalisation transferred ownership not merely of private firms, but also of municipal enterprises (like gas and electricity works and hospitals), to national and sometimes regional organisations, all ultimately responsible to a single national ministry and minister. 'Nation', 'national' and 'nationalise' are terms that recur in this period – particularly in relation to the economy and to the administration of the state: it is hardly surprising that Labour's 1945 manifesto called coal 'Britain's most precious national raw material' or that the 1950 manifesto said: 'Put the nation first'. Harold Wilson claimed that

the Government had asserted its right to ensure that there is a duty on private industry, no less than on socialised industries, to conform to the national interest ... private ownership of industry does not of itself give any guarantee that national considerations will prevail in industrial policy.[156]

that for 1949 the number of civil servants doing civil work in Supply was probably half the number in the Board of Trade and Department of Overseas Trade, is thus likely to be an underestimate (PEP, *Government–industry relations* (London: PEP, 1952), p. 98).
[153] *National income and expenditure 1946–1951* August 1952, table 27; *National income and expenditure 1946–1953*, August 1954, table 37.
[154] Martin Chick, *Industrial policy in Britain, 1945–951: economic planning, nationalisation and the Labour governments* (Cambridge: Cambridge University Press, 1998), p. 43.
[155] See Richard Toye, 'Gosplanners versus thermostatters: Whitehall planning debates and their political consequences, 1945–1949', *Contemporary British History* 14 (2000), 81–104.
[156] 'The state and private industry: memorandum by the President of the Board of Trade', PREM 8/1183, PRO.

There was no question as to whether they should prevail or not. The economy, politics, society, were 'nationalised' in the sense that a powerful alignment of economic and social with political borders was engineered at this time at the expense of both international and sub-national dimensions. The African and other colonies, as well as the commonwealth, also became economically more important.[157]

Such a conception helps point to the continued importance of state purchasing, of radical import controls, of the importance of the idea of 'war potential' in consideration of manufacturing industries and the very great importance of 'strategic' considerations in energy supply and agriculture, to take two important indicative cases. The state acted as a buyer for many imports, including cotton and food. Government ministries were major buyers in the domestic market, indeed sometimes monopoly buyers.[158] In terms of manufactures continued high levels of defence spending were obviously important, but the nationalisation of utilities in particular created large, single, state buyers. Thus the Ministry of Transport through its ownership of the railways, and the Ministry of Health through its ownership of hospitals, and the Ministry of Fuel and Power, through its ownership of electrical systems, the gas works and the coal mines had a crucial say on what was bought. They purchased most of their rolling stock, locomotives, generating sets, boilers, nuclear reactors, telephone equipment, aeroplanes and so on. Needless to say, these state purchases of manufactures were highly nationalistic: the purchase of non-British equipment was not only rare but controversial. The MoS is a key case, not only as the purchasing agent for the armed forces, but for other branches of government too, to such an extent that it was concerned at being overloaded with responsibilities.[159] In late 1946 it was responsible for the supply of civil aircraft to the Ministry of Civil Aviation, prefabricated housing and engineering fitments for housing for the Ministry of Works, as well as motor vehicles, hand tools and medical supplies to the government as a whole.[160] It was soon decided that future house orders should be handled by the Ministry of Works and that medical supplies (which included pharmaceuticals, such as penicillin) should be

---

[157] Hugo Radice, 'The national economy: a Keynesian myth?', *Capital and Class* no. 22 (1984), 120–6. Bob Rowthorn, 'Britain and western Europe', *Marxism Today*, May 1982.

[158] Carlo J. Morelli, 'The illusions, reality and implications of British government expenditure 1948–1968', Working paper 103, Department of Economics, University of Dundee, October 1999.

[159] A. Rowlands to E. Bridges, 14 November 1946, AVIA 49/75, PRO.

[160] 'Functions and responsibilities of the Ministry of Supply', November 1946, AVIA 49/75, PRO.

transferred to the Ministry of Health.[161] But Supply was made responsible for the supply of engineering-based capital goods to two newly nationalised industries, electricity and coal mining.[162] While the ministry was happy to let some responsibilities go, it fought hard to keep control of the purchase of civil aircraft for the now nationalised airlines, a controversial question through the late 1940s.[163] Already at this early stage problems which would plague not only civil aircraft procurement but most of the nationalised industries were becoming apparent. There would be persistent conflict between the industry, the airlines and the supply ministry over civil aircraft down to Concorde and beyond. The ministry wanted to buy British, the airlines were keener on buying from abroad.

After the war the national economy was highly protected by tariffs and quotas, and there was a deliberate aim of promoting national technologies and industries for national needs. The import of any sort of manufacture was exceedingly difficult until the 1960s: before that economic and strategic factors suggested near autarchy in manufactures. Very powerful import quotas, brought to light by Brennan and Milward, were certainly used to discriminate in favour of 'strategic' and modern industries.[164] There was an extraordinary development, or move to Britain, of industries. Oil refining hardly existed in Britain until the late 1940s since petroleum products were imported ready refined, but there was then a boom as big refineries were built by 1956 in the Isle of Grain (BP), Shell Haven (Shell), Stanlow (Shell), Fawley (Esso), Llandarcy (BP), Heysham (Shell) and Grangemouth (BP). They were built to save dollars, but also because they were cheaper to build in the UK than at the oil fields, and more secure.[165] The world shortage of sulphur and pyrites led to three new plants making sulphuric acid from domestic anhydrite to

---

[161] 'Report of the official committee on the civil supply functions of the Ministry of Supply', 26 November 1947, AVIA 49/27, PRO.

[162] L. Hannah, *Electricity before nationalisation* (London: Macmillan, 1979), p. 322; L. Hannah *Engineers, managers and politicians* (London: Macmillan, 1982), pp. 24–5, 27; Winston, 'Defence production', p. 129.

[163] Notes of a meeting held on 10 November 1947, AVIA 55/30; SBAC, 'Procurement of aircraft for the state-owned air transport corporations', AVIA, 55/30, PRO. Peter King, *Knights of the air* (London: Constable, 1989), p. 418. *Interim report*, January 1948, Cmd 7307; *Final report*, July 1948 Cmd 7478, both PP 1947/48, vol. XVII. See also Williams-Thompson, *Was I really necessary?*, ch. 8. Keith Hayward, *Government and British civil aerospace: a case study in post-war technology policy* (Manchester: Manchester University Press, 1983), pp. 18–19.

[164] Alan Milward and George Brennan, *Britain's place in the world: a historical enquiry into import controls, 1945–60* (London: Routledge, 1996), pp. 190–4.

[165] Duncan Burn, 'The oil industry' in Duncan Burn (ed.), *The structure of British industry*, 2 vols. (Cambridge: Cambridge University Press, 1958), I, p. 185.

add to the existing one.[166] Among other new industries set up were alarm-clock-and watch-making, the manufacture of photographic film base and new kinds of colour photographic film.[167] A heavy tractor industry hardly existed in Britain, and Vickers converted Sherman tanks into tractors called 'Sherviks' for the African groundnut scheme. The government also orchestrated a huge scheme whereby Vickers' tank designers would design a large tracked tractor which was built in the Scotswood and other facilities in Newcastle. It was a failure, as these Vickers' Vigor tractors were too expensive and could not break the hold of the US makers.[168] It is interesting indeed that while terms like economic nationalism and autarchy were commonplaces in the interwar years they were rare in the post-war era, despite being rather apt terms to describe the British economy.

Despite all this, accounts of industrial policy focused (and focus) on the issue of controls and what is seen as the lack of discrimination and minor initiatives such as development councils. The general perception in studies of British industrial policy after the war is that there was no discrimination between firms after the war until the late 1960s, and that this was to be regretted.[169] The MoS did, however, continue to choose between firms in both military and civil areas. Where it was the key purchaser the ministry could and did discriminate between products and firms: for example it decided what types of aircraft to produce, where to produce them and so on. The ministry made certain that the industry as a whole, through the Society of British Aircraft Constructors (SBAC), did not have a voice in these key decisions.[170] This is not to say that the SBAC was not important in discussion of general policy, but it could not be involved in the key state–firm relationship since in doing so it would itself be discriminating between its own members.[171]

---

[166] In 1950 in Britain there was one anhydrite sulphuric acid plant (ICI Billingham); of the three new ones, one was built by ICI, and another was connected with ICI. W. B. Reddaway 'The chemical industry' in Burn, *Structure*, I, p. 239.

[167] Glatt, 'Reparations', III, pp. 904–15. See also Winston, 'Defence production', pp. 173–82.

[168] Scott, *Vickers*, pp. 324–6. Christopher Foss and Peter McKenzie, *The Vickers tanks* (Wellingborough: Patrick Stephens, 1988), pp. 148–9.

[169] G. D. N. Worswick 'The British economy, 1945–1950' in Worswick and Ady, *British economy*, pp. 28–9.

[170] Edgerton 'State intervention', chs. 3 and 5. See also John Turner 'Servants of two masters: British trade associations in the first half of the twentieth century' in H. Yamasaki and M. Mijamoto (eds.), *Trade associations in business history* (Tokyo: University of Tokyo Press, 1988), pp. 192–3.

[171] W. P. Snyder, *The politics of British defense policy 1945–1962* (Columbus, OH: Ohio State University Press, 1964), p. 99. In recent years the view has gained ground that state–trade association relations were fundamental to government industry relations in this

The economist and economic adviser to the Board of Trade after the war, Alec Cairncross, has suggested that selection of investment projects was 'largely arbitrary and unrelated to measurable economic criteria such as expected rates of return. There was no question of "picking winners".'[172] However, whatever the nature of the criteria, and whatever the success, the government clearly was discriminating between firms. For example Standard Motors received a shadow factory at low rent (1 per cent of its value per annum), which was used to produce Ferguson tractors, and special help with steel supplies.[173] As we have seen many new industries were established after the war with government help, based on particular firms, often with 'war potential' considerations in mind.

Even critics, and proposers of alternatives, were not clear that alternatives actually existed. Take the instructive case of Harold Wilson, the brilliant and exceptionally well-informed young economist who was President of the Board of Trade between 1947 and 1951. Although known for his much publicised 'bonfire of controls' he wanted to replace non-discriminatory controls over industry with a radically interventionist industrial policy. In a remarkably candid, knowledgeable and wide-ranging memorandum for his senior colleagues written in 1950 on 'the state and private industry' he complained that his subject was 'almost a vacuum in socialist thought'. He rejected general controls, and the development council approach, since they were capable of 'no more than the lowest common factor of industrial agreement', they had no power over individual firms and there was no likelihood of their establishing model factories, as some had hoped and Wilson clearly wanted. Instead Wilson wanted state factories, guaranteed state markets for some capital goods and consumer goods like utility clothing and the appointment of civil servants, forming a new civil service corps, to the boards of the 2,000 to 9,000 largest companies (a proposal dropped from the revised version).[174] Wilson further argued for keeping wartime powers to take over

period. F. Longstreth 'State economic planning in a capitalist society: the political sociology of economic policy in Britain, 1940–1979', unpublished doctoral thesis, University of London (1983), and some of the papers in Mercer et al., *Labour governments and private industry*. The great variety of roles of trade associations just in its dealings with industry, the importance of overlapping memberships and the relative unimportance to large firms of trade associations in dealing with government is apparent from PEP, *Industrial trade associations* (London: PEP, 1957).

[172] Cairncross, *Years of recovery*, p. 461.
[173] Nick Tiratsoo, 'The motor car industry', in Mercer et al., *Labour governments and private industry*, pp. 162–85. Michael French, 'Public policy and British commercial vehicles during the export drive era, 1945–50', *Business History* 40 (1998), 22–44 also shows the continued discrimination.
[174] 'The state and private industry: memorandum by the President of the Board of Trade', 4 May 1950 PREM 8/1183, PRO. See app. B of the 4 May 1950 version, and para. 50.

the management and ownership of inefficient firms, and to 'resist all
attempts to limit them to defence cases or to firms supplying goods for
the public services'.[175] This kind of approach was clearly rejected, but it is
important to note that the Labour government as well as maintaining
emergency legislation for five years (in the Supplies and Services
(Transitional Powers) Act 1945, then renewed annually in 1950),
intended to pass permanent legislation on controls in 1950 and then
1951 but was unable to do so.[176] What is not clear in this document, as
in many others, was that the state was already a huge purchaser of capital
and some consumer goods and already provided competition to the
private sector in some kinds of armaments. Furthermore the state was
in some important cases acting at the level of particular firms to develop
particular technologies and industries. Why Wilson was silent on this is a
mystery.

Defence production

As we have already seen Britain's defence expenditure was much higher
in the years immediately after the Second World War than it had ever
been in peacetime in modern history. From 1950 it rose very sharply and
stayed at these unprecedented peacetime levels, in absolute terms,
through to the early 1990s. The high level of defence expenditure is
well known, though its impact on the nature of the state, and the economy, is not, especially for the first decade after the war.[177] This is perhaps
due to the (entirely reasonable and important) emphasis on the enormous
foreign exchange cost of defence expenditure (since a good deal was spent
stationing troops abroad) and on the impact of conscription on the post-
war labour shortage.[178] Not nearly enough attention has been given to the

---

[175] Ibid.

[176] Neil Rollings, ' "The Reichstag method of governing"? The Attlee governments and
permanent economic controls', in Mercer et al., *Labour governments and private industry*,
pp. 15–36.

[177] Jim Tomlinson, 'The Attlee government and the balance of payments, 1945–1951',
Twentieth Century British History 2 (1991), 47–66. For a contemporary version from the
Communist party see John Eaton (pseudonym for Stephen Bodington), *Economics of
peace and war: an analysis of Britain's economic problems* (London: Lawrence & Wishart:
1952). For a very rare microeconomic analysis of rearmament see Burnham, 'Rearming
for the Korean War'.

[178] On these themes see the excellent discussion in Jim Tomlinson, *Democratic socialism and
economic policy: the Attlee years, 1945–1951* (Cambridge: Cambridge University Press,
1997), ch. 3, which points to the salience of these two arguments, and also to the lack of
contemporary understanding of the significance of the huge export of capital to the white
dominions in the period.

arms industry; indeed it is routinely alleged that in the years after the
Second World War, Britain's forces depended on wartime equipment,
and that it was only from the 1950s that they were re-equipped.[179] Where
the arms industry is dealt with generally commentators have argued that it
suffered from the same lack of initiative and foresight of government as
did civil industry.[180]

Yet the post-war arms industry was kept large, strong and powerful; it was
kept at a higher proportion of wartime output than the US one until the early
1950s. The government was publicly committed to the view that British
defence required a strong arms industry and large-scale R&D.[181] In 1946
the Defence Committee of the Cabinet decided on a ceiling of 650,000
defence workers, a figure that the Foreign Secretary Ernest Bevin wanted
reduced to 500,000, in itself a remarkably high figure.[182] This was about five
times greater than arms employment levels in 1935. In 1947 Barrow was
building new aircraft carriers and submarines; Barrow and Elswick were
making gun-mountings and Elswick had some of the production of the
Centurion tank.[183] The aircraft industry was of central importance: aircraft
and aircraft equipment took 57 per cent of the procurement budget in 1949/
50.[184] In 1948 the manufacture of airframes, engines and parts, as well as
guided weapons, but excluding electrical and electronic equipment,
employed 172,000 workers compared to a 1935 figure of 35,000.[185] In
financial terms the commitment to arms production was huge: even in the
pre-rearmament plans for defence expenditure for 1950–1 of £780 million,
no less than £250 million was for production and R&D.[186]

---

[179] For an example, see Alfred Goldberg, 'The military origins of the British nuclear
deterrent', International Affairs 40 (1964), 600–3.
[180] John Lovering, for example 'Defence spending and the restructuring of capitalism: the
military industry in Britain', Cambridge Journal of Economics 14 (1990), 453–67.
[181] Statement relating to defence, Cmd 6743. See also Julian Lider, British military thought after
World War II (Aldershot: Gower, 1985), pp. 509–16.
[182] Alan Bullock, Ernest Bevin: Foreign Secretary, 1945–1951 (Oxford University Press,
1985), pp. 128, 240. See also George Peden 'Economic aspects of British perceptions
of power on the eve of the Cold War' in J. Becker and F. Knipping (eds.) Power in
Europe? Great Britain, France, Italy and Germany in a post-war world (Berlin: de Gruyter,
1986), pp. 237–60.
[183] Scott, Vickers, p. 354; Select Committee on Estimates, Third Report, 1950/51 Rearmament,
31 May 1951, PP 50/51, vol. V.
[184] Snyder, The politics of British defence policy, p. 89.
[185] Ministry of Aviation, Enquiry into the aircraft industry. Eight aircraft firms had more than
5,000 employees in November 1947: Bristol, de Havilland, English Electric, Fairey,
Avro and Armstrong-Siddeley (both part of the Hawker-Siddeley Group), Vickers-
Armstrong, and Rolls-Royce. 'Production Information on Certain British Aircraft
Firms', AVIA 9/138, PRO.
[186] Statement on defence 1950, Cmd 7895, PP 1950–1, vol. XVI, Annex II.

If there is a standard image of the post-war aircraft industry, it is that it was designing aircraft for the 1950s, rather than building them, and the key examples given tend to be civilian ones – the ill-fated giant Brabazon and Princess flying boat and the pioneering Comet passenger jet are the key examples. Yet in this period, as in all others, military research and development and military production drove the industry. In 1948 the output of the industry was divided between £75 million of British military procurement, £21 million government-funded R&D, £16 million of exports mostly of military types, and only £8 million home civil production, giving a total output of £120 million.[187] Lavish government orders meant that by 1950 the RAF was re-equipped with aircraft of post-war manufacture: 528 Avro Lincolns, a development from the Lancaster bomber, were built between 1945 and 1951; 204 De Havilland Hornet fighters were built between 1945 and 1952; 3,800 Gloster Meteors jet-fighters were built in the decade 1945–55; and some 3,300 De Havilland Vampire/Sea Vampire jet-fighters were built between 1946 and the early 1950s. In terms of exports the British industry did extraordinarily well in the late 1940s. In the first ten months of 1947, for which we have detailed figures, Britain exported £10.9 million worth of complete aircraft, while the USA managed £13.8 million.[188] British dominions were far from being the most important market. Indeed the British outsold the USA in Europe. Most of the sales were of new types of military aircraft in production for the RAF. Some 29 per cent of production of military types introduced between 1944 and 1954 was exported.[189] The great success stories were the Vampire and Meteor jet-fighters: more than 900 Meteors were exported, including 100 to Argentina, and more than 1,000 Vampires (and 500 more were produced under licence).[190] They easily out-sold the most successful British civil aircraft in export markets.[191] 'There can be no question', said *Engineering* in 1952 'about the quality and performance of British aircraft, both civil and military, which are second to none in the world, and, in many cases, are much in advance of

---

[187] Ministry of Aviation, *Enquiry into the aircraft industry*, p. 119.
[188] *Engineering*, 5 March 1948, p. 234.
[189] Ministry of Aviation, *Enquiry into the aircraft industry*, p. 18. The military export successes of the late 1950s were the Canberra bomber (195 exported and 394 produced under licence in the USA and Australia) and the Hunter fighter (more than 600 exported and 460 produced under licence). J. L. Sutton and G. Kemp, *Arms to developing countries 1945–1965* (Adelphi Paper no. 28) (London: Institute for Strategic Studies, 1967), table A, p. 35.
[190] Sutton and Kemp, *Arms to developing countries*, table A, p. 35.
[191] The biggest civil sellers were the Viking (66), Dove/Devon (409), Bristol 170 (174), Heron (103), and the, most successful of all, in terms of value, the Viscount (356). Ministry of Aviation, *Enquiry into the aircraft industry*.

contemporary foreign types.'[192] Such boasting was not unusual in the 1940s, or indeed for most of the 1950s, but it had some justification. In terms of employment the British aircraft industry in the late 1940s employed about half the number employed in the US industry. From 1945 US and British arms dominated the world – not only were they two of the three great powers, but they also provided the arms for most of the rest of the world. The ten years after the Second World War, were as Anthony Sampson rightly says, 'a golden age for British arms exports'.[193]

The immediate post-war levels of arms production, already high by peacetime standards, would soon be boosted by a general programme of rearmament led by the United States. The usually misleadingly dubbed 'Korean war rearmament' had little to do with fighting in Korea and everything to do with building up forces in Europe. The rearmament programme was a major emergency for the British state and the arms industry. From 1950 Vickers civilian work was pushed to one side and by the end of 1951 it had three times the arms work of the late 1940s, and half its workers were on arms.[194] Marconi refurbished the wartime radar stations in the early cold war, and some time afterwards were building a new radar defence system: Marconi was 'virtually on a wartime footing' and new space was acquired, including a former shadow factory in Accrington.[195] As we have seen new factories were built. The aircraft industry in particular boomed. By the early 1950s the RAF was receiving aircraft of post-war design like the Canberra and the Shackleton; by the mid-1950s it was receiving the products of late 1940s' research and development: the V-bombers, and the Hunter, Swift, Venom and Javelin fighters. Employment increased to around 250,000, while the USA raced ahead to 770,000. The British industry declined from around 50 per cent of the size of the US industry to 36 per cent (still a very respectable proportion).

National technological security

We should think about the development of military technology in relation to the positions of particular national states on the geopolitical chessboard.

---

[192] *Engineering*, 15 February 1952, p. 200; 10 March 1953.
[193] Anthony Sampson, *The arms bazaar* (Sevenoaks: Coronet, 1978) pp. 106–8. British surplus small arms, artillery, naval ships were sold around the world. Between 1945 and 1955 Britain and the US controlled the warship market – Britain supplied 51 per cent of the ships – and uniquely sold three new ships: Sutton and Kemp, *Arms to developing countries*, p. 19.
[194] Scott, *Vickers*, pp. 357–8.
[195] W. J. Baker, *A history of the Marconi company* (London: Methuen, 1970), p. 339.

We should also consider the broader national dimensions of technological development. Indeed in the war and post-war years the search for what might be called national technological security was of huge importance to the practices of the state and of industry, not just ideologically.[196] Technonationalism became so powerful an ideology that importing technologies was seen as a national disgrace and would remain so for decades. Yet it also needs to be recognised that the British state, like a number of other powerful nation states, was deliberately creating conditions designed to produce unprecedented rates of nationally based technological change.[197] 'Research and development' was central to these programmes. Central government performed a greater proportion of R&D in its own laboratories than before the war and funded an even higher proportion than pre-war. Much of this shift can be explained by high levels of R&D in weapons. This was the result not only of very high defence spending, but of decisions to spend very high proportions of the defence budget on R&D. In the late 1950s British forces were spending a higher proportion of their resources on R&D than any in the world, including the USA. In the early 1960s the proportion reached 15 per cent, the same sort of level as in the USA, and more than twice French levels; by the late 1960s UK, US and French spending had converged on around 10 per cent of the defence budget.[198] Most of this work was done in industry, though much research was done in national establishments by a hugely expanded state research corps. Industry too was able to upgrade facilities: for example, Barnes Wallis created a new research

---

[196] See Sally Horrocks, 'Enthusiasm constrained? British industrial R&D and the transition from wars to peace, 1942–51', *Business History* 41 (1999), 42–63; David Edgerton and Sally Horrocks, 'British industrial research and development before 1945', *Economic History Review* 47 (1994), 213–38; David Edgerton, *Science, technology and the British industrial 'decline', 1870–1970* (Cambridge: Cambridge University Press, 1996) and 'Science in the United Kingdom of Great Britain and (Northern) Ireland: a case study in the nationalisation of science' in John Krige and Dominique Pestre (eds.), *Science in the twentieth century* (Amsterdam: Harwood, 1997).

[197] Historians and science policy commentators have thought of post-war science and technology policy in terms of a so-called 'linear model', which gives a highly misleading analysis of the history of support for research. A small part of the state machine, that concerned with policy for civilian university-based research, justified its budget by claiming that the research it did would turn into technology which would generate economic growth, but the great bulk of the state's R&D effort was conducted on a quite different basis, as will be obvious. However, it is the case that 'research' increasingly figured much more prominently in all kinds of innovative activity at the expense of 'engineering', 'design', etc. 'Chief scientist' seems to have become more common than 'chief designer' as time went on. See my ' "The linear model" did not exist: reflections on the history and historiography of science and research in industry in the twentieth century' in Karl Grandin and Nina Wormbs (eds.), *The science–industry nexus: history, policy, implications* (New York: Watson, 2005), pp. 31–57.

[198] Stockholm International Peach Research Institute (SIPRI), *SIPRI yearbook 1972* (Stockholm: SIPRI, 1972), table 6A.5, p. 226.

department at Vickers.[199] In aviation there was a huge programme of research and development, as there was in guided weapons.[200] In the nuclear field, British atomic devices were first tested in 1952 and hydrogen devices in 1957. The atomic bomb project cost £140 million between 1946 and 1953, averaging 11 per cent of MoS expenditure over the period 1946–53, with a temporary peak of 23 per cent in 1950/1.[201] In real terms the British bomb cost about half the equivalent parts of the US wartime Manhattan Engineer District project.[202] In 1953 some 15,000 people were directly employed, with a smaller number employed in private industry.[203] Atomic bombs were far from being the only 'weapons of mass destruction' as they were collectively called: new researches were under way on a large scale in chemical and biological warfare. Biological weapons were given very high priority.[204] The new Microbiological Research Department at Porton Down was the largest brick building in Europe, and used 90 per cent of the 1947 imports of teak for its laboratory benches.[205]

The MoS's effort was overwhelmingly defence oriented. But there was perceived as a powerful, potentially commercially exploitable, overlap between new military and civil technologies, notably in aviation and nuclear power. It is important to remember that in the 1940s, 1950s and even 1960s these were also seen as the key civilian technologies of the future, to be used by nationalised electricity suppliers and airlines. In the 1950s Britain had the most ambitious civil nuclear programme in the world: in 1955 it announced plans for twelve stations producing 2,000 megawatts of nuclear electricity by 1965, soon increased to 5,000. Britain also had easily the most powerful civil aircraft industry in the capitalist world outside the USA. In another sector, electronics, the relations between military and civil development were close in certain areas. Indeed, the MoS was instrumental and indispensable in launching the British computer industry.[206] British mandarins felt that it was essential to combine control and funding for both

---

[199] Scott, *Vickers*, pp. 347–50.
[200] S. R. Twigge, *The early development of guided weapons in the United Kingdom 1940–1960* (Amsterdam: Harwood Academic, 1993); Peter Morton, *Fire across the desert: Woomera and the Anglo-Australian joint project 1946–1980* (Canberra: Department of Defence, 1989).
[201] Margaret Gowing, *Independence and deterrence: Britain and atomic energy 1945–1952*. vol. II: *Policy execution* (London, Macmillan, 1974), p. 87.
[202] Ibid., pp. 56–7.   [203] Ibid., p. 37.
[204] Brian Balmer, *Britain and biological warfare: expert advice and science policy, 1930–1965* (London: Palgrave, 2001). Brian Balmer, 'The drift of biological weapons policy in the UK, 1945–1965', *Journal of Strategic Studies* 20 (1997), 115–45.
[205] Robert Bud, *The uses of life* (Cambridge: Cambridge University Press, 1993), p. 112.
[206] B. Lockspeiser to E. Grundy, 26 October 1948, FER/B3, National Archive for the History of Computing, Manchester. On the important electronic analogue computer industry and its close relation to aerospace see James Small, *The analogue alternative: the electronic analogue computer in Britain and the USA, 1930–1975* (London: Routledge,

civil and military aviation, and nuclear power, and related technologies, in a single ministry with wider civil and military responsibilities. Thus, the MoS became the largest single funder of civil R&D too. The civil aircraft programme alone consumed more than the spending of the Department of Scientific and Industrial Research (DSIR). One estimate of MoS civilian aircraft development and spending puts the figure at £78.87 million up to 1955;[207] another at £88.37 to 1959,[208] the Brabazon alone consuming £13 million.[209] Devons estimated that the MoS spent some £30–40 million in the immediate post-war years ordering prototype civil airframes, as well as similar amounts for the development of civil engines.[210] Indeed total expenditure (capital and current) on the nuclear physics research establishment at Harwell was greater than the entire budget of the DSIR. Yet it is around bodies such as the DSIR that the history of British 'science policy' revolves.

Although the programmes of the MoS and their associated private and public industries are the central cases for new highly national programmes they are far from the only ones. In agriculture not only was self-sufficiency strongly pushed, but research funded by the state became increasingly important: in plant breeding private effort was displaced by state development.[211] More generally, industry itself, operating behind powerful import controls, was able in the 1940s, and especially the 1950s and early 1960s, to make huge increases in the research spending.[212] Universities too were nationalised in the sense that they became increasingly dependent on funds from the central University Grants Committee and other central bodies.

2001). Hendry has noted that 'by 1952 [Ferranti] had reached the stage of being Britain's only commercial computer manufacturer, with six firm orders, without having taken any risks and without having invested any significant resources of its own in the venture'. The MoS had paid for the bulk of the development work. J. Hendry *Innovating for failure* (Cambridge, MA: MIT Press, 1990), p. 91. On the role of the MoS in the development of electronics see Jerome Kraus 'The British electron-tube and semiconductor industry, 1935–62', *Technology and Culture* 9 (1968), 544–61.

[207] Keith Hayward, *Government and British civil aerospace: a case study in post-war technology policy* (Manchester: Manchester University Press, 1983), p. 15.

[208] Ministry of Aviation, *Enquiry into the aircraft industry*, p. 125.

[209] Hayward, *British civil aerospace*, p. 17. The Brabazon is routinely condemned as a case of a bad aeroplane inspired by imperial nostalgia. For a very different view see Groves Herrick, 'The Bristol Brabazon air liner', unpublished MSc thesis, university of London (1998). He argues that it should be seen as one of a number of very large projects of the era, including US ones, among them a civil derivative of the B-36 bomber. Furthermore luxury flying across the Atlantic was an appropriate aim into the early 1950s.

[210] E. Devons, 'The aircraft industry' in Duncan Burn (ed.), *The structure of British Industry*, 2 vols. (Cambridge: Cambridge University Press, 1958), II, p. 83.

[211] Paolo Palladino, 'Science, technology and the economy: plant breeding in Great Britain, 1920–1970', *Economic History Review* 49 (1996), 137–53.

[212] See Horrocks, 'Enthusiasm constrained?', 42–63; Edgerton, *Science, technology and the British industrial 'decline'*.

Such funds amounted to around one-third of university income in the interwar years. They rose to more than half by 1946/7, and to 80 per cent by the mid-1960s.[213] The expansion and control of R&D was intimately tied to nationalism and militarism – to the warfare state rather than to the welfare state.

The supply ministries, born from service ministries, had a remarkable impact in the context of highly nationalistic and interventionist policies for industry, science and technology. Historians have systematically discounted these vital ministries and their interventionist role in interwar, wartime and post-war Britain and have often given the impression of a reversion to pre-war conceptions of the role of the state, at least outside welfare. In this rueful story the Treasury regained its power, the innovative temporary intruders were banished and *laissez-faire* was back in bloom. In relation to industry historians and political scientists looked at the feebly interventionist Board of Trade but not the key interventionist ministries.[214] And yet, as we have seen, never before had a British government maintained a peacetime supply ministry, nor charged it with responsibility for very important parts of British industry. And this was a state in which there were many more specialists – from agricultural officers to research physicists – a state which had more power. It is to these men that we now turn.

---

[213] A. H. Halsey (ed.), *Trends in British society since 1900* (London: Macmillan, 1972), table 7.3.

[214] In an interview with the historian of Whitehall Peter Hennessy, Oliver Franks, Permanent Secretary of the MoS, 1945–46 said that civil service colleagues 'from departments which had not been disturbed so much by the war and made to change their ways' did not welcome suggestions for change. (Quoted in Peter Hennessy, *Whitehall* (London: Fontana, 1989), p. 124.) See also W. H. Greenleaf, *The British political tradition.* Vol. III: *A much governed nation*, Part 1 (London: Methuen, 1987), p. 203. But Hennessy, like other critical commentators on the British state, looks too exclusively to these undisturbed departments, and not enough to those that bore the brunt of managing the war economy. Indeed, Hennessy chides as damningly self-congratulatory a document put out by Edward Bridges (then permanent secretary of the Treasury and head of the home civil service), on *The conduct of business in government departments*, despite noting the document's argument that some ministries, – Supply, Food and Works – were operating like large businesses, and that the civil service had to adapt more to that enterprising kind of work. Hennessy, *Whitehall*, p. 126 Another historian, who notes the importance of the wartime supply ministries, and argues, unusually, for the power and coherence of immediate post-war industrial policy, also believes that very soon after the war 'interventionist bureaucracies of the MAP, the Ministry of Economic Warfare, the MoS and the Ministry of Production were simply allowed to melt away.' Glatt, 'Reparations', III, p. 1101. Indeed he claims that Oliver Franks 'lamented the failure to turn the core of MoS into a genuine Ministry for Industry. Only in that way, he believed, would unrelieving pressure for microeconomic efficiency in industry have been maintained': Glatt, 'Reparations', III, p. 1111, citing obituary of Franks in the *Independent*, 17 October 1992.

3   The expert state: the military-scientific complex in the interwar years

> [I]t is remarkable that by 1944 the most brilliant young men from Cambridge and Oxford were already going into the administrative class, there to guide the destinies of the nation; outstanding young men from the provincial universities into the hardly less important scientific and technical grades; worthy young men and women from the grammar schools into the executive grades; the less outstanding joined the junior clerical grades ...[1]

In the standard picture of the British state, there are two groups of senior personnel – the politicians (concentrated in Westminster) and the civil servants (concentrated in Whitehall). When we think of the British civil service we invoke a tripartite hierarchical division into three classes, dating from 1920: the administrative class, the executive class and the clerical class. The austere, incorruptible, member of the administrative class, with his 'Rolls-Royce mind', and his degree in history or classics from Oxford or Cambridge, is at the very centre of our image of the 'civil servant'. Yet these 'mandarins' were also strongly criticised. For example, a group of progressive British scientists, writing in 1940, claimed that the British state was a product of 'Victorian Liberalism'; its 'high administrative officers have a classical training and are almost completely ignorant of technical matters'.[2] The argument was already old and has been repeated many times since. The mandarins were and are seen as 'amateurs' and 'generalists': they were better suited to earlier centuries and to different tasks from those they faced. We need to rethink this common image of the British state which is so central to the technocratic critique of modern Britain. For it is misleading to think of the civil service in these classical terms, especially in relation to expertise. The civil service was made up of many more than these three classes and there were many expert classes. The administrative class may not generally have been experts, but there

---

[1] Michael Young, *The rise of the meritocracy 1870–2033: an essay in education and equality* (Harmondsworth: Penguin, 1961), pp. 19–20 (first published 1958).
[2] Anon, *Science in war* (Harmondsworth: Penguin, 1940), p. 11.

were many experts among the higher administrators of the state. Furthermore, non-civil servants of the state, the military, had important roles in policy making.

The expert officers of the state were and remain remarkably invisible. In 1937 F. A. A. Menzler, who in the late 1920s had been the energetic secretary of their trade union, rightly complained that the standard image left no place for the parallel hierarchies of experts.[3] Even today the problem persists. There is a huge literature on the civil service which still takes it to consist mostly of these three classes, continuing to ignore 'specialists' or 'professionals'.[4] Curiously, much of this same literature on the civil service *condemns* it for under-using experts. For example, Peter Kellner and Lord Crowther-Hunt (a member of the Fulton Commission which influentially examined the civil service in the 1960s) wrote a book on the 'civil servants' criticising the emasculation of the modernising proposals of the Fulton Commission of the 1960s. However, the book was, quite overtly, concerned only with the administrators – the others did not count. Peter Hennessy, in his celebrated history *Whitehall*, lauds the experts and condemns Whitehall for not using them, but his world too is that of the generalist administrators. The experts hardly figure.[5] Menzler's own 1937 article is itself a good example. It gave a very weak account indeed of actual experts in the civil service – it is long complaint about their status. The history of the state's experts needs telling, and if we do tell it the state will look much more expert than is usually believed. The experts were an important feature of the warfare state, and through the warfare state in particular, an important feature of the British state as a whole.

Experts in the state service

That our standard image is awry is evident from the remarkable but little known cases of the four senior British state servants of the interwar years who became government ministers. They were Sir John Anderson,

---

[3] F. A. A. Menzler, 'The expert in the Civil Service', in W. A. Robson (ed.), *The British civil service* (London: Allen & Unwin, 1937), pp. 165–85.

[4] I know of no general account of the British civil service which gives specialist officers due space. For confirmation see Kevin Theakston, *The civil service since 1945* (Oxford: Blackwell, 1995), pp. 191–2. For two studies focusing on technical experts in executive grades see, for the Ministry of Agriculture, Gail Savage, *The social construction of expertise: the English civil service and its influence, 1919–1939* (Pittsburgh: University of Pittsburgh Press, 1996) and on the Treasury Jon Agar, *The government machine: a revolutionary history of the computer* (Cambridge, MA: MIT Press, 2003).

[5] Peter Kellner and Lord Crowther-Hunt, *The civil servants: an enquiry into Britain's ruling class* (London: Macdonald, 1980); Peter Hennessy, *Whitehall* (London: Fontana, 1990).

Sir James Grigg, Lord Chatfield and Sir Maurice Hankey (three of whom have already appeared in our story). Three received high accolades reserved for men of learning: Anderson and Chatfield became members of the Order of Merit; Anderson and Hankey were elected Fellows of the Royal Society (FRS).[6] Of the four, two – Anderson and Grigg – were members of the administrative class of the civil service and both had scientific backgrounds. Both came first in their year in the civil service examination. Sir John Anderson (1882–1958), for much of the interwar period permanent secretary at the Home Office, had studied chemistry in Edinburgh and Leipzig. Sir James Grigg (1890–1964), who spent most of the interwar years in the Treasury, was a Cambridge mathematician who entered the Treasury before the Great War, during which he was in artillery and briefly in the Office of External Ballistics. The remaining two men had backgrounds in the armed forces of a technical nature. Admiral Chatfield (1873–1967), a gunnery expert, rose in the Royal Navy to become Controller, and later First Sea Lord. Colonel Maurice Hankey (1877–1973) was a Royal Marine artilleryman, who joined the Committee of Imperial Defence before the Great War, becoming its second and most famous secretary; he was the first secretary to the Cabinet and served in both posts until 1938.[7] These may be exceptions that prove the rule, but they were very important ones. This example is not meant to show the superiority of technical training, only that key figures in fact had it.

As the interwar head of the civil service, Sir Warren Fisher (1879–1948), put it, there were 'four Crown Services',[8] the three armed or fighting services and the civil service. As Fisher was making clear, civil servants were not the only high officials of the state. Nor yet were they only high administrative officials. Indeed it is sensible to think of the higher administration and policy work of the British state as being carried out by (1) members of the administrative class, (2) senior serving officers of the armed services and (3) senior 'specialist' or 'professional' officers,

---

[6] All have been subjects of biographies or autobiographies: P. J. Grigg, *Prejudice and judgement* (London: Cape, 1948); Admiral of the Fleet Lord Chatfield, *It might happen again*, 2 vols. (London: Heinemann, 1943–8); John W. Wheeler-Bennett, *John Anderson, Viscount Waverley* (London: Macmillan, 1962); S. Roskill, *Hankey: man of secrets*, 3 vols. (London: Collins, 1970–4).

[7] The cabinet secretaryship was not quite the exalted post it was to become after the Second World War.

[8] See *DNB* entry. Warren Fisher was the head of the civil service in the interwar years (and permanent secretary at the Treasury); he was in many ways the creator of the modern administrative class, and the associated doctrines of Treasury control. He epitomises the classical image in another way: schooled at Winchester he read classics at Oxford and entered the civil service on graduation.

including scientists, engineers, doctors and so on. The service departments provide particularly important examples of the roles of all three. Serving officers dominated the highest levels of the three service ministries: they were policy makers and advisers, as well as administrators. Civilian expert officers also had key policy and administrative roles and they were highly concentrated in the service ministries too. In short just as the navy was made up of many 'guilds' or 'professions',[9] and the army of many 'corps', so was the state service as a whole, up to the highest levels.

Specialists, experts and professionals

The British state has long employed experts at many different levels, and in very significant numbers. In the interwar years what we might call the officer and higher non-commissioned officer (NCO) ranks of the civil service were made up of the 1,150 administrative, 4,350 executive, 6,500 technical and scientific grades and 2,150 inspectors.[10] The technical and scientific grades included 1,270 'engineers' (half of them in the Post Office, which ran the telephone system), 740 'chemists and scientific research officers', some 200 'technical officers' engaged in research, 460 medical doctors and 550 legal staff.[11] University graduates were concentrated in two large groups of around 1,000 members: the administrators and the research scientists and engineers.

The administrative class certainly dominated the higher ranks. According to one account, the 'higher civil service' of the 1930s was made up of some five hundred senior members of the administrative class (from the administrative rank of assistant secretary upwards, but including lower ranked private secretaries to ministers) and only about *fifty* expert officers at similar levels, about half of whom were lawyers.[12] This estimate of higher expert officers may be too low: in 1929 there were more than sixty-three technical experts in government paid at least the £1,000 per annum basic salary of assistant secretaries, and at least fifty-one of these posts were scientific, technical or medical.[13] There were six experts

---

[9] J. D. Scott and R. Hughes, *The administration of war production* (London: HMSO, 1955), pp. 3–8, 81–134.

[10] A. M. Carr-Saunders and P. A. Wilson, *The professions* (Oxford: Oxford University Press, 1933), p. 242.

[11] *Introductory memorandum relating to the Civil Service submitted by the Treasury*, appendix to part I of the *Minutes of evidence, Royal Commission on the Civil Service (1929–1930)*, Para. 57.

[12] H. E. Dale, *The higher civil service of Great Britain* (London: Oxford University Press, 1941), pp. 10–11, 16.

[13] Statement submitted by the IPCS, appendix IV. This document is itself appendix XI, *Minutes of evidence, Civil Service*.

paid more than £2,000 basic salary: the director of naval construction, the government actuary, the chief medical officer, the secretary of the DSIR, the director of Ordnance factories, and the civil engineer-in-chief at the Admiralty.[14] In the departments where the experts were concentrated the proportions of higher personnel who were experts was very high. In the Admiralty there were eleven administrators who were assistant secretaries or higher but there were at least twenty-one expert civilians on at least the same salaries, including six naval constructors.[15]

The administrative class saw itself as a state-specific cadre, and not, say, a specialised form of higher manager. By contrast many of the experts were 'professionals' and thought of themselves, and were seen as, members of a wider profession who happened to work for the state. Whereas the primary identification of the administrator was with the civil service, an expert would often identify first with his profession and then the civil service. We should not, however, fall into the trap of believing that all state expertise was largely external to the state. Some forms of technical expertise were found only within the state, others very largely so. The expertise of soldiers, sailors and airmen is clearly a state-centred expertise, and so was that of tax and patent officers, but so too was much scientific and technological expertise. Ballistics, meteorology, oceanography, aerodynamics and so on, were state sciences and technologies, in a way which chemistry or medicine were not (at least in modern Britain). Some of these complexities can be illustrated from the history of civil service trade unionism. In 1918 a Federation of Professional Officers (Admiralty) was formed which included the naval constructors, who had had an association since the 1880s. By the end of the year this body decided to extend membership to all engineers in the state service, and in 1919 the 'Professional Alliance, HM Civil Service' was formed. This soon changed its name to the Institution of Professional Civil Servants (IPCS).[16] Its monthly journal was called *State Technology* until 1926, when it was renamed *State Service*.[17] However, among 'scientists' in government service, the IPCS had a competitor, the AScW, formerly the National Union of Scientific Workers, which organised all scientists, including academics. In 1928 the IPCS had 803 government scientists (out of

---

[14] Ibid.

[15] Admiralty evidence, *Minutes of evidence, Civil Service.*

[16] J. E. Mortimer and V. Ellis, *A professional union: the evolution of the Institution of Professional Civil Servants* (London: Allen & Unwin, 1980), pp. 1–2. On the early years of the National Union of Scientific Workers, from 1927 the AScW, see Roy and Kay MacLeod, 'The contradictions of professionalism: scientists, trade unionism and the First World War', *Social Studies of Science* 9 (1979), 1–32.

[17] Mortimer and Ellis, *Professional union*, pp. 20, 38.

5,000 members), while the AScW had 316, with 61 in both.[18] This
question of internality or externality to the state of scientific and technical
expertise was, as we shall see, of some importance to the nature of the
recruitment process, pension arrangements and self-image of the experts.

Technical experts and the armed services

Within the armed services there are particular specialisations, not only in
say infantry and cavalry, but in more technical spheres, such as engineering
and artillery. The uniformed technical corps often acted as technical
advisers for their service as a whole. In the army the Royal Artillery
and the Royal Engineers provided not just gunners and sappers in the
field, but also key personnel for supply and research and development
positions; they also spawned newer technical corps.[19] In the navy gunnery
and torpedo officers were particularly noted for their technical expertise,
and the gunnery school, HMS *Excellent*, and the torpedo school, HMS
Vernon, became centres for research and development.[20] 'Engineer' officers, in naval terminology the men who operated the propulsion machinery of the ship, were 'permanent specialists' with their own branch with
very limited roles.[21] In the interwar air force nearly all officers were pilots.
Some had specialist training in such matters as signals, engineering
and navigation. In 1940 a separate technical branch, including engineer
officers, was created.[22] Like other serving officers, technical officers were
generally internally trained.[23] They were recruited from public schools
and in the case of the navy often preparatory schools.[24] Artillery and

[18] Ibid., pp. 55, 57.
[19] For example, the Royal Corps of Signals (1920) and to a lesser extent, the repair and
recovery Royal Electrical and Mechanical Engineers (1942).
[20] R. F. Pocock, *The early British radio industry* (Manchester: Manchester University Press,
1988).
[21] See Andrew Nicholas, 'Engineer officer education in the Royal Navy, 1902–1926: status,
expertise and technological change', unpublished MSc thesis, Department of Science
and Technology Policy, University of Manchester (1988).
[22] John James, *The paladins* (London: Futura, 1991), pp. 194–5.
[23] Since the Second World War, and especially in recent years, the armed forces have
recruited many more graduates to the officer corps. Indeed the forces have externalised
some historically internal training. In 1968 the training for the Royal Corps of Naval
Constructors was taken over by University College London. In 1984 the now Royal
Military College of Science, which moved to Shrivenham, was put under the management of Cranfield Institute of Technology (now university), itself created in 1946 as the
Cranfield College of Aeronautics by the government.
[24] The very early education of naval cadets at Osborne and Dartmouth was 'monstrously
mechanical and included a great deal of practical and theoretical engineering' (Stephen

engineer officers were trained at Woolwich, separately from the infantry and cavalry officers who went to Sandhurst. In the navy and the air force all officers had a common initial training, followed by specialised education. Further technical training was available for some already commissioned officers, including in the case of the air force and army university training, principally, it seems, at the University of Cambridge Engineering Department.[25] An unusual but very interesting example is (Sir) Frank Whittle (1907–1996) FRS 1947, who became a general duties RAF officer, went on to engineering specialisation, a degree in engineering at Cambridge and the design of some of the first jet-engines.[26]

The service departments also had civilian technical corps. The Royal Corps of Naval Constructors was a special case. The corps was 'recruited almost entirely from the dockyard towns, mainly from secondary or technical schools'.[27] The constructors came up through a highly competitive system of royal dockyard apprenticeships, from which a very few of the very best were taken away to the Royal Naval College at Greenwich for higher training as constructors. They were a tightly organised and highly specialised public sector profession, perhaps the only British near equivalent to the French technical corps, though very small and much inferior in status. They designed and built warships and they were navy's key technical advisers.[28] Other, less state-specific corps included the electrical engineers in the navy and the technical staffs of the Ordnance factories.

One of the most significant new civilian corps was the emerging body of research scientists and engineers. Even before the Great War, the technical side of the fighting services was being strengthened by research and experimental units. They included on their staffs some civilian graduate scientists and engineers. Examples would be the new 'research department' at the Woolwich Arsenal, the Royal Aircraft Factory,

King-Hall, *My naval life, 1906–1929* (London: Faber and Faber, 1952), p. 45). King-Hall argued that this education produced a naval officer incapable of speaking or writing, and without strategic or tactical understanding.

[25] Werskey cites a Cambridge publication of 1934 which states that 30 per cent (presumably of the students) in the engineering department were army officers: Gary Werskey, *The visible college* (London: Allen Lane, 1978), p. 340.

[26] Whittle was very unusual as an RAF officer in that he entered through a very restrictive scheme which allowed a very few RAF apprentice technicians to go on to officer training. See John Golley, *Whittle: the true story* (London: Airlife, 1987).

[27] D. K. Brown, *A century of naval construction: the history of the Royal Corps of Naval Constructors, 1883–1983* (London: Conway, 1983), p. 154.

[28] One account states that in the interwar years the DNC 'quietly installed himself as the principal technical adviser to the Board, although in Sir John Fisher's day it is clear this eminence had been shared with the Engineer in Chief of the Navy' (Vice-Admiral Sir Louis Le Bailly, *From Fisher to the Falklands* (London: Institute of Marine Engineers, 1991), p. 51).

Farnborough, and various naval facilities.[29] That civilians would be employed was not wholly a foregone conclusion. In 1920 the Admiralty briefly considered putting its scientists in uniform.[30] Even in the 1930s uniformed RAF engineer officers wanted to have the civilian research and development posts at Farnborough reserved for them.[31] The number of such civilians grew very rapidly in the Great War and after the war it was clear that large numbers would be permanently employed in both old establishments and newly created ones like the chemical warfare establishment at Porton Down, and the new Admiralty Research Laboratory opened in 1921. Indeed a majority of civilian research scientists and engineers employed by the British state were in the service departments. Most of the rest were in the National Physical Laboratory (NPL) which was put under the new DSIR in 1918 (see table 3.1).

I will call the expert staff of these laboratories, and the headquarters organisation, the research corps, rather than the scientific civil service (as the researchers became known after the Second World War). Many graduate and non-graduate scientists worked in non-research jobs in other parts of the civil service; many of those engaged in research, and sometimes labelled 'scientific officers', had degrees in engineering rather than science. There were also many called 'technical officers', among other things, who were engaged in research. It would be very misleading to suggest there was a unified research corps in the interwar years: for example each department recruited separately and on different terms. But there were clear moves towards such a corps. The pay scales adopted by the NPL for its research staff (who were far from

---

[29] The army and joint-service bodies like Woolwich had long employed civilian experts. It appears that the first four civilian research scientists in the Admiralty, three from Trinity College, Cambridge, were appointed to HMS *Vernon*, the torpedo school, before the outbreak of war. Naval lieutenants specialising in torpedoes did most of the work. W. Hackmann, 'Sonar, wireless telegraphy and the Royal Navy: scientific development in a military context, 1890–1939' in N. Rupke (ed.), *Science and public policy* (London: Macmillan, 1988), pp. 95–7. For the extraordinary importance of radio to the navy and vice versa see R. F. Pocock, *The early British radio industry* (Manchester: Manchester University Press, 1988). On aircraft see Percy Walker, *Early aviation at Farnborough*, 2 vols. (London: Macdonald, 1971, 1974); Takehiko Hashimoto, 'Theory, experiment and design practice: the formation of aeronautical research, 1909–1930', unpublished doctoral thesis, Johns Hopkins University (1990). On the research department see Guy Hartcup, *The war of invention: scientific developments, 1914–18* (London: Brassey's, 1988), pp. 6–10. The first head was Oswald Silberrad. He was succeeded, though in a somewhat different capacity, by a long-term War Office scientist: (Sir) Robert Robertson (1869–1948), who in 1921 went on to become Government Chemist.

[30] W. Hackmann, *Seek and strike: sonar, anti-submarine warfare and the Royal Navy, 1914–1954* (London: Science Museum, 1984), p. 112. See also Scott and Hughes, *Administration*, p. 130.

[31] James, *The paladins*, pp. 189–91.

Table 3.1 *The distribution of the government research corps by department, 1929–30*

	Admiralty	Air Ministry	War Office	Total services	DSIR	Total
'Scientists' in FSSU	81	85	267[a]	433	316	749
'Technical' staff (most established)[b]	61	143	–	204	–	204
Total	142	228	267	637	316	953

Notes:
[a] All except the most junior in FSSU.
[b] 75 per cent established. The term 'technical' here does not mean technician – these technical posts were equivalent to 'scientific' posts.

Source: H. M. Treasury, *Report of the Committee on the Staffs of Government Scientific Establishments* (1930) (Carpenter Committe), appendices I, II, IV.

all being physicists) were adopted by the navy and air force (though terminology varied), and the army had similar scales. The Admiralty appears to have led the way in creating a unified corps: by the late 1920s all the Admiralty's scientific, technical and analytical staffs, were put into separate 'pools' all under the director of scientific research (DSR). The DSR now had influence over appointments, promotions and so on, across the navy.[32] Another key step was the appointment of a committee on scientists in the civil service, under Professor H. C. H. Carpenter of Imperial College, which reported in 1930 and provided the basis for the cross-government grading scheme which was fully introduced by 1936 and applied until 1945.[33] This scheme divided staff into scientific grades (engaged in research), technical grades (in development) and chemist grades (analysis and inspection). In 1943 a report of a committee under the Treasury official Sir Alan Barlow recommended important changes which were put into effect in 1945.[34] A unified 'scientific civil service' was created for the scientists and engineers engaged in R&D. One could, and perhaps should, see this as reflection of the rising status of researchers with respect to both administrators and serving officers, and indeed other technical branches.

[32] Hackmann, 'Sonar', p. 109; Scott and Hughes, *Administration*, pp. 130–1.
[33] Mortimer and Ellis, *Professional union*, p. 73.
[34] Chancellor of the Exchequer, *The scientific civil service: reorganisation and recruitment during the reconstruction period*, Cmd 6679, September 1945. Includes as an annex the *Report of the Barlow Committee on scientific staff*, April 1943.

R&D in the forces

It is important to distinguish, as we have in effect already done, between expertise and research. The conflation of science and research – enshrined in the name 'scientific civil service' – has impoverished our understanding of both. The twentieth-century belief that 'Science implies the breaking of new ground',[35] has led to scientific intellectuals using 'science' and 'scientific' to refer to scientific research. Too often the history of science in business, or of science in government or the university is, without this being clear, the history of research.[36] Although only a small proportion of scientists were ever engaged in it, we are beginning to recognise the importance of the research revolution since the late nineteenth century, as one that extended right across the field of knowledge and to many kinds of institution.[37] But we should not ignore the continuing importance of non-research technical expertise.[38] Nor should we underestimate the novelty of research in science, as well as engineering, medicine or even history: even in the 1930s research was not universal in university departments of arts or sciences.[39] In some respects industry and government led the academy in research. The views of a critic will help us understand the transformation that was taking place. The former submariner Captain Bernard Acworth, an all-round reactionary who was critical of Darwinism and aviation, saw not only aviation but 'modern science' and 'research' as a gigantic rip-off: 'modern

---

[35] Hyman Levy, *Modern science* (London: Hamish Hamilton, 1939), p. 710.

[36] See D. E. H. Edgerton, 'Introduction' in D. E. H Edgerton (ed.), *Industrial innovation and research in business* (Chelternham: Edward Elgar, 1996).

[37] See my 'From innovation to use: ten (eclectic) theses on the history of technology', *History and Technology* 16 (1999), 1–26, first published in *Annales HSS* juillet–octobre 1998, nos. 4–5, 815–37; John Pickstone, *Ways of knowing* (Manchester: Manchester University Press, 2000); Robert Fox and Anna Guagnini, *Laboratories, workshops and sites: concepts and practices of research in industrial Europe, 1800–1914* (Berkeley, CA: University of California, 1999); Elsbeth Heaman, *Making medicine at St Mary's: the history of a London teaching hospital* (Montreal: McGill-Queen's University Press, 2003); Mark Pendleton, '"A place of teaching and research": University College London and the origins of the research university in Britain, 1890–1914', unpublished doctoral thesis, university of London (2001). For the business case see the papers in Edgerton, *Industrial innovation*.

[38] Or indeed in many other fields, technical and otherwise. Indeed the distinction between research and non-research can help clarify the debates within interwar British medicine discussed by Chris Lawrence in his 'A tale of two sciences: bedside and bench in twentieth century Britain', *Medical History* 43 (1999), 421–49 and 'Still incommunicable: clinical holists and medical knowledge in interwar Britain' in C. Lawrence and George Weisz (eds.), *Greater than the parts: holism in biomedicine 1920–1950* (New York, 1998), pp. 94–111.

[39] For the low place of research in the British university in the interwar years see Bruce Truscott (Pseud.), *Red brick university*, 2nd edn (Harmondsworth: Pelican, 1951), ch. 4. See also J. D. Bernal, *The social function of science* (London: Routledge, 1939).

science' was 'the modernist title for what was once called engineering' he claimed.[40] He lamented that in the navy:

[h]ulls, machinery, instruments, devices, weapons, explosives, gas, aircraft, sea-lions, hydrophones – all these show the cloven hoof of scientific research, represented by a huge bureaucratic department presided over by the usual Director and Administrative Staff, and manned by no less than sixty-two gentlemen called senior and junior scientists and sixty-eight further gentlemen known as 'technical officers' ... At the Signal School alone, of all places, no less than fifty-nine of these gentlemen are employed, while in the Vernon, Mining School, Anti-Submarine establishment, and Gas Experimental Station at Porton ... scientists and technicians swarm.[41]

By the interwar years Britain's armed forces indeed had formidable research and experimental facilities.

The broad outlines of interwar 'scientific research, technical development and experiment' in the forces are remarkably easy to establish from the annual estimates given to Parliament. Indeed each of the service estimates included a summary table of funding. Because these tables were presented in different ways, and because they overlap, they need to be used with caution, but the overall picture is very clear.[42] I have taken data from the very early 1930s, in part to make the point that the military-scientific complex was strong well before rearmament (as one would expect from the previous chapter). I have estimated total expenditure (see table 3.2) as £2.8 million, about the same as the best estimates for industry's own funding of research and development in the mid-1930s.[43] The Air Ministry was very clearly the largest single research and development funding organisation in Britain. It spent many times more than the largely civilian DSIR, and more too than any British industrial firm. The total cost of running the Royal Aircraft Establishment (RAE) at Farnborough in 1932 was to be no less than £430,000, while the Woolwich Research Department (including proof work) cost £241,000. ICI, one of the world's great chemical combines, and easily the largest industrial researcher in Britain, was spending £500,000 on all its research in the early 1930s. In terms of staff numbers too the arms laboratories

---

[40] Captain Bernard Acworth, *The navies of today and tomorrow: a study of the naval crisis from within* (London: Eyre & Spottiswode, 1930), p. 119.

[41] Ibid., p. 117.

[42] This is a lesson I have learnt from James, *The paladins*, who points out that in failing to use RAF estimates historians have not only missed an important source, but missed some of the most obvious issues. James makes the additional very important point that politicians did not use this published information either (pp. 233–6).

[43] D. E. H. Edgerton and S. M. Horrocks, 'British industrial research and development before 1945', *Economic History Review* 37 (1994), 213–38.

Table 3.2 *Expenditure on scientific research, technical development and experiment (£ 000)*

	1931	1932
Air Ministry	1,574.0	1,458.0
Admiralty	804.4	734.4
War Office	668.8	617.0
Total (estimated)	–	2,800.0

Note:
These estimates are gross, and any total would involve double counting since departments contributed to each other's efforts, as did other departments. Woolwich research department (including proof work) received some £116,000 from other departments. In 1932 the navy was to pay some £155,000 to other departments, largely the War Office. It might be reasonable to deduct some £200,000 from the total, giving a total spend of around £2.8 million.

Source: Air, Navy and Army Estimates, PP 1931/2, vols. XV and XVI.

were huge. Farnborough had 150 qualified civilian scientific and techni-cal staff (and a total staff of 448). (For a list of laboratories see table 3.3.) The research branch of the Research Department at Woolwich had 161 civilian qualified staff, and its Proof and Experimental Establishment had 6. The Porton Down chemical warfare establishment and its outstation at Sutton Oak together employed 66 civilian scientists and technologists.[44] We have no comparable breakdown for the navy, but it had at least 196 civilian scientists and technologists in research and development work.[45] In 1921 the Admiralty Research Laboratory had 39 scientific staff.[46]

Farnborough and the Research Department *each* had about the same number of qualified staff as there were teachers of science in the whole University of Cambridge; each was much larger than any single university laboratory and at least the size of the very largest laboratories in industry. Only the smaller military laboratories were comparable to some of the larger academic laboratories, and the smaller research performing firms, places like the Signals Experimental Establishment, Woolwich, with 24 researchers, and the Air Defence Experimental Establishment at

[44] In 1922 Porton had twenty-three civilian scientific and technical officers; the number had doubled by 1925 (G. B. Carter, *Porton Down: 75 years of chemical and biological research* (London: HMSO, 1992), p. 28).
[45] All data from Air, Navy and Army Estimates, pp 1931/2, vols. XV, XVI.
[46] From John Buckingham, 'The scientific research department in the time of the first director, 1920–29', *Journal of the Royal Naval Scientific Service* 7 (1952), 101, reproduced in Charles Goodeve, 'Frank Edward Smith', *Biographical Memoirs of Fellows of the Royal Society* 18 (1972), 532–33.

Table 3.3 *Military R&D establishments, 1932, by administering department*

War Office
Research Department, Woolwich
External Ballistics Establishment, Woolwich
Design Department, Woolwich
Signals Experimental Establishment, Woolwich
Chemical Defence Research Establishment, Porton Down and Sutton Oak
Experimental Establishment, Shoeburyness
Small Arms and Machine Gun Experimental Establishment, Hythe
Mechanical Warfare Experimental Establishment
Air Defence Experimental Establishment, Biggin Hill
Experimental Bridging Establishment, Christchurch

Air Ministry
Royal Aircraft Establishment, Farnborough
Aircraft and Armament Experimental Establishment, Martelsham Heath,
Marine Aircraft Experimental Establishment, Felixstowe
Air Ministry Laboratory, South Kensington

Admiralty
Admiralty Research Laboratory, Teddington
Admiralty Engineering Laboratory, West Drayton
Mine Design Department, HMS *Vernon*, Portsmouth
Torpedo Experimental Establishment, HMS *Vernon*, Portsmouth
Signal School, Portsmouth
Anti-Submarine Establishment, HMS *Osprey*, Portland
Admiralty Experiment Works, Haslar (Naval Constructors)
Royal Observatory, Greenwich
Cape of Good Hope Observatory
Hydrographic Department
Admiralty Chart Department
Compass Department, Slough

Source: Air, Navy and Army Estimates, PP 1931/2.

Biggin Hill with 23, and others.[47] These figures may underestimate the research strength of the universities because they exclude postgraduate students. Nevertheless the overall picture is clear.

It is impossible to get a good overall picture of the funding of R&D in the arms industry by the service ministries, or indeed the extent of arms research funded in industry itself, or the civilian research undertaken in

---

[47] For the data on which these comparisons are made see Edgerton and Horrocks, 'Industrial research', 213–38 and Bernal, *Social function*, p. 417.

major arms contractors.[48] Vickers claimed in 1936 that it was spending £200,000 on research, which would have placed it second to ICI in any early 1930s' research and development spending league.[49] The main aero-engine firms would have had research and development expenditures which would probably have placed them in the top ten. The airframe firms spent a great deal on new designs, and some had wind tunnels, even research departments. Fairey opened a new research department in 1938 – made up of sections dealing with aerodynamics, structures and metallurgy – which was claimed to be 'by far the largest' in a private firm; the wind tunnel was the 'largest in private use'.[50] At the Vickers-controlled ESC research was expanded in the early 1930s, with a staff of about eighty, which would place the firm in the top ten.[51] The Brown-Firth research laboratories, created in 1908, continued to be of very great importance; they reported spending £35,000 per annum in the 1930s, putting them in the top twenty.[52] Hadfields too had long been a leading firm in steel research. By the end of the 1920s the optical firm Barr and Stroud had a scientific staff of twenty, including those working on military and naval optics.[53]

Although the details given above were not all available to contemporaries, the degree to which research was funded by the military could be estimated by those who cared to do so. In a pioneering early 1930s' survey of research funding undertaken by the academic biologist Julian Huxley, he noted,

if you are willing to pay for more men and more facilities in war research than in, say, medical research, you will get more results adapted to killing people and less adapted to keeping them alive. And it is when we look at the amounts of expend-iture in different fields that we begin to realise what a large share of the nation's scientific brains is occupied with war. It is very difficult to obtain exact figures; but I have attempted to reach rough estimates which I think are not too far from actuality to be of service. I submit them with reserve, and as subject to an error of at least 15 to 20 per cent. For research in industry, and in the sciences mainly basic to industry, like physics and chemistry, the country spends perhaps 2 1/4 or 2 1/2 millions a year. War research comes next to this, with certainly over a million pounds, perhaps a million and a half. Research in agriculture and the agricultural

[48] The wartime survey which is the source of the best 1930s' data excluded arms suppliers. See Edgerton and Horrocks, 'Industrial research'.

[49] Royal Commission on the Private Manufacture of and Trading in Arms 1935–6, Minutes of Evidence, p. 353.

[50] 'The new Fairey Research Laboratories', The Aeroplane, 2 November 1938, 531–3.

[51] G. Tweedale, Steel city: entrepreneurship, strategy and technology in Sheffield 1743–1993 (Oxford: Clarendon Press, 1995), p. 253.

[52] Tweedale, Steel city, pp. 254–6; Edgerton and Horrocks, 'Industrial research', p. 223.

[53] Mari Williams, The precision makers: a history of in the instruments industry in Britain and France, 1870–1939 (London: Routledge, 1994), p. 161. Williams severely underestimates the significance to Barr & Stroud of continuing naval and other service orders. See Michael Moss and Iain Russell, Range and vision: the first hundred years of Barr & Stroud (Edinburgh: Mainstream, 1988), ch. 4.

side of biology take somewhere around three-quarters of a million; research in health and the physiological side of biology about half a million or probably less. And research in the specifically human sciences like psychology and sociology probably accounts for well under a hundred thousand. Money talks: and these figures tell a tale. Science is being applied on a large scale to the ends of destruction, not because science is essentially destructive or scientists particularly militarist, but because the nation, through its appointed government, is paying handsomely to secure that it shall be so applied.[54]

As we have seen, Huxley may have underestimated the significance of military research. The Marxist academic physicist J. D. Bernal also highlighted the extent to which British science was funded by the military: 'It would not be unfair to say that something between one-third and one-half of the money spent on scientific research in Britain is spent directly or indirectly on war research ... And this in peace time'.[55] Let us remember these proportions.

The academic elite and the military-scientific complex

In the 1920s the academic scientific elite was not particularly concerned about warlike research. An editorial in the key journal of scientific opinion, *Nature*, argued in 1926:

The intelligent man in the street must see that to abandon investigations on lethal weapons while other nations pursue them is to court disaster, if not extinction. However much we may detest these weapons, the calls of home, of country, and of Empire must come first. In these circumstances the responsibility of the scientific workers concerned appears to be confined to the observance of strict secrecy in their work.[56]

J. B. S. Haldane, the biologist nephew of the great pre-war army minister R. B. Haldane, published a defence of chemical warfare which argued that to be killed by gas was no worse than being killed by other means, and that gas warfare would lead to more decisive, and therefore more humane, wars.[57] In the 1930s, however, the relations of science and the military became an important source of concern for some scientific intellectuals. One reason was that, as *Nature* put it in 1931: 'There is a

---

[54] Julian Huxley, 'Peace through science', in Philip Noel-Baker et al., *Challenge to death* (London: Constable, 1934), pp. 292–3.

[55] Bernal, *Social function*, p. 173.   [56] *Nature*, 117, 23 January 1926, p. 110.

[57] J. B. S. Haldane, *Callinicus, a defence of chemical warfare* (London: Kegan, Paul, Trench, Trubner, 1925). See Ronald Clark, *J. B. S.: the life and work of J. B. S. Haldane* (London: Hodder & Stoughton, 1968). The humanisation of war through science was also a theme developed in the United States as Hugh Slotten has ably shown in his 'Humane chemistry or scientific barbarism? American responses to World War I poison gas, 1915–1930', *The Journal of American History* 77 (1990), 476–98. Positive moral arguments were still used,

widespread tendency to hold science, and possibly chemistry in particular, responsible for many of the worst evils of modern warfare, which is perhaps the more dangerous to society because it is apt to discredit the voice of science.'[58] But there was another, very particular context. The outbreak of new wars, especially in the Far East and South America, and the Geneva disarmament conference, gave the issue of war a new salience for intellectuals. At this time the tiny pre-Popular Front communist movement sought to mobilise intellectuals, including scientists, on anti-war platforms.[59] Anti-war groups sprung up, including the Cambridge Scientists' Anti-War Group, founded in 1932. Its key figure, J. D. Bernal, gave evidence to the Royal Commission on the Private Manufacture of and Trading in Arms. This grouping was responsible for interesting many Cambridge scientists in the wider social relations of science and political activity more generally.[60] By the mid-1930s a new view of scientists' ideas of the relations of science and war was being given historical antecedents. An article in *Nature* in 1937 argued that:

Already in the time of the Great War the prostitution of science to warfare was deeply felt by many British men of science, some of whom refused altogether to participate either as soldiers or scientific workers. The same attitude would again be taken by many, should we be cursed by another war; even in the present time of uneasy peace, the activity in rearmament is renewing in the minds of many men of science the same tension of feeling, the same problems of conscience.[61]

The article did not point out that during the Great War *Nature* had shown no such scruples; nor did it name any conscientious objector (though there were some). Bernal's view was very different:

The attitude of scientists during the last war has seemed, in retrospect, a most pathetic spectacle. Every shred of scientific internationalism was lost, and

though apparently extremely rarely, in official documents in the war with respect to biological weapons in the 1930s. See Brian Balmer, *Britain and biological warfare: expert advice and science policy, 1930–1965* (London: Palgrave, 2001), p. 18.

[58] *Nature* 127, 7 March 1931, p. 333.

[59] Martin Ceadel, 'The first communist "peace society": the British anti-war movement 1932–1935', *Twentieth Century British History* 1 (1990), 58–86.

[60] Werskey, *The visible college*, pp. 217ff.; E. H. S. Burhop, 'Scientists and public affairs' in Maurice Goldsmith and Alan Mackay (eds.), *The science of science* (Harmondsworth: Penguin, 1966), pp. 32–46. The Cambridge University and city branches of the Communist party of Great Britain were formed in 1931/2, with Trinity College men, including David Guest, John Cornford and Maurice Cornforth, playing a leading role. Guest was a mathematician. Guest and Cornford died in Spain. Neal Wood, *Communism and the British intellectuals* (London: Gollancz, 1959), pp. 85–6. A misprint on p. 86 kills off Cornforth rather than Cornford. See David Guest, *Lectures on Marxist philosophy* (London: Lawrence and Wishart, 1963; first published under different title, 1939).

[61] *Nature* 139, 1937, p. 980, quoted in P. G. Werskey, 'The perennial dilemma science policy', *Nature* 233 (1971), p. 531.

scientists were not content with helping material destruction, but were obliged to vilify the scientists and even the science of enemy countries.[62]

Yet at the same time as they condemned warlike research many scientific intellectuals criticised the forces for not being scientific enough. J. B. S. Haldane, who was extremely unusual in discussing the relation of science to strategy ('Lovers of peace often make the disastrous mistake of refusing to study the technique of war because they regard it as wicked or disgusting'),[63] criticised Britain's commitment to a bomber fleet as both morally and technically wrong, explaining that it was the result of old-fashioned militarism and the lack of scientific culture among Britain's ministers and civil servants.[64] Julian Huxley suggested the establishment of a War Services Research Council along the lines of the civil research councils to give scientists a greater say in, indeed control of, warlike research policy.[65] The progressive authors of *Science in war*, a manifesto for science published in 1940, claimed that the 'permanent technical advisers' were 'not infrequently cut off from the more active streams of scientific thought'.[66] As we shall see, academic scientists went to great lengths to get some control of services research.

Running warlike R&D

For the huge state R&D effort was not in the hands of academics, nor indeed the DSIR or the administrative class. The senior scientific and technical officers in the navy and air force had access to and reported to either a member of, or the whole, Admiralty Board or Air Council. These boards or councils generally contained one senior officer, usually, in modern parlance, a two-star admiral, general or air marshal, responsible for both the supply and development of weapons. To outsiders the positions they occupied had exotic and unrevealing job titles: in the navy, the Third Sea Lord, also known as the Controller of the Navy; in the army, the Master-General of the Ordnance, an artillery or engineer officer[67] and later the director-general of munitions production. In the air force, the key figures were the Air Member for Supply and Research until 1934, the Air Member for Research and Development until 1938 and then the Air Member for Development and Production (Air Member means airman

[62] Bernal, *Social function*, p. 182.
[63] J. B. S Haldane, *ARP* (London: Gollancz, 1938), p. 247.   [64] Ibid., p. 247.
[65] J. H. Huxley, *Scientific research and human needs* (London: Watts, 1934), pp. 152–3, 167.
[66] Anon., *Science in war*, p. 11.
[67] Three interwar masters-general were artillerymen, the remaining two engineers.

member of the Air Council).[68] The role of the administrators was minimal. The director of scientific research in the Admiralty, who had direct access to each member of the Admiralty Board, claimed that 'in fact I saw the First Sea Lord five times as frequently as the Permanent Secretary to the Admiralty'.[69] The IPCS wanted to extend the Admiralty model to other departments, without making clear that the bulk of scientists in government were in structures which did not report to administrators.[70]

What directors of scientific research directed was something rather different from what we might think of as 'science' or 'science and technology' or 'research and development'. They directed only a small part even of the civilian scientific and technical work of their ministries, even the R & D work. They were among many directors controlling research and development. In the case of the navy the directors of naval construction, signals, torpedoes and mining, naval ordnance and the engineer-in-chief all had significant research and development roles. In the army research was split between the director of artillery and the director of mechanisation until 1938; in that year a DSR was appointed, who took on only part of their responsibilities. The Air Ministry had a director of scientific research, a director of technical development and from 1938 a director of communications development (in fact radar) as well. Of these directors only the DSRs of the three services, the director of communications development and the director of naval construction were civilians. The civilian DSRs controlled only some of the service research laboratories. In the navy the DSR's department ran only the Admiralty Research Laboratory. In the air force the civilian DSR shared the RAE at Farnborough with the airman director of technical development. The staffs of both directorates concentrated at Farnborough, were civilian scientific and technical officers, who intermingled.[71] In the army, the laboratories came under the director of artillery or the director of mechanisation.[72] All the army laboratories were headed by military (or naval) officers, none by a civilian scientist or engineer.[73] The very large research department at Woolwich was headed by a military or naval chief

[68] The Air Council, like the Army Board and the Board of Admiralty, had civilian members in the form of the responsible ministers, and the permanent secretary.
[69] Dr F. E. Smith, Secretary DSIR, *Minutes of evidence, Civil Service*, Q 16,699.
[70] Statement submitted by the IPCS, *Minutes of evidence, Civil Service*.
[71] Scott and Hughes, *Administration*, p. 34.
[72] The director of artillery was responsible for the Research Department, the Design Department and the Chemical Defence Establishment; the director of mechanisation had the remainder, including those concerned with signals.
[73] Scott and Hughes, *Administration*, p. 31

superintendent, who had three senior civilian directors under him.[74] Only the Admiralty Research Laboratory, Farnborough, and later the radar laboratory were headed by civilian scientists and engineers.

Despite the vast internal effort devoted to research, 'science' was thought of by the military as something associated with the external civilian world. Indeed it was a recurrent theme that the services should remain in close touch with it. Thus the DSRs had responsibilities for liaison with 'science'.[75] There was a dense network of committees on which external scientists sat, usually with departmental representatives. One of the most important was the Advisory Committee on Aeronautics, created in 1909, to advise and guide research at Farnborough and the NPL. Under changing names, it was to exist until 1980.[76] Although routinely left out of accounts of British science policy it should have an honoured place. Its most famous chairman was (Sir) Henry Tizard,[77] who served between 1933 and 1943, while Rector of Imperial College. He had been a member since 1920.[78] The other services were less connected to the academic world, but even without a director of scientific research the War Office had formal links with academic science: both the Ordnance Committee and the Chemical Warfare Committee (in fact inter-service bodies) had academics on them permanently, while other committees had them as necessary.[79] For example in 1932 the Ordnance Committee had Professors L. Bairstow, C. V. Boys and R. H. Fowler on it.[80] The Chemical Warfare (later Defence) Committee and its sub-committees had many distinguished civilian scientist members. In 1932

---

[74] H. M. Treasury, *Committee of Civil Research, Report of the Research Co-ordination Sub-committee* (1928), para. 137.

[75] Scott and Hughes, *Administration*, p. 130 for the Admiralty case.

[76] Hashimoto, 'Theory, experiment'.

[77] In what follows I give dates to allow easy access to the biographical information. I add reference to Fellowship of the Royal Society, with date of election, and reference to high honours such as peerages, knighthoods. When knighthoods and peerages are put in brackets – (Sir) or (Lord) – this indicates that the person concerned was not at the time referred to thus distinguished.

[78] In this regard it is important to note the dense networks of acquaintance and friendship between scientists, and engineers inside and outside of the service ministries, often formed during the Great War. The wartime theoretical department H at Farnborough and the Chudliegh mess seem to have been particularly important. At the Chudliegh Mess were (Sir) G. I. Taylor, (Sir) W. S. Farren, H. Glauert, (Sir) R. H. Fowler, (Sir) G. P. Thomson, (Sir) B. Melvill Jones, Teddy Busk, F. M. Green, F. W. Aston, (Lord) F. Lindemann and others. From a lecture by G. I. Taylor first given in 1971, reproduced in ch. 6 of George Batchelor, *The life and legacy of G. I. Taylor* (Cambridge: Cambridge University Press, 1996). (Lord) E. D. Adrian, also lived at the Chudliegh Mess; he worked at the military hospital in Aldershot (*DNB*). See also John Bradley, 'The history and development of aircraft instruments – 1909 to 1919', unpublished doctoral thesis, University of London (1994).

[79] *Committee on civil research*, paras. 130–3.   [80] *Army List 1932.*

the committee had eighteen members of whom seven were FRSs.[81] There were many shorter-lived committees set up under the Committee of Imperial Defence, or particular service ministries, among them the Committee on Air Defence of the 1920s, the Tizard Committee of the early 1930s and for example the committee set up by Hankey to look into biological warfare in 1934.[82] In addition there were many informal contacts at many different levels. The state machine was to resent deeply the claims of parts of the academic scientific community that new committees were needed to bring the services into contact with academic science.

The identification of science with the civilian, and with the external world, can also be seen in other ways. Some of the research officers were enrolled in the universities' pension scheme, the Federated Superannuation Scheme for Universities (FSSU) rather than having the pension arrangements of established state servants.[83] The assumption was that researchers might only be temporarily in the civil service. But to assume that it was thought that government scientists were on a par with university teachers, or that they were likely to go on to university careers, would be a mistake. The key point about the universities' scheme was that it allowed a researcher to leave the civil service without complete loss of pension contributions.[84] Movement on to industry was typical and the universities pension scheme policy was crucial in this.[85] In the six years to May 1930, seventy-three, mostly junior, scientists left the research department, Woolwich – out of a complement of 150.[86] The Admiralty lost fifteen in the same period, six to other parts of government.[87] Quite

[81] Which included professors A. J. Allmand, J. Barcroft, Robert Robinson, and J. F. Thorpe: Carter, *Porton Down*, p. 30; *Army List*, September 1932. In 1939 the membership excluding *ex officio* government people was F. W. Bain of ICI, the Cambridge physiologist Professor Sir Barcroft, the Imperial College meteorologist Professor D. Brunt, F. H. Carr of British Drug Houses, C. J. T. Cronshaw of the British Dyestuffs Corporation (ICI), the Oxford physiologist C. G. Douglas, Sir Harold Hartley of the LMS Railway, Professor Ian Heilbron of Imperial College, Harry Pollitt of ICI, J. Davidson Pratt a former chemical warfare official, the Oxford chemist Professor Robert Robinson, the Cambridge biologist Lord Rothschild, the Imperial College chemist Professor J. F. Thorpe and Professor A. M. Tyndall of Bristol. *Army List*, October 1939.
[82] Balmer, *Britain and biological warfare;* Philip Chaston, 'Gentlemanly professionals within the Civil Service: scientists as insiders during the inter-war period', unpublished doctoral thesis, University of Kent (1998); David Zimmerman, *Britain's shield: radar and the defeat of the Luftwaffe* (London: Sutton, 2000); Alexander Rose, 'Radar and air defence in the 1930s' *Twentieth Century British History* 9 (1998), 219–45.
[83] Hackmann, *Seek and strike*, p. 113.
[84] *Committee of civil research*, para. 108. H. M. Treasury, *Report of the Committee on the staffs of government scientific establishments* (1930) (Carpenter Report), para 16.
[85] Dr F. E. Smith, Secretary DSIR, *Minutes of evidence, Civil Service*, Q 16,770.
[86] *Report of the Committee on the staffs of government scientific establishments*, paras. 10–13.
[87] Sir Oswyn Murray, PS Admiralty, *Minutes of evidence, Civil Service*, Q 17,633.

a number of them went on to very successful industrial careers.[88] A very few future academics had also spent time in the War Office laboratories.[89] Movement to and from universities was very unusual, except in the special case of aeronautics, where state employment dominated the field.[90] Against the conceit of an external world of science we must put the sheer dominance of the state corps of scientists and technicians in key areas.

[88] Among the Woolwich men who went to industry were (Sir) Stanley Hooker (1907–1984) FRS 1962, who, with a first degree from Imperial and an Oxford engineering doctorate, joined the Admiralty Research Laboratory in 1935 and was transferred to Woolwich to work on rockets. He joined Rolls-Royce in 1938. See Sir Stanley Hooker, *Not much of an engineer* (Shrewsbury: Airlife, 1984). (Sir) Eric Mensforth (1906–2000), a Cambridge engineer, was briefly at the Woolwich Arsenal before going to various engineering companies, including John Brown and Westland (obituary in *Guardian*, 1 March 2000); see also Eric Mensforth, *Family engineers* (London: Ward Lock, 1981). (Sir) William Thomas Griffiths (1895–1952) from the university of Wales was a metallurgist, research department, Woolwich, 1921–6, before setting out on a career with Mond Nickel.

[89] (Professor) P. A. Sheppard (1907–1977) CBE 1963, FRS 1964, a Bristol physicist, was a meteorologist at Porton between 1934 and 1939 before going to Imperial College, where he would become Professor of Meteorology, 1952–1974. (Professor) J. B. Speakman (1897–1969), a graduate of Manchester, worked on chemical warfare from 1921 to 1924 before moving to a career in textile chemistry at Leeds. (Professor) Harold Burton (1901–1966) trained in Sheffield, spend the years 1924–6 at the Chemical Warfare Research department before taking up an academic career in organic chemistry at the University of Leeds. (Professor) J. M. Coulson (1910–1990), educated at Cambridge and Imperial College, joined Woolwich in 1935, before returning to teach chemical engineering at Imperial in 1939. Later he was Professor of Chemical Engineering, University of Newcastle-upon-Tyne (formerly University of Durham), 1954–75. (Professor) John Coales (1907–) CBE (FRS 1970) is an important naval case. He returned to the Cambridge engineering department after the war.

[90] Hashimoto, 'Theory, experiment'. The connections between Cambridge and Imperial, which dominated training in aeronautical engineering, with the Air Ministry were extremely close. The Cambridge programme was headed by (Sir) Bennett Melvill Jones (1887–1975) FRS 1939 who was a professor at Cambridge from 1919 to 1952. The Imperial programme was run by (Sir) Leonard Bairstow (1880–1963) FRS 1917, who was head of department and Zaharoff Professor between 1923 and 1945. Both were active members of the Aeronautical Research Committee. Among the Air Ministry staff who taught at Imperial was Haynes Constant (1904–1968) FRS 1948, another key figure in jet-engines and a future director of the National Gas Turbine Establishment: he joined in 1928, and spent the two years 1934–6 as a lecturer at Imperial College. Among those who left the RAE for academic jobs were W. J. Duncan (1894–1960) FRS 1947, a University College London engineer who joined in 1926 and left in 1934 for an academic job in aeronautical engineering at Hull, and Professor A. V. Stephens (1908–1992) a Cambridge engineer who joined RAE in 1930, before returning to Cambridge in 1934, as a fellow of St John's College until 1939; he later held chairs in aeronautics in Sydney and Belfast. Some post-war academics had started their careers in the military labs, including (Professor) R. V. Jones, who joined the Air Ministry in 1936, as did (Professor) Robert Hanbury Brown. See R. V. Jones, *Most secret war* (London: Hamish Hamilton, 1978); R. Hanbury-Brown, *Boffin* (Bristol: Adam Hilger, 1991).

The civil service research scientists and engineers

The interwar research corps appears in the literature by and about academic scientists as an inferior breed. For example, the biologist Solly Zuckerman complained at the beginning of the Second World War that the state's scientists did not want to upset the military and state authorities and that outside scientists who wanted to do war research, 'had to face the opposition created by the vested interests of second-rate people in the Service departments'.[91] A wartime Treasury committee on scientific civil servants noted: 'All the evidence before us points to one main conclusion, that the Government failed in peace-time to attract into and retain in its service a proper proportion of the best scientists produced by the universities.'[92] More recently R. V. Jones, who joined the research corps in the late 1930s, claimed that the

research establishments were not well supported up to 1935, in that they tended to be staffed by men who had gone into them during or shortly after the first war, and who had since lived in a closed environment without many contacts with their colleagues in universities; and the speed of their activities limited by the normal procedures of the Civil Service.[93]

It is a damning consensus. And yet such criticisms are misleading for the research corps as a whole, and wholly wrong for some important elements. The popular idea of the 'boffin' or 'backroom boy' is more helpful than the *de haut en bas* sneering of the academics.[94]

Who were the boffins? Let us start at the top. The interwar directors of scientific research had broadly speaking two things in common. First, few would accurately be described as scientists – most were graduate engineers. Second, all were long-term servants of the state whose earlier careers had concentrated on research and development. The first DSR was appointed in 1920, to the Admiralty. He was (Sir) Frank Smith (1876–1970) FRS 1918, a Royal College of Science physicist, who had been at the NPL since 1900, where he was an expert on electrical measurement and

[91] Solly Zuckerman, *From apes to warlords* (London: Hamish Hamilton, 1978), p. 110.
[92] *Report of the Barlow Committee on scientific staff*, April 1943, para. 5 in Chancellor of the Exchequer, *The Scientific Civil Service: reorganisation and recruitment during the reconstruction period*, Cmd 6679, September 1945.
[93] R. V. Jones, 'Research establishments', in *Proceedings of the Royal Society* A, 342 (1975), 482–3. He clearly recognises, however, that it was these same scientists who made the key contributions to radar, itself the key scientific innovation in war.
[94] A note for younger and non-British readers. 'Boffin' was originally an endearing name given by RAF officers to their research scientists and engineers, which later came to be applied, affectionately, to research scientists and engineers in general. See R. W. Clarke, *The rise of the boffins* (London: Phoenix House, 1962).

standards. He left the navy in 1929 to become secretary of the DSIR, succeeding Sir Henry Tizard. He retired in 1939 but was to be a very important scientific adviser and administrator during the war.[95] His successor, Charles Drysdale (1874–1961), was trained at the Central Technical College (later, like the Royal College of Science, part of Imperial College): he too was an expert in electrical measurement devices. He joined the Admiralty in 1918 from the Northampton Institute (London, now City University), and became the first superintendent of the Admiralty Research Laboratory, a position he held until he replaced Smith in 1929. He owes his place in the *Dictionary of national biography* (*DNB*) as much for his espousal of eugenics and birth control as his naval service. In 1921 he replaced his mother as President of the Malthusian League, a post he held until 1952. He became a member of the National Birth Control Council in 1930. He served as DSR until 1934 and was succeeded by (Sir) Charles Wright (1887–1975), a Canadian who had studied at Toronto and at the Cavendish Laboratory 1908–10. He was a member of the British Antarctic Expedition, 1910–13, spent the war in the Royal Engineers, and joined the Admiralty in 1919, becoming superintendent of the Admiralty Research Laboratory in 1929. He was DSR for the whole period between 1934 and 1946.[96]

The Air Ministry DSRs had long associations with aeronautics, and particular connections to Cambridge. H. E. Wimperis (1876–1960), educated at the Royal College of Science – at the same time as Frank Smith – and Cambridge (in engineering) spent the war in the Royal Naval Air Service and invented an important bombsight. He became the first superintendent of the Royal Naval Air Service/Air Ministry laboratory in Imperial College, becoming DSR in 1925.[97] He retired in 1937 and was replaced by (Sir) David Pye (1886–1960) FRS 1937, his deputy since 1925. Pye was also a Cambridge engineer; he had been a lecturer in engineering at both Oxford and Cambridge. In 1938 the Air Ministry created a job which paralleled DSRs to cover what was called communications development, but was in fact RDF, later known by the

---

[95] After retirement he became an adviser to the oil major BP. During the Second World War he played a very important role as one of the most senior scientific advisers. From 1941 to 1947 he was Chairman of the Scientific Advisory Council of the MoS, and of the Technical Defence Committee of MI5, 1940–46. But he was also director of instrument production, MoS, and between 1940 and 1942 Controller of Communications at MAP, as the overall head of the radar programme (see ch. 8).

[96] He is not in the *DNB*.

[97] He went to the Air Ministry as deputy director of scientific research in 1924 at a time when there was no director.

Americanism 'radar'. The first incumbent was (Sir) Robert Watt (1892–1973) FRS 1941, or Watson-Watt as he became. He was a career scientific civil servant who joined the Meteorological Office (which was, in the interwar years and beyond, part of the Air Ministry) in 1915, having studied at University College, Dundee. In 1927 he became head of the DSIR Radio Research Station at Slough. He was a very active trade unionist with the IPCS. In 1936 he transferred to the Air Ministry's new Bawdsey Research Station, the inter-service laboratory under the Air Ministry which developed radar. The War Office DSR, Herbert Gough (1890–1965) FRS 1933, had been a Vickers apprentice and had a London engineering degree. He had been in the Royal Engineers (Signals) during the war. He spent most of his career at the NPL where he headed the engineering department from 1930.

The most senior men in the laboratories were rather similar. The key figures at Woolwich, the directors of explosives, metallurgy and ballistics, and the interwar directors of Farnborough, were all longstanding members of the research corps, though mostly recruited before the Great War.[98] A good number of the senior men were recruited from men who had been in some kind of technical role in the services in the Great War. Examples are (Sir) Alwyn Crow of Woolwich, (Sir)Charles Wright of the Admiralty Research Laboratory or (Sir) Nelson Johnson of Porton Down, as well as many of the key naval scientists like B. S. Smith or A. B. Wood. But many more were recruited in the interwar years.

---

[98] The senior civilian figures at Woolwich research department were Harold Moore (1878–1972), director of metallurgical research, 1919–32, who joined the research department from Beardmore in 1904; Godfrey Rotter, (1879–1969) director of explosives research, 1921–42, had been at the War Office since 1903 and was a graduate of University College, North Wales; and (Sir) Alwyn Crow (1894–1965), a Cambridge physicist who joined Woolwich in 1917 after war service; he was director of ballistics research between 1919 and 1939, where he led the rocket work; during the war he was in charge of the rocket programme. He became chief superintendent projectile development 1939/40, was director and controller of projectile development from 1940 to 1945 and director of guided projectiles at the Ministry of Supply, 1945–6. He was knighted in 1944. The chief superintendent of Farnborough 1918–28 was the graduate engineer and former factory inspector W. S. Smith (1866–1945). He was succeeded by A. H. Hall (1876–1945), a public schoolboy who studied engineering at Cambridge, did an apprenticeship with the shipbuilders Denny and had been in continuous government service since 1905. He was first at Woolwich, and the Air Ministry airship works at Cardington (where the R101 was built), before being appointed to Farnborough in 1928 where he was stayed until 1941. (Sir) Nelson Johnson (1892–1954) became director of experiments at Porton Down in 1928, and later chief superintendent of the Chemical Defence Research Department (the most senior scientific post in chemical warfare, based in London). He became director of the Meteorological Office in 1938. He was a Royal Flying Corps pilot in the war and joined the Meteorological Office in 1919. In 1921 he went to Porton Down in charge of the meteorological station.

And as we shall see many, particularly from Farnborough, went on to successful careers.

There was, however, a recognition within government that the best scientists did not go into government laboratories. Sir Oswyn Murray, the permanent secretary at the Admiralty, noted in the late 1920s that: 'the sinister symptom, I think, is that we have not recently had any candidates from Oxford or Cambridge, and the candidates we have had from the newer universities have not been, we felt, the highest products of these universities'.[99] The Admiralty DSR noted the particular difficulties in recruiting the brightest research scientists.[100] In March 1939 A. P. Rowe, the superintendent of the radar research station at Bawdsey, was complaining to Sir Henry Tizard that he was having great difficulties recruiting good science graduates from the universities to what were still regular civil service positions, and that he felt that the academic scientific elite discouraged their best students from such a course. Tizard replied admitting that 'I certainly used not to encourage the very best men to go for service under the government because in normal times I think it is better for them to get experience of the outside world first'.[101] Yet, the data in table 3.4 suggest that in the late 1930s some 30 per cent of the scientific officers came from Oxford and Cambridge. As table 3.5 shows, of the members of the interwar research corps who went to certain distinction (which here means an entry in *Who's who* or the *DNB*),[102] 26 per cent were educated in Cambridge and 20 per cent at Imperial College.[103] However, aeronautics appears to have been quite different from the naval and military state sciences, not only in apparently continuing to recruit strongly from Cambridge and indeed Imperial College, but also in

[99] Sir Oswyn Murray, PS Admiralty, *Minutes of evidence, Civil Service*, Q 17,634, see also 17,632.

[100] Dr F. E. Smith, Secretary DSIR, *Minutes of evidence, Civil Service*, Q 16,717.

[101] A. P. Rowe to Sir Henry Tizard, 17 March 1939; and reply by Tizard, 21 March 1939, in Tizard Papers, Imperial War Museum (IWM), HTT 106.

[102] An entry in *Who's Who* followed from high civil service rank, and less certainly from distinction in other fields.

[103] Even before the Great War, there was a particular connection between Farnborough and Cambridge, and Trinity in particular. E. T. Busk joined in 1912, R. H. Mayo in 1913; both were engineers. Wartime entrants who had studied mechanical sciences at Cambridge included R. McKinnon Wood, H. L. Stevens, B. Melvill Jones, W. S. Farren, H. M. Garner and R. V. Southwell. Other mechanical science graduates elsewhere connected with the air services were David Pye, Harry Ricardo and H. E. Wimperis. Farnborough also had a significant contingent of Cambridge scientists and mathematicians, including F. W. Aston, H. Glauert, T. C. Keeley, Keith Lucas, Searle, G. I. Taylor and G. M. B. Dobson. John Bradley, 'The history and development of aircraft instruments – 1909 to 1919', unpublished doctoral thesis, University of London (1994), has the most complete listings. There was a particular Oxford connection through Tizard at other establishments (ibid., pp. 23–4).

Table 3.4 *The two principal graduate classes of the civil service; characteristics of the scientific officer class and administrative class in post in mid-1960s, but established before 1940 (%)*

	Scientific officers	Administrative class
Father's occupation[a]		
I and II	68	77
III (i)	16	15
III(ii) IV & V	16	7
	100	100
School		
Secondary modern/Comprehensive	6	2
LEA grammar	50	28
Direct grant	21	20
Public/fee paying	23	50
	100	100
University[b]		
Oxbridge	31	85
London	24	5
Other English and Welsh	29	0
Scottish	13	9
Irish and Foreign	7	2
Other	3	0

Notes:
[a] Registrar general's classification of occupations.
[b] Adds to more than 100, since some attended more than one university, non-graduates not included

Source: A. H. Halsey and I. M. Crewe, 'Social Survey of the Civil Service' published as vol. III (1) of *The civil service* (1969), Fulton Committee; various tables in chs. 3 and 10.

Table 3.5 *Interwar members of the military research corps born after 1880 who achieved listing in* Who's who, *and how trained*

	Cambridge	Imperial College	London	Scottish	Other	Total
RAE/NPL aeronautics/						
Air Ministry	12	10	4	5	13	44
War Office	1	3	5	0	8	17
Admiralty	5	0	0	0	0	5
Total	18	13	9	5	21	66
Of which, FRS (by 1945)	9 (3)	2 (2)	4 (1)	0	7 (2)	22 (8)

Source: See appendix 1.

providing the key senior technical cadres for the state. Fully two-thirds of the interwar research corps members who went on to distinction were associated with the Air Ministry. Eight interwar RAE men went on to become FRSs, together with three others from the Air Ministry, and four aerodynamicists from the NPL. The other services achieved five in total (see table 3.5). Certainly some were elected to fellowships on the basis of their seniority in government service, but even then a measure of scientific distinction was required.

The status of scientists and technicians in the interwar civil service

The world of the armed forces, and indeed the civil service, was, as one would expect, deeply concerned with rank, and its very close relation, social class. There is no doubt that the question of status has been important for those technical experts. They have often been disingenuous, or perhaps merely naive, in portraying the issue as being one of respect for technical expertise. Social class, type of school and type of university attended left a very clear set on markers which mattered, often painfully, to individuals and to professional groups. However, professional groups were far from uniform in background, and for that reason often divided internally. Thus a public school and Oxbridge-educated scientist, teaching at Oxbridge, and advising the armed forces, was easily distinguished from a grammar-school/red-brick scientist working in a government laboratory. Each had a quite different position with respect to the high authorities in government. They were also different from the often extremely well-paid senior engineers in the private arms industry, quite often public schoolboys, like (Sir) Roy Fedden (Clifton College), the great engine designer of Bristol Aeroplane Company, or Sir John Carden Bt, an old Harrovian, the key tank designer who worked for Vickers from 1928 and inventor of the remarkable 'Flying Flea' aeroplane.[104] Aircraft industry entrepreneurs and engineers like (Sir) Richard Fairey and (Sir) Thomas Sopwith (both well-known sailors) were in yet another category. Social connections were obviously important too. Intriguingly, Harold Nicolson, in his biography of King George V, notes that only once did the king ask that an honour be conferred on a particular subject, in this case an inventor of flying boats known to him personally.[105]

---

[104] C. F. Foss and P. McKenzie, *The Vickers tanks* (Wellingborough: Patrick Stephens, 1988), pp. 54–6.

[105] Harold Nicolson, *King George V: his life and reign* (London: Constable, 1952), p. 514.

Fiction gives us little hints on these matters of status. Harold Nicolson's novel about rockets and atomic bombs of 1932, *Public faces*, has funny portraits of diplomats and politicians, but the only scientist in the text, a Professor Narteagle of Glasgow, a member of the Aeronautical Research Committee, hardly figures. He is characterised by little more than the fact that he wears a pince-nez.[106] A second atomic bomb novel of the 1930s, Eric Ambler's *The dark frontier*, has a Professor Henry Barstow, FRS, DSc, an 'eminent physicist' who lives in Park Lane, but in Wimbledon, Surrey, rather than the aristocratic central London street.[107] Ambler's *Journey into fear* features a protagonist who had a

> highly paid job with a big armaments manufacturing concern, a pleasant house in the country an hour's drive from his office and a wife whom everyone liked ... He was, though you would never think it to look at him, a brilliant engineer; quite an important one if some of the things you heard were true; something to do with guns.

His father was a schoolmaster, he was able to go to university, went on to a doctorate (on a problem in ballistics) and 'by the time he was thirty he was in charge of one of his employer's experimental departments, and a little surprised that he should be paid so much money for doing something that he liked doing'.[108] Here was an example of the upward mobility of the technical middle class, a key feature of the twentieth century.

Some hints about the world of the civilian technical man in the services and government can be got from memoirs and histories by participants. Commander Stephen King-Hall recalled of the late 1920s that

> [t]here was virtually no contact between the naval staff on floor one and the Royal Corps of Naval Constructors on floor two [of the Admiralty building]. The two groups of people never met each other: there was an immense gulf psychologically, and in status, between the designer and user of warships ... they might have been living in different continents so far as personal intercourse was concerned.[109]

The naval engineers provide one of the most interesting case-studies in the complexities, and importance of, status: the new style engineering officers (educated alongside other naval officers) who were just coming into being after the Great War found that they were demoted in 1925 to

---

[106] Harold Nicolson, *Public faces* (London: Constable, 1932).
[107] Eric Ambler, *The dark frontier* (London: Hodder & Stoughton, 1936).
[108] Eric Ambler, *Journey into fear* (London: Hodder & Stoughton, 1940).
[109] Stephen King-Hall, *My naval life, 1906–1929* (London: Faber and Faber, 1952), p. 264.

a status where they could no longer command men. The United Services Club in London now banned them from membership.[110] Such divisions are not so simple as division between experts and non-experts, nor did they remain the same over time.[111] The divisions and distinctions were highly graded: naval engineering specialists in training looked down on trainee constructors: trainee constructors could eat in the engineers' mess, but were not permitted use of the anterooms.[112] At higher levels too questions of status were of vital importance, though the pecking order might be quite different. For example 'Successive Directors of Naval Construction came to regard themselves as technological Popes to whom, they seemed to assume, the Engineer-in-Chief (uniformed) and the Director of Electrical Engineering (civilian) should always defer', while the constructors and engineers both took the scientists to be living on another planet.[113] The Director of Naval Construction (DNC) was given a knighthood; it was also 'traditional' that he be elected to the Athenaeum, the London club of the elite scientists, which as it happens, stood opposite the United Services.[114] The DNC was indeed in a special position: a permanent secretary at the Admiralty noted that 'I do not know of any position of higher status under the Board [of Admiralty] than that of the Director of Naval Construction', noting with approval that at times the DNC had been paid more than the permanent secretary.[115] Crucially though, that DNC was Sir Eustace Tennyson D'Eyncourt (1868–1951) FRS 1921, who served between 1912 and 1924 and had a background in the private sector (Armstrongs) and was related to the poet Tennyson. The naval and air force directors of scientific research, although at some level formally equivalent, were paid considerably less than the DNC, and certainly did not have his status. Something of the complexities of class and status relations is caught by comments made by the academic physiologist A. V. Hill on Sir Frank Smith, the first DSR. Hill expressed surprise that someone who had risen so far had kept his Birmingham or Cockney accent, it is not clear which. Hill claimed to recall receiving a letter addressed to 'Ivy Hill' – Smith's poor secretary presumably being unused to his pronunciation of 'A. V.'.[116] In the army

---

[110] Le Bailly, *Fisher to the Falklands*, p. 39.

[111] Thus in the early 1930s it was apparent that future naval officers, from Dartmouth and the public school entry, became much keener on the engineering specialisation (ibid., pp. 60–3).

[112] The distinction was abolished in 1934. Ibid., p. 51.

[113] Ibid., p. 51

[114] Scott and Hughes, *Administration*, p. 89. See also Brown, *A century of naval construction*.

[115] Sir Oswyn Murray, PS Admiralty, *Minutes of evidence, Civil Service*, Q17,868.

[116] See letters to Sir Charles Goodeve, Smith's Royal Society biographer, from A. V. Hill and Sir Robert Robinson (4 November 1970), B/SMITH, Imperial College Archives.

the division between civilian scientist and soldier was clear. A. P. Rowe, an Imperial College graduate at the Air Ministry, later to be director of the main radar laboratory, recalled 'how astounded he was' at the 'humble and subservient manner of the head of one of the scientific establishments' belonging to the army.[117]

Researchers versus administrators

Despite the fact that the majority of the research corps worked in the service departments or under the scientist-controlled DSIR, they complained about control by the administrative class. The administrative class, with around 1,200 members in the interwar years, and the only slightly smaller research corps, were by far the largest groups of university graduates in state service. The research corps constantly compared themselves with the administrative class, bemoaning their relatively low status and prospects compared with the mandarins. The research corps considered itself to be a comparable elite corps, by virtue of its university education and its involvement in research. Thus the AScW complained that 'The status of the specialist is definitely lower than that of his administrative colleague, despite the comparability of the two in training and in mental calibre.'[118] They too compared researchers in the civil service with the administrators.[119] Sir Richard Gregory (the editor of *Nature*, educated at the Royal College of Science) and Major A. G. Church MP (educated at University College London) of the AScW got themselves into interesting and revealing problems in their evidence to the Tomlin Commission on the civil service. They were forced to claim that the science questions in the administrative class examination were more difficult than those in classics as an explanation for the low number of scientists in the administrative class.[120] There was no evidence for this. They could not answer other key questions: was the entry standard for a scientist higher or lower for entry to the administrative class or the research class? Would they advise a scientist son to join the administrative or research classes? They were stumped because their argument about the higher status of the administrators would lead them to push their sons in that direction; on the other hand they could not

---

[117] Guy Hartcup, *The challenge of war: scientific and engineering contributions to World War Two* (Newton Abbot: David and Charles, 1970), p. 159.
[118] Statement submitted by the AScW, *Minutes of evidence, Civil Service*, para. 31.
[119] Evidence of Sir Richard Gregory and Major Church, *Minutes of evidence, Civil Service*, Q 16,910.
[120] Ibid., Q 17,011.

admit that the scientific standard required for the research corps was lower than that for the administrative corps. From their position they could not explain why science graduates did not apply in large numbers for entry to the administrative class.[121] It was, however, acknowledged that in practice the civil service exam was more difficult for scientists because it included general papers and it tested writing skills.[122] However, the science entry route did exist, and was used, as the cases of John Anderson and P. J. Grigg suggest. Grigg took his degree in mathematics at St John's College, Cambridge, in 1913. In the same year he took the civil service exam, of no fewer than 19 three-hour papers and three practical tests. He took his exams in maths, physics, chemistry and botany and came first in the year. Interestingly Grigg found learning a lot of what he called elementary science for the civil service exam distasteful, and saw this as a

foretaste of the intense distrust I have since acquired of the ultra-scientific outlook. I hate the terrible materialism into which the Western world is plunging as a result of the combination of science and Marxism, and I am terrified lest the restoration of the humanities to at least parity should come too late to save the civilization which we have inherited from Greece and Palestine. But I did not in those days know what a tyrant science was to become.[123]

There were many who disagreed that the status, and the promotion prospects of the scientists and professionals, should be similar to that of the administrators, or that they were in fact comparable in training or mental calibre. The administrators formed a state-wide *corps d'élite*, while the scientists were viewed as professional men, tied to particular departments, and to their professional tasks. The Anderson Committee on pay of state servants of 1923 was categorical: the professional man 'should, in our judgement, relate his pay and position with those of his professional brethren in the outside world, and in doing so should remember all that the Civil Service offers in addition to its pay', and went on to say that when a man with professional experience joined the civil service 'he has no cause to complain because some other servant of the state who is not a professional man and has been selected for a different kind of work at a

---

[121] Ibid., Q 17,026, 17,042.   [122] *Minutes of evidence, Civil Service*, Q 22,334.

[123] P. J. Grigg, *Prejudice and judgement* (London: Cape, 1948), p. 33. On these questions see Anna-K. Mayer '"A combative sense of duty": Englishness and the scientists' in Christopher Lawrence and Anna-K. Mayer (eds.), *Regenerating England: science, medicine and culture in interwar Britain* (Amsterdam: Rodopi, 2000); Andrew Hull, 'Passports to power: a public rationale for expert influence on central government policy-making: British scientists and economists, c 1900-c1925', unpublished doctoral thesis, University of Glasgow (1994).

different age and in a different way, seems to him to be better paid than himself'. The report went on to make an emphatic attack on the claim for greater power for professionals:

We do not agree that an officer appointed for his technical knowledge is necessarily the best man to control a Department. The duties and outlook of an administrator differ from those of the technical man. Although men with high technical qualifications occasionally prove themselves to be first-rate administrators, the head of a Department should, in our view, be so detached from technical bias that he can weigh the advice of his various officers and judge correctly between competing claims, each of which may, to its technical advocate, seem paramount. There is a danger that if a man is appointed head of a department because of his technical qualifications he may not be able to free himself from his technical outlook and that the Service may not gain, but suffer by his special knowledge in one direction.[124]

Not surprisingly, the administrative class trade union quoted the above paragraph in their evidence to the Tomlin Commission on the civil service. The First Division Association, as they called themselves, also claimed: 'There is a fundamental difference between assigning wider administrative powers to technical officers, as such, in connection with their technical duties, and admitting them to the general field of work for which the Administrative Class is recruited and trained.' They objected even to the 'creation of avenues by which men whose training and early experience is technical would pass to the administrative career' because this was 'contrary to the principles on which the Administrative Class is recruited and to the teaching of experience.'[125] As we shall see the issue of the place of the specialist in the civil service would have even greater salience after the Second World War. But the arguments remained much the same.

The administrative class and the research corps really were very different in all sorts of ways. While the administrators were recruited centrally, by examination, the scientists were recruited departmentally, without examination.[126] Furthermore they lived in very different worlds. While the administrators inhabited Whitehall in central London, the bulk of the research corps were working in DSIR laboratories, the largest of which

---

[124] *Report of the Committee on pay etc. of state servants* (1923), para. 28. The members of the committee were Sir Alan Anderson (chairman), Gen the Hon. Sir Herbert Lawrence and Sir W. Peter Rylands.

[125] Association of First Division Civil Servants, statement to the Royal Commission on the Civil Service, *Minutes of Evidence, Civil Service*, appendix VIII, para. 26.

[126] On the historian administrators from Balliol, Oxford and King's, Cambridge, see R. B. Soffer, *Discipline and power: the university, history, and the making of an English elite, 1870–1930* (Stanford: Stanford University Press, 1994). See also Peter Gowan, 'The origins of the administrative elite', *New Left Review* no. 162 (1987), 4–34.

was the NPL in Teddington, or in laboratories close to or in military areas such as Woolwich, Farnborough, Portsmouth and Porton Down. The research corps hardly came into contact with administrators; they were much more likely to deal with military officers. Data generated for the Fulton Commission on the civil service in the 1960s shows just how different young interwar recruits to the research corps were from those entering the administrative class (see table 3.4). The two classes were similar in that (as we have already noted) both were made up overwhelmingly of graduates, but otherwise they were remarkably different. The research corps simply did not have the extreme social and especially educational exclusiveness of the administrators (50 per cent public school and 85 per cent Oxbridge): the scientists were typically grammar school and non-Oxbridge (50 per cent and 69 per cent). Although the contrast is clearly important one must insist too that nearly a quarter of the scientists came from public school and a third from Oxbridge. It is worth noting that 13 per cent of the administrative class had degrees in science or technology.

It has been claimed that 'scientists' were an inferior class in the civil service, but we need to beware this argument. Scientists could and did join the administrative class; the distinction was between those doing scientific research work and those whose job was administration and policy. Those engaged in the administration of research policy, who often had science backgrounds, were on a par with administrators or were themselves in the administrative class.[127] Such a man (until 1929) was Sir Henry Tizard, secretary of the DSIR. Yet he too complained during the Second World War about the relative status of scientists in the forces, and in government establishments, and of both with arts graduates.[128]

The results of state R&D

How important was the expert state in innovation in armaments in the interwar period? How important was it in developing the new technologies of war in use in the Second World War? How important was the

[127] Eric Hutchinson, 'Scientists as an inferior class: the early years of the DSIR', *Minerva* 8 (1970), 396–41, misses this key point.
[128] Sir Henry Tizard to Minister, 19 November 1941; Sir Archibald Rowlands to Minister, 20 November 1941, 12 December 1941. Tizard Papers, IWM, HTT 313. Tizard's confused arguments were comprehensively demolished by Rowlands, who noted that junior administrative officers joined at the same sort of pay as junior scientific officers, noting too that the only such male administrators joining during the war were unfit for military service.

contribution of uniformed officers, and of the civilian research corps? How important were the arms firms? What was the role of purely civilian industries, and of the universities? Making an assessment is obviously difficult and would mean entering into all sorts of controversies – for example between the private aircraft makers and Farnborough.[129] But we can ask a simpler question which allows of a readier answer: did bodies outside the military-industrial-scientific complex – the warfare state and the arms industry – make significant contributions to the development of weapons of war in the interwar years? No one appears to doubt, even implicitly, that artillery, warships, armour plate, even tanks, were products of the complex in our period. Although in the interwar years ICI was seen as part of the military-industrial complex, it is clear that it was not responsible for developments in chemical warfare, and no such claim has since been made. As we have seen, and will discuss again, the aircraft industry was seen as civilian, but we have already noted that it is best treated as fully part of the complex.

Let us consider, in the British case, some possible cases of new techniques from outside the complex, focusing on what are taken to be the most important innovations. Let us start with jet-engines, by any account an important innovation. Here the answer is clear: Farnborough played a significant role, and of course Frank Whittle, the key British inventor, was a state servant, indeed an airman. In anti-aircraft fire control, the Kerrison predictor was the work of Colonel A. V. Kerrison, a gunner. In rocketry British development was clearly concentrated at Woolwich. Radar too came from inside the state: it came out of the NPL/DSIR rather than the Air Ministry itself.[130] But it was developed by the services from the mid-1930s: by May 1938 the Bawdsey Research Station, newly created in 1936 for radar research, was already large, with thirty-seven scientific staff.[131] Operational research too was first conceived of within the warfare state by members of the research corps.[132] ASDIC (later better known as sonar) submarine location was developed by the

---

[129] Out of the Design Department, Woolwich came new 14-inch guns for the new battleships, 8-inch guns for the cruisers and 4.5-inch guns for use first on aircraft carriers; the 4.5-inch army gun, the 4.5-inch anti-aircraft gun, a tank gun and the 25-pounder field gun, which became the standard artillery piece of the Second World War. Scott and Hughes, *Administration*, p. 273.

[130] Zimmerman, *Britain's shield*; Rose, 'Radar and air defence in the 1930s'.

[131] James, *Paladins*, p. 190. See E. G. Bowen, *Radar days* (London, 1986); Hanbury-Brown, *Boffin*; A. P. Rowe, *One story of radar* (Cambridge, 1948); Sir Robert Watson Watt, *Three steps to victory: a personal account by radar's greatest pioneer* (London: Odhams. 1957). The key book is now Zimmerman, *Britain's shield*.

[132] Maurice W. Kirby, *Operational research in war and peace: the British experience from the 1930s to the 1970s* (London: ICP and the Operational Research Society, 2003), ch. 3.

Admiralty.[133] There are no claims for significant civil development in explosives: the research department at Woolwich developed a new flashless propellant and the important new high explosive RDX (research department explosive).[134] These observations are consistent with one study of forty-one military innovations which were significant in the Second World War, since all can be traced back to interwar scientific establishments.[135]

There are three remaining major cases, which on the face of it are more promising as innovations external to the warfare state: the cavity magnetron, nuclear weapons and biological weapons. The cavity magnetron was a generator of high-power very short-wave radio frequency radiation for radar. In the crudest summaries of its history and impact it is written about as if it comes straight out of the University of Birmingham in 1940, and was *the* key war-winning innovation. It is a particularly interesting case. As is well known, the cavity magnetron was not a new invention and what was done in Birmingham was to improve it. Less well-known is that the work was done on Admiralty contract, and was allocated to Birmingham, which had no particular expertise in the area. Furthermore, (Sir) John Randall (1905–1984), the key co-improver, was not a typical academic scientist. After graduating from Manchester he worked at the General Electric Company's (GEC) research laboratories for the whole period from 1926 to 1937. GEC was one of the leading electrical companies, and was one of the very largest performers of industrial research. From 1937 to 1939 he was at Birmingham on a Royal Society fellowship, and remained there on Admiralty funding until 1943. His co-worker Henry Boot was a doctoral student at Birmingham who after the war joined the naval scientific service. The exact nature of the improvement they made is disputed, but Randall was clearly aware of the work that had long been done on magnetrons at the GEC laboratories, notably by E. S. Megaw. GEC already had Admiralty contracts for magnetrons, and would be critical in developing the Randall–Boot version.[136] In short, even if Randall and Boot did make

---

[133] Hackmann, *Seek and strike.*

[134] R. P. Ayerst, M. McLaren and D. Liddell, 'The role of chemical engineering in providing propellants and explosives for the UK armed forces' in William F. Furter (ed.), *History of chemical engineering* (New York: American Chemical Society, 1980), pp. 376–8.

[135] Hartcup, *The challenge of war.* Of course, the sample may be biased in this direction anyway.

[136] *Biographical Memoirs of Fellows of the Royal Society* 33 (1987), pp. 491–535. See also the useful reflections by Walter Kaiser, 'The development of electron tubes and of radar technology: the relationship of science and technology', in Oscar Blumtritt, Hartmut Petzold and William Aspray (eds.), *Tracking the history of radar* (IEEE-Rutgers Centre

a decisive contribution, neither the cavity magnetron nor its improvement can be fully credited to academic physics. Nuclear weapons are much more clearly an academic case, though it is worth noting that British universities did none of the key work that led to the idea of the atomic bomb in the late 1930s. British academics did pick up the possibility of a bomb, and contacted the government, and this led to work being put in hand even before the war under government auspices.[137] Proposals for biological weapons appear to have come from outside the military-scientific complex as well.[138]

The contribution of the civilian world to military innovation can also be addressed by international comparisons. In 1940, Sir Henry Tizard, by then of the MAP, went to the United States in the hope of getting a military technology regarded as hugely important, the Norden bomb-sight. Tizard and his team took with them many of Britain's key military technologies, including the cavity magnetron and jet-engines. Despite the case of the Norden sight, Tizard, returning from his mission, believed that the USA was behind in the development of military technology.[139] After the war he was clear that the service establishments had been crucial in establishing this clear lead.[140] In the wider context of 1930s' innovation Tizard's claim is more remarkable than it might seem. For the contribution of the United States to civilian technical development was clearly already enormous, and by any standard greater by then than that of Great Britain. For example, US industry spend some ten times more than British industry on research and development, though we should certainly not deduce that it was therefore ten times as innovative. In other words the crucial variable was probably, as Tizard implied, the investment in military innovation, not innovation in general. No one has claimed superiority for the other key belligerents – France, Italy, Japan and perhaps even Germany.

The British forces built up a remarkable research corps, which should be included in accounts of the origins of what is often rather misleadingly

for the History of Electrical Engineering and Deutsches Museum, 1994), pp. 217–36. See note 26, p. 234, where he argues that future research needs to ask how these academic physicists were able to come up with this device without training in radio – he is unaware of Randall's background in industry, in itself significant, since he is clearly in command of the sources.

[137] M. M. Gowing, *Britain and atomic energy* (London: Macmillan, 1964), ch. 1.

[138] Balmer, *Britain and biological warfare.*

[139] David Zimmerman, *Top secret exchange: the Tizard mission and the scientific war* (Stroud: Alan Sutton Publishing, 1996), p. 169.

[140] In addition, he noted that university education and research was much stronger. See draft letter to 'Chancellor' (Tizard was confusing the historian J. M. Butler with his cousin, the Chancellor R. A. Butler), 8 December 1953, Tizard Papers, IWM, HTT 696.

called 'big science'. For the research corps did what might better be called 'big research', on a scale at least equal to that of industrial laboratories. The British military research facilities were among the very largest research institutions of their time. As we shall see, it was the research corps into which young science graduates, and some senior academic researchers, were inducted during the war. These new, temporary, members of the research corps typically worked on programmes already well established within the existing military laboratories. Furthermore, the research corps provided the key leaders (with a few exceptions) of the research sections of the warlike ministries, and of the key wartime laboratories. Yet as we shall also see all this was rather hidden by the standard historiography of the relations of science and war which concentrated on the contribution of academic scientists working in atyptical areas.

Whether the future will offer to the scientific civil servants the power and the glory which some of them would unhesitatingly claim as their due is less certain. Politicians may praise them to the skies, crediting them with almost supernatural powers, to be devoted to raising the living standards of the masses, and setting up official "panels" of expert advisors on subjects ranging from the mass production of prefabricated pigsties to the improvement of human relations in coal mines: the man in the street remains a little sceptical. If scientists do succeed in increasing production and wages while lowering prices – a gift with which they are freely credited – he will be disposed to regarding them with a certain degree of favour. If they succeed only in getting us off to a shaky start in an atomic war, which seems equally feasible, those who are left may quite well be lynched. In either event the prospects for the scientific civil service are not without interest.[1]

The warfare state which emerged so strengthened by the Second World War was, as we have seen, highly interventionist and directive. It pursued highly nationalistic economic and innovation policies. Except for the wartime period, the image we have of the British state and in particular of its personnel in itself makes this seem unlikely. We have a picture of a wartime state invigorated by the entry of Labour ministers into political office with the creation of the coalition government in May 1940, and by the entry of energetic temporary civil servants. For Hennessy, whose work *Whitehall* gives the most complete existing account of the wartime civil service, the Second World War saw a civil service reformed by 'temporaries'; alas, the opportunity to reform permanently was lost.[2] Despite its historiographical significance, the personnel of the wartime state are hardly known, and not easily deduced from the usual sources. Political histories do not look enough at non-political ministers; the official histories of war production and administration

---

[1] Roy Lewis and Angus Maude, *The English middle class* (London: Phoenix House, 1949), pp. 122–3.
[2] Peter Hennessy, *Whitehall* (London: Fontana, 1990).

are silent on the all-important details.[3] The literature is particularly poor on the role of businessmen in government, reflecting a more general indifference to the history of business.[4] Perhaps the best is the work on the academic economists, and especially those at the centre of government.[5] The literature on and by scientists systematically plays up the role of academic scientists in advisory roles, without this being at all clear, and plays down the history of state employees and research and development more generally.

Against the standard images of a temporary temporaries' revolution, I propose a very different and more complex picture.[6] The first key point, made in ch. 2, is that already specialist-oriented departments were becoming more important overall. After the war these departments remained more important than they had been. To that extent the technocratic critique is right – the state did require more technical experts. But it did so not because it was generally short of them or resistant to them. Rather it needed more technical experts to expand its already expert departments. The standard image is that the key experts were civilians and outsiders. Here I want to argue for equally important revisions. First, at the most senior levels military men had crucially important roles in supply and R&D, as did long-standing state civilian scientists and engineers. Secondly, the crucial senior recruits from the outside were businessmen, not academics, let alone socialist academics, and many of them came straight from the arms industry. If the warfare state was civilianised it was through the increased influence of long-standing civilian associates of the military. The standard arguments are particularly strong and misleading with respect to science: the academic scientific left, it turns out, was hardly involved at all in the main scientific effort of the war.

[3] The subject is treated in J. D. Scott and R. Hughes, *The administration of war production* (London: HMSO, 1955).

[4] George Peden's valuable paper 'Arms, government and businessmen, 1935–1945' in John Turner (ed.), *Businessmen and politics: studies of business activity in British politics, 1900–1945* (London: Heinemann, 1984), pp. 130–45, does not unfortunately cover the war. Contemporary criticisms by communists in the 1939–41 period are nearly the only contemporary accounts, and they underestimate and misunderstand the significance of businessmen. See for example, Ivor Montagu, *The traitor class* (London: Lawrence & Wishart, September 1940), pp. 93–104.

[5] Sir Alec Cairncross and Nita Watts, *The economic section 1939–1961: a study in economic advising* (London, Routledge, 1989).

[6] The key sources are the *Imperial Calendar and Civil Service List* for the war years (this is unavailable in most places – presumably it was on restricted circulation during the war. Copies for 1941, 1943 and 1945 are available at the IWM and the PRO); *Whittakers' Almanac*, which has listing of some of the most senior people; *Who was who*; *Biographical Memoirs of Fellows of the Royal Society*; the *DNB*; and the *Dictionary of business biography*, which while not comprehensive, is surprisingly and perhaps interestingly, unhelpful for the businessmen in government.

Overall there were important changes in which experts gained power and influence at many levels. They gained power over politicians: many were appointed to important ministerial positions. In crucial cases experts bypassed ministerial heads of department. For example, Churchill severely downgraded the role of the service ministers and raised the power and status of the professional heads of the services, individually and collectively. For Churchill these 'fundamental changes in the machinery of war direction were more real than apparent'.[7] The Chiefs of Staff committee operated directly with Churchill as self-styled Minister of Defence as well as Prime Minister and ran the war and the armed forces, while the service ministers – who were in any case not in the war cabinet – ceased to have any significant role in either strategic planning or in day-to-day operations.[8] Overall, the expert officers, established and temporary, gained power over the administrators, old and new; the directors were gaining over the secretaries. Thus wartime saw the emergence of a huge number of directors-general, as well as controllers, controllers-general and chief executives, and of course a multiplication of directors, deputy directors, assistant directors, chief superintendents and so on and so forth. The administrative class of permanent secretaries, deputy secretaries, principal assistant secretaries and more junior ranks was also expanded, but much less so. Still the 'the classiest class of the civil service',[9] it recruited arts academics (for example Oliver Franks, John Maude and John Fulton) or lawyers, accountants, journalists and some economists (for example, Hugh Gaitskell, Douglas Jay and R. W. B. Clarke), though most economists went to specialist jobs (for example, Lionel Robbins, Alec Cairncross, John Jewkes). The expansion of expert departments, and of the number of specialists, went hand in hand with Treasury loss of power, for the Treasury was not only the guardian of money, but also the upholder of the power of the administrative class, which was responsible for financial control in departments.[10] There

[7] Winston Churchill, *The Second World War*. Vol. II: *Their finest hour*, (London: Cassell, 1949), p. 15.
[8] Churchill, *Their finest hour*, p. 16. The key servicemen were Air Marshal Portal (1940–5); General Sir Alan Brooke (December 1941–5) and Admirals Pound (1939–43) and Andrew Cunningham. On these matters see Alex Danchev, 'Waltzing with Winston', *War in History* 2 (1995), 202–30, and the papers by him in John Sweetman (ed.), *Sword and mace: twentieth century civil–military relations in Britain* (London: Brassey's, 1966) and Paul Smith (ed.), *Government and the armed forces in Britain* (London: Hambledon, 1996). See also Field Marshal Lord Alanbrooke (Sir Alan Brooke), *War diaries, 1939–1945* (ed. Alex Danchev and Daniel Todman) (London: Weidenfeld & Nicolson, 2001).
[9] As William Cooper put it in his novel set just after the war, *Scenes from metropolitan life* (London: Macmillan, 1982).
[10] Scott and Hughes, *Administration*, p. 315.

was also a shifting balance of power between experts. The research corps
in particular was able to increase its power and range of operations. It was
also able to take over, after the war, positions which in previous eras
would have been the prerogative of the military – the control of R&D
and indeed procurement in certain key areas. Here too there was a
civilianisation, but by internal experts. At the same time there was a
change within the civilian technical branches. While the director of
naval construction once ruled the roost as the supreme technical officer
of the state, he was displaced by a number of senior researchers, at whose
peak after the war were the 'nuclear knights'. The 1960s was a key period
in which the research corps attained high influence; paradoxically, as we
shall see, this was their last moment of glory.

The state research corps was just one part of a hugely expanded
scientific and technical effort associated with the warfare state. This
warfare state, not the welfare state, had the decisive influence on the
wartime and post-war development of the British university. The university became a much more scientific place, and a more masculine place
than it had been before the war, and by the 1960s a majority of male
students were studying science or technology. The notorious arts/science
dichotomy, so central to the study of the university, also remained crucial
in discussions of the civil service, particularly in the struggles between the
research corps and the administrators. Yet such dichotomies, so central
to the technocratic critique of the British state, higher education and the
elite, were very misleading not only in describing what was happening,
but also what was at stake.

New ministers

There is a case to be made that in wartime the 'technocrats' were more
important than the 'socialists' even at the political level. For one of the
most remarkable features of British government during the war was
the entrance of non-party-politicians into high ministerial office. One of
the most important, the businessman Oliver Lyttelton (later Lord
Chandos), recalled joining 'the small and select club of those who made
their maiden speeches from the Front Bench. In those days it included
Anderson, Duncan, Bevin, Grigg and me in the Commons, and Woolton,
Leathers, and Cherwell in the Lords.'[11] The wartime club of non-politician
ministers was somewhat larger in that it should include earlier appointments such as Lords Chatfield, Hankey, Reith and others. They were

[11] Oliver Lyttelton, Viscount Chandos, *The memoirs of Lord Chandos* (London: Bodley
Head, 1962), p. 209.

numerically more important than Labour politicians in the highest level of wartime government, the war cabinet. Only three established Labour politicians were war cabinet members, five if we include both Ernest Bevin and Sir Stafford Cripps.[12] A total of seven men (including Bevin) were new to political office. These seven represented two out of the ten men who served at some time in Neville Chamberlain's war cabinet and five out of fifteen of Churchill's. Three came from Whitehall, three from business and one, Bevin, from the trades unions. All, except Bevin, were conservatives. The state servants were Lord Chatfield, Lord Hankey and Sir John Anderson.[13] Anderson was easily the most important, serving as Lord President from 1940 to 1943 and Chancellor of the Exchequer from 1943 to 1945. As Lord President and later as chairman of the Manpower Committee, he took the lead in manpower allocation, at the very least sharing the task with Bevin.[14] He was Churchill's designated successor after Foreign Secretary Anthony Eden.[15] Chatfield was Minister for the Coordination of Defence into the beginning of the war, but did not last long; Hankey was a minister without portfolio in the war cabinet, 1939–40, and remained a minister until 1942. The three businessmen were Lord Beaverbrook, Lord Woolton and Oliver Lyttelton. The newspaper tycoon Beaverbrook (like Churchill a minister in the Great War) went straight into government as Minister of Aircraft Production, later becoming Minister of Supply, and very briefly Minister of Production. Frederick Marquis, of Lewis's department stores, known as Lord Woolton from 1939, was recruited to government as director-general of equipment and stores at the MoS. He became Minister of Food in 1940, and spent the period 1943–5 as Minister for Reconstruction. Oliver Lyttelton came from an aristocratic political family, had been to Cambridge as well as Eton, and spent the interwar years in the metals business in the City. He was controller of non-ferrous metals at the MoS from the beginning of the war: he became President of the Board of Trade, and was Minister of Production between 1942 and 1945.

---

[12] Bevin was brought in as a trade unionist and was not a member of Parliament. Cripps, while a Member of Parliament, and a politician, had been expelled from the Labour party in 1939.

[13] Sir John Anderson became Lord Privy Seal with special responsibility for air raid precautions before the war. Admiral Lord Chatfield served between 1939 and 1940 as Minister for the Coordination of Defence, the first First Sea Lord to become a minister since the Napoleonic wars. Maurice Hankey was in the Cabinet between 1939 and 1942 as Minister without Portfolio, Chancellor of the Duchy of Lancaster and Paymaster-General, with particular responsibilities in the scientific area.

[14] John Wheeler Bennett, *Sir John Anderson: Viscount Waverley* (London: Macmillan, 1962), pp. 266–7.

[15] Ibid., pp. 315–17.

The trade unionist, Ernest Bevin, leader of the Transport and General Workers' Union, was Minister of Labour and National Service from 1940 to the end of the war.

The role of the MoS, and to a lesser extent that of the MAP, in feeding businessmen into government is evident in the above, confirming the importance of new blood in these ministries. Indeed many of the new ministers outside the war cabinet were concentrated in the supply and related economic and industrial ministries, again confirming the traditional story of a state unable to undertake these functions effectively. For example, Sir Andrew Duncan was, with a brief interruption, Minister of Supply from October 1940 to 1945. Duncan was a barrister, but was best known as a former chairman of the Central Electricity Board (which had created the National Grid) and the British Iron and Steel Federation. He became controller of iron and steel at the MoS on the outbreak of war, and became President of the Board of Trade in January 1940. Sir Stafford Cripps, who had been expelled from the Labour party in 1939, was the closest approximation these ministries had to a long-serving traditional politician. He was Minister of Aircraft Production from November 1942 to the end of the coalition. He had been a very successful barrister and had a degree in chemistry from University College London. The other outsiders to become ministers were also concentrated in clearly war-related ministries. Lord Reith, a Scottish engineer who had briefly worked for Beardmore, though of course better known as director-general of the BBC, was Minister of Information, Minister of Transport and of Works between 1940 and 1942.[16] The civil servant Sir James Grigg, as we have noted a mathematician, became Secretary of State for War in 1942. The businessman Lord Leathers was Minister of War Transport from 1941 to 1945. The businessman Lord Portal (not to be confused with the chief of the air staff), was Minister of Works from 1942 to 1945. The Oxford physicist Lord Cherwell was Paymaster-General from the end of 1942. He had previously been Churchill's scientific adviser at the Admiralty and in Downing Street. It is worth noting the number that had a measure of technical education, again confirming the usual thesis.

Serving officers, businessmen and the supply departments

And yet we need to be careful for as we have seen the state created new supply and industrial ministries out of parts of two of the service

---

[16] See Andrew Boyle, *Only the wind will listen: Reith of the BBC* (London: Hutchinson, 1972).

ministries. Despite the emphasis on the need for such ministries because of the service ministries' lack of ability to manage industry, there were continuities of senior expert personnel of very great importance. Pre-war civil servants, including many members of the research corps and serving officers, remained important, indeed became more important. The service and supply ministries followed, with one exception, the pre-war practice of service ministries in that the permanent secretary was not necessarily the most senior official. This was true of the MAP, where the permanent secretary was just one of a number of senior officials of formally similar seniority,[17] and of the Admiralty which continued on pre-war lines. Only in the MoS did the permanent secretary always rank higher than any other official. Long-established administrative civil servants served as permanent secretaries of all the supply departments.[18] It was only after the war that an outsider, the philosopher Professor Oliver Franks, briefly became the permanent secretary at MoS/MAP, having risen remarkably quickly.[19] Some overall impression of the key men can be gained by considering some names associated with a wartime lunch club of senior procurement officers called 'the boilermakers': it started as lunches bringing together Sir James Lithgow, a businessmen in the Admiralty, with the Controller of the Navy, but extended to include, at various times, Commander Sir Charles Craven of Vickers and the Ministry of Aircraft Production, Vice Admiral Sir Harold Brown of Supply, Lt-Gen. Sir Ronald Weeks of the War Office, Sir Robert Sinclair (of the War Office, and later Ministry of Production), Sir Graham Cunningham (MoS), Air Marshal Sir Wilfrid Freeman (MAP), Sir George Turner (MoS) and Sir Cyril Hurcomb (Ministry of War Transport).[20] The figures named above were among the most senior

[17] In the period 1940–2 as one of five or six key officials. See appendices to Scott and Hughes, *Administration*.

[18] Sir Arthur Robinson, the first permanent secretary of the MoS, had long worked with Neville Chamberlain, who had brought him into the Cabinet Office as Chairman of the Supply Board. The longest serving permanent secretaries were Sir William Douglas, who was at Supply between 1942 and 1945; Sir Archibald Rowlands who headed the MAP between May 1940 and November 1943, and Sir Henry Markham at the Admiralty. Others were Sir R. H. Carter 1936–40 at the Admiralty; Sir William Brown at Supply; Sir Harold Scott (1943–5) and Sir Frank Tribe (1945–6) at the MAP and at Production, Sir Henry Self (1942–3) and Sir John Woods (1943–5).

[19] See Alex Danchev, *Oliver Franks: founding father* (Oxford: Clarendon Press, 1993). Franks's rise was similar to that of another don: John (Redcliffe-) Maud, Master of Birkbeck before the war, who rose through the civil service just as fast. He stayed as a permanent secretary after the war, at Education. No science don achieved such an elevated civil service rank so quickly.

[20] J. M. Reid, *James Lithgow, master of work* (London: Hutchinson, 1964), p. 212.

in the supply ministries. The absence of trade unionists, and indeed of academic or government scientists, should be noted.[21]

At the military level, the continuities with the service ministries were particularly remarkable and important. The key army and air force supply officers of the rearmament period transferred to key roles in the new ministries, and served in them for most of the war. Engineer Vice Admiral Sir Harold Brown, the then Engineer-in-Chief of the navy, was appointed to the Army Council in 1936 as director-general munitions production, and as such created the core of the MoS.[22] In the MoS he was the most senior specialist official, with the title of controller-general of munitions production, and later senior supply officer. Air Marshal (Sir) Wilfrid Freeman was responsible for aeronautical research and development from 1936 and all development and production from 1938. He created, with (Sir) Ernest Lemon of the London, Midland and Scottish Railway, the core of the MAP within the Air Ministry. Freeman's position was downgraded in 1940, both by the fact of Beaverbrook's appointment as Minister of Aircraft Production, and because of Beaverbrook's actions, and he left after a few months, to become Vice Chief of the Air Staff. Under a different minister Freeman returned to the MAP in 1942 and stayed until 1945, with the new title of chief executive. Before Freeman went back to the MAP he arranged that he would be equal or higher status than the permanent secretary in all branches except finance and secretariat. As might be expected there was distrust and a fight.[23] Freeman won, and the permanent secretary, Archibald Rowlands, left. His biographer claims it was probable, on the basis of family evidence, that Freeman was offered but turned down a peerage at the same time as the three chiefs of staff – a signal honour.[24] As well as Freeman, the MAP had senior air force officers responsible for aircraft research and development, who also sat on the Air Council. In the navy, which retained its procurement and research responsibilities, the key officer remained the Controller of the Navy, the longest serving in wartime being Admirals Fraser (1939–42) and Wake-Walker (1942–5). However, even in the MoS, certain artillery, engineer, ordnance and service corps officers had senior positions; sometimes the posts were simply transferred from the War Office. The artillery officer

[21] The only cases I have come across are the appointment of J. W. Bowen to the Air Ministry panel before the war, and a G. Thompson who was a member of the Tank Board (see M. M. Postan, D. Hay and J. D. Scott. *Design and development of weapons* (London: HMSO, 1964), pp. 331–3). Both roles were essentially advisory.
[22] Remarkably he is not in the *DNB*.
[23] Anthony Furse, *Wilfrid Freeman: the genius behind allied survival and air supremacy* (Staplehurst: Spellmount, 2000), p. 255.
[24] Ibid., p. 291.

Major-General (Sir) E. M. C. Clarke (1885–1971) was from 1938 director of artillery and from 1942 director-general until the end of the war. He was physically transferred from the War Office only in December 1939.[25] The artillery officer (Lt-Gen. Sir) George Wrisberg (1895–1982), who had from 1929 been either in the Air Defence Experimental Establishment or headquarters, was director of gun and carriage production, and then director and then director-general of weapons and instrument production. He went on to become controller of supplies (for the army) at the MoS from 1946 to 1949, that is to say the senior procurement officer for the army. The ministry also had a senior military adviser.[26]

Businessmen were important in army supply, but many of the key people had long connections with the warfare state. (Lord) Ronald Weeks (1890–1960) of the glass makers Pilkington became a staff officer at the beginning of the war, becoming in 1941 director-general of army equipment, and in 1942 the deputy chief of the Imperial General Staff, the member of the Army Council with responsibility for supply. Weeks was no ordinary businessman: as well as being a Cambridge natural scientist, he served with distinction in the Great War, and remained in the territorial army in the interwar years, commanding a territorial battalion in the 1930s.[27] In April 1940 a new Air Minister brought in Commander Sir Charles Craven (1884–1944), chairman of Vickers-Armstrong, as civil member for development and production.[28] Craven was not merely chairman of the greatest armourer in the land, but had

---

[25] See the Clarke Correspondence in the Brigadier G. MacLeod Ross papers 78/46/5, IWM.

[26] Among the holders were the engineer General Sir Maurice Taylor (1881–1960) 1939–41, the artillery officer Lt-Gen. (Sir) Wilfred Lindsell (1884–1973) in 1941, the infantry officer Lt-Gen. Laurence Carr (1886–1954), 1942–4, and Lt-Gen. (Sir) John Evetts, formerly assistant CIGS 1944–6. On retired pay he went to Australia as Head of British Ministry of Supply Staff in Australia, 1946–51, and chief executive officer Joint UK–Australian Long Range Weapons Establishment, better known as the Woomera rocket range, 1946–9.

[27] He wrote *Organisation and equipment for war* (Cambridge: Cambridge University Press, 1950).

[28] A very few businessmen had come to executive government jobs before the war. Industrial advisers were appointed to the Committee of Imperial Defence machinery, including Viscount Weir who had been a minister in the Great War, and a key adviser on supply and aircraft production in the 1930s. In June 1938 the Air Ministry appointed a Panel of Industrial Advisers, and the Prime Minister set up his own Panel of Industrial Advisers in December. Air Ministry Panel: Sir Amos Ayre (shipbuilder); S. R. Beale (GKN), J. W. Bowen (retired trade unionist), Sir Charles Bruce Gardner (SBAC), Lord Cadman (Anglo-Iranian), Lt-Col. J. H. Greenley (Babcock and Willcox), Sir Robert McAlpine (Sir Robert McAlpine and Sons). The Prime Minister's panel was J. Addison (Courtaulds), Sir George Beharell (Dunlop), P. F. Bennett (Lucas and ICI), Sir Geoffrey Clark (P&O), J. O. M. Clark (J. and P. Coats), and R. J. Sinclair (Imperial Tobacco) (who replaced F. D'Arcy Cooper of Unilever, who resigned). Source AVIA 10/91, and press reports. Colonel Greenley, who was on both panels, chaired the Prime

been the most visible British 'merchant of death' in the 1930s. Craven was a crucial figure in the early years of the MAP, though not in the Beaverbrook regime. He returned to Vickers in November 1940, but was back in the MAP in June 1941 with the title of controller-general. He was succeeded in July 1942 by another Vickers man, (Sir) Alexander Dunbar (1888–1955) who served until June 1943, when he too returned to Vickers. The high point of external business influence in the MAP was under Beaverbrook, when the ministry was overrun by business helpers of all sorts.[29] (Sir) Patrick Hennessy (1898–1981), from the Ford Motor Company, and Trevor Westbrook (1901–1978), who had been general manager of the Vickers aviation, were the most senior.[30] Beaverbrook's regime of business cronies, where generic businessmen were thought to be able to work wonders, in practice disrupted a well-ordered machine that was in many respects put together again after Beaverbrook left, with the return of key people like Craven, and especially Freeman.

At the MoS, Admiral Brown was succeeded in 1941 as controller-general by (Sir) Graham Cunningham (1892–1978), chairman of Triplex Safety Glass, described by one military colleague as an 'arch windbag' who would not do 'anything except strut around'.[31] It is rather difficult to characterise the many senior businessmen in the ministry, and yet a great number, like Cunningham himself, ran firms from the Midlands region. W. T. Avery Weighing Machines gave the ministry (Lord) Percy Mills (1890–1968); BSA (Sir) Alexander Roger (1878–1961) and (Sir) Geoffrey Burton (1893–1954); Joseph Lucas (the electrical component maker who supplied the car and aircraft industries) (Lord) Peter Bennett (1880–1957) and Oliver Lucas (1891–1948); the rolling stock maker Metropolitan Carriage and Wagon (Sir) Archibald (John) Boyd

---

Minister's panel. It is significant that these men were not in the arms trade. It appears that the War Office had a panel of 'expert' advisers chaired by Sir Frederick Marquis (Lewis's) who advised specifically on clothing. He brought in Lewis Ord, and T. S. Smith, a Bedaux specialist. See Sebastian Ritchie, *Industry and air power* (London: Cass, 1997) for details. At the Air Ministry, Lt-Col. H. A. P. Disney (1893–1974) a Cambridge graduate and former Royal Flying Corps pilot who worked in the radio industry was appointed in 1936 to be the first director of aeronautical production. From 1938 to 1940 (Sir) Ernest Lemon (1884–1954), of the LMS railway, was director-general of aircraft production, and a member of the Air Council.

[29] F. R. Banks, *I kept no diary* (Shrewsbury: Airlife, 1978). The second, unpublished volume of Commander Sir Stephen King-Hall's unpublished memoirs, contains a vivid chapter on his time at MAP under Beaverbrook. King-Hall was then a Member of Parliament and worked as Director of the Factory Defence Section. I am grateful to the late Ann King-Hall.

[30] Westbrook was paid £2,250, but most businessmen were unpaid. Westbrook seems to have flourished under Beaverbrook, he left in 1941, to go to Supply, and from 1942 worked for De Havilland.

[31] Major-General E. C. M. Clarke (ex-director-general artillery) to Brigadier G. MacLeod Ross, 8 March 1946, Brig G. MacLeod Ross Papers 78/46/5, IWM.

(1888–1959); the car maker Rootes (Lord) William Rootes (1894–1964) and the chocolate firm Cadbury's (Sir) Hugh Weeks (1904–1992).[32] ICI men were particularly important on the chemical and ammunition side, and ICI's ammunition works were in the Midlands too. In 1942 there were two ICI directors, five chairmen/directors of groups and thirty-three other staff seconded to ministries, including the MoS.[33] Peter Bennett, Andrew Duncan, John Anderson and Viscount Weir were all non-executive directors of ICI around the war period. Among those concerned with tank supply were Commander (Sir) Robert Micklem (1891–1952)[34] of Vickers, (Sir) Claude Gibb (1898–1959), FRS 1946,

---

[32] On the Birmingham productionist nexus see Richard Davenport-Hines, *Dudley Docker: the life and times of a trade warrior* (Cambridge: Cambridge University Press, 1984). On the remarkable pair of Peter Bennett and Oliver Lucas see Harold Nockolds, *Lucas: the first hundred years*. Vol. I: *Kings of the Road* (Newton Abbott: David & Charles, 1976), pp. 236–46. Bennett was the more commercially and politically oriented, indeed he succeeded Neville Chamberlain as MP for Edgbaston. Lucas, the engineer, was very oriented towards his business, but was 'fiercely patriotic' (p. 245).

[33] W. J. Reader, *ICI: a history*, 2 vols. (London: Oxford University Press, 1975), II, pp. 252–3. ICI men were particularly important in the MoS, on the chemical and ammunition side. The one-armed Frederick Bain (1889–1950) was chairman of the Chemical Control Board, 1941–4; H. O. Smith (1882–1952) was director-general ammunition production, 1941–2, as was (Sir) Arthur Smout (1888–1961) – all three were wartime directors of ICI. Other senior ICI men in Supply were Charles Robinson, Chairman of ICI (General Chemicals) as director-general filling factories, 1941–5; Dr J. W. Armit as director-general explosives and chemical supplies, (Lord) Christopher Hinton, the Cambridge educated chief engineer at ICI alkali division, and later a key figure in the nuclear programme as deputy director-general filling factories, 1942–6; (Sir) Leonard Owen was engineering director, filling factories, 1940–5.

[34] Among those who spent time at the MAP were, in addition to those mentioned above, W. C. Devereux (1893–1952) of High Duty Alloys (a firm which supplied the aircraft industry), (Lord) Sir Robert Renwick Bt (1904–1973) a young old-Etonian stock-broker, who became controller of telecommunications equipment (radar): Scott and Hughes, *Administration*, p. 299. Others include (Sir) Eric Bowater (1895–1962) 1940–45, of the paper firm Bowater, (Sir) Archibald Forbes (1903–1989), an accountant who was a deputy secretary, 1940–3, Eric Fraser (1896–1960) of ICI was director-general equipment production and then director-general aircraft production. (Lord) Edwin Plowden (1907–2001), a Cambridge-educated businessman, who had been in the MAP since 1941, became chief executive in 1945/6 on a salary of £3,200, a figure well above the deputy secretary pay point, £2,500. Oliver Franks as permanent secretary in the just merged Supply and Ministry of Aircraft Production was on the permanent secretary's salary of £3,500. Sir Charles Bruce Gardner was controller of labour allocation and supply from 1943, but had long been linked to the ministry. Bruce Gardner had been forced on to the aircraft industry trade association, the SBAC in December 1937, as an 'independent chairman' by the government. He was described as 'executive chairman' and his brief was to act as a bridge between the industry and the government – a remarkable role for the chair of a trade association. See the file on Bruce Gardner's appointment in the Handley Page Papers, HP AC 70/10/67, RAF Museum, Hendon.

the Australian engineer and head of C. A. Parsons of Tyneside, and (Sir) George Usher (1889–1963), an engineer and businessman.[35] In the Admiralty, where they were much less in evidence, the key businessman was Sir James Lithgow. He served from 1940 to 1946 as the Controller of Merchant Shipbuilding and Repair, and became a member of the Admiralty Board. A shipbuilder and armourer (he became chairman of Beardmore in 1936, and his firm also took over Fairfield), had been one of the industrial advisers of the Principal Supply Officers' Committee since 1933.[36] The coordinating Ministry of Production had from 1943 both a permanent secretary – (Sir) John Woods, a career civil servant – and a chief executive – (Lord) Sir Robert Sinclair (1893–1979), of Imperial Tobacco. Nearly all of these men were knighted for war service, an honour which was very important to them.[37]

Running R&D

Important continuities can also be seen in the direction of wartime research and development. In the Air Ministry/Ministry of Aircraft Production, the key senior figure in research was usually an airman, occupying posts called director-general of R&D and later controller of R&D.[38] On the radar side civilians were in charge, but not academic

[35] He had been controller of light alloys and magnesium, then director-general of materials production, for the MAP.

[36] He was also temporarily chairman of the Tank Board and headed the tank division of the MoS. See Reid, *James Lithgow, master of work*.

[37] 'Witness the pathetic jealousies between Rootes, Graham Cunningham and Usher, during the war, when any one of them got a knighthood before the rest': Major-General Sir E. C. M. Clarke (ex-director–general of artillery) to Brigadier G. MacLeod Ross, 2 March 1949, Brigadier G. MacLeod Ross papers 78/46/5, IWM. The economist James Meade noted 'sundry other men (many with spanners sticking out of their pockets and oil dripping from their fingers – or so it seemed) from the Supply Departments' (James Meade, in Susan Howson (ed.), *The collected works of James Meade* (London: Unwin Hyman, 1980), p. 85, quoted in Carl Glatt, 'Reparations and the transfer of scientific and industrial technology from Germany: a case study of the roots of British industrial policy and of aspects of British occupation policy in Germany between post-World War II reconstruction and the Korean War, 1943–1951', unpublished doctoral thesis, European University Institute, Florence (1994), in three volumes, vol. III, pp. 1068–79. p. 1023). Some senior recruits from business came with knighthoods, including Sir Cecil Weir (1890–1960), a Scottish businessman was director-general equipment and stores, 1942–6, Sir Kenneth Lee (d. 1967) a Manchester businessman (and member of the Royal Commission on the Private Manufacture of and Trading in Arms) was director-general raw material controls, 1942–5, the Liberal party activist (Lord) Sir Walter Layton (1884–1966), chairman of the *News Chronicle* (and former economics don and editor of *The Economist*) was director-general programmes 1940–2.

[38] Scott and Hughes, *Administration*, p. 305. Renwick occupied a parallel post at the Air Ministry at the same time, making a nonsense of the arguments for a separate supply ministry. So too, in many ways, the fact that Air Marshal Sir Wilfrid Freeman was chief

scientists. From 1940 Sir Frank Smith, whom we have already met several times, was controller of telecommunications equipment, responsible for all aspects of radar. He was succeeded in 1942 by (Lord) Sir Robert Renwick (1904–1973) Bt, a young businessman. At a lower level of both aeronautical and radar development career established technical civil servants dominated.[39] The directors of technical development, always airmen before the war, were civilians during it, a significant change.[40] The equivalent level in radar was also held by technical civil servants.[41] In the Admiralty (Sir) Charles Wright remained DSR through the war, his pay rising from £1,700 to £2,000 (see table 4.1, which gives pay levels for many key figures, as an indicator of seniority), but Professor (Sir) Charles Goodeve (1904–1980) FRS 1940, Professor of Chemistry at UCL, who joined 1939, was appointed to a new post of assistant (and later deputy) controller (research and development) (£2,000) from October 1942.[42] His job was to supervise research in the departments under the Controller and indeed the navy as a whole.[43] Goodeve had been a reserve officer in the Royal Canadian Navy, and subsequently in the Royal Navy; Charles Wright had been with Captain Scott in Antarctica and Frederick Brundrett, his wartime deputy, had been in the naval volunteer reserve before and during the Great War.[44] In the MoS the picture was more complex and fluid. In 1940 the (military)

executive from 1942 onwards. (Marshal of the RAF Lord) Arthur Tedder (1890–1967), a post-war Chief of the Air Staff, was director-general of research and development from 1938 to 1940. Tedder was an unusual officer in having a degree – from Cambridge, in history. Tedder was succeeded between 1940 and 1941 by (Air Chief Marshal Sir) Roderick Hill (1894–1954), later (like Tizard) rector of Imperial College. In 1941 (Air Marshal Sir) Francis Linnell (1892–1944) took over as controller of research and development (who like the old Air Member for Research and Development was a member of the Air Council); he was succeeded by (Air Marshal Sir) Ralph Sorley (1898–1974) in 1943.

[39] On the aeronautical side David Pye (£1,900) remained director of scientific research, his two deputies (on £1,400) were Ben Lockspeiser (who took over as DSR later in the war) and (Lord) Harold Roxbee-Cox, another long-time civil servant, and Imperial graduate, who was made director of special projects, covering jet engines, in 1943. (The figures in brackets are their basic salaries, which give an indication of rank, see table 4.1.)

[40] W. S. Farren (1940–1), had joined from Cambridge in 1937, N. E. Rowe (£1,400), who succeeded him, was a long-serving Farnborough engineer, who had trained at Imperial.

[41] Robert Watson-Watt, was succeeded as director of communications development in 1940. Watson-Watt was given the titles scientific adviser, and vice-controller communications equipment. After the war he went into private practice. He was succeeded as director of communications development in 1940 by Sir George Lee (1879–1967) the retired engineer-in-chief of the Post Office, who served until 1944.

[42] Goodeve had to give up his naval rank of Commander, but his post was at rear admiral level, a remarkable promotion for a scientist under 40. Gerard Pawle, *The secret war, 1939–45* (London: Harrap, 1956), p. 196.

[43] Scott and Hughes, *Administration*, p. 132.

[44] Patrick Blackett, the naval director of operational research, had been a career naval officer through the Great War.

Table 4.1 *Administrators and research officers, comparative pay and ranks, 1939–51 (£)*

Administrative class rank	1939		1946		1951	
	Administrators	Scientific and technical	Administrators	Scientific and technical	Administrators	Scientific and technical
Permanent secretary to the Treasury	3,500		3,750		3,750	
Permanent secretary	3,000	DNC, 2,500	3,500		3,500	Chief Scientist, MoS, 3,000; Director of AERE (Cockcroft) 2,750; CSAR (Penney) 2,650
Deputy secretary	2,200		2,500	DNC	2,500	DNC; Director, RAE
Under secretary	na	DSRs 1,700	2,000	DSR/ DGSR	2,000	Chief RNSS, 2,250; DGTD (air) 2,250
Principal assistant secretary	1,450–1650	Chief Superintendent, RAE 1,450	1,700		na	CSO (principal directors, etc.)

Grade	1939		1946		1951	
	administrative	scientific	administrative	scientific	administrative	scientific
						DCSO 1,600–1,800
Assistant secretary	1,150–1,450	Director Explosives Research, 1,400; Chief Superintendent Chemical Defence Research Department, 1,400; Deputy DSRs 1,400	1,200–1,700		1,320–1,700	SPSO 1,320–1,520
Principal	800–1,100	Superintendents 1,050–1,250[a]; PSO 850–1,050; SSO 680–800	800–1,100	1,050–1,250; PSO 850–1,050; SSO 680–800	950–1,250	PSO 950–1,250; SSO 700–900
Assistant principal	275–625	SO 400–680			400–750	

Note:

[a] This includes the scientific heads of all the naval laboratories, the senior scientist at Porton (the Superintendent of Experiments)

AERE, Atomic Energy Research Establishment; CSAR, Chief Scientist Armament Research (Head of Woolwich/Fort Halstead); SO, scientific officer; SSO, senior scientific officer; PSO, principal scientific officer; SPSO, senior principal scientific officer; DCSO, deputy chief scientific officer; CSO, chief scientific officer; RNSS, Royal Naval Scientific Service; DGTD, Director-general, Technical Development; DGSR, Director-general, Scientific Research.

Source: Imperial Calendar and Civil Service List, 1939, 1946 and 1951.

directors of artillery and mechanisation controlled the bulk of R&D. The director of scientific research, a career civil servant, still had limited responsibilities.[45] In mid-1941 Lord Beaverbrook, briefly minister, made the engineer and businessman Oliver Lucas (1891–1948) controller-general of research and development. Such central control of R&D did not last very long, and was again divided between departments, including the directorate (soon directorate-general) of scientific research and development (under Herbert Gough, DSR since 1938), now on £2,000 a year.[46] Towards the end of the war Gough was re-titled chief scientific officer and relieved of most executive responsibility.[47] These positions, were with the exception of that of secretary of the DSIR (£3,000) were the highest paid positions in government research. They were all held by civil servants with the exception of Goodeve, and a second academic, Professor (Sir) John Lennard-Jones (1894–1954) FRS 1933, Professor of Theoretical Chemistry at Cambridge, a Manchester-trained applied mathematician. In 1943 he became chief superintendent of armament research, the head of the Armament Research Establishment (ARE), the renamed and moved Woolwich research department, the only major laboratory run by an academic, other than the army's radar establishment. The key wartime change was the shift from military to civil direction of the main laboratories, from military to civil servants of the state (see appendix 4).

Academic science

A hugely expanded research corps remained central to warlike R&D. Universities did not become significant R&D contractors, as happened in the USA where, for example, parts of the bomb project were officially run as contracts with the universities of California and Chicago, and radar development was concentrated at the Massachusetts Institute of Technology (MIT).[48] Only relatively minor contracts went to British

---

[45] (1) Physics and engineering research; (2) general chemical and metallurgical research; (3) patents; (4) inventions; (5) secretariat of the Advisory Council; (6) administration of scientific research staff. It also ran the extra-mural research scheme. Scott and Hughes, *Administration*, 273.

[46] Ibid., p. 283.

[47] Responsibility other than for general chemical and physical research, metallurgy, the allocation and use of the staff for scientific research, and various common services: Scott and Hughes, *Administration*, p. 285.

[48] On the US case see Paul Forman, 'Behind quantum electronics: national security as a basis for physical research in the United States, 1940–1960', *Historical Studies in the Physical and Biological Sciences* 18 (1987), 149–229; Stuart W. Leslie, *The cold war and American science: the military-industrial-academic complex at MIT and Stanford* (New York:

universities: for example the director of scientific research at Supply told the press in November 1939 that there were twenty-seven university teams with a total of 139 staff working for the ministry.[49] A significant exception was the early relatively small-scale work on the British bomb project.[50] To be mobilised for war research British academics generally had to leave the universities. Yet the proportion of established academic staff mobilised was remarkably low, even in Imperial College with its close links to the warfare state. In January 1940 Imperial College had 105 teaching staff, all scientists or engineers, still teaching full time, 9 combining teaching with government work and 28 working for government. In 1942 as few as 35 staff were devoting more than 70 per cent of their time to government work.[51] In 1944 it had 8 (out of 22) professors on government work, 6 readers, and 26 other academic staff (including part-time work), that is to say about one-quarter of its staff.[52] The main role of the universities was teaching. Their most important task was to continue to produce science and engineering graduates to feed into government scientific service, including the research corps. The overwhelming majority of wartime recruits to the research corps were young very recent graduates. To take an example, the physicist (Sir) Nevill Mott's group at the ARE was made up of two senior permanent civil servants, one well-established academic, five doctors (PhD) and ten wartime graduates.[53]

The image of the 'mobilisation of science' conjures up the image of scientific reserves being recalled to the colours. However, many academic scientists presented academic science as mobilising itself to fight the war on its own terms, and having to argue with government

Columbia University Press, 1993); E. Mendelsohn, M. R. Smith and P. Weingart (eds.), *Science, technology and the military*, 2 vols. (Dordrecht: Kluwer, 1988), the journal *Historical Studies in the Physical and Biological Sciences*, for the 1990s in particular, and the special issue on science in the cold war, of *Social Studies of Science* 31 (2001), 163–97; Michael Aaron Dennis, '"Our first line of defence": two university laboratories in the postwar American state', *Isis* 85 (1994), 427–55; Everett Mendelsohn, 'Science, scientists and the military' in J. Krige and D. Pestre (eds.), *Science in the twentieth century* (London: Harwood Academic, 1997); Larry Owens, 'The counterproductive management of science during WWII', *Business History Review* 68 (1994), 515–76; David Hart, *Forged consensus: science, technology and economic policy in the United States, 1921–1953* (Princeton: Princeton University Press, 1997).

[49] 'We have a secret weapon', *Daily Mail*, 9 November 1939.
[50] M. M. Gowing, *Britain and atomic energy 1939–1945* (London: Macmillan, 1964).
[51] Imperial College Papers, GXD/2, Imperial College Archives.
[52] See Imperial College to Appleton, 8 May 1944, CXE/3/13 (Penney), Imperial College Archives. I am also indebted to Paul Brandon, 'The scientists and engineers of Imperial College during World War Two', Imperial College MSc dissertation (1996).
[53] Ian Sneddon (one of those who had a doctorate) in his 'Fort Halstead: superintendent of theoretical research in armaments' in E. A. Davis (ed.), *Nevill Mott: reminiscences and appreciations* (London: Taylor and Francis, 1998), pp. 36–8, on p. 36.

to bring forward scientific volunteers and reserves.[54] In the standard view the academic left were particularly important, and saw their ideas about the planning of science justified in practice. Academic scientists have since seen government establishments as mere 'nuclei for the aggregation of the university scientists'.[55] Yet the small number of academics who were seconded to the research corps, as well as the large numbers of recent graduates, joined existing research programmes. The state sciences and technologies including radar, ballistics, meteorology, chemical warfare, aeronautics, had been developed by large teams pre-war and involved techniques into which academic scientists and young graduates had to be inducted. This process predated the war. In the summer university vacations of 1938 and 1939 the Air Ministry invited selected academics to work at several of its establishments (and not just radar stations).[56] War was declared in the long vacation of 1939, finding many of them already in place: thirteen were immediately recruited at scientific officer and junior scientific officer levels; twenty-two senior scientific officers (lecturers) and eleven principal scientific officers (professors) very quickly followed them.[57] The recruitment of research talent was very significant. About thirty academics who were already FRSs or would be by 1950, were recruited to the laboratories and headquarters research staffs of the supply ministries (see appendix 3). This compares with some eleven FRS-level civil servants (by this definition) doing military research in the existing research corps as of 1939.[58] Most of these recruits were in their thirties and forties, marking them off from most existing Fellows, and indeed many prospective ones too. The Air Ministry/MAP got eleven, mostly physicists (six from the Cavendish) and mathematicians/engineers. Seven went first to Farnborough (and not radar),

[54] See Tizard Papers, HTT 65 (correspondence with Professor Lennard-Jones in 1938) and HTT 125 (also 1938 – including scheme by G. T. R. Hill and Charles Goodeve of UCL), IWM.

[55] R. V. Jones, 'Research establishments', in *Proceedings of the Royal Society* A 342 (1975), 484. He clearly recognises, however, that it was these same scientists who made the key contributions to radar, itself the key scientific innovation in war.

[56] Recruitment to radar work started in 1935, but my impression is that permanent civil service jobs were being offered. Here I am interested in academics being drawn in for temporary positions.

[57] Scott and Hughes, *Administration*, p. 313. (Sir) Bernard Lovell joined in 1939 as a junior scientific officer from Manchester; he left the Telecommunications Research Establishment in 1945 as a principal scientific officer, to take up a lectureship in physics at Manchester, at half the salary (Bernard Lovell, *Astronomer by chance* (Oxford: Oxford University Press, 1992), pp. 49, 107).

[58] Griffith, Farren, Pye, Gates, Constant, Watson-Watt all of the Air Ministry, Relf, Fage, Frazer, of NPL, and Sutton and Gough of the War Office.

including physicists with no direct connection to aeronautics. For example, Professor (Sir) G. P. Thomson (1892–1975) FRS 1930, head of the physics department at Imperial College, went to the RAE as a principal scientific officer with a salary of £850. The head of the Manchester physics department, Patrick Blackett, went to the Instrument Department where he worked on bombsights. Indeed he was credited with being the co-inventor of the new Mark XIV bombsight which became the standard equipment of Bomber Command in its strategic bombing of Germany (it was known as the T-1 in the US manufactured version). Blackett is much better known as an opponent of strategic bombing. Only three of the thirty senior academics went straight into radar, with a fourth joining from Farnborough. The MoS got seventeen FRS–level scientists, but only three were Cavendish products – most were mathematicians and chemists.[59] The greatest concentration was at the ARE at Fort Halstead – at least ten went there mostly in the Lennard-Jones period. By contrast, Porton Down had only three. The Admiralty did far less well, with only five FRS-level men in R&D, from a variety of disciplines, led by the University College London chemist Charles Goodeve. For comparison, there were six FRS-level scientists working on the British atomic bomb project as of 1940: three were refugees from Germany.[60] Around five of the thirty, including Blackett and Thomson, would leave R&D to become advisers to the services.

The most famous academic names in wartime science were advisers rather than researchers or managers of research groups. Scientific advisers were concerned with many broad questions including strategy, especially 'operational research', but not with the control or direction of R&D. They were often not attached to supply ministries, but service and other ministries. For example Professor Frederick Lindemann of Oxford was Churchill's scientific adviser (and statistician) at the Admiralty and later at Downing Street. Sir Henry Tizard of Imperial College was 'scientific adviser' to the Chief of the Air Staff from 1939 (for which Imperial College were paid £2,000 per annum).[61] Tizard resigned from the Air Ministry in June 1940, and transferred to the MAP.[62] From early 1942 Tizard convened informal meetings of what

---

[59] Professor John Cockcroft of the Cavendish, the leading early recruit was in fact an interesting mixture – a Manchester electrical engineer who had worked for Metropolitarn Vickers, he had a Cambridge mathematics degree as well as a doctorate from the Cavendish.
[60] Gowing, *Britain and atomic energy*, p. 53.
[61] See the correspondence in B/TIZ/1, Imperial College Archives.
[62] Tizard Papers, HTT 250, IWM.

were called 'independent scientific advisers' which were concerned overwhelmingly with 'operational research'.[63] Towards the end of war the senior 'scientific advisers' were brought together officially, under Tizard's chairmanship, as a committee to look at the future of war. But its members – Tizard, Patrick Blackett (navy) Charles Ellis (army), G. P. Thomson (air force) and J. D. Bernal (combined operations) – were not allowed access to nuclear work.[64] A second group of advisers were concerned with R&D programmes. The Aeronautical Research Committee, chaired by Tizard from 1933 until 1943, was as we have seen of long-standing importance.[65] The MoS appointed three academic scientific advisers when it was set up,[66] and an Advisory Council on Scientific Research and Technical Development in early 1940.[67] As first constituted, the Council had no fewer than seventeen FRSs as well as the directors of mechanisation and artillery, and the senior military adviser among its members.[68] In many ways this committee was like the Aeronautical Research Committee, covering a vast range of research looked over by, many sub-committees.[69] The MoS also had a Chemical Board – a reconstituted Chemical Defence Committee – chaired by James Davidson Pratt – which included nine FRSs.[70] In

---

[63] Regular attenders were Blackett, Darwin, Schonland, Bernal, Fowler, Ellis, Pye, Watson-Watt and R. S. Capon of the MAP. See Tizard Papers, HTT 298, IWM.

[64] As the Future of Weapons sub-committee of the Joint Technical Warfare Committee of the Chiefs of Staff. The restrictions on nuclear access are very clear in correspondence between Ismay and Tizard, e.g. 10/4/45 Tizard Papers, HTT 401, IWM. But even with a new government, Tizard was not permitted to have the nuclear secrets. See Ismay to Tizard, 22 August 1945.

[65] See Andrew Nahum, 'Two-stroke or turbine? The Aeronautical Research Committee and British aero-engine development in World War II', *Technology and Culture* 38 (1997), 312–54.

[66] Professor Andrade of London, Professor Cockcroft of Cambridge, and Professor Heilbron of Imperial, each on a salary of £850: *British Imperial Calendar and Civil Service List, 1940.*

[67] Scott and Hughes, *Administration*, p. 272. Its first chairman was Lord Cadman (1877–1941) FRS 1940, friend of Lord Rutherford, former chairman of BP and former Professor of Mining at Birmingham. He was succeeded by the ever present Sir Frank Smith, who on retiring from DSIR had become an adviser to BP.

[68] Five of the ten academics were from Cambridge. See the list attached to the minutes of the first meeting (4 January 1940), in Tizard collection, B/TIZARD/3/3, Imperial College Archives.

[69] See for example the committee's *Report for the Year 1942* in Tizard Papers, HTT 309, IWM.

[70] For members in June 1940 see Tizard collection, B/TIZARD/3/2, Imperial College Archives. See also the wartime *Army Lists*, which reveal that in 1943 the members included Professors E. D. Adrian, A. C. Andrade, D. Brunt, C. G. Douglas, Robert Robinson, Ian Heilbron and Cecil Hinshelwood, as well as Lord Rothschild, B. Mouat Jones and R. E. Slade (ICI).

1941 the navy followed suit, setting up an Admiralty advisory panel on scientific research.[71]

The distinctions between the research corps and the academics, between the researchers and the advisers, and different kinds of advisers, are crucial. As we shall see there were continuing divisions between them. They are also essential to understanding the campaigns of academic scientists. Some academic scientists had wanted a higher-level sort of 'scientific general staff' to advise on and coordinate all the warlike research and development effort. The Royal Society had been agitating from the late 1930s for a sort of services research council attached to the new Ministry for the Coordination of Defence, proposals which were strongly resisted by the research corps in the navy and air force.[72] The scientists were given a sop in the form of the War Cabinet Scientific Advisory Committee formed in 1940, chaired at first by Lord Hankey.[73] It was called a 'brains trust' by the press.[74] It was a committee of the senior officers of the Royal Society, and the heads of the civil research councils. It was advisory, and was not concerned with the running of the services' R&D programmes.[75] After the war it was turned into the Advisory Council on Scientific Policy, which dealt with civil matters only. In 1942, in response to further agitation by the Royal Society, a group of three full-time scientists, attached to the Ministry of Production, and thus potentially overseeing the supply ministries, was

---

[71] Including DSR, (Sir) Edward Appleton (1892–1965) FRS secretary of the DSIR, and Professor (Sir) Ralph Fowler (1889–1944) FRS of Cambridge. W. D. Hackmann, *Seek and strike: sonar anti-submarine warfare and Royal Navy, 1914–1954* (London: HMSO, 1984), p. 245.

[72] Sébastien Soubiran, 'De l'utilisation contingente des scientifiques dans les systèmes d'innovations des Marines française et britannique entre les deux guerres mondiales. Deux exemples: la conduite du tir des navires et la télémécanique', 3 vols., unpublished doctoral thesis, Université de Paris VII-Denis Diderot (2002), for the naval response.

[73] William McGucken, 'The central organisation of scientific and technical advice in the United Kingdom during the Second world War', *Minerva* 17 (1979), 33–69. It consisted of Sir William Bragg (replaced by Henry Dale, when he became President of the Royal Society), A. C. G. Egerton; A. V. Hill, and the secretaries of the DSIR, Aeronautical Research Committee and Medical Research Council. An Engineering Advisory Committee was formed in 1941, also under Lord Hankey's chairmanship: the members were Lord Falmouth (an engineer as well as a hereditary peer), Sir Henry Tizard, A. P. M. Fleming, W. T. Halcrow, C. C. Paterson (GEC), H. R. Ricardo and Dr A. Robertson. It soon died.

[74] *Daily Telegraph* and *Daily Herald*, 3 October 1940.

[75] One claim to fame it has, is that under Hankey, the Scientific Advisory Committee received details about the British bomb project. These were promptly leaked to the Soviets by the committee's secretary, John Cairncross. See David Holloway, *Stalin and the bomb: the Soviet Union and atomic energy, 1939–1956* (London: Yale University Press, 1994), pp. 82–3.

convened. Their influence on war research programmes was meant to be, and was, minimal.[76]

What happened to the wartime technocrats?

The British state recruited many new men to its ranks in wartime, but their influence was less temporary than has been allowed. Many of the senior experts brought into government as ministers and officials continued in public life after the war. Of the ministers Lord Woolton, Oliver Lyttelton (Lord Chandos), Lord Cherwell and Lord Leathers were all significant figures in the Conservative party and Conservative governments after the war. A number of men who held senior positions in the supply ministries went on to public and/or political careers, notably Lords Edwin Plowden and Robert Renwick of Aircraft Production, and Lords Peter Bennett, Oliver Franks and Percy Mills of the MoS. Bennett and Mills became Conservative MPs and ministers, as did Lord Errol, who had held a junior official position in Supply; Renwick was a Conservative party figure.[77] Plowden and Franks were classic examples of the centrist great and good, chairing many government committees, ranging from those on public finances and the aircraft industry (Plowden) to those on the University of Oxford and the Falklands war (Franks).[78] Some key figures in the post-war Labour party had middle ranking administrators outside the key supply ministries: Hugh Gaitskell, an academic economist, was a principal assistant secretary at the Board of Trade, Harold Wilson, a specialist, was director of economics and statistics (ranked as assistant secretary) at the Ministry of Fuel and Power, and the financial journalist Douglas Jay was an assistant secretary in Supply, before moving to the Board of Trade as a principal assistant secretary.

Few of the important temporaries stayed on as civil servants, as opposed to politicians and advisers. That is true of the academics

---

[76] They were Professor (Sir) Ian Heilbron FRS (1886–1959), Professor (Sir) Thomas Merton FRS (1888–1969) and (Sir) William Stanier (1876–1965). William McGucken, 'The central organisation of scientific and technical advice in the United Kingdom during the Second world War', *Minerva* 17 (1979), pp. 33–69. See also Oliver Lyttelton, Lord Chandos, *The memoirs of Lord Chandos* (London: Bodley Head, 1962), pp. 169–70. For Chandos's snobbish comments on the engineers and senior managers of Associated Electrical Industries, which he headed for a long period after the war, see R. Jones and Oliver Marriott, *Anatomy of a merger* (London: Cape, 1970), p. 234. See also Nigel Balchin, *The small back room* (London Collins, 1962) pp. 26–7, 84–5 (First published 1943).

[77] Anthony Sampson, *Anatomy of Britain* (London: Hodder & Stoughton, 1962), p. 606. Renwick became a key figure in early commercial television.

[78] Edwin Plowden, *An industrialist in the Treasury: the post-war years* (London: Deutsch, 1989); Alex Danchev, *Oliver Franks: founding father* (Oxford: Clarendon Press, 1993).

scientists also. The post-war research corps kept very few of the academic FRS-level researchers, and most, but not all returned to university jobs, and some went on to industry.[79] Still, six of the thirty stayed, but by the end of 1950 only two were left. Their presence brought the number of FRSs in the military part of the research corps to eight in 1950.[80] The state also lost some of its own FRS-level staff, mostly to more lucrative positions. (Sir) David Pye retired to run University College London, but W. S. Farren, Λ. Λ. Griffiths, Robert Watson-Watt, Frank Whittle and Herbert Gough left in their forties or early fifties for the private sector.[81] Other senior figures also retired or soon went abroad, like Sir Charles Wright or A. P. Rowe.[82] The two academic FRS-level men who stayed beyond 1950 were John Cockcroft and William Penney. Cockcroft ran the new MoS Atomic Energy Research Establishment at Harwell while Penney took over the ARE, with a brief to design atomic bombs.[83] At least twelve more academics stayed, among them a future director of Harwell, the most senior naval scientist between 1946 and 1964, a chief scientist at the MoS, two key scientists in the atomic bomb project, and the head of the post-war bacteriological warfare effort. Four became FRSs for government service.[84]

The key to the story of government science is not what happened to the academic recruits, but to the research corps as a whole. This was expanded during the war by the influx of young scientists and engineers,

---

[79] Many more junior staff also returned to university positions, often with a promotion. F. C. Williams returned to Manchester as a professor. Philip Dee went to Glasgow and Goldstein to Manchester. Some, like Charles Goodeve, went to industry.

[80] The others were career civil servants in aeronautics (Relf, Fage, Gates, Constant, Frazer) and the a meteorologist with a background in chemical warfare (Sutton).

[81] We should also note (Sir) Alfred Pugsley, a London engineer who spent most of his career in the state service, mostly at RAE. In 1945 he went to a chair in civil engineering at the university of Bristol; elected FRS in 1952; chairman of the Aeronautical Research Council, 1952–57.

[82] Rowe succeeded Goodeve as deputy controller, R&D, Admiralty 1946–7; he went to Australia as Chairman, Defence Research and Development Policy Committee and Defence Science Adviser to the Australian government 1947–8, becoming Vice-Chancellor, university of Adelaide 1948–55.

[83] Patrick Linstead became director of the Chemical Research Station, though he went to Imperial College in 1949, becoming rector a little later. Herbert Skinner who also went to Harwell, where he was a division leader, 1945–50, before going to a chair in physics at Liverpool. Otto Frisch was a division head and Deputy Chief Scientific Officer at Harwell, 1945–7 'the post was roughly equivalent to a professorship; I took to travelling first class on trains' (Otto Frisch, *What little I remember* (Cambridge: Cambridge University Press, 1979), p. 195). Wilfrid Lewis took over as chief superintendent of the Telecommunications Research Establishment but went to Canada to replace Cockcroft (Sir Bernard Lovell and D. G. Hurst, 'Wilfred Bennett Lewis', *Biographical Memoirs of Fellows of the Royal Society* 34 (1988), 453–509).

[84] Robert Spence, Monty Finniston, Robert Smith and David Henderson.

Table 4.2 *Numbers of administrators and scientific officers, 1929–66*

	1929	1937	1950	1956	1966
Administrative	1.1	1.3	3.0	2.5	2.5
Professional, scientific, technical I[a]	6.5	9.6	23.1	22.4	25.2
of which, scientific officers	0.7	–	3.3	3.4	4.1

Note:
[a] This includes scientific officers, works group, accountants and lawyers.

Source: The Civil Service (Fulton Report), IV, *Factual, Statistical and Explanatory Papers* (London: HMSO, 1968), p. 271.

and remained much larger after the war than before it. Among the very junior people who stayed on, and they were many, was one future Nobel Prize winner, (Sir) Francis Crick (1916–) a University College London graduate who had joined the Admiralty in 1940 and stayed until 1947. Indeed the size of the research corps dropped very little after the war. The administrative class more than doubled in size by the 1960s, but the research corps grew much more (table 4.2). From around 700–1000 before the war, the research corps had grown to 3,300 in 1951, up to 3,900 in 1954, whence it fell to 3,400 largely as a result of to the transfer of the UK AEA out of the civil service. It stayed at about this level before climbing in the 1960s to reach 4,100 in 1965.[85] These numbers refer to the scientific officer class, and exclude experimental officers and assistants as well as the many qualified scientists and engineers in other classes.

At one level the research corps and the administrative class, the two main graduate classes, had become more like each other. The nature, grading and pay of the research corps was aligned with that of the administrative class. The salaries scales of scientific officer entrants were the same as those for assistant principals, and the principal scientific officer equated to the administrative class principal. The research corps were also integrated with the rest of the civil service in that from 1 January 1953 all new appointees would go into the civil service superannuation scheme. The universities' pensions scheme (FSSU) was kept only for those who wanted to stay in it and for temporary staff.[86] Recruitment of

---

[85] *The civil service* (Fulton Report), vol. IV: *Factual, statistical and explanatory papers*, Cmd 9613 (London: HMSO, 1968), p. 275. The *Fulton Commission Report and Evidence* volumes will be cited hereafter as *The civil service*.

[86] Memorandum of Evidence submitted by H.M. Treasury on Civil Service Superannuation, *Royal Commission on the Civil Service (1953–1955), Minutes of evidence*, para. 15. Hereafter cited as *Minutes of evidence, Civil Service (1953–1955)*.

scientific officers was centralised through the civil service commission. Furthermore, more senior positions were created in the scientific civil service. As we have seen at the end of the war, the highest salaries were paid to the head of the DSIR (£3,000), while there were a number of posts at £2,000. The new scientific civil service would have a number of posts at £2,250 and £2,500 (above under secretary, and at deputy secretary level) and two or three at £3,000 (between deputy and permanent secretary) (see table 4.1).[87]

In the post-war state they continued to rise in the hierarchy, became the most senior technical officers of the state and took over some key procurement positions. In addition the individual service ministries began to appoint research corps members as scientific advisers to their ruling boards.[88] The scientific advisers to the coordinating Ministry of Defence were also sometimes research corps members. Sir Henry Tizard returned to Whitehall in a more senior position than he had ever had before. He was full-time chairman of a new Defence Research Policy Committee, in the new Ministry of Defence.[89] In the area of weapons of mass destruction the top procurement and policy jobs went at first to outsiders. Sir John Anderson was chairman of the committee concerned with atomic energy, and Lord Hankey, chaired the biological weapons committee.[90] Tizard was succeeded in 1950 by Sir John Cockcroft, who was followed in 1954 by Sir Frederick Brundrett (1894–1974), a Cambridge mathematician who had been in the naval scientific service since 1919, rising to be its head after the war. He was succeeded in 1960 by a partial outsider, Sir Solly Zuckerman, who was himself followed in 1966 by a rather odd double structure in which another career scientific civil servant, Sir William Cook, was particularly influential. (Sir) W. R. Cook (1905–1987) FRS 1962, was a Bristol mathematician, who went in 1928 to the External Ballistics Section of Woolwich, where he worked on problems with naval guns. From 1935 and through the war he worked on rockets. Like Brundrett he headed the Royal Naval Scientific Service. He would also play a very important role as deputy director of Aldermaston, during H-bomb

[87] *Report of the Barlow Committee on scientific staff*, April 1943, in Chancellor of the Exchequer, *The scientific civil service: reorganisation and recruitment during the reconstruction period*, Cmd 6679, September 1945, para. 11.

[88] Sir Ewen Broadbent, *The military and government: from Macmillan to Heseltine* (London: Macmillan, 1988), pp. 148–60.

[89] Jon Agar and Brian Balmer, 'British scientists and the cold war: the defence research policy committee and information networks, 1947–1963', *Historical Studies in the Physical Sciences*, 28 (1998), 1–40. Tizard was still not privy to nuclear matters.

[90] The Bacteriological Research Advisory Board (BRAB). Hankey chaired it until 1951: Roskill, *Man of secrets*, III, p. 603.

development.[91] In 1971 the practice of appointing a succession of academic scientific advisers was made permanent. The chief scientific adviser, the permanent secretary and the chief of the defence staff were the three senior advisers to the secretary of state for defence.[92] These scientific advisers were still not concerned with the running of the defence R&D programme as such, which was in the hands of the supply ministries or other branches of the service ministries.

Looking at the very top of all of government, there were seven non-administrative posts at permanent secretary level in 1953 – of which four were scientific/technical – the secretary of the DSIR, the deputy controller atomic energy (production) (Christopher Hinton), the director of Harwell, who was also chairman of the Defence Research Policy Committee (John Cockcroft), and the director of Aldermaston (William Penney).[93] In contrast to the interwar years, it was the nuclear leaders, rather than the director of naval construction, who were the highest paid technical officers of the state. At the MoS, and the succeeding Ministry of Aviation, the chief scientists ranked higher than the old combined service/supply ministry DSRs. They were with perhaps one exception career civil servants. At the level of the headship of state laboratories the war saw the research corps and academics take over many such positions from the military and they kept them after the war. Research corps members dominated these posts after the war. In 1960 the seven main military laboratories, other than Farnborough and Harwell, were in the hands of civil servants: of these seven three were trained at Imperial College, and one each at the University of Manchester Institute of Science and Technology, Cambridge, Manchester and Glasgow. Scientific civil servants were also able to take over from servicemen some important positions in procurement. The key officials were the Controller of the Navy, and allowing for

[91] In 1935 he transferred to work on a high priority programme on rockets, and he contributed to the development of the 3-inch AA rocket which came into service in 1940/41. During the war he continued on rockets, and in 1946 because first director of Westcott. In 1947 he went to the Admiralty as director of Physical Research, and in 1950 became head of the Royal Naval Scientific Service. In 1954 went to become deputy director of Aldermaston; in 1958 replaced Hinton at the AEA; from 1964 was senior adviser at the Ministry of Defence. See in particular his Royal Society *Biographical Memoir* (1988).
[92] This structure was somewhat weakened with the move of Sir Solly Zuckerman in 1966, when his post was divided in two, but he was replaced on the Defence Council by Sir William Cook. From 1971, the post of Chief Scientific Adviser was filled by academic scientists. Although they remained members of the Defence Council, from 1985, the CSA was no longer (formally) one of the direct advisers to the minister. Broadbent, *Military and government*, ch. 10.
[93] Senior posts outside the administrative class: Note by the Treasury, *Minutes of evidence, Civil Service (1953–1955)*.

some changes in title, the Controller of Munitions/Master-General of the Ordnance, the Controller Aircraft, and the Controller Guided Weapons and Electronics.[94] The Controller Guided Weapons and Electronics was nearly always a research corps member,[95] as were the two Controllers, Aircraft, serving between 1959 and 1966.[96] An overlapping way of making the point is that in the Ministry of Technology of the 1960s, the key supply ministry of the period, research corps people had many key positions.[97] Of the four controllers, three were research corps officers: (Sir) Ieuan Maddock (1917–1988), FRS 1967 Controller (Industrial Technology) 1967–1971, had been in the Ministry of Supply from 1940, and had been a key figure in the British bomb project;[98] the Controller (Research) – was (Sir) George MacFarlane (ex-Telecommunications Research Establishment); the Controller, Guided Weapons and Electronics, was (Sir) Merion Morgan (ex-RAE). The remaining controller was the Controller, aircraft, Air Marshal Sir Christopher Hartley (1913–), an unusual airman in that he had an Oxford degree in zoology, and had been a member of the 1932 Oxford expedition to Sarawak led by Tom Harrison. These were, in the military parlance, 'three star' positions.[99]

[94] There was also for a time a Controller of Production, Atomic Energy. On the latter see M. M. Gowing, *Independence and deterrence: Britain and atomic energy, 1945–1952*, 2 vols. (London: Macmillan, 1974), I, pp. 40–46. The Controller was Lord Portal, wartime Chief of the Air Staff.

[95] Between 1951–6 and 1959–62 it was (Sir) Steuart Mitchell (1902–1990) who had been Chief Engineer at the Armament Design Establishment, 1945–51 (admittedly he had been a naval officer before that). (Sir) Robert Cockburn held the post between 1956 and 1959, (Sir) Morien Bedford Morgan (1912–1978) between 1966 and 1969. His successor was (Sir) Clifford Cornford (1918–) another pre-war Cambridge RAE man, who had joined in 1938. He was in OR during the war, but was working on guided weapons at the RAE between 1945 and 1960.

[96] (Sir) George Gardner, a former director of Farnborough, was Controller, Aircraft, 1959–1963, and was succeeded by (Sir) Morien Morgan, 1963–6.

[97] Six out of nine of the top men had a technical degree: the permanent secretary Sir Richard 'Otto' Clarke (1910–1975) was a Cambridge mathematician, who joined as a temporary administrator in 1939 from the *Financial News*; Sir Ronald Melville, the secretary (Aviation), was a Cambridge classicist. Below were three deputy secretaries, one of whom had a BSc.

[98] He was chief scientist in the successor Departments of Trade and Industry, and Industry, 1971–7.

[99] Broadbent, *Military and government*, p. 49. In the 1970s, with a unified procurement executive, three controllerates were established, one each for land, sea and air systems, under in some cases officers with the historic titles, Master-General of the Ordnance, and Controller of the Navy, and the more recent Controller, Aircraft. A fourth controllership, first of Research and Development Establishments and Research, and then of Research and Development Establishments, Research and Nuclear, was established as the Atomic Weapons Research Establishment was brought within the Ministry of Defence. The guided weapons controllership was dispersed. Broadbent, *Military and government*, pp. 47–50, and *passim*.

Table 4.3 *Permanent secretaries of Whitehall departments (excluding second permanent secretaries and other civil servants with permanent secretary rank, and excluding research councils, including the DSIR)*

	1900–19	1920–44	1945–64	1965–86	Total 1900–86
No.	75	74	75	80	304
No. entering from other professions	36	11	12	11	70
Of which					
Lawyers	13	3	2	4	21
Army	5	1	–	–	6
Business					4
Academic/research	5	–	6	2	13
Colonial service					5
Engineers	1	–	–	1	2
Politics	2	–	–	–	2
From lower civil service ranks	5	6	10	6	27
From specialist grades[a]	9	1	5	5	20[b]

Notes:
[a] There is some overlap with entry from external professions.
[b] Nine lawyers, three engineers, one scientist, one statistician.

Source: Kevin Theakston and Geoffrey K. Fry, 'Britain's administrative elite: permanent secretaries 1900–1986', *Public Administration* 67 (1989), 129–48.

In the 1970s too the research corps had a strong tendency to fill controller posts.[100] In the early 1970s a new higher level procurement position was established. Although not the first holder of the post, (Sir) Clifford Cornford, formerly of the RAE, made the post his own, serving as chief executive and permanent secretary of the procurement executive (1975–7) and chief of defence procurement, Ministry of Defence (1977–80). The other research corps member who made it to permanent secretary level (at Education and Science) was (Sir) James Hamilton (1923–) who had been director-general Concorde 1966–70.[101] Hamilton is the only one of the above to figure in table 4.3.

The new class, the warfare state and the university

The twentieth century saw, in Britain as elsewhere, the emergence and growth of a new technical middle class, which grew very fast indeed,

[100] Ibid., p. 159.
[101] See Hennessy, *Whitehall*, p. 203 for more, including Harold Wilson's special interest in Hamilton.

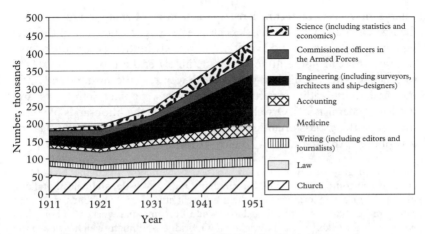

Figure 4.1 Higher professionals in Britain, 1911–51

Source: Guy Routh, *Occupation and pay in Great Britain 1906–60* (Cambridge: Cambridge University Press, 1965), table 5, p. 15.

much faster than the also expanding 'old' professional middle class of doctors, lawyers, or indeed administrative civil servants (see fig. 4.1). This new class has been barely studied, partly because the majority were not elite enough to figure in elite studies and were too elevated to be captured by studies of white-collar trade unionism.[102] The emergence of

---

[102] We have no studies of the depth of those of the French state and academic elites by Pierre Bourdieu, (*Homo academicus* (Cambridge: Polity, 1988) and *The state nobility* (Cambridge: Polity, 1996)) but British empirical sociologists – particularly A. H. Halsey – have produced a surprising amount of (hardly known) data on the servants of the state and university graduates. On white-collar unionism see George Bain, *The growth of white collar trade unionism* (Oxford: Clarendon Press, 1970) and on 'technical workers' see Chris Smith, *Technical workers: class, labour and trade unionism* (London: Macmillan, 1987). The closest we have are histories of professional institutions and trades unions, a very different matter. For the late nineteenth century the situation is much better. See Hannah Gay, 'Association and practice: the City and Guilds of London Institute for the Advancement of Technical Education', *Annals of Science* 57 (2000), 369–98; 'Brothers in science: science and fraternal culture in nineteenth-century Britain' (with John W. Gay), *History of Science* 35 (1997), 425–53; 'East End, West End: science, culture and class in mid-Victorian London', *Canadian Journal of History* 32 (1997), 153–83. For the twentieth century see Robin MacKie, '"What is a chemical engineer?" Profiling the membership of the British Institution of Chemical Engineers, 1922–1956', *Minerva* 38 (2000), 171–99, and Robin MacKie and Gerrylyn Roberts, 'Professional careers in twentieth century Britain: the case of chemists and chemical engineers, 1890–1960', mimeo. Thanks to Gerrylyn Roberts. Her online database of chemists will be an invaluable resource. Ross McKibbin, while certainly recognising the emergence of a new scientific and technical middle class by the late 1930s, has little specific to say on this stratum (*Classes and cultures: England 1918–1951* (Oxford: Oxford University Press,

a large new class of technicians was a feature of many commentaries. George Orwell saw a new classless class emerging, particularly in the new light industry areas around London: 'To that civilisation belong the people who are most at home in and most definitely *of* the modern world, the technicians and the higher paid skilled workers, the airmen and their mechanics, the radio experts, film producers, popular journalists and industrial chemists'.[103] Orwell noted for example the 'thousands of young men of working class origin graduating into the technical middle class by way of the RAF' in the war.[104] Harry Hopkins observed in the 1960s,

the men in grey pullovers and grey raincoats who now filled the First Class carriages en route to cities like Birmingham and Newcastle, shamelessly talking in highly miscellaneous accents their unintelligible shop. The odds would be rather more than even that their fathers had been manual workers. Their *alma mater* was more likely to be redbrick than Oxbridge, and might well have been the 'White Tile' of some large, bleak, provincial 'Tech'. They were as different from the old 'professional man' as a Glasgow Scot from a Home Counties Englishman. Builders of a new world, they were not so foolish as to expect its divisions to coincide with those of the old one.[105]

Hopkins himself noted that 'In the twenty years between 1931 and 1951 the number of scientific workers alone multiplied more than three times and, as the *Situations Vacant* columns bore daily witness, the demand was still far from met.'[106] Indeed, in contrast to pre-war, in the early 1950s it was commented on that: 'Today it is only the weaker type of arts graduates who may have difficulty finding employment normally regarded as befitting a graduate: scientists and technologists are eagerly pursued by would-be employers and can pick and choose.'[107]

These changing demands – which were driven by the warfare state and industry, and not by the welfare state – had a profound effect on the university and on the nature of the male graduate. Although, as we have seen, universities were not centres of wartime research and development, and remained important as teaching institutions, they did see some important differential changes. As the pseudonymous author of *Red Brick* put it:

1998), chs. 2 and 3). See also Alan Kidd and David Nichols (eds.), *The making of the British middle class? Studies of regional and cultural diversity since the eighteenth century* (Stroud: Sutton, 1998), in particular the essays by Quail, Trainor and Distenfass.

[103] George Orwell, 'The lion and the unicorn', *Collected Essays*, II, p. 98.
[104] Ibid., III, p. 36.
[105] Harry Hopkins, *The new look: a social history of the forties and fifties in Britain* (London: Secker & Warburg, 1964), p. 159.
[106] Ibid., p. 159
[107] PEP, *Graduate employment* (London: PEP, 1956), p. 1.

Comparatively few professors went on war service; many lecturers remained with us whom we might have expected to lose; the undergraduates' military education was planned so skilfully that it disorganised lectures considerably less than the pre-war preparations for Panto day. Most graduate work came to an end, but both research funds and direction were still at the disposal of those who were able to use them, and the learned reviews which Red Brick publishes went on appearing, though in a queerly shrunken form. Some of the Faculties, such as Medicine and Engineering, which the Government considered of national importance actually 'registered students' (to use Red Brick's unlovely language) in greater numbers than ever before. The chief casualty was the Faculty of Arts.[108]

He went on to note that fit young men who were studying arts went to war:

Had they been engaged in sciences which would enable them to build bombers or manufacture poison gases, they would have been left to finish their courses undisturbed. Because their studies were in languages, history, economics, and foreign civilisations – the only studies which will teach the nations how to live together in peace – they were ruthlessly truncated.[109]

As we can see in fig. 4.2, the male arts student virtually disappeared (he went into the forces) while the male scientist, engineer and medical students remained and were joined by new cohorts.[110] As far as men were concerned, the wartime university was a very technical place.[111] After the war the universities saw a very noticeable bulge of male arts students whose studies had been interrupted or deferred by war service; for science and engineering the bulge was much smaller.[112] Crucially, there was no systematic replacement of men by women, least of all in science, technology and medicine, where the increase in the numbers of women was particularly small. However the increasing proportion of women students temporarily reversed a little-known trend: the

[108] Bruce Truscott, Red brick (Harmondsworth, Penguin, 1951) (First published 1943 and 1945), pp. 256–7.

[109] Ibid., pp. 260–1.

[110] For example, Oxford history student Noble Frankland studied full time for one term, and then had two terms of life split between history and the university air squadron, before full time aircrew training. He returned to complete his degree after the war (Noble Frankland, History at war: the campaigns of a historian (London: Giles de la Mare, 1998), pp. 9, 35); the literary critic Raymond Williams studied for two years at Cambridge, then went into army, returning to complete his degree after the war.

[111] Indeed, special provision was made to train first radio and radar engineers, and then technical specialists more generally, with a new system of bursaries for these shortage subjects named after Lord Hankey, chairman of the Technical Personnel Committee.

[112] One consequence was that a whole generation of administrative class entrants to the civil service had experience of serving as officers during the war, often before completing their studies. An example is Roy Denham, who was at Cambridge for a year before joining the army. See his The Mandarin's tale (London: Politico's, 2002), pp. 5–8, 246.

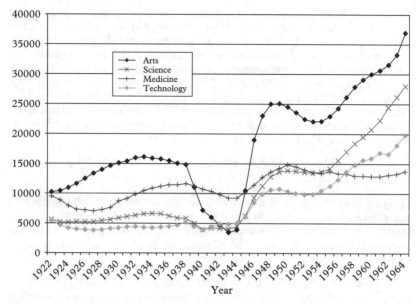

Figure 4.2 Number of male university students by faculty, 1922–64

masculinisation of the student body (see fig. 4.3).[113] The proportion of male students was higher in the late 1940s and 1950s than it had been in the 1920s and 1930s, and was still higher in 1964 (72 per cent) than it had been in the mid-1920s (69 per cent). Even sexually segregated Oxford masculinised: the Franks (Oliver Franks, needless to say) Report on Oxford University of the mid-1960s noted that 'the proportion

---

[113] Robert Anderson notes, almost in passing, that: 'cuts in public expenditure after 1931 made school teaching an unattractive career. This particularly affected the recruitment of women: the percentage of women students reached a peak at the end of the 1920s, but then declined, and remained stuck at 23–24% until the 1960s.' Anderson's analysis is speculative, and does not explain why the proportion of women stuck at the low 1930s' levels, and somewhat misleading about causes and timings: R. D. Anderson, *Universities and elites in Britain since 1800* (London: Macmillan, 1992), p. 23. Carol Dyehouse, *No distinction of sex? Women in British universities, 1870–1939* (London: UCL Press, 1995) takes her analysis of the proportion of women students from Anderson, but gives the issue no prominence (pp. 17–18). R. M. Blackburn and J. Jarman, 'Changing inequalities in access to British universities', *Oxford Review of Education* 19 (1993), 197–215 cover the period from 1938, and for the proportion of women the period from 1948, thus missing most of the masculinisation: they do however comment on the erratic feminisation after 1948. Clearly much larger changes, and with longer-term effects, than the attractiveness of school teaching to women were taking place, though Anderson's analysis of the 1930s is plausible. University graduates destined for teaching were particularly hit by poor job opportunities in the 1930s: see PEP, *Graduate Employment*, p. 1.

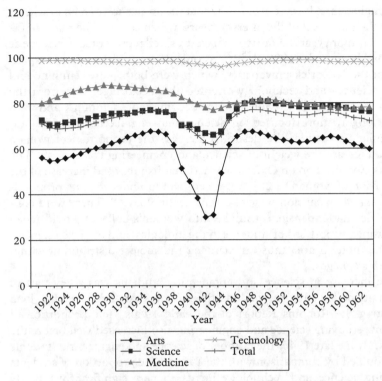

Figure 4.3 Proportion of male students in British universities, by faculty, 1922–64

of women at Oxford was 18 per cent forty years ago [i.e. in the mid-1920s]; it was 16 per cent in 1963/4'.[114] That is surprising enough, but a breakdown by subject and gender reveals a particularly strong masculinisation in the notoriously masculine subjects of science, and

[114] University of Oxford, *Report of Commission of Enquiry*, 2 vols. (Oxford: Clarendon Press, 1966), I, para. 101. There was in fact an interesting difference in trends between Oxford and the university system as a whole. At Oxford the proportion of women was constant at between 17 and 18 per cent through the interwar years, it dropped after the war, reaching a low of 14 per cent in 1958/9: *Report of Commission of Enquiry*, II, table 4.4, p. 13. Remarkably, the recent history of Oxford University in the twentieth century does not make these points (nor indeed does it comment on the fact that after the war male undergraduates had usually done their military service, making them older than the undergraduates we are used to, as well as in many cases having experience of command): Brian Harrison (ed.), *The history of the University of Oxford*. Vol: VIII, *The twentieth century* (Oxford: Clarendon Press, 1994).

even engineering. It was only in 1962 that the proportion of men in science fell to the *peak* level of the interwar years, which came in the mid-1930s, and many more years before women were as well represented in science as they had been in the 1920s.[115] It was only because of the relative expansion of the red brick universities, which were both more feminine and more science- and technology-oriented than Oxbridge, that from the 1950s universities as a whole were to become more feminine, and for a while longer, more focused on science and engineering too. But for particular universities the desire to increase the proportion of women and to increase the weight of science and engineering could clash. The Franks Commission on Oxford worried that its proposed increase of the proportion of women to 20–25 per cent would undermine its proposals for a relative expansion of science and technology.[116] There were concerns too that expansion of intake into women's colleges would mean increasing proportions of students in the biological and medical sciences, and the modern arts, thus unbalancing the subject distribution within women's colleges.[117]

The increase in science and engineering students was a key part of university policy after the war, and the numbers expanded steadily, long predating the Robbins Report of the early 1960s. The proportion of students studying science and engineering also increased well before the 1960s. By the late 1940s the number of science and engineering students had doubled by comparison with the 1930s. The proportion of students studying science and technology increased very significantly too. By international standards the post-war British university was a very

[115] A similar sort of pattern is evident in the United States. We have compelling though partial evidence that such a process took place to an astonishing degree at doctoral level in the United States. In the case of chemistry, a maximum of 10 per cent women was reached in 1929, which apart from one exceptional year was not exceeded until 1972. By 1933 the figure had dropped to 5 per cent, and reached a minimum of 2 per cent in the 1940s (Marelene F. Rayner-Canham and Geoffrey W. Rayner-Canham, 'Women in chemistry: participation during the early 20th century', *Journal of Chemical Education* 73 (1996), 203, citing K. G. Everett and W. S. DeLoach, *Journal of Chemical Education* 68 (1991), 545). See also V. B. Haas, and C. C. Perucci (eds.), *Women in scientific and engineering professions* (Ann Arbor: University of Michigan Press, 1984). In the case of physics participation was lower, but the trend similar: 4 per cent of physics PhDs were women in the 1920s, but the proportion fell to less than 2 per cent in the 1950s. Again recovery came only in the 1970s (Rayner-Canham and Rayner-Canham, 'Women in chemistry', 203, citing V. Kistiakowsky, *Physics Today* 33 (1980), 32.

[116] It was considerations to the effect that Oxford could tap the pool of women scientists more effectively which led them to the cautious conclusion that: 'It would appear that, although Oxford has not much leeway, increasing the entry of women need not lead to a worsening of the balance of subjects': University of Oxford, *Report of Commission of Enquiry*, II, p. 85, para. 148.

[117] Janet Howarth, 'Women', in Harrison, *History of the University of Oxford*, pp. 358–9.

scientific and technical place, contrary to the usual impression.[118]
Combining the subject story and the gender story is necessary to
bring out something very important which has not been visible – the
radical transformation of the male graduate. While in 1929–30 some
30 per cent of men were studying science or technology (excluding
medicine and agriculture) by 1967/8 the figure was up to 52 per cent;
the comparable figures for women were 16 per cent and 23 per cent.
Male students moved to science and technology more strongly than did
women: the male graduate was ever more likely to be a scientist or
engineer than the female graduate.[119] That the majority of new male
graduates were, by the late 1960s, scientists or engineers, counters
particularly strongly the view that British education was dominated
by the arts and social sciences. The shift to science and technology,
and away from the arts and medicine, could also be usefully seen as a
shift towards industry and the warfare state and away from the welfare
state which required not scientists and engineers, but teachers and
doctors.

The warfare state and industry wanted male graduates. Indeed a 1950s'
PEP survey on graduate employment which is cited above restricted itself
to male graduates on the grounds that patterns of employment for men
and women were very different and industry, a particular focus of interest,
was primarily looking for men.[120] Government wanted men too, especially in the scientific and engineering branches. During the war the
number of scientific women of the rank of scientific officer or above was
fourteen in the defence departments, up from four in 1940, reaching a
peak of around 1 per cent of the total.[121] In 1967 there were seventy-six
women in the post-war scientific officer class (2.3 per cent) compared
with 206 in the administrative class (8.3 per cent).[122] The male science
and engineering graduates went, if scientists, in to manufacturing industry (34 per cent), teaching (19 per cent), government scientific service
(16 per cent) and universities (6 per cent); if technologists they went to
manufacturing industry (45 per cent), the building industry (9 per cent)
and local government (8 per cent). For male arts students the pattern
was strikingly different: teaching dominated (33 per cent), followed

---

[118] See David Edgerton, *Science, technology and the British industrial 'decline', 1870–1970*
(Cambridge: Cambridge University Press, 1996), ch. 5.
[119] A. H. Halsey (ed.), *Trends in British society since 1900* (London: Macmillan, 1972), table 7.14.
[120] PEP, *Graduate employment*, pp. 15–16.
[121] Grace Pickering, 'Women in wartime science: Britain, 1939–1945', unpublished MSc
thesis, University of London (2001).
[122] *The Civil Service*, IV, pp. 242, 232.

by commerce (13 per cent), manufacturing (10 per cent), the churches (8 per cent) and the law (8 per cent).[123]

The new class of male graduate scientists and engineers was significantly different in terms of class background and its close corollaries – type of school and university attended – from the male arts graduates, on average. Grammar-school boys who went to university were more likely to study science and technology than public schoolboys, although they had equal probabilities of studying technology.[124] Looking at it the other way, 39 per cent of male arts graduates had been to public school, compared with 20 per cent of male science graduates and 27 per cent of male technology graduates.[125] Part of the explanation is that non-Oxbridge institutions produced a far higher proportion of scientists and engineers than they did arts graduates. While 14 per cent of male scientists had been to Oxbridge, the figure for arts was 37 per cent.[126] In terms of class background there were also differences: science undergraduates as a whole were more likely than arts to have manual worker fathers (26 per cent arts and social sciences; 33 per cent science).[127] Such differences were apparent overall, but not necessarily within particular universities: at Oxford in the early 1960s the school backgrounds of arts and science students were almost identical (in the cases of both men and women, though these may not be compared directly). The subject with a distinctively strong public school orientation was 'social studies', which in Oxford meant politics philosophy and economics (PPE) and jurisprudence.[128] The crucial point was that grammar schools and red brick universities, largely but not only through scientific and technological education, provided an important route for post-war social mobility. Understanding the important emerging differences between male arts and science graduates is essential to understanding not only the notorious 'two cultures' issue (to be discussed in the next chapter), but also the specific nature of the supposed conflict between administrators and the research corps within the state machine.

---

[123] PEP, *Graduate employment*, table 28, p. 71.
[124] Of men at university studying science, technology or arts in the late 1940s, 51 per cent studied science or technology, for public school boys the proportion was 37 per cent. Interestingly, the proportion of grammar and public school boys taking engineering was the same. PEP, *Graduate employment*, table 5, p. 28.
[125] Calculated from PEP, *Graduate employment*, tables 5, 6, p. 28.
[126] Calculated from ibid.
[127] A. H. Halsey and I. M. Crewe, *Social survey of the civil service*, in *The civil service*, III (1): *Surveys and investigations* (London: HMSO, 1969), p. 314n, citing the Robbins Report. Hereafter cited as Halsey and Crewe, *Social survey of the civil service*.
[128] University of Oxford, *Report of Commission of Enquiry*, II, tables 36, 37, pp. 51–2 (Franks Report).

Table 4.4 *Distribution of scientific officer and administrator grades,*
1967

Scientific officers	Administrators
24 senior posts	28 permanent secretaries
	72 deputy secretaries
55 chief scientific officers	270 under secretaries
157 deputy chief scientific officers	
	798 assistant secretaries
549 senior principal scientific officers	
1464 principal scientific officers	1001 principals
856 senior scientific officers	255 assistant principals
226 scientific officers	
3433 total	2524 total

Source: The civil service, III(1), pp. 3, 5.

Two civil service corps: researchers and administrators

The scientific officers continued to complain about their relative status
and conditions compared to the administrative class. This was a central
theme of the evidence of the scientists to both the Priestley and Fulton
enquiries into the civil service of the 1950s and the 1960s. The DSIR in its
evidence to the Priestley Commission noted that the 'normal' scientific
officer entrant was likely to rise through the ranks more slowly, and reach
a lowlier grade, than the 'normal' administrative entrant.[129] The scientific officers' trade union, the IPCS, complained to the Fulton commission that scientific officers were less likely to make it to the very top.[130]
Indeed the evidence is clear. In April 1953 there were 319 administrators
at under-secretary or above, and 59 equivalent scientific officer posts, at a
time when there were 3,721 scientific officers and 2,594 administrators.[131] Much the same imbalance, if such it was, was present in the
1960s (see table 4.4). The scientific officers assumed that there should
have been equivalence in rank distribution between administrators and
scientific officers.[132] In the 1950s they even wanted to increase the

[129] Memorandum of Evidence submitted by the DSIR, *Minutes of evidence, civil service*
(1953–1955), para. 19.
[130] Memorandum no. 42, IPCS, 'Comparative career values of administrative, works group
and scientific officer classes', *The Civil Service*, v(1), *Proposals and opinions* (London:
HMSO, 1968), pp. 359–78.
[131] Introductory factual memorandum on the Civil Service, submitted by HM Treasury,
Royal Commission on the Civil Service (1953–55).
[132] *Report of the Royal Commission on the Civil Service 1953–55*, Cmd 9613, paras. 523–32.
This was rejected.

relative rank of the research grades making a chief scientific officer a deputy secretary and deputy chief scientific officer an under-secretary.[133]

Senior administrators of the professional intensive parts of government were keen, at least in the 1950s, to distinguish the two roles. Sir John Lang, permanent secretary of the Admiralty put it thus – professionals

have to know how to plan a research programme or a new construction programme, but within the ordinary civil service meaning of administration, which is policy making and ensuring that the business of government is carried on, frankly I would not have said that the professional departments have any appreciable contact with that.[134]

He was happy to have professionals under 35 transferring to the administrative class, but 'I should be very hesitant about taking a leading engineer or scientist and putting them into the Admiralty as an under secretary or deputy secretary'.[135] Sir James Helmore, permanent secretary of the MoS, said that most of the work that came the way of the department was in the nature of management – 'The pure policy does not come our way perhaps so much in the sense of things being highly political – leaving aside things like the steel industry where clearly it was the administrators' job right the way through.'[136] All this is in some ways a little strange since, as Denis Healey has written of his time at the Ministry of Defence in the 1960s, permanent secretaries had little personal experience of defence problems, and they

like the other civil servants in the ministry, tended to confine themselves to administration and finance rather than plunge into policy. Even so, I find it difficult to forgive Sir Edward Playfair for saying he was glad to leave Defence in 1961 after only one year as Permanent Secretary, because "it lacked intellectual challenge"![137]

It is certainly worth noting that here the administrators appeared not to be central to policy making, supposedly their key role.

The Treasury, the representative of the administrative class, argued that there was no reason why progression should be the same and that the two classes were not equivalent. Although the formal qualifications were the same the administrator was chosen on the basis of 'potential for general management', that is for the senior posts. Scientific officer entrants were judged on their ability to undertake particular kinds of

---

[133] *Report of the Royal Commission on the Civil Service 1953–55*, para. 540. This proposal was rejected by the Commission.
[134] *Minutes of evidence, Civil Service (1953–1955)*, Q 2779.
[135] Ibid., Q 2780.   [136] Ibid., Q 2480.
[137] Denis Healey, *Time of my life* (London: Michael Joseph, 1989), p. 263.

work – the degree was more significant and was 'more akin to a professional qualification'.[138] This was a replay of debates of the 1920s. It was not just the administrators who objected to ideas of putative equality. The Gibb-Zuckerman Report on the management of R&D (and both Sir Claud Gibb and Sir Solly Zuckerman were FRSs) commented that the comparison made by the scientific officers downplayed key differences, and that there were good reasons why there was an unequal distribution of ranks.[139]

The administrators continued to see themselves as higher beings than the researchers. Indeed a Treasury document of 1954 bluntly claimed that 'the average AP [assistant principal] entrant is a superior article to the average SO [scientific officer] entrant'. This has been cited as demonstrating the unthinking and damaging prejudices of the administrators, but the Treasury official is more likely to have been expressing a disdain for the ordinary graduate, rather than the ordinary scientists.[140] For, while the administrators were a highly selected group of (typically) arts graduates the scientific officers were broadly representative of male science graduates. The proportions recruited from Oxbridge were very different. The proportion of administrators from Oxbridge remained roughly constant over time and thus notoriously high. The proportion of scientific officers from Oxbridge was falling quickly, from 31 per cent pre-war to less than 10 per cent in the 1950s, reflecting in part the differential expansion of non-Oxbridge colleges.[141] Scientific officers were less likely to have been to Oxbridge than scientists and engineers in private industry.[142] It is not possible to compare class origins of the two groups, but the scientific officers were of distinctively lower-class origin than the generality of professionals in class I,[143] indeed only 15 per cent had fathers in their own social class I; one-third were sons (the proportion of women was of course negligible) of manual workers.[144] Interestingly, the small numbers of Oxbridge-trained scientific officers were marginally

---

[138] Memorandum no. 43, submitted by HM Treasury, November 1967. *The civil service*, v (1), *Proposals and Opinions* (London: HMSO, 1968), pp. 364–5.

[139] Office of the Minister of Science, *The management and control of research and development* (London: HMSO, 1961) (Gibb–Zuckerman Report), para. 279. There was a distinct R&D management problem – an R&D workforce which was more heavily weighted to older men than other labs, and which therefore faced the problem of transferring older less productive staff out of R&D, and indeed out of the civil service (paras. 280–3).

[140] 'Points in favour of the Administrator, as opposed to the Specialist', quoted in Hennessy, *Whitehall*, p. 159, where he comments: 'Of all the Treasury files I have read that one takes the prize for smugness, narrowness, arrogance, and restrictive practice'.

[141] Halsey and Crewe, *Social survey of the civil service*, table 10.21, p. 322. In these statistics the administrative class is lumped in with other administrators and managers in class II.

[142] Ibid., table 10.23, p. 321.   [143] Ibid., p. 314.   [144] Ibid., p. 313.

Table 4.5 *Comparison of the main graduate classes of the civil service in the mid-1960s (percentages)*

	Administrators	Scientific officers
Reading		
The Times	88	23
Guardian	36	24
Telegraph	72	39
Economist	68	12
New Statesman	25	9
Spectator	17	3
New Society	33	5
Universities attended if graduate		
Oxbridge	64	16
London	9	27
School		
LEA grammar	40	57
Direct grant	19	15
Public	36	20
Place of work		
Inner London	87	17
Outer London	0	15
England and Wales, other than north	4	60

Source: Halsey and Crewe, *Survey of the Civil Service*, various tables.

more socially and educationally exclusive than administrators (unfortunately we cannot compare with Oxbridge-trained administrators only) (see table 4.5): one-third had fathers in social class I and half had been to public school.[145]

It is worth noting that the scientific advisers to government were in general very similar in educational background to the administrative class (that is to say overwhelmingly Oxbridge trained).[146] These advisers were scientific generalists, indeed scientific mandarins. They, and some research corps members, were generally admirers of the administrators and/or critical of the research corps. One government scientist claimed in the 1950s that it was 'still true today that . . . [among schoolboys] a greater proportion of the better intellects among them choose the classical side. This, of course, is reflected – among other ways – in

[145] Ibid., tables 10.26 and 10.27; tables 3.21, 3.35.
[146] Elite studies of civil scientific advisers show the extreme representation of Cambridge graduates – see Stuart Blume, *Towards a political sociology of science* (New York: Free Press, 1974), p. 200.

the superb intellectual quality of the Administrative Class of the Civil Service.'[147] Sir Solly Zuckerman's memoirs, far from praising the scientific civil service, criticise it.[148] In a lecture in the 1980s he was blunt: 'Some scientists are more ignorant of the work of others than would be a well-read layman'; he reasoned that 'a scientific education, and still less a technological obsession, is not a sufficient condition for wise judgement' and thought that 'Ministers and civil servants not only need dispassionate scientific advice, but maps of the hidden rocks of vested and prejudicial scientific opinion'.[149] Other academic scientists with experience of government scientific advice are generally either silent or disparaging about the scientific civil service.[150] Generally there seem to be few if any complaints about the role of the scientists in high level advice in the forces: indeed Sir Frederick Brundrett celebrated the high place of the scientific adviser in the forces, compared to the low place in the other departments of state.[151] Yet Brundrett was clear that 'The right man to be at the top is the man who takes the broadest view of the whole thing, and that is the administrator.'[152] This was not unusual: Sir Henry Tizard's admiration for the administrative class is also evident. He clearly did not want scientists to dominate administration, though he wanted some science to be taught in 'modern greats', to give future administrators a more rounded view.[153] It is notable that while celebrations of the brain power of the administrators are a cliché – for example in the number of references to 'Rolls-Royce minds' – they are not extended to scientific officers.

---

[147] E. C. Williams, 'Science and defence', *Public Administration* 34 (1956), p. 265.

[148] Solly Zuckerman, *Monkeys, men and missiles* (London: Collins, 1988).

[149] Lord Zuckerman, 'Scientists, bureaucrats and ministers', *Proceedings of the Royal Institution of Great Britain*, 56 (1984), 205–29, on 221. For an important analysis of the significance of monopolistic scientific advice within government see P. D. Henderson, 'Two British errors: their probable size and some possible lessons', *Oxford Economic Papers* 29 (1977), 186–94.

[150] The key people are, apart from Zuckerman, R. V. Jones and Blackett.

[151] 'Government and science', *Public Administration* 34 (1956), 245–56. It should also be noted that the technical advice of service officers was strongly encouraged after the war, including the non-technical branches. E. H. W. Cobb, 'Science and the services', *Brassey's Annual, 1955* (ch. XIX). The title refers to the scientific and technical training of uniformed officers. The role of the Cambridge engineering department in training of specialists in all three services is notable.

[152] *Minutes of evidence, Civil Service (1953–1955)*, Q 3421. See also Sir Frederick Brundrett, 'Rockets, satellites and military thinking', *Royal United Services Institute Journal*, (August 1960), 332–43; 'Government and science', *Public Administration* 34 (1956), 245–66.

[153] His other recommendations were equally mild. See his 'A scientist in and out of the Civil Service', Haldane Memorial Lecture, Birkbeck College, 1955, pp. 18–21; Sir Henry Tizard, 'The influence of science on strategy', *Brassey's Annual, 1951*, pp. 112–15.

The non-war between administrators and scientific officers

Just before the 1964 election the Labour politician Richard Crossman, who was a central figure in discussions of policy for science, urged that 'we need to avoid ... a very simple piece of self-deception which is often offered to us by scientists themselves. The main thing wrong with Whitehall, they say, is its "anti-scientific bias".' Indeed, as we have seen this was an old theme, and one which would be played again and again. But Crossman maintained that there were ministries – Defence, Aviation, DSIR and Works – where scientists had no complaints.[154] Crucially, however, and Crossman did not spell it out, the research corps was highly concentrated into these same few departments. In the mid-1950s more than half were in the service and supply ministries: 1,135 in R&D only in the MoS[155] and in 1960 there were 1,937 in R&D in the main service and supply ministries, divided as follows: Admiralty (417), War Office (437) and Aviation (1,083).[156] If we look at these ministries, we find scientific officers and other technical officers very well represented in the upper ranks, as they had been in the interwar years. In the Admiralty in the early 1950s there were, at under-secretary rank and above, nine administrators, seven scientific officers and seven naval constructors, among other technical grades. There were six under-secretary posts and five equivalent chief scientific officer posts. At the lower level there were twenty-two assistant secretaries and sixty-nine scientific officer equivalents.[157] The MoS in 1953 had thirteen under-secretaries and fourteen chief scientific officers; lower down it had forty-two assistant secretaries, and no fewer than two hundred and nine scientific officers of equivalent rank.[158] In the post-war Air Ministry, of the hundred or so senior posts (director and air rank upwards) the ratios were three administrators to two serving officers to one specialist.[159]

---

[154] R. H. S. Crossman, 'Scientists in Whitehall: thoughts on the eve', *Encounter* 23 (July 1964), 3–10. He clearly did not want to give the existing scientists more power; he wanted a new kind of senior civil servant.

[155] And 1,379 in total. Memorandum submitted by the MoS on the Scientific, Professional and Technical Staffs employed by the Department, *Minutes of evidence, Civil Service (1953–1955)*, para. 2 and app. I.

[156] Office of the Minister of Science, *The management and control of research and development*, app. 2.

[157] Memorandum submitted by the Admiralty on civilian professional, technical and scientific staffs, *Minutes of evidence, civil service (1953–1955)*.

[158] That is senior principal scientific officers and deputy chief scientific officers. Memorandum submitted by the MoS on the scientific, professional and technical staffs employed by the department, para. 2, and evidence of Sir James Helmore, permanent secretary, MoS, *Minutes of evidence, Civil Service (1953–1955)*, Qs. 2534–5.

[159] B. Humphreys-Davies 'Internal administrative services in the Air Ministry', *Public Administration* 33 (1955), 363.

We should recall too that as in the interwar years, the research corps and the administrators worked in different worlds. The great majority of the administrative class (and the scientific advisers) worked in the central head-quarters buildings – 'Whitehall' in the jargon – the name of the road that links Parliament Square and Trafalgar Square, where many headquarters of ministries were and are. In the 1960s each department had around 50–150 administrators. As we have noted the research corps was much less evenly spread between departments, and most members worked a very long way from Whitehall, in laboratories increasingly spread around southern English suburbia, small towns and the countryside.[160] The Telecommunications Research Establishment and the Army Radar Establishment ended up in Malvern, Worcestershire. The Woolwich Research Department and Design Department moved to Fort Halstead, Sevenoaks (in Kent), while Tank Design went to Chertsey, on the western edge of London. The main new nuclear research facilities were at Harwell in Oxfordshire, and Aldermaston in Berkshire. A new Aeronautical Establishment went to Bedford and the new National Gas Turbine Establishment to Pyestock in Hampshire.[161] The world of the scientific officers was quite self-contained and local. Indeed much recruitment was local and regional rather than national. The character of each laboratory varied. Some remained closely connected to military bases, and indeed there were significant differences between them for this and other reasons. In some laboratories there were many serving officers present, in others very few. Unlike other government research establish-ments some of the military ones became 'royal': the RAE was royal from the beginning: the Royal Radar Establishment from 1957; the Royal Armament Research and Development Establishment from 1962.[162] The navy began to style its laboratories His/Her Majesty's Establishments, for example HM Underwater Warfare Establishment. The administrative civil service was absent.

Despite the differences there was some movement into the adminis-trative class. Between the end of the war and the early 1950s eleven scientific officers transferred in the MOS, and fourteen specialists in the Ministries of Transport and Civil Aviation and Works.[163] 'It is clear,

---

[160] Government laboratories continued to be very highly concentrated in the south-east Carol E. Heim, 'R&D, defense, and spatial divisions of labor in twentieth century Britain', *Journal of Economic History* 47 (1987), 365–78.

[161] The exceptions are worth noting. There were some Admiralty establishments on Clyde, the additional chemical warfare establishment at Sutton Oak (near St Helens) replaced in early 1950s by site in Nancekuke, Cornwall.

[162] ARDE was created by the merger in 1955 of the Armament Design Department and ARE.

[163] Access of professional staff to administrative posts – note by the Treasury, *Minutes of evidence, Civil Service (1953–1955)*, para. 7.

therefore' claimed the Treasury, 'that there is no ban in principle on the appointment of professional staff to the administrative class, and that in practice such appointments are made.'[164] The Treasury's explanation for the low numbers was that it took a long time to become a good administrator, that good professionals would not take the risk of becoming perhaps poor administrators and the longer someone spent as a professional the more difficult to adapt to the 'rather different attitude of mind required of the administrator'.[165] It appears that transfers continued to take place, and in 1964 the Conservative government organised a simultaneous transfer of around fourteen professionals to the administrative class.[166]

When he became Prime Minister in the 1960s, the former wartime temporary civil servant Harold Wilson appointed another former temporary, John Fulton, to head a royal commission enquiring into the civil service. In its report the Fulton Commission echoed, even amplified, the old technocratic criticisms of the administrative class, and these were to resonate strongly in the subsequent literature too. Among many recommendations, Fulton proposed breaking down the distinctions between the 'generalist' administrators, and the 'specialist' professionals in the higher levels of the civil service – proposing open competition for high-level appointments from all classes.[167] Fulton endorsed the standard picture of the low place of the expert, yet did not recognise the extent to which experts and administrators were already operating in unified hierarchies in certain ministries, and the extent to which experts were involved in policy making.[168] An article which

---

[164] Ibid., para. 9.   [165] Ibid., paras. 11–12.

[166] I owe this information to one of the fourteen, Mr Colin Hughes. He worked on the British bomb project, went into the nuclear industry and returned to the civil service as a principal scientific officer in the Ministry of Agriculture. In 1964 he became a principal in the newly merged Ministry of Defence.

[167] One member of the Commission, Sir William Cook, wanted the technically intensive ministries to be run by a board (the analogy he made was with industrial companies, not – perhaps surprisingly, the service ministries), chaired by the minister. The permanent secretary would thus be one of a number of senior advisers, and his functions would be restricted. At the level of finance too the heads of professional functional groupings would be financially responsible. Thus instead of making some professionals administrators he wanted senior professionals 'heading the technical administration divisions with full responsibility and equal status with the secretary'. W. R. Cook to P. M. S. Blackett, 20 March 1967, Blackett Papers, E69, Royal Society Archives. Cook was a member of the Fulton Commission, and was writing to Blackett to set out his views, which were, in his view more radical than those of Blackett, who had talked to the Commission.

[168] Even in the 1950s in rebutting claims that professional officers were not involved in policy advice, the Treasury pointed out that the Post Office engineer in chief was involved in policy, so were the medical officers in Health, and that in the MoS, 'as regards access to the minister, and the formulation of policy, senior professional men are in much the same position as members of the administrative class of equivalent status'. Access of professional staff to administrative posts – note by the Treasury, Minutes of evidence, Civil Service (1953–1955), para. 14.

predated Fulton, published in *Public Administration*, correctly notes that the 'traditional' separation of professional and administrative structures, and the subordination of the latter, was 'traditional' only in civil ministries.[169] The article went on to chart a history of integration in some ministries. It showed how from 1949 the architects and buildings branch of the Ministry of Education was jointly headed by a professional and an administrator, and how this model was used from 1958 in the works directorate of the War Office, from 1962 in much of the Ministry of Public Building and Works, from 1963 in part of the Ministry of Housing and Local Government, and from the early/mid-1960s in the highways department of the Ministry of Transport.[170] Fulton could have noted a number of other military and civil cases. The Polaris executive created in 1963 to manage the nuclear submarine and missile project mingled administrators with professionals.[171] The original Ministry of Technology had a single organisation structure and all senior posts were 'opportunity posts', that is could be filled either by the administrative class, or other classes.[172] In the later Ministry of Technology the integration went deep, with scientific officers in senior administrative posts although they retained their membership of scientific or professional grades: 'they do not become under secretaries, assistant secretaries etc, even though their work may be virtually indistinguishable from that of administrative officers with these ranks.'[173] In 1968 the ministry had two permanent secretaries and below them three deputy secretaries and four controllers. These officials controlled a number of divisions each, headed by either a director-general or an under-secretary, which in turn had branches under them, run by either directors or assistant secretaries. There was a great deal of mixing of these professional and administrative grades, so that a director might report to an under-secretary who might report to a controller.

The idea that the British state was entirely dominated by an arts-trained elite who illegitimately kept down the professionals is an enduring legacy of a long-standing interested critique which has found extraordinary resonance. And yet, as this chapter has shown, it cannot be as simple as that. Indeed international comparisons are, as ever, revealing. The US sociologist Robert Putnam carried out a fascinating study in the 1970s of

---

[169] D. E. Regan, 'The expert and the administrator: recent changes in the Department of Transport', *Public Administration* 44 (1966), 149–68.

[170] Ibid.

[171] John Simpson, 'The Polaris Executive: a case study of a unified hierarchy, *Public Administration* 48 (1970), 379–90, ignores the other precedents listed by Regan, 'Experts and administrators'.

[172] Sir Richard Clarke, *New Trends in Government*, HMSO 1971 (Civil Service Department. Civil Service College Studies 1). See also, Philip Gummett, *Scientists in Whitehall* (Manchester: Manchester University Press, 1980), ch. 3, a useful survey, p. 26.

[173] Regan, 'Expert and administrator', p. 153.

the mentalities of the top two ranks of civil servants in Britain, Germany and Italy (for the year 1970–1). Putnam found the British administrative elite distinctive in its composition, by having a high proportion of scientists, engineers and mathematicians, and arts graduates. The British elite had easily the highest proportion of scientists, engineers and mathematicians (26 per cent) – Italy had 10 per cent and Germany 14 per cent. In the latter two countries lawyers dominated (53 per cent and 67 per cent respectively), but they had virtually no arts graduates. In this sample, among the British officials it was historians, not the classicists of the cliché, which formed the single largest group. Putnam found that in all three countries educational background shaped attitudes. Scientists were much more likely to take a negative view of politics; to believe in political neutrality, to believe in the primacy of technical considerations, and to be more elitist in their approach to the world than arts graduates.[174] In short they displayed classic technocratic attitudes. In that sense we might speak about two cultures. There was another important cultural dimension, which we have already found much comment on in this book, concerning identification. Senior British civil servants with an arts background, obviously overwhelmingly members of the administrative class, associated themselves, in Putnam's study, with the civil service in general, and only then with their department. Scientists, by contrast, tended to put science/technology in general as their primary affiliation, followed by their own department.[175] Thus the distinction between in effect 'civil servant' and 'professional' ran deep, and was not just a creation of the administrators to put down the experts.[176] How these significant and complex differences came to be turned into the standard simplistic 'two cultures' polarisation, and how the research corps was written out of the history of British science and of the British state, is the subject of the next chapter.

---

[174] See the various tables in Robert Putnam, 'Elite transformation in advanced industrial societies: an empirical assessment of the theory of technocracy', *Comparative Political Studies*, 10 (1977), 383–412.

[175] Putnam, 'Elite transformation', p. 390

[176] An earlier study showed that the research corps members were generally committed to research as their job and despised administration. There was a huge cultural gap between the two. Z. M. T. Tarkowski and Avice V. Turnbull, 'Scientists versus administrators: an approach towards achieving greater understanding', *Public Administration* 37 (1959), 213–31.

5   Anti-historians and technocrats: revisiting the technocratic moment, 1959–64

The central problem of social spring cleaning needed at the moment is how to replace the literary-legal intelligentsia of old school tie socialism by a technical 'expertensia' in tune with the aspirations of the salaried middle class ... Fundamentally, my dear Kingsley, you and your entourage expect your readers to pick up an elusive reference to the seventh mistress of a 17th century minor French poet, and refuse to reckon with the fact that hundreds of people who don't give a damn for your French poet or his mistress know much more about a kilowatt, a calorie or a bacteriophage than you do.[1]

For the American political scientist Samuel Beer twentieth-century political culture had two strands: the technocratic and the populist. But in Britain, he argued, the technocratic strand only appeared briefly. The 'opening salvo' of this technocratic moment was C. P. Snow's 'two cultures' lecture of 1959; also important was the special issue of *Encounter* on the 'suicide of a nation' of 1963.[2] The results were, the [Lionel] Robbins Report on the expansion of higher education of 1963, reform in the 'science policy' machinery (including the creation of the Ministry of Technology) of 1963/4, and most important of all, the [John] Fulton Report on the Civil Service, of 1968.[3] According to Beer, the ambition and impact of the technocratic programme had faded by the 1970s. This description is notable for its clarity but it is a commonplace of British historiography and political comment. The failed technocratic moment of the 1960s, is one of the key explanatory foci of Britain's account of itself. It is taken, within the dominant technocratic tradition, as the exception that proves the rule that British political and administrative culture was anti-technocratic. But it was the technocratic

---

[1] Lancelot Hogben to Kingsley Martin, editor of the *New Statesman*, Christmas/New Year 1937/8, quoted in C. H. Rolph, *Kingsley: the life, letters and diaries of Kingsley Martin* (London: Gollancz, 1973), pp. 283–4.
[2] Samuel H. Beer, *Britain against itself* (London: Faber, 1982), pp. 121–3.
[3] Ibid., pp. 123–5. Robbins and Fulton were academic entrants into the state machine during the war; others that will feature as chairmen of committees and advisers in this and the next chapter include Blackett, Franks and Zuckerman, to which we need to add two business entrants – Gibb and Plowden.

moment which itself defined Britain in this way. The technocratic moment was ideologically much more significant than has been recognised, and much less significant in policy terms: it defined a whole mode of thinking about the British elite and state, and British science, technology and industry in particular. It gave us at least thirty years of technocratic and declinist historiography, and indeed analyses like Beer's where British technocracy hardly exists except in this brief moment. It generated clichés such as 'two cultures' and the 'white heat', and criticism of the 'establishment', the 'traditional culture', the 'stagnant society' and the 'sick man of Europe' which are still remarkably current. The arguments have been repeated as if nothing had happened in the interim, and as if they were credible in the first place.[4] It is hardly surprising then that Snow's *The Two Cultures* is still in print now with an introduction by a Cambridge intellectual historian.[5] The special issue of *Encounter* was issued as a paperback in 1994.[6]

The technocratic moment primarily was one where the technocratic critique of British institutions was very prevalent, rather than one where British technocrats were celebrated. This technocratic critique is a central common feature of declinism, which some historians have associated with other proximate causes.[7] For declinism, the view that the relative decline of Britain was due to British failings, almost always took those failings to be ones which more, and more powerful, technocrats would have avoided.[8] Central to the technocratic critique is what might be called the anti-history of British technocracy.[9] Historical accounts are surprisingly important in

---

[4] Anthony Sampson, *Anatomy of Britain* (London: Hodder & Stoughton, 1962); Michael Shanks, *The stagnant society* (Harmondsworth: Penguin, 1961); Andrew Shonfield, *Modern capitalism: the changing balance of public and private power* (London: Oxford University Press, 1965); Thomas Balogh, 'The apotheosis of the dilettante' in Hugh Thomas (ed.), *The establishment: a symposium* (London: Anthony Blond, 1959), pp. 83–126.

[5] Indeed it has been re-issued with an introduction by a Cambridge intellectual historian: C. P. Snow, *The two cultures and the scientific revolution* (Cambridge: Canto, 1993) with an introduction by Stefan Collini. Originally published by Cambridge University Press in 1959.

[6] Arthur Koestler (ed.), *Suicide of a nation* (London: Vintage, 1994).

[7] For example the loss of world leadership, resistance to structural change, the failure to meet aspirations and the appearance of comparative economic data. See Barry Supple, 'Fear of failing: economic history and the decline of Britain', *Economic History Review* 67 (1994), 441–58; Jim Tomlinson *The politics of decline: understanding post-war Britain* (London: Longman, 2000). Tomlinson sees the Snow declinism as a particular version because of its focus on science: *Politics of Decline*, p. 24. True, others might be a bit less gung-ho specifically about natural science, but the technocratic tenor was shared with declinism in general. See my 'The prophet militant and industrial: the peculiarities of Correlli Barnett', in *Twentieth Century British History* 2 (1991), 360–79.

[8] For discussion of this definition of declinism, see my *Science, technology and the British industrial 'decline', 1870–1970* (Cambridge: Cambridge University Press, 1996), pp. 3–5.

[9] E. P. Thompson uses the term in a different sense, that of weeders of official documents: E. P. Thompson, *Beyond the frontier: the politics of a failed mission to Bulgaria* (Woodbridge: Merlin, 1997), pp. 14, 20.

this tradition, as we shall see, but they are very strange histories in that they typically obliterate the past and present of the technocratic institutions they most care about. The emphasis is on the strength of the forces that are taken to oppose these technocratic institutions, hence the term anti-history. Such anti-histories involve a gross distortion of the historical record by denying the strength of technocracy and overestimating the significance of opposition to them. British technocracy, whose existence was denied in these anti-histories, thus ceased to be open to ordinary historical questions. The technocratic anti-histories were themselves anti-historical in that they denied their own place in a historical tradition of technocratic critique. The resulting invisibility of technocracy, and of the anti-historical tradition of writing about it is, paradoxically, a measure of the power of this tradition in Britain. For these anti-histories, I suggest, have played a crucial role, and are themselves expressive of, technocratic values. Declinism, imbued as it is with the technocratic critique, is in itself an expression of measure of strength of the technocratic tradition in Britain. That declinism has been of enormous significance in Britain's intellectual culture, and indeed political and civic culture since at least the early 1960s, should not be read as evidence that its theses are correct, but that they are profoundly wrong. If that is so, our account of British culture needs a radical overhaul since so much existing work accepts declinist arguments.

We have already come across some examples of anti-histories: the historical works of Sir Basil Liddell Hart and Major-General Fuller downplayed the existence of the pro-tank forces in the British army and portrayed that army as being dominated by blimps. Many accounts of the civil service called for a greater role for experts, argued against the dominance of the arts-trained administrators and blamed them for the low status and power of the experts, but as we have seen were blissfully ignorant of the work of such experts. Indeed the Fulton Commission provided an anti-history of state experts. But there are many others: studies of British culture regretting the weakness of science, but revealing a knowledge of science no deeper than the works of C. P. Snow, advocates of strong industrial policy, writing histories of industrial policy, who were utterly convinced that Britain had never had them and that the Treasury had won every battle. In the repetition of these stories, science, technology, industry and experts became ever weaker, while pacifists, literary intellectuals, the administrative class, Bloomsbury, the Treasury, loomed ever more grotesquely large. These anti-histories worked because the historians had accounts of British society which themselves ignored technology, trusting the accounts of the anti-historians. They deferred to the experts, propounding the experts' own theses. In doing so they propagated their argument, but inadvertently undermined it too. For the (anti-) historians argue that the arguments of the technocrats have not been heeded by the arts-based intelligentsia, historians included. If British culture had been as the anti-historians suggested, anti-history would have been doomed.

The writers of anti-histories were a new kind of public intellectual looked down on by old-style elite intellectuals.[10] Think for example of Gramsci's 'organic intellectuals' or 'technicians', or consider the brutal and insightful comment by Ortega y Gasset on the new mass-man, the specialist, who

is a learned ignoramus, which is a very serious matter, as it implies that he is a person who is ignorant, not in the fashion of the ignorant man, but with all the petulance of one who is learned in his own special line ... In politics, in art, in social usages, in the other sciences, he will adopt the attitude of primitive, ignorant man; but he will adopt them [sic] forcefully and with self-sufficiency, and will not admit of – this is the paradox – specialists in those matters ...[11]

British intellectuals, particularly in the interwar years, also worried about the narrow-minded specialist or professional, and indeed we have seen strong echoes of this in debates between experts and mandarins within the civil service.[12] These concerns should not be interpreted, as they often are, as hostility to specialism or worse still to 'science'. They address the pretensions of some specialists as intellectuals. It is little wonder that broad intellectuals have not been concerned with the content of the claims of the experts. Historical studies of what they have said are rare and much such work is sympathetic to the arguments of the particular experts studied, if not to experts in general.[13] Yet the

---

[10] Jonathan Harwood, *Styles of thought: the German genetics community 1900–1933* (Chicago: Chicago University Press, 1993), p. 363.

[11] And he went on: 'Anyone who wishes can observe the stupidity of thought, judgement and action shown today in politics, art, religion, and the general problems of life and the world by the "men of science" and behind them, the doctors, engineers, financiers, teachers, and so on.' José Ortega y Gasset, *The revolt of the masses* (London: Allen & Unwin 1961), p. 86 (trans anon.); first Spanish edn 1930; British 1932.

[12] Distinctions between old-style and new-style intellectuals, the former broad and the latter narrow in their thinking, has been a theme of commentary on the twentieth century. See A. N. Whitehead, *Science and the modern world* (London: Fontana, 1975), p. 233 (first published 1926); R. G. Collingwood, *An autobiography* (Oxford: Oxford University Press, 1939); Anna-K. Mayer '"A combative sense of duty": Englishness and the scientists' in Christopher Lawrence and Anna-K. Mayer (eds.), *Regenerating England: science, medicine and culture in interwar Britain* (Amsterdam: Rodopi, 2000), pp. 81–3 especially.

[13] P. G. Werskey, *The visible college: a collective biography of British scientists and socialists of the 1930s* (London: Allen Lane, 1978); W. McGucken, *Scientists, society and the state* (Columbus, OH: Ohio State University Press, 1984); D. S. Horner, 'Scientists, trade unions and the labour movement policies for science and technology, 1947–1964', unpublished doctoral thesis, University of Aston (1986). Studies of futuristic literature include discussion of the work of scientific intellectuals, but such studies often place a

historiographical significance of the accounts of the experts is often much greater than is realised.[14] Experts, and particularly what I will call scientific intellectuals, have provided not just the evidence, but the intellectual framework for most studies of expertise in twentieth-century Britain. Frank Turner's warning that the 'uncritical reading of the documents of public science has led historians to take at face value speeches, reports, and essays by scientists about the condition of science when in fact those writings simply repeated arguments and polemics that had been long in the public domain' is still often unheeded.[15] The result is that traditional humanistic intellectuals have come to endorse the claims of the experts; the historians for example have incorporated the anti-histories of the technocrats into their historical accounts of twentieth-century Britain.

It would thus be very misleading to see the issue as one of experts versus traditional humanistic intellectuals. Yet, as Jonathan Harwood points out, distinctions are usually made between disciplines in which intellectuals are trained, most notoriously between the humanities and science, and only more rarely between 'styles of thought' within disciplines which are also found in many disciplines.[16] In post-war Britain there were indeed many different kinds of scientific intellectuals and technocrats, though we hardly have a measure of the range of opinion, not least because of the vulgar assumption, encouraged by many scientists, that science is unitary and implies a singular scientism. Yet it will be obvious from the last chapter that even within government there were very different kinds of scientists ranging from the most intellectual of the scientific advisers to narrow professional bench scientists. The difficulty for the historian is that only some of the former became public or scientific

premium on the supposed prescience of their subjects. See W. H. G. Armytage, *Yesterday's tomorrows: a historical survey of future societies* (London: Routledge and Kegan Paul, 1968); I. F. Clarke, *Voices prophesying war: future wars, 1763–3749*, 2nd edn (Oxford: Oxford University Press, 1992) (first edition 1966); I. F. Clarke, *The pattern of expectation: 1763–2001* (London: Cape, 1979). For more recent accounts see Daniel Pick, *War machine: the rationalisation of slaughter in the machine age* (London: Yale University Press, 1993); D. P. Crook, *Darwinism, history and war: the debate over the biology of war from the 'Origin of Species' to the First World War* (Cambridge: Cambridge University Press, 1994); Lawrence and Mayer, *Regenerating England*.

[14] I take scientific intellectuals to be scientists (overwhelmingly academic scientists) who as a second or parallel career did a good deal of writing on science and society issues, and the large number of men of scientific background who were full-time writers/journalists on and for science, like Norman Lockyer, Richard Gregory, J. G. Crowther, H. G. Wells, C. P. Snow and others.

[15] Frank M. Turner, 'Public science in Britain, 1880–1919', *Isis* 71 (1980), 589–608. As I will show this is no less true of the period after 1918. See also Andrew Hull, 'Passports to power: a public rationale for expert influence on central government policy-making: British scientists and economists, c 1900–c1925', unpublished doctoral thesis, University of Glasgow (1994).

[16] Harwood, *Styles of thought*.

intellectuals, while the latter are largely silent. In mid-twentieth-century Britain the ranks of the scientific intellectuals were dominated by the scientific left and centre, who told very particular stories about the place of science in British life.

As examples of scientific intellectuals I will take the two important cases of C. P. Snow (1905–1980) and Patrick Blackett (1897–1974). Of very different class origins, both were products of interwar Cambridge science, both were wartime temporaries, both became peers, both were famous as spokesmen for 'science', both were at the Ministry of Technology in the mid-1960s. Snow was a minister and Blackett served briefly as a civil servant and longer as an adviser. They were the most influential scientific intellectuals of the post-war year in terms of general impact among the intellectuals. They were both key figures in articulating the technocratic critique of Britain which was hugely influential, not only ideologically but in terms of practical politics and policy. One, Snow, was an exemplary declinist anti-historian; the other, while also prone to anti-history, used science to criticise policies for science. Both were critical in downplaying the history of research and development and promoting 'operational research' as central to accounts of science in the Second World War. Indeed partly in this way they did much to shape how British science in the Second World War was written about, not least in their criticisms of strategic bombing as anti-scientific. Also partly through their work war they provided critical evidence of the potential service that science, and not just research, especially in the hand of socialists, could yield the nation. What was taken as the scientisation and civilianisation of war stood as a model for the forging a new peacetime world. What the scientific left did in the war, and particularly what academic science did, assumed a key place in the thinking about British science in the twentieth century. It was a story of brilliant successes but also of profound failures to influence the unreformed British state. British technocrats conceived of their own relation to the state in very odd ways, systematically, and influentially, distorting our accounts of the place of experts and indeed war in the British state. They took the warfare state out of the history of British expertise, but they also wrote the history of expertise out of that of warfare.

C. P. Snow, anti-historian

Britain has had a remarkable number of novelists with backgrounds in science and engineering. By far the most significant as a novelist was H. G. Wells, but in the 1930s and 1940s a new generation emerged, including Eric Ambler, William Cooper, Nigel Balchin, Neville Shute and C. P. Snow. Cooper, Balchin and Snow all studied science at Cambridge; Shute studied engineering in Oxford; Ambler engineering in London.[17] Snow was and is easily the most famous and certainly the most influential as an ideologue. He was an exemplary new man: he came from a modest provincial background, graduated in chemistry through University College, Leicester, before going on to a doctorate in physical chemistry at Cambridge. He became a fellow of his college, Christ's, but gave up research in the mid-1930s.[18] During the war he was director of technical personnel at the Ministry of Labour. After the war, and until 1960, he continued part-time in a similar role, as the first civil service commissioner with responsibility for science and engineering recruitment. He was thus an important figure in the growth of the new centrally recruited research corps. Sir Charles Snow, as he became in 1957, was a very significant public man – as novelist, sage and administrator. Snow can usefully be taken as the new technical middle classes' spokesman, and symbol of their importance and success in the new world. He articulated, to the great satisfaction of many of them, what they thought ought to be said about science and technology, Britain, the world and the future. Further, he spoke for and with the approval not only of the new class, but also with that of the majority of Britain's humanistic intellectuals. There was a 'bland scientism' in his work, notably, the *Two cultures* essay[19] which appealed to many, showing that such ideas were very widely shared in post-war Britain. Snow told a story which was already familiar and continued to be familiar.

Snow's account of the place of science in British culture drew in part on his experiences with the scientific civil service. In his famous Rede Lecture of 1959, *The two cultures and the scientific revolution*, he described a sample of thirty or forty thousand scientists and engineers, still largely under forty years old, whom he and his colleagues had interviewed

---

[17] Cooper (Harry Hoff) worked with the Civil Service Commission and later the Atomic Energy Authority dealing with scientific personnel. He wrote a trilogy *Scenes from provincial life* (1950), covering pre-war, *Scenes from metropolitan life* (1982) dealing with the MoS after the war, and *Scenes from married life* (1961), also set in the 1940s. His novel *Memoirs of a new man* (1966) set around nuclear power/electricity generation and an Oxbridge college not unlike Churchill College, Cambridge, usefully divides the world into three cultures – scientists (in R&D), engineers and administrators. It also makes the point that all three tended to come from similar backgrounds and were not of the old gentry. None of these novelists wrote, as the Italian industrial chemist Primo Levi did, about technical work as such. For a memoir which is revealing of émigré technical industrialists in Britain see Oliver Sacks, *Uncle tungsten: memories of a chemical childhood* (London: Picador, 2001). See also Michael Frayn, *The tin men* (London: Collins, 1965).
[18] W. H. Brock, 'C. P. Snow – novelist or scientist', *Chemistry in Britain* (April 1988), 345–7.
[19] *Spectator*, 4 October 1963, p. 406.

during and after the war.[20] Snow said of them that 'Their culture ... doesn't contain much art, with the exception, an important exception, of music. Verbal exchange, insistent argument. Long-playing records. Colour photography. The ear, to some extent the eye. Books, very little ...'[21] Snow was in a position to compare his scientists with the recruits to the administrative class, but he did not do this. He contrasted these potential scientific civil servants not with the administrative class, but with novelists who stood not just for the 'literary intellectuals' but for the whole 'traditional culture' which, in his view, ran the country. Oddly enough Snow did write extensively about the administrators in his own novels, though the administrator Sir Roy Denman warns us acidly that they 'purport to offer leeringly knowing pictures of Whitehall life but are about as authentic as fake Chippendale'.[22] In fact Snow's comparison between 'two cultures' is exceedingly badly specified on both sides. For the thousands of scientists hoping to enter state service are only briefly his concern: academic physics usually stands for science. Furthermore it is often not clear what Snow was saying about the distinction between 'cultures': for example he insisted that the 'two cultures' distinction cut across class.[23] However, while at one point he says that the 'two cultures' were 'not grossly different in social origin',[24] at another he notes that 'Compared with the rest of the intellectual world, considerably more scientists in this country ... come from

---

[20] C. P. Snow, *The two cultures and a second look* (Cambridge: Cambridge University Press, 1969), p. 11. From other data we can conclude that recruits to the scientific civil service after the war were reasonably representative of science graduates. Entrants to the scientific civil service (who were presumably reasonably representative of Snow's sample) around 1950 were 65 per cent grammar school, and 17 per cent public school; 10 per cent were Oxbridge. PEP, *Graduate employment* (London: PEP, 1956), table 42, p. 105.

[21] Snow, *Two cultures and a second look*, p. 13. It is often pointed out that Snow's analysis of the 'two cultures' was not at all original. This is certainly right, but it is more important to note that some writers had earlier criticised not only the narrowness of scientific intellectuals but scientific education too. For example 'So long as the universities persist in turning out scientists so specialised, so ignorant of anything outside a narrow sector of "science" itself as to be totally unaware even that they lack culture, a vast expansion of science faculties may well prove a mixed social blessing.' And, continued Lewis and Maude, while the universities should provide vocational training one should ask whether they ought to turn out half-baked 'scientists' who are largely ignorant of literature and who have but the haziest idea of the historical processes which gave rise to scientific discoveries and of the social and ethical frameworks in which operates to-day; or whether the lawyer who is ignorant of the structure of science, or the doctor who is a stranger to philosophy are really cultured beings.

Roy Lewis and Angus Maude, *The English middle class* (London: Phoenix House, 1949), pp. 243–4.

[22] Roy Denman, *The mandarin's tale* (London: Politico's, 2002), p. 3.

[23] Snow, *Two cultures and a second look*, p. 9.   [24] Ibid., p. 2.

poorer families.'[25] Snow could have made use of existing research to show that social class, type of school and type of university attended were vital factors, especially in mid-century, and that the average science student was different from the average arts student. Indeed he could also have pointed to research which showed the lack of general interests of male science and technology students of the late 1940s – they were only about half as likely to join religious, music, drama, art, literature, political or debating societies, than arts students.[26] Much of the evidence used in the last chapter was publicly available by the late 1950s. What is interesting and significant is that Snow could reduce a multiplicity of differences, even within the state machine, to a matter of degree subject studied. Even more remarkable is the success of the concept.

Among some intellectuals and experts, Snow was treated, in private, with contempt for his lack of understanding. Solly Zuckerman, another key scientific intellectual, recalled that on a committee considering 'scientific manpower' in the 1950s Snow

always felt we were not doing enough, and that the scale of our effort compared poorly with that of other countries, even, I remember, with that of Italy.[27] In private Otto [Clarke, another committee member – and as we have seen a mathematician by training] was scathing about Snow's views. 'If he tells us that we should be moving in that direction,' he would say, 'turn smartly round and go the opposite way – we are more likely to be right.'[28]

There was of course a famous public criticism, but it came not from a scientific intellectual but from F. R. Leavis, a Cambridge literary intellectual. Also of modest background, Leavis argued in a celebrated polemic that Snow had to be taken seriously because he was taken seriously, and not because of any intrinsic quality or interest of his writings. His concern was that a 'nullity' like Snow should be taken for a sage: it indicated

---

[25] Ibid., p. 10. Snow provided no detailed evidence, noting merely that the distribution of schools attended by FRSs was markedly different from that of the Foreign Service or QCs (note 5). The comparison is of course an extreme one.

[26] PEP, *Graduate employment*, table 9, p. 32. Some insights are produced by various studies and observations. English grammar schoolboys of the 1960s were famously found to be psychologically different depending on whether they studied science or arts. Liam Hudson, *Contrary imaginations: a psychological study of the English schoolboy* (London: Methuen, 1966).

[27] I remember a senior British scientist (in the 1990s) giving a talk in which figures were presented showing Italy doing more R&D that Britain. To my astonishment a letter to the *The Times Higher Educational Supplement* took up the point not as the obvious absurdity that it was but as evidence of the decline of British science.

[28] Solly Zuckerman, *Monkeys, men and missile: an autobiography, 1946–1980* (London: Collins, 1988), p. 111. I was amused by this part too, as I had made this same argument about the whole declinist literature on British science and technology (*Science, technology and the British industrial 'decline'*, p. 69).

a corrupted culture, a corrupted university, a corrupted Cambridge.[29] Leavis's attack is often presented as being unpleasantly personal and/or as an exemplification of Snow's point about there being 'two cultures'. That is to read Leavis through Snow's eyes, and to misunderstand and underrate Leavis's exemplary dissection of the technocratic genre Snow represented. Far from exemplifying Snow's claimed 'gulf of mutual incomprehension' between the two cultures, Leavis understood Snow only too well, recognising him as a vulgar technocrat, who affected to speak from science, with the authority of science and for science, but without any justification for so doing. Snow claimed, for example, that the argument of scientists was more rigorous and operated at a higher conceptual level than that of literary intellectuals. Leavis noted that Snow's own conceptual level was extremely low and denied him his role as spokesman for science; indeed Leavis's published lecture was accompanied by another by a scientist.[30] Leavis was right to be dismissive of Snow. His significance lay precisely in what Leavis said it did, in his being taken seriously.[31] One might add too that for all his talk of scientists having 'the future in their bones' Snow's own account was antiquated in style and substance: he was a technocrat with the past in his bones.

Snow's 'two cultures' analysis of 1950s' Britain was only a small part of his essay and most of it was placed in the past. Much was a history of the place of science in British life. Although Leavis noted Snow's ignorance of history, and the journalist Henry Fairlie his ignorance of the history of science,[32] the extraordinary nature of Snow's account needs spelling out.

---

[29] F. R. Leavis, *Two cultures? The significance of C. P. Snow*, with an essay by Michael Yudkin (London: Chatto & Windus, 1962). The lecture was given in Downing College, Cambridge. The Richmond Lecture was named for the naval historian and strategist Admiral Sir Herbert Richmond, who had been master of the college. See also the important new work by Guy Ortolano, 'Two cultures, one university: the institutional origins of the "two cultures" controversy', *Albion* 34 (2002), 606–24; 'Human science or a human face? Social history and the "two cultures" controversy', *Journal of British Studies* 43 (2004), 482–505.

[30] Leavis, *Two cultures?*, p. 15.

[31] A neat and much better comparison of 1950s' intellectuals is due to Jonathan Rée, who compares two overrated lecturers of the time: 'If Snow was an emblematic plebeian technocrat ... [Isaiah] Berlin was an archetypal cosmopolitan intellectual who had fallen in love with British cultural and political traditions.' Berlin's *Two concepts of liberty* were given in Oxford in 1958. Jonathan Rée, 'Talking philosophy', *Prospect* (May 2002), 34–7.

[32] Henry Fairlie, 'Cults not cultures', *The Spectator*, 1 November 1963, p. 554. Fairlie – who is credited with coining the term 'The Establishment' – had a nice line in anti-declinism (see his contribution to Koestler, *Suicide of a nation*) and in debunking the scientists and their propaganda more generally. In one article he said: 'He is already a buffoon: Dr Ernest Braindrain, one of Britain's "top" scientists, which he has somehow managed to become while remaining in an obscure or minor post in what we were once allowed to

For, as in his account of the 'two cultures', many readers take Snow to have put his finger on something important, even if crudely. Yet Snow was portentously wrong on the history of British science as on so much else, and yet his account is worth analysing because of the ubiquity of similar arguments. Snow's history of British science and technology is exemplary of anti-histories of British science and technology.

His account is centred on an 'industrial revolution' which lasted from the mid eighteenth century to the early twentieth century and a 'scientific revolution' which, following the fashion of the 1950s, Snow placed no earlier than 1920–30.[33] The 'scientific revolution' was continuing and was creating an 'industrial society of electronics, atomic energy, automation', which was profoundly different from what had gone before.[34] According to Snow, in Britain the 'traditional culture' ignored or disliked the industrial revolution and did not contribute to it. It

trained its young men for administration, for the Indian Empire, for the purpose of perpetuating the culture itself, but *never in any circumstances* to equip them to understand the revolution or take part in it. Far-sighted men were beginning to see, before the middle of the nineteenth century, that in order to go on producing wealth, the country needed to train some of its bright minds in science, particularly in applied science. *No one listened.* The traditional culture *didn't listen at all*: and the pure scientists such as there were, didn't listen very eagerly ... the story ... in spirit continues down to the present day [emphasis added].[35]

Furthermore, 'the academics *had nothing to do with* the industrial revolution [emphasis added]';[36] only in Germany was it different and able men got education in applied science, some of them, like Ludwig Mond, making their fortunes in Britain.[37] Let us recall that the industrial revolution that Snow had in mind lasted into the early twentieth century.

Needless to say, in the later twentieth century Britain was also failing. 'Why aren't we coping with the scientific revolution?' asked Snow. 'Why are other countries doing better?'[38] If Britain did not adjust it would, he claimed, suffer the fate of the Venetian republic in its last half-century.[39] He had Russia and the USA in mind as successes and comparators.[40] On Snow's diagnosis the prognosis for Britain was bleak: other countries,

call a provincial university' (Henry Fairlie, 'Dr Braindrain – Bon Voyage', *Spectator*, 21 February 1954, p. 243). The *Spectator* was in this period an extremely interesting journal, with a consistent hostility to scientism. Its air correspondent was Oliver Stewart, who was essentially nostalgic for a pre-war, smaller and more competitive aircraft industry. The *Spectator* was not then reactionary or fogeyish. It published Leavis's Richmond Lecture. See Roy Jenkins, *A Life at the centre* (London: Macmillan, 1991), pp. 117–18.

[33] *Two cultures and a second look*, p. 29.
[34] Ibid., p. 30. This periodisation is unfamiliar to us now, because historians have subsequently pushed back the second industrial revolution to the late nineteenth century.
[35] Ibid., p. 23.   [36] Ibid., p. 23.   [37] Ibid., p. 24.
[38] Ibid., p. 33.   [39] Ibid., p. 40.   [40] Ibid., pp. 34–6.

including poor countries, were forging ahead. Given his account of the 'industrial revolution' it is extraordinary to find that Snow claimed that the division between the 'two cultures' was getting worse, but so it was: Cambridge was 'a good deal more flexible between 1850 and 1914 than it has been in our time' he maintained.[41] In Snow's Britain 'it was more difficult *than in any other*' country to restructure education [emphasis added];[42] and it had an elite 'far smaller proportionally that in any comparable country'.[43] He attributed this to continued specialism in the educational system and the British 'tendency to let our social forms crystallise'.[44] 'Crystallise' recurs many times: the term sums up his analysis of twentieth-century Britain.

Snow's was an extreme form of anti-history in which he managed to erase the history of the development of British science and technology from the historical record. Science is always failing, engineering even more so. The active agency in British history, if one can call it that, was the traditional culture with its crystallising properties. Also typically of techno-declinist arguments then and since, its policy prescriptions were weak and confused, and out of proportion with the diagnosis. For all the huffing and puffing Snow's policy was further expansion of scientific and technical education, especially within the university. The 'two cultures' issue, of such supposedly monumental importance, barely came into his programme: 'fourth and last' in his prescriptions, Britain needed 'politicians, administrators, an entire community, who know enough science to have a sense of what the scientists are talking about'.[45]

Snow's anti-historical techno-declinism is not a particular version of the declinism of the 1960s but characteristic and exemplary. Its themes, arguments and character were very similar to those of the mass of declinist literature produced at this time. Most was produced by intellectuals trained in the arts. Thus Anthony Sampson (1926–2004), who read English at Oxford, in his *Anatomy of Britain* of 1962 dissected Britain in exactly the techno-declinist, two-culture mode that Snow represented.[46] He claimed that 'the Ministry of Aviation is run by Latin and History scholars, headed by an unscientific minister'.[47] He went on:

The experts not surprisingly resent this *apartheid* and in the last fifteen years a cold war has existed between the two sides. This conflict between amateurs and professionals, between gentlemen and players, runs through many British

---

[41] Ibid., p. 21.   [42] Ibid., p. 18.   [43] Ibid., p. 19.   [44] Ibid., p. 17.   [45] Ibid., p. 38.
[46] Obituary in the *Guardian*, 21 December 2004.
[47] Sampson, *Anatomy*, p. 227. Sampson's father was an ICI chemist. He noted that 'The Ministry of Aviation is much more like ICI than the Home Office, and it employs 3,000 scientists. ICI's board of 22 includes 18 former research scientists.'

institutions– more than on the continent or in America – but it has its most troubled frontier in the civil service.[48]

He could have pointed out that the Ministry of Aviation was the largest funder of R&D in Britain. Nearly all the contributors to *Suicide of a nation* invoked the usual technocratic critiques of the civil service and of Britain more generally, and yet the great majority were trained in the arts and in some cases social sciences, and needless to say from Oxbridge: the Imperial College educated engineer and Labour MP Austen Albu (1903–1994)) was quite atypical.[49] Lord Fulton, the arts academic and wartime administrative civil servant, famously made much of the 'generalist' amateur and the specialist professional in his report. Many claimed that Britain did not have an interventionist industrial policy because it was stuck with outmoded parliamentarism, as put forward in the work of Andrew Schonfield.[50] Furthermore, two-cultures thinking powerfully influenced studies of business, the state and the civil service undertaken by historians, themselves of course usually trained in the arts.[51] That arts-trained intellectuals believed in, indeed promoted, the technocratic critique is a point of some importance. For it itself undermines the significance of the 'two cultures' distinctions at the centre of this literature. One could argue that at a very deep level this point reinforces the fundamental technocratic critique – that in Britain the arts establishment has been so powerful that it even created its own oppositionist discourse. But a simpler explanation (also technocratic in spirit) points to the influence of technocrats' analysis and the credulity and amateurishness of public intellectuals and indeed politicians when it comes to science, technology and industry. Snow was a great beneficiary of an arts-based high culture that accepted the claims of the technocratic critique.

Snow's career and the success of his arguments refute his own theses. Snow crossed between the academy and the state, the state and industry,

---

[48] Sampson, *Anatomy*, p. 227.
[49] See Koestler, *Suicide of a nation*, pp. 249–53. Apart from Albu, the others were one journalist without higher education, ten Oxford graduates, none studying anything more technical than PPE, and four Cambridge graduates, including an economist and a medic. Shonfield did not specify, but he was at Oxford. Tomlinson, *The politics of decline*, p. 23 tells us that this point was made at the time.
[50] Shonfield, *Modern capitalism*.
[51] D. C. Coleman, 'Gentlemen and players', *Economic History Review* 27 (1973), 92–116, was influential in studies of British business. The key data are challenged in Edgerton, *Science, technology and the British industrial 'decline'*, p. 27. As yet unpublished work by Clive Cohen based on the *Dictionary of business biography* confirms the importance not only of scientists and engineers amongst the leaders of British industry, but specifically of Oxbridge-trained ones.

science and letters, with the greatest of ease. His thesis required him to have used superhuman effort. He refutes himself in a deeper sense, for it was not by virtue of being a novelist that he was a civil service commissioner or a member of the board of EE (as we have seen a very important armourer) or, as Lord Snow, a junior minister in the Ministry of Technology, but as a scientist or at least expert on science.[52] Culturally too his own success refutes his own thesis. In a properly literary culture Snow's lecture would hardly have been noticed, and Leavis would not have bothered with it. Had he bothered, in the Britain Snow claimed existed Leavis's attack would have been famous: Snow would be remembered only like some Feuerbach or Duehring, as the unfortunate butt of a brilliant analysis.[53] In the real Britain it is Snow that makes Leavis famous for most of the lay population.[54]

The two cultures was far from Snow's only venture into history, or rather anti-history. His *Science in government*, a series of lectures given in Harvard in 1960, were of greater importance, for they gave an account of British science in the Second World War which, while long challenged, still resonates. *Science in government* was not a survey of the place of scientists in British government, much less an account of the scientific civil service Snow was familiar with. It is concerned with operational research and the morality and effectiveness of strategic bombing. Operational research involved teams of mostly young scientists analysing data about military, naval and air operations (say, searching for submarines) and giving advice to military commanders on such operations. These scientists were attached to particular service commands and not to the research laboratories of the supply departments. The emphasis on operational research was not new in the literature on science and the Second World War. Indeed, since most of the well-known scientific

[52] Thomas Inskip's son Robert (1917–) Lord Caldecote, an Etonian and Cambridge engineer, who served in the navy during the war, was at Greenwich and the Vickers yard on the Tyne after the war and became a lecturer in engineering at Cambridge from 1948 to1955. He joined the board of EE in 1953 and stayed until 1969, representing the company on BAC's board from 1960 to1969.
[53] Noel Annan claims that Leavis did succeed in destroying Snow's standing as a novelist with 'middle-brow opinion': *Our age* (London: Weidenfeld and Nicolson, 1990), p. 284. This seems doubtful. Annan and Robbins were particularly loathsome to Leavis, as is clear in his essays following up the two cultures critique (F. R. Leavis, *Nor shall my sword: discourses on pluralism, compassion and social hope* (London: Chatto & Windus, 1972)).
[54] In 2002, the fortieth anniversary of the Richmond Lecture was marked in the *Guardian* newspaper by a pro-Snow piece that argued that Snow was so right, even about 2002. See Martin Kettle, 'Two cultures still', *Guardian*, 2 February 2002. It was noted in *Prospect* by a plague on both their houses reflection, which again misses the significance of Snow. See Geoffrey Wheatcroft, 'Two cultures at forty', *Prospect* (May 2002), 62–4. F. R. Leavis had long complained, and rightly, that he was misunderstood, and that the misunderstanding revealed the ubiquity of Snow-like analyses: see his *Nor shall my sword*.

intellectuals of the left were involved in it, rather than in R & D work, it figured in work by them and work about them: examples are Blackett (who was styled 'the father of operational research'), Tizard, Bernal, Zuckerman, C. H. Waddington and many others. From very soon after the war operational research was much talked about, particularly by the scientific left, as a general contribution not just to war but potentially to peace.[55] For some it was an alternative not only to traditional military decision making but also to the price mechanism.[56] It was in such accounts pure scientific method unencumbered by association with things, and especially with weapons, and thus a potent example of what science could bring to statesmanship. Two other reasons for its import-ance can be suggested. Tizard stressed that operational research was the novel application of science in the Second World War, and that it was a uniquely British achievement. Tizard told the government scientists' trade union in 1946 that there was an area in which science 'has reached a stage in this country far ahead of any other is its influence on policy and strategy. It is the scientific method of solving problems ... that now finds a welcome in the Service Departments.'[57] Tizard claimed 'for the first time in history, I believe, scientists were able to influence military tactics and strategy' and indeed that the first scientific body concerned with tactics was his own radar committee of the 1930s.[58] Of course novelty and Britishness are not the same as significance, but they are certainly taken as such in accounts of British science and war. Conversely, the use of scientists for the design and development of weapons was not novel in the Second World War, nor uniquely British, and thus less likely to be made use of in arguments for science in Britain.

Snow's *Science in government* constructed the so-called Tizard/ Lindemann dispute over strategic bombing in 1942 and made it central to thinking about British science and war. It represented an extraordinary moralisation of a story best told otherwise, and as such is a British parallel to stories told of the US atomic bomb, which highlight the apparent moral

---

[55] Neal Wood, *Communism and British intellectuals* (London: Gollancz, 1959) perceptively observes the use made of operational research (p. 133). See J. G. Crowther and R. Whiddington, *Science at war* (London: HMSO, 1947); Air Ministry, *Origins and devel-opment of operational research in the RAF* (London: HMSO, 1963); C. H. Waddington, *OR in World War 2: operational research against the U-Boat* (London: Elek, 1973).

[56] Jonathan Rosenhead, 'Operational research at the cross-roads: Cecil Gordon and the development of post-war OR', *Journal of the Operational Research Society* 40 (1989), 3–28.

[57] Sir Henry Tizard, address to the annual conference of the IPCS, July 1946, Reprinted in *State Service* (July 1946), copy in Tizard Papers, HTT 596, IWM. Here he also argued that the civil departments were behind, and also argued against the view that Britain needed more research.

[58] Tizard to Chancellor, 8 December 1953, Tizard Papers, HTT696, IWM.

objections of some participants to the use of the bomb against civilians.[59] Snow very clearly put science and the scientific left on the side of good, and anti-science and bad science on the side of evil strategic bombing. In Snow's account Tizard was the goody who opposed strategic bombing and Lindemann the baddy who supported it; while Tizard was the 'English of the English', Lindemann was 'quite un-English'; Tizard was poor, Lindemann rich; Lindemann was strange, Tizard normal; and, of course, Tizard was the better scientist.[60] Snow claimed that strategic bombing was 'an unrationalised article of faith', not a matter of science or reason, and that 'Lindemann had always believed in this faith with characteristic intensity'.[61] The key to the story was that Tizard together with Blackett had demonstrated that Lindemann's calculations justifying strategic bombing were wrong; but that neither Lindemann nor the government accepted this and therefore bombing was stepped up. Blackett strongly supported this account, and wrote:

I confess to a haunting sense of personal failure, and I am sure Tizard felt the same way. If we had only been more persuasive and had forced people to believe our simple arithmetic, if we had fought officialdom more cleverly and lobbied ministers more vigorously, might we not have changed this decision?[62]

This was no trivial matter for Blackett, since he felt that 'So far as I know, it was the first time that a modern nation had deliberately planned a major military campaign against the enemy's civil population rather than against his armed forces.' Blackett too came to forget his history, for he claimed that 'During my youth in the Navy in World War 1 such an operation would have been unthinkable.'[63] For the navy's major role in that war was the blockade of Germany, and this was central to naval policy from well

[59] For a particularly repellent example see Jacob Bronowski, *The ascent of Man* (London: BBC, 1973), p. 369. See my discussion in 'British scientific intellectuals and the relations of science, technology and war ' in Paul Forman and J. M. Sánchez Ron (eds.), *National military establishments and the advancement of science: studies in twentieth-century history* (Dordrecht: Kluwer, 1996), pp. 1–35.
[60] C. P. Snow, *Science in government* (London: Oxford University Press, 1961), pp. 8–12.
[61] Ibid., p. 47.
[62] P. M. S. Blackett, 'Science in government', review of Snow, *Science in government* reprinted in P. M. S. Blackett, *Studies of war* (Edinburgh: Oliver & Boyd, 1962), p. 126. This argument is congruent with that in the excellent paper by Paul Crook, 'Science and war: radical scientists and the Tizard–Cherwell area bombing debate in Britain', *War and Society* 12 (1994), 69–101, which concentrates on the post-war debates. The paper adds many fascinating details, including J. D. Bernal's involvement. On the significance of naval operational research, showing that in itself it was not as important as is usually implied, see Peter Hore (ed.), *Patrick Blackett: sailor, scientist, socialist* (London: Cass, 2003) and especially the contributions by Jock Gardner and by Malcolm Llewelyn-Jones.
[63] Blackett, *Studies*, p. 123.

before the Great War. Snow and Blackett came to believe that there was a moment of decision when reason (or just arithmetic) was overlooked.[64]

Snow's account has stood the test of time, despite being immediately and devastatingly challenged. In fact, the official history of strategic bombing, published in 1961, using Tizard's own papers, stressed the crude nature of the assessments made on both sides, and the fundamental agreement on the potential efficacy of bombing.[65] From these papers it is indeed clear Tizard had no objections to strategic bombing in principle: his objection to a particular calculation was that he believed that to be decisive bombing would have to be 'carried out on a much bigger scale than is envisaged'. Cherwell responded: 'I am glad to see that we do not differ in arithmetic, or even in our general conclusion.'[66] Blackett, it should also be noted, was unable to corroborate his account of the debate on strategic bombing in the face of private and public criticisms from R. V. Jones, a strong defender of Lindemann.[67] In his own memoirs Zuckerman too dismissed the Snow account.[68]

There is however, a deeper critique to be made. It is that the Snow/ Blackett accounts read as if science, newly inserted into the state, was fighting the forces of backwardness. It is the failure of science which allows unprecedented horrors to be visited on the world. These accounts did not explore the history of scientific advice or indeed the continuing association of science with the military. They are anti-histories of military science. For example, Snow did not make clear that Tizard had been the senior scientific adviser to the Air Ministry since 1933, or that the

---

[64] Michael Sherry has noted the importance of this kind of moral thinking about air warfare and nuclear weapons, but comments that decisions 'certainly resulted from choices but not from a moment of choice'. Michael Sherry, *The rise of American air power: the creation of armageddon* (New Haven: Yale University Press, 1987), p. 363.

[65] C. Webster and N. Frankland, *The strategic air offensive against Germany* (London: HMSO, 1961), I, pp. 331–6, is a very clear summary of the correspondence between Tizard and Cherwell, in Tizard Papers, HTT 353, IWM. For a defence of Lindemann against Snow's quite bizarre arguments and insinuations see Thomas Wilson, *Churchill and the Prof* (London: Cassell, 1995).

[66] See Tizard, 'Estimates of bombing effect', 20 April 1942; and Cherwell to Tizard 22 April 1942, in Blackett Papers, D66, Royal Society. Nowhere is there any reference to moral questions. See also Tizard Papers, HTT 353, IWM. Tizard and Blackett were arguing, in different ways, for the use of bombers against both submarines and enemy merchant ships (Tizard particularly emphasising the latter), rather than the bombing of land targets, but in the very particular context of early 1942.

[67] Blackett Papers, J44, Royal Society, collects the crucial correspondence and papers from the early 1960s.

[68] Solly Zuckerman, *From apes to warlords* (London: Hamish Hamilton, 1978), pp. 139–48. Zuckerman complains that Lindemann's preliminary analysis of his and Bernal's survey of the effect of bombing, incorrectly claimed that morale was strongly affected by bombing.

ministry had been deeply committed to strategic bombing for two decades. Snow later admitted that he was not really sure whether Tizard had any fundamental objections to strategic bombing, without realising the damage that this did to his whole case.[69] Equally, this literature did not make clear that the greatest contribution to the development of operational research had not come from the academics, but from government scientists and businessmen, or indeed that not all operational researchers were academics.[70] It is interesting that hardly any attention has been given to one of the very largest operational research sections, that attached to RAF Bomber Command itself. But in a memoir the physicist Freeman Dyson, who had been a junior member of the section, told a parallel story to the Snow one. He recalled how his advice on reducing the losses of aircrew, by taking out guns and making escape hatches better, was ignored. In a scathing attack on Bomber Command he said 'it might have been invented by some mad sociologist as an example to exhibit as clearly as possible the evil aspects of science and technology'. The root was the doctrine of strategic bombing which had been 'attractive to political and military leaders', though not, it is implied, to scientific leaders.

Bomber Command was an early example of the new evil that science and technology have added to the old evils of soldiering. Technology has made evil anonymous. Through science and technology, evil is organised bureaucratically so that no individual is responsible for what happens ...

Even he had no feeling of personal responsibility.[71] Dyson is unsparing in criticism of himself, but nevertheless he exonerates himself to some extent by his insistence on the lack of individual responsibility in a bureaucracy, and above all because he believes that the scientist is trying to save life, while the soldier or airman is profligate with it. The wartime commander of Bomber Command, much criticised by Dyson as an antediluvian militarist, was, hardly surprisingly for a man in his position, in fact very committed to science.[72] That cannot be recognised for in these accounts science is clearly on the side of good, and cannot be

---

[69] C. P. Snow, *Postscript to science and government* (London: Oxford University Press, 1962), p. 27.
[70] Maurice Kirby, *Operational research in war and peace* (London: Imperial College Press, 2003) makes clear these aspects of the origins of operational research.
[71] Freeman Dyson, 'The children's crusade' in *Disturbing the universe* (New York: Harper & Row, 1979), pp. 29–30.
[72] As he wrote in 1947: a new Defence Force

must obviously become more and more dependent on science, and must make it its main business, as the only condition of winning the next war, to exploit the best contemporary weapons that science has to offer, with no more regret when it relinquishes an older

associated with evil, except by the intercession of sociologists, or society or most obviously the military.

The writer Nigel Balchin, himself a Cambridge-trained scientist then working in the War Office, produced an illuminating scene in his wartime novel *The small back room* which helps us to read the accounts of Snow and Blackett:

'That's right,' said the old boy, brightening up. 'A scientist isn't a man who understands physics, or chemistry, or biology. He's a man whose training had taught him to think in a scientific way . . . '

He went on giving Selling Talk Number One for about twenty minutes . . . When Mair had finished the long and short of it seemed to be that we were Scientists and Scientists were God's Own People, if they weren't God Himself. It made me feel pretty sick, particularly after the way he'd been cursing every other research man we mentioned.[73]

'The main thing is,' said Pinker, 'that these things ought to be ironed out before they go to the Minister. Otherwise we shall get to the point where people say, "Oh, don't let's ask the scientists. They never agree." '

[Sir Lewis] Easton nodded, 'Precisely. It was to avoid these purely individual expressions of opinion that the National [Scientific] Council was set up – so that science could speak with one authoritative voice.'

I said, 'Wouldn't it be better if the voice were a bit less authoritative and a bit better informed? Sometimes I think we try rather to teach the production and services people their job.'

Easton turned his head very slowly and gave me the flat hard stare that served him as an expression of anger, surprise, interest and amusement, depending on the context.

'You regard science as a humble handmaid, to speak when she is spoken to?' he said coldly.

'No. But I don't think a scientist's opinion is worth any more than any one else's when he isn't talking on scientific grounds.'

'*Are* there grounds which are not, in the end, scientific?' asked Easton oracularly.[74]

---

weapon than a scientists shows when a hypothesis is exploded, or when he finds a quick and easy method to replace one that was inefficient and laborious.

(Marshal of the RAF Sir Arthur Harris, *Bomber offensive* (London: Collins, 1947), p. 278)

[73] Nigel Balchin, *The small back room* (London Collins, 1962) pp. 26–7 (first published 1943).
[74] Ibid., pp. 84–5.

These are not analyses to be found in either Snow or Blackett.

It is important to recognise the general significance of the critique of strategic bombing for the left and the intellectuals in the early 1960s. This was the period of the great anti-nuclear campaigns by the Campaign for Nuclear Disarmament (CND), and the connections between strategic bombing and nuclear bombing were obvious to all. For the scientists, and particularly the radical ones, distinguishing between science and weapons of mass destruction was clearly important. Here we can connect the story to the welfare state. For one of the intellectuals most closely associated with CND was the historian A. J. P. Taylor. His hostility to strategic bombing is evident in his *English history*, as we shall see in detail in ch. 7, and yet it is treated as something new, not something implicit in the policies of the pre-war state, nor is it something which tells one about the nature of wartime Britain. In Taylor's account it is a terrible anomaly, as it is in the work of Snow and Blackett.

P. M. S. Blackett, the state and the left

As a critic and analyst Blackett was in a different class from Snow; he stands comparison with J. D. Bernal. Blackett was also different in that he was an insider, an example of a scientist recruited from the English elite. He started his career in the navy, going through the reformed naval education system of the Edwardian years. He served at sea in the Great War and after it was sent to Cambridge with many other young naval officers to complete his education. He decided to resign from the navy and stayed at the Cavendish laboratory until the early 1930s; thereafter he held chairs and headed departments at Birkbeck (1933–7), Manchester (1937–53) and Imperial College (1953–63).[75] Blackett was a commanding patrician figure; his demeanour is often traced back to his naval experience; for others there 'remained about him [in the 1950s] a vestigial air of the intelligentsia of the twenties', he was an 'archbishop of science'.[76] Blackett was also a man of the intellectual left, in ways in which Snow was not.[77] Blackett was a scientific mandarin, who could think politically and could also turn scientific method

---

[75] Blackett retired in 1965. Generally see Peter Hore (ed.), *Patrick Blackett: sailor, scientist, socialist* (London: Cass, 2003).

[76] *The Times*, 15 July 1974. One of his obituaries noted that he had once been called 'the Archbishop of Science', *The Sunday Times*, 14 July 1974. No source is given, nor any more detail.

[77] In the 1930s he occasionally visited (as did J. D. Bernal) *New Statesman* editor Kingsley Martin's flat in Bloomsbury – Blackett had beaten Martin to a King's fellowship in 1923. C. H. Rolph, *Kingsley: the life, letters and diaries of Kingsley Martin* (London: Gollancz, 1973), pp. 175, 102.

on science (something which Snow in particular could never do). He was also an active and open opponent of key scientific policies of the state.

Blackett, who was certainly a premature anti-fascist, was to call himself a 'premature military realist'.[78] Indeed despite the radical politics (for a man in his position) he was in many ways a conservative. His obituary in *The Times* noted his continuing interest in 'old fashioned' problems in physics, citing his interest in the measurement of specific heats.[79] He was indeed sceptical, certainly ambivalent, about claims for the transformative role of science and technology in war. One can detect in Blackett's commitment to operational research a critique not only of the unscientific armed services for conducting operations on 'gusts of emotion' as Blackett put it,[80] but also of the claims made for new weapons:

'New weapons for old' is apt to become a very popular cry. The success of some new devices has led to a new form of escapism which runs somewhat thus – 'Our present equipment doesn't work very well; training is bad, spare parts non-existent. Let's have an entirely new gadget!' Then comes the vision of the new gadget, springing like Aphrodite from the Ministry of Aircraft Production, in full production, complete with spares, and attended by a chorus of trained crews.

One of the tasks of an Operational Research Section is to make possible at least an approach to a numerical estimate of the merits of a change over from one device to another, by continual investigation of the actual performance of existing weapons, and by objective analysis of the likely performance of new ones ... In general, one might conclude that relatively too much scientific effort has been expended hitherto in the production of new devices and too little on the proper use of what we have got.[81]

Indeed Blackett argued that many mistakes had been made by considering the effects of new weapons, before considering possible changes in tactics: 'a new weapon may be demanded which promises an improved yield over existing weapons with existing tactics, but which may prove to give a lower yield compared with existing weapons with improved tactics'.[82] It is hardly surprising that Blackett conceived of operational

[78] In a BBC lecture in 1958, cited in Bernard Lovell, 'Patrick Maynard Stuart Blackett', *Biographical memoirs of Fellows of the Royal Society* 21 (1975), 75.
[79] *The Times*, 15 July 1974.
[80] 'The scientist can encourage numerical thinking on operational matters, and so can help to avoid running the war by gusts of emotion' ('Scientists at the operational level' (December 1941), reprinted in *The Advancement of Science*, 5(17)(1948), 28). From the context it seems unlikely that the accusation is directed only at service personnel.
[81] Blackett, 'Scientists at the operational level', 27–9.
[82] P. M. S. Blackett, 'A note on certain aspects of the methodology of operational research' (1943), reprinted in *The Advancement of Science*, 5(17) (1948), 31. See Erik P. Rau, 'Technological systems, expertise and policy making: the British origins of operational

research, among other things, as a bridge between operations and the technical departments of the services.

But this crucial contrast between operational research and R&D is missing from Blackett's and indeed other scientific intellectuals' own reflections. But it was important, and is something which linked Blackett and Tizard. Already in 1938 Tizard stressed that in the war 'the main things to do will be to get on even faster with the job of applying the results of research'.[83] In 1942 he told the newly appointed Ministry of Production scientific advisers that the 'able scientific young men' in the establishments produced weapons 'unsuited for efficient large-scale production'; what was needed was weapons to be used so that it 'followed that the development branches of industry ... were of supreme importance in the war', but were neglected.[84] More strongly still at the first meeting of the 'independent scientific advisers' in June 1942 he told them that 'by far the greatest contribution that scientists could make at this stage was to do everything possible to improve the operational efficiency of equipment and methods now in use'. Therefore, 'on the whole if there were men available who were valuable for operational research, they were better employed on it in the interests of the war than on experimental work however important it might appear.' This was agreed, with Blackett clearly supporting 'taking the best people away for operational research as soon as possible'.[85] It is hardly surprising that both Tizard and Blackett were both opposed to the building of a British atomic bomb.[86] As we shall see, in the 1960s both Blackett, and another scientific mandarin, Solly Zuckerman, came to accept that Britain was doing too much rather than too little R&D.

Blackett had been a member of the wartime Maud Committee which concluded that building an atomic bomb was indeed possible, but had alone argued that Britain could not hope to build a bomb on its own during the war.[87] Blackett, one of Britain's leading nuclear physicists, soon to be a Nobel Laureate, did not work on the British wartime bomb project; he did not go to Los Alamos or Harwell or Woolwich or

research' in Michael Allen and Gabrielle Hecht (eds.), *Technologies of power: essays in honor of Thomas Parke Hughes and Agatha Chipley Hughes* (Cambridge, MA: MIT Press, 2001), pp. 215–52 and Crook, 'Science and war', 69–101.

[83] Sir Henry Tizard to Professer J. Lennard-Jones, 11 October 1938, Tizard Papers, HTT 65, IWM.

[84] 'Note of meeting with the Ministry of Production scientific advisers', Tizard Papers, HTT 19/39, IWM.

[85] 'Notes of First Informal meeting of independent scientific advisers held in Sir Henry Tizard's office, MAP, on Monday 8 June 1942', Tizard Papers, HTT 298, IWM.

[86] For Tizard's opposition see note dated 8 July 1943, Tizard Papers, HTT 20/21, IWM.

[87] Margaret Gowing, *Britain and atomic energy* (London: Macmillan, 1964), pp. 78, 80. It was Blackett's minority view which was accepted by the MAP, then responsible for the project (p. 92).

Aldermaston.[88] He was a member of the Advisory Committee on Atomic Energy, 1945–7, but his opposition to a British bomb, cogently expressed, 'undoubtedly led to his almost total exclusion from the inner advisory circles of government for the next sixteen years'.[89] His *Military and political consequences of atomic energy* published in 1948 was the public expression of his dissent from a key policy of the state.[90] What was interesting and important in Blackett's arguments was that he linked atomic bombing with strategic bombing; he did not, as so many scientific propagandists have done then and since, argue that the atomic bomb ushered in a new era of warfare. He was also a distinctive voice on the left, and the scientific left in particular, in his approach to war. He was one of the very few, in either category, who concerned themselves with strategy, and one of the few who was a military-technological, as well as geopolitical, realist.[91] Another way in which he shows his realism was in his analysis of the role of science and technology in development. He argued the need for poor countries to adopt 'old technology' rather than 'new science'.[92]

Blackett was very much a man of the left, and as such was certainly aware of and critical of the claims of technocrats. In a broadcast republished in *The frustration of science* in 1935 Blackett held, in a classic bit of reductionist Marxist prejudice, that the peasants and lower middle classes were against science. Capitalism, requiring their political support, was becoming anti-scientific and leading to fascism. The only alternative was large-scale socialist planning:

You are now being told – and in the next few years you will be told again a thousand times – that there is a third way, neither Socialism nor Capitalism, but something called a planned economy, which will benefit everyone equally. You

[88] His 1948 Nobel prize was one of many Britain picked up in physics in the late 1940s: Appleton in 1947, Powell in 1950, and Cockcroft and Walton in 1951. Britain's interwar physics prizes were C. T. R. Wilson, 1927; Sir Owen Richardson 1928; Paul Dirac 1933; James Chadwick, 1935, and G. P. Thomson 1937. Britain won no further physics prizes in the remainder of the 1950s or 1960s, but picked up a clutch in the 1970s. On how these men got these prizes, and why they got them when they did, see Robert Marc Friedman, *The politics of excellence: behind the Nobel Prize in science* (New York: Times Books, 2001).
[89] Lovell, 'Blackett', p. 71; see M. M. Gowing, *Independence and deterrence*, (London: Macmillan, 1975), I, pp. 115, 171–2 and app. 8.
[90] (London: Turnstile, 1948). Mary Jo Nye, 'A physicist in the corridors of power: P. M. S. Blackett's opposition to atomic weapons following the war', *Physics Perspectives* 1 (1999), 136–56.
[91] Michael Howard, 'P. M. S. Blackett' in John Baylis and John Garnett (eds.), *Makers of nuclear strategy* (London: Pinter, 1991), pp. 153–63.
[92] Alexis De Greiff, 'The International Centre for Theoretical Physics, 1960–1979: ideology and practice in a United Nations institution for scientific cooperation and Third World development', unpublished doctoral thesis, University of London (2001).

will be told, for instance, that unemployment insurance and housing policy should be taken out of politics and treated objectively, scientifically. As if such questions are not the very essence of politics![93]

'I believe there are only two ways to go, and the way we seem to be starting leads to fascism ... Scientists have not perhaps very long to make up their minds on which side they stand.'[94] Clearly, for Blackett, as for others, only socialism was compatible with the continued advance of science. But socialism required not only a political understanding, but also political action. Importantly he did not mean by this that scientists should have a greater role in government as such: what he was calling for was political commitment:

We cannot look to the scientists for salvation. Mr Wells at one time appeared to think that the scientists might save us. Then more recently it was going to be international financiers. But so many committed suicide. So now it is going to be the aviators. Perhaps soon we will be told to pin our hopes on a dictatorship of midwives.[95]

As President of the AScW (1943–6), Blackett wrote in his introduction to *Science and the nation*, that he, and the anonymous contributors to the volume, were

frankly and proudly partisan in our attitude to the main social tasks of today ... we find little to admire in those of our scientific colleagues who, faced by the great social problems of our time, are so frightfully scientific that they are unable to make up their minds on which side they stand.

He hoped that 'one of the results of the book will be that more of our scientific colleagues will be persuaded to stop sitting on the fence'.[96] Blackett did indeed stand with the left, in Britain and elsewhere, notably India.[97]

Yet *Science and the nation* found the military problematic. It claimed that

the real lesson which the development of 'scientific weapons' should make as clear as daylight is: when sufficiently large resources of finance, organisation and scientists are used there are few problems of the control and exploitation of Nature that cannot be solved, and often with unexpected speed.[98]

---

[93] P. M. S. Blackett, 'The frustration of science' in Sir Daniel Hall et al. *The frustration of science* (London: Allen & Unwin, 1935), p. 139.

[94] Ibid., p. 144.   [95] Ibid., p. 134.

[96] Association of Scientific Writers, *Science and the nation* (Harmondsworth: Penguin, 1947), p. xviii.

[97] R. S. Anderson, 'Patrick Blackett in India: military consultant and scientific intervenor, 1947–1972', *Notes and Records of the Royal Society of London* 53 (1999), 253–73 and 345–59. C. Butler, 'Recollections of Patrick Blackett, 1945–1970', *Notes and Records of the Royal Society* 53 (1999), 143–56.

[98] AScW, *Science and the nation*, p. 243.

Although putting 'scientific weapons' in quotation marks, suggests a desire to distinguish science from weapons, there was no hint of inefficiency or wastefulness of wartime research, nor indeed was there any particular objection to the way science had been used in the war on the British side, only perhaps of opportunities forgone.[99] The only two examples I know of doubts as to whether science or engineering in fact advanced come from Sir William Stanier, a member of the wartime Engineering Advisory Council, and from Sir Henry Tizard.[100]

Yet despite the radical plans proposed to mobilise science in the service of the nation, *Science and the nation* did not wish to highlight that research activity already so mobilised: only a passing reference was made to post-war services research, despite it being so central a part of the nation's actual research effort.[101] The most obvious features of the relations of science and the nation could not easily be addressed. Indeed most scientific intellectuals of the 1940s and 1950s ignored the post-war military R&D effort, and with it the bulk of the state research corps. The problem was that highlighting the significance of the military in post-war British R&D, dwelling on science–military relations, was to engage in communist propaganda. There was a very significant deradicalisation of intellectual politics in

---

[99] Ibid., p. 243. This asked readers to balance the scientific war effort against an equally large war on disease which might have been launched. There was no sense of setbacks here, only the possibility of greater progress still.

[100] 'It is a mistake to suppose that science advances rapidly in a war. Certain branches of science may receive a special stimulus, but on the whole the advance of knowledge is slowed.' Sir Henry Tizard, 'The passing world', Presidential Address to the British Association for the Advancement of Science, September 1948. Widely published, including in *The Advancement of Science*, 5(19) (1948), 155–64 and *Nature*. In a 1956 article in which he gave many examples of the way in which the two world wars advanced British engineering Stanier wrote:

> The foregoing may suggest that the influence of war on the advancement of engineering is wholly beneficial. But it should be noted that though war stimulates advances it does so only in restricted fields. In other fields advance is brought almost to a halt not merely 'for the duration' but for long afterwards ... during the war, the thoughts of many brilliant men had to be turned away from the creation of things beneficial to the human race and concentrated upon devising new means of destruction or new means of averting an enemy's destructive intentions ... But little was learnt from much of that activity which can be applied in peace, certainly not nearly as much as could have been learnt had all the brains and insight been applied to the advancement and construction of peaceful appliances. In short, the influence of war upon engineering advancement is to distort rather than to further it. The benefit, so very apparent in certain fields, is, in this writer's opinion, more than over-balanced by the setbacks suffered in other fields and the wastage of talent inherent in the design of destructive instead of constructive things.

Sir William Stanier, 'The influence of war', *The Engineer*, Centenary Number (1956), 172.

[101] AScW, *Science and the nation*, p. 166.

'Natopolitan culture', and this turning a blind eye was one of the consequences.[102] A particularly clear official example is given by the 1956 Reith lectures, given that year by Sir Edward Appleton, former secretary of the DSIR (1939–49). He called his lectures, 'Science and the nation', but felt that he had to explain his title, because science was obviously international. His lecture on science and war implies that before the war scientists were all civil; his lecture on government and science is mostly concerned with civil science.[103] As we will explore more fully in a later chapter, that is exactly how most historians of British science have understood British science and British science–war relations.

Blackett, Labour and science policy

The Labour party had lost the 1959 general election – the third one in a row. Following that defeat there were divisions within the party on many key issues, but they were particularly focused on the issue of public ownership (centred on a proposal to change the famous clause 4 of the party constitution) and on nuclear disarmament (this was the era of CND). Long before the election of Harold Wilson as leader there was a proposal to defuse ideological divisions by developing a 'forward-looking policy' centred on the 'scientific revolution'. These were the key ideas in the policy part of the fascinating document presented to the 1960 party conference by its general secretary, Morgan Philips, called *Labour in the sixties*. The document claimed:

The central feature of our post-war capitalist society is the scientific revolution. Both its pace and its extent are beyond the dreams of previous generations. New

---

[102] E. P. Thompson, 'Outside the whale' (1960), reprinted in *The poverty of theory and other essays* (London: Merlin, 1978), pp. 1–34. There is a striking contrast between the flourishing Marxist historiography of the 1950s, in which E. P. Thompson played a leading part, and the weakness of Marxist studies of science. It is also interesting to note that the Marxist historians did not engage with the history of science and technology, despite the pioneering work of J. D. Bernal. See Eric Hobsbawm, 'The Historians' Group of the Communist party' in Maurice Cornforth (ed.), *Rebels and their causes: essays in honour of A. L. Morton* (London: Lawrence & Wishart, 1978), pp. 21–48.

[103] Sir Edward Appleton, *Science and the nation: the BBC Reith Lectures for 1956* (Edinburgh: Edinburgh University Press, 1957). The 1953 Reith lectures involved a similar evasion. Given by J. Robert Oppenheimer, they were expected by the public at least to be about the bomb, and Oppenheimer's troubles. Instead they got history and philosophy of science. See Freeman Dyson, preface to J. Robert Oppenheimer, *Atom and void: essays on science and community* (Princeton: Princeton University Press, 1989), which reprinted the lectures, which were published in 1954 as *Science and the common understanding*. Freeman Dyson approved of Oppenheimer's evasion. Oppenheimer is of course the key case of the scientist whose involvement in war is moralized away.

discoveries and inventions now produce upheavals in five or ten years which previously took a century to complete ... In the 1960s mankind is conquering nature, releasing new sources of energy and even voyaging out into space in ways which were still no more than schoolboy fantasies when the war ended. This scientific revolution has made it physically possible, for the first time in human history, to conquer poverty and disease, to move towards universal literacy and to achieve living standards for the masses higher than those enjoyed by tiny privileged classes in previous epochs. The central issue of politics throughout the world today is not merely how the new riches shall be distributed with and between the nations but – just as important – how the new powers and energies now released by science shall be controlled.[104]

This typical futuristic banishing of all existing politics was extremely useful. Philips went on to claim that Labour's new 'criticism of contemporary capitalism' was based 'on the demands of the new world towards which we are moving, and our indictment is that scientific progress is being throttled and distorted by obsolete policies'. This was a bizarre claim, given that the central argument was that scientific progress was happening faster than ever! Yet it was necessary to make the argument to justify a policy, even a very vague one, of greater state involvement. And here too the futuristic emphasis on the radically new present banished any reflection of past policies for these matters. There was no recognition of the already central role of the British state in science.[105]

By 1964, especially under the leadership of Harold Wilson from 1963, the association between socialism and the scientific revolution was central to Labour's arguments, and this was the key theme of Wilson's 'white heat' speech, one of the two or three most famous political speeches in the history of post-war Britain. Blackett, like Snow, was closely associated with Labour's thinking on the scientific revolution, and saw himself as one of the key creators of Labour's science and technology policy, and especially the Ministry of Technology. Blackett was sitting at Harold Wilson's side when he gave the 'white heat' speech at the Scarborough conference in 1963, and it was incorrectly rumoured that he had written it.[106] It was later thought that Blackett would enter the government (as in fact did C. P. Snow and Vivian Bowden), and some newspapers commented that Whitehall still regarded Blackett as a security risk.[107]

Blackett had a very particular conception of what Labour needed to do in government. He developed a distinct personal conception, based on this wartime experience and his association with the National

---

[104] Morgan Philips, *Labour in the sixties* (1960), pp. 5–6.   [105] Ibid., p. 6.
[106] Lovell, 'Blackett', p. 78n. Wilson wrote it himself in the early hours of the same day.
[107] Solly Zuckerman, *Six men out of the ordinary* (London: Peter Owen, 1992), p. 34. See also Lovell, 'Blackett'.

Research Development Corporation (NRDC). The NRDC had been created by Harold Wilson in 1948 under the Board of Trade.[108] It had very limited functions: it was charged with the commercialisation of patents derived from public sector work. It gave funds to the private sector to develop new technologies, analogous to launching aid for aircraft, but on a much smaller scale. From at least the very early 1960s the NRDC was at the centre of Labour plans for technical modernisation, for example in Labour's policy document of 1961, *Signposts for the sixties*.[109] Wilson made a number of references to NRDC in 1963/4 as the example of what could be done, talking of Hovercraft, the Atlas computer and fuel cells.[110] This was the standard list of innovative technologies cited by Labour, and they were all NRDC projects.[111] For Blackett the NRDC could provide the core of a new government ministry, and a new policy for state research. In January 1964 Blackett produced a paper in which he called for Ministry of Industry and Technology to be made up of the NRDC (which a hugely expanded budget) and possibly the industrial research associations funded by the DSIR. The clear central aim was to put finance for industrial research into industry. Indeed he hoped that government researchers would *transfer to industry* as government projects were cut back. He saw a paper he had written on the lack of R&D in British industry in 1959, as a key step in this argument.[112] Blackett was in effect expressing a serious disillusionment with all government research, and wanting to keep most of it away from his proposed ministry. Blackett thought there might be a case for the transfer to his proposed

[108] S. T. Keith, 'Invention, patents and commercial development from governmentally financed research in Great Britain: the origins of the National Research Development Corporation', *Minerva* 19 (1981),92–122.

[109] David Horner, 'The road to Scarborough: Wilson, Labour and the scientific revolution' in R. Coopey, S. Fielding and N. Tiratsoo (eds.), *The Wilson governments 1964–1970* (London: Pinter, 1993), p. 59.

[110] In various speeches and in private, for example, 'Notes of a meeting with Harold Wilson on October 7th 1963', Hetherington Papers, 5, LSE archives, where he refers to 'digital computers', Hovercraft and fuel cells. The 1964 manifesto also mentioned the NRDC in the context of 'The Hovercraft and the Atlas computer', *Let's go with Labour for the new Britain*, p. 9. On the computer project see John Hendry, 'Prolonged negotiations: the British Fast computer project and the early history of the British computer industry', *Business History* 26 (1984), 280–306, and *Innovating for failure* (Cambridge, MA: MIT Press, 1990).

[111] For example in 1961 Blackett referred to 'superfast computers, fuel cells, hovercraft, etc', in 'Notes for a speech in support of A. W. Benn, Bristol South East, 28 April 1961', Blackett Papers, H89, Royal Society.

[112] In December 1966 Blackett prepared a mimeographed volume on *Science, technology and government: some lectures and speeches* addressed to people in government. It consisted of a 1959 paper on the need for more R&D in industry; two articles from 1964 on technology, and an account of the first year of Mintech. See Blackett Papers, H123, Royal Society Archives.

ministry of Ministry of Defence laboratories in the future, and if defence work reduced; he thought it possible that the AEA should be split up between different ministries in the future; and that the DSIR (minus its university responsibilities) should be kept going just to run the big government laboratories, especially the NPL.[113] The key emphasis was on making private industry more efficient: 'this may be emotionally distasteful at times, but the challenge must be faced', he wrote to Crossman.[114] Blackett maintained his particular vision of what a Labour government should do. On the eve of the election, in September 1964, he prepared an argument for a 'Ministry of Technology'. Again he wanted a new ministry, rather than a new part of the Board of Trade or a new organisation around the Ministry of Aviation, now on the grounds of 'speed'. He also claimed that the Board of Trade was notoriously unscientific, and the Ministry of Aviation solution was unsuitable because of the 'commercial attitude needed in the civil field, compared with the cost-plus tradition of the MoA'. What was needed was a 'new and small Ministry of Technology' made up at first of the NRDC and an 'intelligence division' of some fifty specialists.[115] Labour went into the election promising the creation of a Ministry of Technology of undefined scope and powers.

The Ministry of Technology was created, and although it included the NRDC, it was very different from what Blackett proposed, and indeed would become something completely different very quickly. The Ministry of Technology, as the following chapter will show, is better seen on quite another trajectory than as the embodiment of the techno-declinist rhetoric of Snow, Blackett and Wilson. More importantly still, the ministry's own understanding of technocratic modernisation was to be very different from Blackettt's, and indeed of the techno-declinists as a whole. It was no longer believed that British industry had underspent on R&D. Blackett was later to echo these conclusions in speeches, with some conviction, as the scientific adviser to the Minister

---

[113] P. M. S. Blackett, 'The case for a Ministry of Industry and Technology', 17 January 1964. Although the form is different, the content of 'The case for a Ministry of Technology' September 1964 is very similar. Both are in Blackett Papers, E49, Royal Society Archives.

[114] P. M. S. Blackett to R. H. S. Crossman, 23 February 1964, Blackett Papers, E49, Royal Society Archives. In the letter Blackett makes the argument in the two papers above. In a letter to T. Pitt at the Labour party on the following day, he notes that 'Dick convinced me over the telephone today that it would be better to transfer the AEA and DSIR complete to the MOIT at the start'. Blackett soon returned to his original idea, though the new ministry as set up was very close to Crossman's suggestion.

[115] 'The case for a Ministry of Technology', September 1964, Blackett Papers, E49, Royal Society.

of Technology, and at the same time, as president of the Royal Society. He argued forcibly for a greater role for the private sector and a running down of the public sector. As Hilary and Steven Rose pointed out in *Science and society*, published in 1969, it was a bit rich for Britain's great socialist scientist to argue this way.[116] Tony Benn, the second Minister of Technology, later the great standard bearer for the left, congratulated Blackett noting warmly that it 'was a sign of the times that a PRS [President of the Royal Society] should be talking about industry and be reported on "Business News"'.[117]

The politics of technocratic modernisation revisited

The implication of the technocratic critiques from the left was that Labour's opponents were anti-scientific or indeed anti-modernisation. A brilliant political move, it is clearly misleading as an account of the practice of Conservative governments, their ideological positions and of the politics of the experts. There were differences between Labour and Conservative intellectuals, though, and they are rather interesting. Indeed the politics of science around 1960 was much richer than the standard readings suggest, and indeed very surprisingly different from the standard accounts in some respects.

Conservative intellectuals denied any necessary connection between socialism and the scientific revolution, as would be expected, but some also rejected declinism and the 'two cultures' arguments. The lawyer Lord Hailsham (or Quintin Hogg, as he reverted to), who in the crucial period 1959 to 1964 was the Minister for Science and briefly Minister of Education and Science, is a particularly pertinent example.[118] In 1963 he published a small book on *Science and politics* which clearly shows the influence of liberal concern with state encroachment on science. Indeed he accepted but questioned the powerful linkages between state and science already existing:

there is a sense in which I continue to regard the results of Government patronage as something of a paradox, and I am tempted to speculate whether, in the end, the

---

[116] H. Rose and S. Rose, *Science and society* (Harmondsworth: Penguin, 1969), pp. 120, 122, 153.

[117] Minister of Technology to Blackett 21 February 1968, referring to the coverage of a speech the previous evening. Blackett Papers, H89, Royal Society Archives.

[118] He was also Lord President of the Council, 1960–64, the senior post which traditionally carried responsibility for the research councils. Hailsham's grandfather, also Quintin Hogg, had founded the Regent Street polytechnic (now part of the University of Westminster).

influence of and interest by Government so obviously materially motivated will not obscure the very insights on which creative science is essentially based.[119]

Noting the very great importance of government and the uses to which it put science he asked: 'Who will deny that, in the process, both the state, and science, have to some extent been corrupted?'[120] He went on:

I remain obstinately of the opinion that, in the long run, the marriage between science and defence is corrupting, and will at best turn science from a liberating to a destructive force, and at worst ultimately dry up the wells of inventiveness in the scientist himself.[121]

It is significant too that Hailsham derided what he called the 'legend of the "two cultures"', with a typically pompous put-down:

Sir Charles Snow's diagnosis of the 'two cultures' is thus perhaps more a reflection of the politics in the Senior Common Room, than of life in the real world. Neither in exegetical nor in fundamental terms does it stand up to examination.[122]

After calling for a thorough modernisation of Britain he decisively rejected declinist exaggerations – only the USSR and the USA were possibly better and that was largely a question of scale – 'No one should think that the Europeans have yet matched us' he asserted.[123]

Hailsham's critique was, it seems, influenced by the impressive intellectual counter-revolution led by the émigré chemist and philosopher Michael Polanyi, which denied the equation of science with socialism and planning, condemned the planning of science, and the failure to distinguish science from technology, and science from scientism. It comes as no surprise that Polanyi was hostile to the Snow's 'two cultures'.[124] For Polanyi, as for the scientific left, arguments about science were intimately related to particular political economies and historiographies of science.[125] Like other 'Austrian' philosophers of science, and like

---

[119] Lord Hailsham, *Science and politics* (London: Faber and Faber, 1963), p. 13.
[120] Ibid., p. 14.   [121] Ibid., p. 15.   [122] Ibid., p. 33.   [123] Ibid., p. 59.
[124] See his comments in 'Two cultures', *Encounter* 13 (1959), 61–4; reprinted in Marjorie Green (ed.), *Knowing and being: essays by Michael Polanyi* (London: Routledge & Kegan Paul, 1969). Thanks to Guy Ortolano.
[125] On this see Anna-K. Mayer, 'Setting up a discipline: conflicting agendas of the Cambridge History of Science Committee, 1936–1950', *Studies in the History and Philosophy of Science* 31 (2000), 665 –89, and also Jessica Reinisch, 'The Society for Freedom in Science, 1940–1963', unpublished MSc thesis, university of London (2000). The key members of the Society for Freedom in Science were closely tied emotionally and intellectually with the anti-Marxist, anti-Keynesian and anti-technocratic economists, notably Friedrich von Hayek, John Jewkes and Lionel Robbins. The connections ran deep – for example Polanyi was a close friend of his Manchester colleague John Jewkes, and was an important member, like Jewkes, of Hayek's Mont Pèlerin Society. See Richard Cockett, *Thinking the unthinkable: think*

the 'Austrian' economists, Polanyi was deeply committed to liberalism, and to anti-holistic, micro-thinking. However, Polanyi and his colleagues did not concern themselves with the research that went on in government and industrial laboratories. The latter, they acknowledged was and should be directed, but it was not 'science'.[126] Interestingly enough in the 1950s John Baker, a founder of the Society for Freedom in Science, thought the society needed a statement of policy in reconciling 'freedom in science on the one hand, and the necessity for secrecy in certain parts of nuclear research on the other' – without it the society was in a weak position, 'at the mercy of communists and fellow travellers who pretend to be interested in the freedom of science'. Nothing would come of this, for perhaps obvious reasons.[127]

The *Spectator*, the Conservative-leaning intellectual weekly which had published Leavis's attack on Snow, had a nice line in criticising the technocratic pretensions of the Labour party. Commenting on Harold Wilson's 'white heat' speech it observed that there was very little between the parties in terms of commitments to science. This view is supported by later research.[128] But the *Spectator* regretted, doubtless disingenuously, but nevertheless effectively, the disappearance of traditional Labour themes from Wilson's rhetoric: 'the big magic of scientific progress was there to divert attention from part of the traditional attitudes of the Labour Party disappearing into the gullet of a technocratic Moloch', it pithily noted. It went on –

the image presented at Scarborough of a Britain pulsing with dynamic energies where technologists and scientists will be valued at their proper financial worth is hardly that of a more just or a more humane society. It is a society of technocratic privilege, high salaries and early coronary thrombosis, of men with Sir Charles Snow's future lurking in their bones, like strontium-90 ... it was the ad-man's image of an efficient Britain that was stamped upon the conference, unexpectedly

---

tanks and the economic counterrevolution 1931–1983 (London: Fontana, 1995; first published 1994), *passim*. For the role of the Congress of Cultural Freedom (and thus the CIA) in supporting Polanyi's International Society for Freedom in Science, and later in supporting the journal *Minerva* see Frances Stonor Saunders, *Who paid the piper? The CIA and the cultural cold war* (London: 2000).

[126] See William McGucken, 'On freedom and planning in science: the Society for Freedom in Science, 1940–1946', *Minerva* 16 (1978), 42–72. John R. Baker, *The scientific life* (London: Allen & Unwin, 1942) and Michael Polanyi, 'The republic of science: its political and economic theory', *Minerva* 1 (1962), 54–73, both ignore, not always explicitly, the vast bulk of scientific activity.

[127] J. R. Baker to H. H. Dale, 26 September 1951; and SFS document of 1955 quoted in Reinisch, 'The Society for Freedom in Science'.

[128] Norman J. Vig, *Science and technology in British politics* (Oxford: Pergamon, 1968) is good on this.

reviving the language of *laissez-faire* and the iron laws that regard an expanding economy as self-sufficient and self-explanatory.

It went on to make the point that Wilson's speech was no guide to what needed to be done, but noted 'something which even political opponents of the Labour Party may be allowed to regret, that this year's slogan should represent the movement's abandoning of concern for the quality of life and its direction in favour of one of the more vulgar myths of our time'.[129] This explicitly anti-technocratic message is, however, combined in this case, as in Hailsham's arguments, with a commitment to rapid economic growth. It is hard to find a genuine reactionary in the debates of the 1960s, except in the propaganda of the left.

Moving to the left the picture is also somewhat different from the usual image. One group with a particular interest in the politics of science and technology was the small British Communist party. They did indeed hold distinctive though changing critical positions on British science. In 1945 J. D. Bernal, the most committed and influential of the communist scientists, celebrated the fact that in the war in democratic countries the total and voluntary mobilisation of science, 'for a purpose which scientists recognised as a valid one', 'enriched the content and method of science'; during the war 'scientific effort flourished'. He lauded, and embraced as a model for the future, research organised in large interdisciplinary teams, with no financial restrictions, and controlled by scientists. There is not a hint of criticism or concern about wartime research.[130] Bernal had enthused not just about the organisation of research in the war, but welcomed the dropping of the atomic bombs on Japan, following the line of Communist parties everywhere. However, as the cold war got under way, the Soviet Union and Communist parties condemned atomic weapons, and military research more generally.[131] In the late 1940s Bernal criticised British research policy, characterising what was happening as 'firstly, the trend toward predominant concentration on war research; secondly the trend towards an emphasis on immediate export production and away from long-term development in industry; and lastly the trend

---

[129] 'Shadow and substance', *The Spectator*, 11 October 1963.
[130] J. D. Bernal 'Lessons of the war for science', first published in *Reports on Progress in Physics*, 1945 and reproduced in *Proceedings of the Royal Society* A 342 (1975), 555–74, on 555.
[131] Lawrence Wittner, *One world or none* (Stanford: Stanford University Press, 1993), pp. 171–5. For the Soviet view see also 'Dr Einstein's mistaken notions: an open letter from Sergei Vavilov, A. N. Frumkin, A. F. Joffe and N. N. Semyonov' (1947) reprinted in Albert Einstein, *Out of my later years* (New Jersey: Citadel Press, 1956), pp. 161–8.

towards increasing colonial research'.[132] While we can dispute some aspects of this analysis – in particular the second point – Bernal's account was broadly correct. The AScW, during Bernal's presidency, which followed Blackett's, highlighted the importance of warlike R&D in the British post-war research effort.[133] Bernal himself regularly pointed to the relatively high levels of defence expenditure in the UK, and the very high proportion of the R&D budget spent by the military.[134] Bernal now upheld a view of a pristine science which the bomb corrupted: war increasingly had the object of 'blind slaughter without even military excuse'; this was 'foreign to the whole tradition of science' but if accepted would lead to scientists losing 'all sense of social responsibility and moral value in science'. It also gave 'apparent justification to the non-scientific public to associate science with war in its most horrible aspects'. The bomb would also, through military secrecy, destroy free scientific communication.[135]

Communists continued to stress the weight of defence in British R&D: in 1967 it was claimed by the *Morning Star* science correspondent that half of all R&D was for the military, and a quarter of scientists and engineers were on military projects (an exaggeration by 1967): 'This represents a monstrous perversion of science ... [weapons] represent frustration of science rather than fulfilment'.[136] A key sub-argument was that military involvement delayed and distorted civilian technology. For example, Bernal regretted that military nuclear development was delaying civil use.[137] As we shall see a version of this argument became very influential from the 1960s and 1970s, well outside the Communist party. More generally, the party argued that even Labour governments had proved incapable of planning science. For example, it was claimed that 'each post-war British government has feared and fought against real planning of science. Important inventions have been starved of support and sometimes have been handed over to the Americans, who have developed them'; Quintin Hogg, the Conservative Minister for Science was really a 'Minister for anti-science', Harold Wilson's 'white heat' led to 'no real planning of science, "purposive" or otherwise'.[138] As we shall see, in less stark terms, this analysis was to become quite common on the left.

---

[132] J. D. Bernal and Maurice Cornforth, *Science for peace and socialism* (London: Birch Books, 1949), p. 31.
[133] D. S. Horner, 'Scientists, trade unions and the labour movement policies for science and technology, 1947–1964', unpublished doctoral thesis, University of Aston (1986), ch. 1.
[134] J. D. Bernal and Maurice Cornforth, *Science for peace and socialism* (London: Birch, 1949); J. D. Bernal, *World without war*.(London: Routledge & Kegan Paul, 1958).
[135] Bernal and Cornforth, *Science for peace and socialism*.
[136] John Moss, *The scientific revolution* (London: Lawrence & Wishart, 1967), p. 8.
[137] Bernal, *World without war*, p. 47.   [138] Moss, *Scientific revolution*, pp. 53, 5.

Much of the New Left which emerged in the late 1950s was as committed to a technocratic declinist account of Britain as the old left. That might seem surprising, for it is notorious that the New Left took no interest in science[139] or indeed the warfare state.[140] It was perhaps precisely this lack of engagement that allowed the standard old left arguments to be accepted by the New Left, and has led historians of the New Left to ignore this crucial aspect of its ideological make-up. Taking it into account allows us to shed new light on one of the key controversies within the New Left, the famous exchange between Perry Anderson, Tom Nairn and E. P. Thompson in the mid-1960s. Perry Anderson had dismissed the British intellectuals and technocrats as useless. He discounted the importance of British intellectual Marxism of the 1930s, which was, in his view, dominated by 'poets and natural scientists – the two vocations most unsuited to effect any lasting transformation of British culture'. He went on: 'where there was a bid to "apply" their formal beliefs, the outcome was frequently bad art and false science: at its worst the rhymes of Spender and the fantasies of Bernal'.[141] For all this dismissal of British intellectual traditions, Anderson was a very British analyst of his time, reproducing in his own distinctive language the key theses of the techno-declinists: 'Today Britain stands revealed as a sclerosed, archaic society, trapped and burdened by its past successes' he claimed; the causes were old 'under-investment at home, lagging technological innovation since the end of the last century'; the Treasury, after the City of London (the great financial centre), was 'the second great albatross round the neck of British economic growth'. The British state needed to be interventionist, technocratic, but all it offered was 'universal dilettantism and anachronistic economic liberalism', while the British educational system was only belatedly scientific. And so on and so forth.[142]

Just as Anderson's polemic is not known for its techno-declinism nor is E. P. Thompson's famous response known for its anti-declinism. Thompson contended that political economy and science were central to English ideology in the nineteenth century and beyond. In close relation with these points he contended that Anderson (and Nairn) also

---

[139] Hilary Rose and Steven Rose, 'The radicalisation of science', *Socialist Register 1972*, pp. 117–18.

[140] See Lin Chun, *The British new left* (Edinburgh: Edinburgh University Press, 1993); Michael Kenny, *The first new left: British intellectuals after Stalin* (London: Lawrence & Wishart, 1995); Dennis Dworkin, *Cultural marxism in post-war Britain: history, the new left, and the origins of cultural studies* (Durham, NC: Duke University Press, 1997).

[141] Perry Anderson, 'Components of the national culture', *New Left Review* 50 (July-August 1968), 11.

[142] 'The origins of the present crisis', *New Left Review* 23 (January-February 1964).

ignored the Protestant and bourgeois democratic inheritance, and that they confused the British empirical idiom with an empiricist ideology.[143] Thompson noted the 'uncomfortable affinity of tone' between the pronouncements of Perry Anderson and Tom Nairn on the one hand, and 'the journalistic diagnosticians of the British malaise whom they profess to despise ... Mr David Frost, Mr Shanks, and Comrade Anderson are saying different things but there is the same edge to the voice'. Thompson worried that they all overlooked 'certain strengths and humane traditions' in Britain, but more importantly, in attacking what they saw as left-overs from Old Corruption, they were blind to the reality that a 'new, and entirely different, predatory complex occupies the state'. He asked whether it was not to this new Thing of vast power and influence, 'rather than to the hunting of an aristocratic Snark, that an analysis of the political formations of our time should be addressed?'[144] Interestingly he did not give the Thing a more specifically modern name – nor indeed did he complain of a British military–industrial complex or a British warfare state; he had a wide and rather vague concept in mind. But there was an inkling here of something the rest of the left implicitly denied existed, except as yet another archaic remnant.

Part of the power of the vast technocratic Thing was that when necessary it could fit neatly into the preferences of left and right, having no independent ideological charge of its own, being largely invisible in British intellectual culture. It was also invisible because both the left and right were very nationalistic about technology, and no area of technology was more national than military and related technology. Not surprisingly it is neo-liberals who identified the syndrome. The economist David Henderson, who worked in the Ministry of Aviation in the early 1960s, dubbed it 'bipartisan technological chauvinism'.[145] Samuel Brittan, a well-known economic journalist of the 1960s, was to call attention to, with respect to state support of the arms trade, 'a near perfect fusion of the right-wing belief in "my country right or wrong" and the left-wing belief in industrial intervention and subsidy'.[146] Certainly, the aeronautical engineers, when they put pen to paper, struck a powerful right-wing techno-nationalist note.[147] For example, the aero-engine designer Sir Roy Fedden wrote an alarmist pro-air and pro-technology

---

[143] E. P. Thompson, 'The peculiarities of the English' (1965), reprinted in *The poverty of theory* (London: Merlin, 1978), p. 57.

[144] E. P. Thompson, 'The peculiarities of the English', in *The poverty of theory*, p. 56.

[145] See his *Innocence and design* (London: Economist, 1986).

[146] Samuel Brittan, 'Lessons of Iraqgate', *Financial Times* 23 November 1992.

[147] Prince Philip is often found as a signatory to congratulatory prefaces to books about the aircraft industry. In the 1950s Prince Philip, in an echo of Victoria's consort, became the

tract in the late 1950s.[148] Sir Frank Whittle, though once a socialist, became a partisan of the right.[149] A particularly extraordinary case was that of (Sir) Barnes Wallis, the aircraft designer famous for inventing the bouncing bomb used in the 'Dambusters' raid, and the subject of one of the most famous British war films of the post-war years. Between the late 1950s and the early 1970s Wallis gave versions of a lecture with the all-too revealing title 'The strength of England'. He argued that England had the 'opportunity to regain our supremacy at sea' through the building of merchant nuclear submarines which could make Britain not only invulnerable to blockade, but would make England the centre of the trading world, for these submarines could travel under the north polar ice cap. Furthermore, Britain could become the 'Clapham Junction of the air' if it developed a small, supersonic, short take-off and landing airliner – with it Britain would 'dominate the world, in the manner that pessimists now suggest must be the prerogative of the USA'. By contrast 'Not the Strength, not even the Weakness, but the Death of England' would follow the giving up of aircraft design to the USA. Finally, automation would also renew English strength. This extraordinary talk was first given at Eton in the 1950s, but the quotations are from the version he gave as his presidential address to section G of the British Association for the Advancement of Science in 1965.[150] Dramatically supporting the theses of David Henderson and Samuel Brittan, his speech was noted approvingly by Communist party daily *The Morning Star*. Wallis was presented as an inventor let down by government, and one who was keen to stop the Americans controlling British technology.[151] Wallis's political sympathies, incidentally, turned to the extreme right: he addressed the Monday Club in the late 1960s.[152]

'Prince Albert of the jet age' playing a big role stressing the importance of science and technology for Britain's future. See Richard Weight, *Patriots: national identity in Britain 1940–2000* (London: Macmillan, 2002), p. 236.

[148] Roy Fedden, *Britain's air survival: an appraisement and strategy for success* (London: Cassell, 1957); see also the papers of Barnes Wallis, Science Museum library. See generally, my *England and the aeroplane* (London: Macmillan, 1991).

[149] His biographer points out that he spoke in support of a Conservative candidate in 1955, and of another in 1964, and that on both occasions his comments were widely reported in the press on election day. The biographer notes that in 1964 he wrote an 'open letter to the voters of Smethwick which was a fierce attack on the Labour candidate, Patrick Gordon-Walker': John Golley, *Whittle: the true story* (Shrewsbury: Airlife, 1987), pp. 210–11. Golley does not say that Gordon-Walker lost due to a viciously racist campaign, which remains notorious. The Tory victor, Peter Griffiths, was famously called a 'parliamentary leper' by Harold Wilson, and he lost his seat in 1966.

[150] Barnes Wallis Papers, BNW H25, Science Museum Library. See also J. E. Morpurgo, *Barnes Wallis* (London: Longmans, 1972), ch. 17.

[151] Moss, *The scientific revolution*, p. 53.

[152] He gave a lecture to the Monday Club in the very late 1960s. 'Is there any hope that you will once more be willing to address the Monday Club? ... we all remember your

It is clear that the common implication that the British technocratic tradition, if it exists at all, is a left-wing one, cannot be right. One can draw an intellectual and policy line from J. D. Bernal's work of the 1930s, through the AScW's *Science and the nation* and the Labour party's discussions of science policies in the late 1950s and early 1960s, to the Ministry of Technology, seeing it as a failed application of the 'Bernalism' of the 1930s, but that is to miss most of the history of British technocracy, and most of the history of British science and technology policy.[153] Technocrats of the right have been less obviously political, but right-wing techno-nationalism has been a powerful strand of thinking.[154] More importantly, it is clear too that we should not confuse particular arguments about the nature of the state's policies for research with the state's actual policies. There was, putting it mildly, a gap between the commentary of the scientific intellectuals and the practices of the state.

As ever, the ideological story is more complex the more one looks into it, but in this particular case complexity needs particular stressing because of the impact of 'two cultures' thinking on the analysis of science itself. It keeps coming back imposing a fearful simplicity. Thinking does not correlate on science versus humanities lines at all, but it does help to note the centrality of certain forms of argument, notably, I have argued, the anti-history. The main effect has been to take the world of the scientist and engineers away from critical empirical gaze. Significantly, the key criticisms (however limited) of science as it was done (as opposed to general notions of science and what it did) came not from humanists, but from scientific and social scientific students of science. The neo-liberal students of science around Polanyi were among the most critical of scientism, for example. While the culturally oriented New Left consistently ignored the analysis of science and technology (Thompson being a partial exception), the old scientific left proposed a 'science of science', which was critical of the existing science policies of the state, in ways dating back to Bernal's *Social function*.[155] The sociology of *scientific*

wonderful lecture two years ago.' Meetings secretary, Monday Club to Sir Barnes Wallis, 22 March 1971, BNW H82, Science Museum Library. Wallis agreed but later had to cancel. The biography does not mention any of this.

[153] Werskey, *The visible college*; Horner, 'The road to Scarborough: Wilson, Labour and the scientific revolution'; Horner, 'Scientists, trade unions and Labour Movement policies for science and technology: 1947–1964', and Fred Steward and David Wield, 'Science, planning and the state' in Gregor McLennan, David Held and Stuart Hall (eds.), *State and society in contemporary Britain* (Cambridge: Polity, 1984), pp. 176–203.

[154] Roy Sherwood, *Superpower Britain* (Cambridge: Willingham Press, 1989).

[155] See Maurice Goldsmith and Alan Mackay (eds.), *The science of science* (London: Souvenir Press, 1964) (Penguin edn 1966).

knowledge which emerged in the late 1960s saw itself as coming from within: 'If we want an account of the nature of scientific knowledge, surely we can do no better than to adopt the scientific method itself' said one of its leading exponents.[156] It was the economists, not the literary intellectuals, who discredited, temporarily, the claim that more research and development meant more economic growth. Of course, ideological constellations were later to change positions in this ideological zodiac, though the conjunctions and oppositions always remained more complex than is immediately apparent.

The techno-declinist, anti-histories were central to the modernisation project in British politics in the early 1960s. They did indeed result in new policy proposals and new policies. Among them were the extension of higher education, the reform of the higher civil service, the reform of the science policy machinery and the creation of the Ministry of Technology in 1964. The latter, as we have already seen, was particularly directly associated with the techno-declinist critique, and would indeed have both Blackett and Snow on its staff. But the Ministry of Technology as it developed was more a product of the warfare state, and soon ceased to believe in the arguments that led to its creation. Yet it too was to be a victim of the anti-historians, as it had to be. For its nature and practices undermined the arguments that led to its creation, and thus some of the most influential theses about the nature of post-war Britain. It is to 'Mintech' that we now turn.

---

[156] David Bloor, *Knowledge and social imagery* (London: Routledge, 1976), p. ix. See also M. Mulkay, *Sociology of science: a sociological pilgrimage* (Milton Keynes: Open University Press, 1991), p. xv.

6 The warfare state and the 'white heat', 1955–70

> In this Conference, in all our plans for the future, we are re-defining and we are re-stating our Socialism in terms of the scientific revolution. But that revolution cannot become a reality unless we are prepared to make far-reaching changes in economic and social attitudes which permeate our whole system of society. The Britain that is going to be forged in the white heat of this revolution will be no place for restrictive practices or for outdated methods on either side of industry.
>
> Harold Wilson, Scarborough 1963[1]

Introduction

The history of the Ministry of Technology (Mintech), created in 1964 and lasting until 1970, is a key example of the programme of technocratic modernisation of the 1960s, which ended in disillusion and failure. At least that is how it is seen within the standard framework in which British politics and British technocracy is understood, a framework which was formed by the techno-declinist arguments which shaped Labour's rhetoric in the 1960s and which has shaped much of the historiography since. Within a different framework, shaped by different assumptions about the history of the British state and British technocracy, it looks very different. From the perspective of the arguments of this book, far from injecting for the first time a technological dimension into the British state, Labour set about redirecting the state's already massive technological effort. Mintech, as the ministry came to be called, came out of the warfare state the scientific intellectuals so downplayed and was to be a key agent in this redeployment of resources. Mintech was a recreation of the supply ministries of the war and post-war years. But it was a recreation in a different context – one of falling defence expenditure and of pulling out of vast military techno-nationalist projects. As the hugely

---

[1] Harold Wilson, 'Speech opening the science debate at the party's annual conference, Scarborough, 1963', in Harold Wilson, *Purpose in politics: selected speeches* (London: Weidenfeld and Nicolson, 1964), p. 27.

inflated warfare budgets of the early 1950s started to fall, welfare budgets started to increase significantly and the British state could begin, with more justification, to be labelled a welfare state. Let us recall, nevertheless, that only in 1970 was the welfareness of the state, the ratio of welfare to warfare spending, back to the levels of the early 1930s.

Even more significantly, Labour's industrial and technological policies came to be based, within a remarkably short period, on a rejection of key techno-declinist arguments. Under Labour there was a distinct commitment to cut back on techno-nationalist projects, a scaling back of the research corps and an attempt to part-privatise it. Of even more general significance it became well established, especially within Mintech, that there was no positive correlation between national research and development spending and national rates of economic growth, a crucial unspoken assumption of arguments for national research and development policies in history, today and in the historiography. The whole Mintech experience thus fatally undermined not only the analyses that led to its creation but the analyses which form the basis of the way in which it has been studied, and indeed most accounts of the history of British science and technology in the twentieth century. Only because Mintech, the product of anti-historical accounts of British technology and technocracy, has itself been a victim of similar anti-histories, has this story and its significance not been clear.

Technological futurism and the British military-industrial complex, 1955–64

By 1955 the post-war rearmament programme was over and defence spending started to fall as a proportion of GDP. In absolute terms it remained very roughly constant for the period lasting until the late 1980s, but there was a distinct fall in the late 1960s, under the Labour governments of that period. The shift away from high defence expenditures, as a proportion of GDP, went hand in hand with increased emphasis on ever more advanced weaponry and indeed a distinct technological enthusiasm in defence. The technocratic moment in armaments long predated Harold Wilson. In 1955 the government announced its intention of building a hydrogen bomb in that year's Defence White Paper. In the post-Suez 1957 Defence White Paper it was announced that conscription would go, and that Britain would rely on H-bomb deterrence to a unprecedented degree.[2]

---

[2] L. Martin, 'The market for strategic ideas in Britain: the "Sandys era"', *American Political Science Review* 56 (1962), 23–41; S. J. Ball 'Harold Macmillan and the politics of defence: the market for strategic ideas during the Sandys era revisited', *Twentieth Century British History* 6 (1995), 78–100.

Britain led the way in what some saw as adopting the logic of nuclear war. The American political scientist Samuel P. Huntingdon observed in 1961:

Changes in American military policy often came two or three years after changes in British military policy. The New Look originated with Churchill and the British Chiefs of Staff in 1951 and 1952; it became American policy in 1953 and 1954. The British began to reduce and redesign their reserve forces in 1955; the Americans followed suit in 1958. The British announced in 1957 their intention of eliminating conscription by 1962; in 1960 American policy was edging in this direction. While the wealthier country was able to develop new weapons earlier than the poorer one, nonetheless, the poorer one, largely because of its more limited resources, often was first in adjusting its military policies to the new technological requirements.[3]

Leaving aside the issue of the 'requirements' of technology this is an intriguing analysis with much to commend it. The emphasis on the speed of development of technology is also important, for Britain probably did not lag in initiating military research programmes. The British state had felt itself to be strong, and believed that it needed its own nuclear weapons for its own specific strategic reasons.[4] Far from being conservative in technology and armaments, post-war Britain was radical. Central to Britain's development policy, or at least a justification for it, was 'leap-frogging' the Americans. The idea was that British genius would jump a generation of technology. At the very beginning of the cold war Britain started designing jet-bombers and abandoned the piston-engined bombers that the USA continued to develop. In fast fighter aircraft, there was a direct move from the subsonic Hawker Hunter to the very supersonic English Electric Lightning. In helicopters, Britain relied on US types, hoping to capture a future market with its own designs.[5] And in the civil field too Britain went for leapfrogs like the huge Bristol Brabazon trans-atlantic airliner and the jet-powered De Havilland Comet. In other areas, for example electronic switching for telephones, it sought to jump a generation.[6] The 1957 Defence White Paper is a particularly clear example of British defence futurism. Not only would Britain become very dependent on H-bombs, it would abandon development of many

---

[3] Samuel P. Huntingdon, *The common defence: strategic programmes in national politics* (New York: Columbia University Press, 1961), p. 118.

[4] Ian Clark and Nicholas Wheeler, *The British origins of nuclear strategy 1945–1955* (Oxford: Clarendon Press, 1989).

[5] Matthew Uttley, 'British helicopter developments 1945–1960: government technology policy in a changing defence environment', in R. Coopey, G. Spinardi and M. Uttley (eds.), *Defence science and technology: adjusting to change* (Amsterdam: Harwood, 1993), pp. 125–41.

[6] Geoffrey Owen, *From empire to Europe: the decline and revival of British industry since the Second World War* (London: HarperCollins, 2000), pp. 282–8.

manned aircraft and go straight to missiles. By contrast the US would continue to develop long-range bombers and supersonic fighters. Britain would develop new kinds of aircraft like the the BAC TSR2, a very complex multi-role aircraft, and the Hawker P1154, a supersonic vertical take-off fighter.[7] In these years Britain also developed a long-range missile, the Blue Streak, and the hydrogen weapons it would carry. All these leapfrogs failed and Britain acquired US technology instead.

Over and above the connection with the abolition of conscription, the commitment to the H-bomb signalled the demilitarisation of Britain and its economy. The place of the economy and industry in war was reconsidered. The old policy of maintaining reserve capacity and war potential would give way to emphasising more short-term preparedness. There was no point in having industries ready to gear up to large-scale military production when wars would be decided in quick and deadly H-bomb exchanges. The impact on the arms industry of this shift in policy was rapid. In 1955 the MoS had lost its responsibilities for civil industry to the Board of Trade, as it focused on its immediate defence responsibilities. It itself ran down reserve capacity: within a very few years after 1957 one-third of the remaining wartime ordnance factories were closed down.[8] In the private arms industry attitudes also changed. In Vickers, a commitment to 'Service' – in the sense of the armed services and 'service' to the nation as an arsenal – was rethought in the light of 1957: Vickers was no longer necessarily ready to turn over to arms.[9] Indeed Vickers ceased to be dominated by armaments, and it did not dominate arms production as it had in the interwar years. For all this, Vickers in the late 1950s and early 1960s was still a powerful industrial presence, in both aircraft and ship-building and much else, and it built itself a huge new headquarters building, just along the Thames from Westminster and Whitehall to reflect this – the Millbank Tower. This was later to be occupied in part by the Ministry of Technology.

Dependence in high technology

The cold war was a supremely transnational effort which involved major surrenders of national sovereignty in military matters, on both sides of the iron curtain. Major powers now routinely stationed troops on territory

---

[7] See Michael Pryce, 'Feeling supersonic: the rise and fall of the Hawker P1154: a case study of the place of technological failure in aircraft design and development', unpublished MSc thesis, University of London (1996).

[8] Seven in the period 1958–60, leaving at least ten which survived into the 1980s. Twenty-two closed after the war.

[9] J. D. Scott, *Vickers: a history* (London: Weidenfeld and Nicolson, 1962), pp. 368–70.

other than their own: Western Germany had US, Canadian, British and French troops. There were large numbers of US facilities of great importance on British soil.[10] Yet national and nationalist armament policies remained hugely important. The geopolitics of technology in the cold war were not bipolar: there was competition between the Western powers in weapons development, and from the British point of view especially, the key technological competitor was not the Soviet Union but the USA. This is reflected in the public politics of post-war arms development, where the ostensible enemy is almost wholly absent. Yet for all the huge importance of the national efforts made, there was a great deal of sharing of technology. Even Britain, with the second most powerful arms industry in the North Atlantic Treaty Organisation (NATO), had chosen to acquire US technology. During the Second World War it used very large numbers of US transport and naval aircraft and it equipped many of its tank formations with US Grant and Sherman tanks. In the post-war years not only did specially enlarged British bases host US B-29 bombers,[11] but they were also supplied free (as was the logistic support) to the RAF under the US Mutual Defence Assistance Program.[12] Eighty or so B-29s were in RAF service from 1950 to 1954.[13] In the case of fighters too US aircraft proved crucial stopgaps: no fewer than 430 North American Sabres (F-86) of Canadian manufacture were in RAF service from 1953 to around 1956. In helicopters Britain depended on the production of US models by the British firm Westland.[14] US finance had a powerful influence on British domestic production. Under the Special Aircraft Assistance Programme (1953–7) British-designed and built Javelin, Hunter, Valiant and Canberra aircraft, as well as F-86s, were made for NATO air forces.[15] Britain Centurion tanks were also made for NATO forces under US offshore procurement. British arms technology was licensed

---

[10] With respect to the Common Market, see Alan Milward, *The European rescue of the nation state* (London: Routledge, 1992).

[11] Patrick E. Murray, 'An initial response to the cold war: the build-up of the US Air Force in the United Kingdom, 1948–1956' in Roger G. Miller (ed.), *Seeing off the bear: Anglo-American air power co-operation during the cold war* (Washington DC: US Air Force, 1995), pp. 15–24. Ulrich Albrecht, *The Soviet armaments industry* (Chur, Switzerland: Harwood Academic Publishers, 1993).

[12] William W. Suit, 'The transfer of B-29s to the Royal Air Force under the Mutual Defense Assistance Programme' in Miller, *Seeing off the bear*, pp. 101–15.

[13] US bombers following were the Convair B-36, the Boeing B-47 and the Boeing B-52.

[14] Uttley, 'British helicopter developments 1945–1960', pp. 125–41.

[15] Jacqueline McGlade made me aware of the importance of this issue. I am grateful to her for copies of unpublished papers. See also Till Geiger and Lorenza Sebesta, 'A self-defeating policy: American offshore procurement and integration of western European defence production, 1952–56', *Journal of European Integration History* 4 (1998), 55–73.

to allies; for example jet technology was licensed to Pratt and Whitney of the US and other firms as well as other countries.[16] Although it is well known that joint Anglo-American work on nuclear weapons ended in 1946, in the other 'weapons of mass destruction' of the period, chemical and biological weapons, there were close links to the US programmes.[17] The supposedly independent British Blue Streak missile was dependent on the transfer of technology from US missile contractors: the engine was a scaled down copy of a US one, for example.[18] In fact the three major armourers of the post-war world – the USA, Britain and the Soviet Union – shared a remarkable amount of arms technology. In rocketry and of course in other fields too all had access to and used German technology and technicians. In the atomic field, what had been a remarkably multi-national project was further internationalised, not by scientific interna-tionalists but political internationalists, who helped ensure that the Soviet Union was able to detonate a near copy of the US plutonium bomb in 1949.[19] Britain's bomb, tested in 1952, was also a plutonium bomb, and was not radically different from the wartime US model either. But that was not all: in the early 1950s all three main powers used versions of the same long-range bomber, the Boeing B-29, the first atomic bomber. Britain, as we noted above, used them between 1950 and 1954. The USSR had a fleet of Tu 4s, copies of B-29s forced down on Soviet territory during the war. In addition British Nene and Derwent jet-engines (and also copies) powered Soviet jet aircraft, notably the MiG15 over the skies of Korea (the transfer was authorised in 1946).[20]

From the late 1950s British dependence on the USA increased very greatly. The momentous decision to equip British forces with a British thermonuclear weapon would, within a very few years, be radically chan-ged. Britain had developed an independent atomic (fission) bomb, and deployed a weapon which went by the name of Blue Danube (1953–61) and a tactical derivative called Red Beard (1961–71). Also all-British was the very powerful Green Grass uranium fission warhead used more briefly

---

[16] Peter Pugh, *The magic of a name: the Rolls-Royce story, part two: the power behind the jets, 1945–1987* (Cambridge: Icon Books 2000), p. 35.

[17] Brian Balmer, 'The drift of biological weapons policy in the UK, 1945–1965', *Journal of Strategic Studies* 20 (1997), 115–45; Rob Evans, *Gassed* (London: House of Stratus, 2000), p. 133.

[18] S. R. Twigge, *The early development of guided weapons in the United Kingdom 1940–1960* (Amsterdam: Harwood Academic, 1993), pp. 56, 191.

[19] David Holloway, *Stalin and the bomb: the Soviet Union and atomic energy, 1939–1956* (London: Yale University Press, 1994).

[20] The politics of these transfers is nicely explored in Jeffrey A. Engel, '"We are not concerned who the buyer is": engine sales and Anglo-American security at the dawn of the jet age', *History and Technology* 17 (2000), 43–68.

in the Violet Club bomb (this was a Green Grass warhead in a Blue Danube casing) and Yellow Sun Mk 1 bombs.[21] But although Britain tested a thermonuclear device in 1957 no all-British weapon was ever deployed. Britain entered into remarkably close cooperation with the USA in 1958 and stopped developing its own thermonuclear weapons. As the official historian, Lorna Arnold, puts it:

Britain's megaton quest was over in 1958, and by 1959 the Anglo-American nuclear partnership was already being closely integrated. After 12 years of isolation and independence, a unique and lasting nuclear relationship was beginning which – through many vicissitudes and through changing world conditions – continues to the present day.[22]

All this was deeply secret, and is still not wholly clear. The first thermonuclear bomb in British service was derived from the American W28 (it was codenamed Red Snow, and fitted into the Yellow Sun casing making it Yellow Sun Mk 2 (which was in service 1961–1972); Red Snow was the weapon which would have gone on to the British Blue Streak ballistic missile as well, and it was also used in Blue Steel (1962–9).[23] The American Mk 44 was also to be copied to be used in tactical missiles, but these programmes were soon stopped. The long-serving British small thermonuclear weapon WE177 (1966–98) is of unclear provenance, but appears to be based on a British-designed primary and a US-designed thermonuclear part, plus many other US parts.[24] A version of this primary device appears to have been used on the semi-British Polaris warhead (ET317), which were derived from the 0.4 megaton US W47; here again, the thermonuclear part appears to have been US designed.[25] In addition the USA transferred nuclear propulsion technology. The first nuclear-powered submarine, with a US built reactor (HMS *Dreadnought*), was finished in 1960; the following ones had British reactors based on US designs. Between 1958 and 1963 the RAF deployed, under a 'dual key'

---

[21] J. Mellisen, 'The restoration of the nuclear alliance: Great Britain and atomic negotiations with the US, 1957–8', *Contemporary Record* 6 (1992), 72–106, makes clear that the first operational British megaton range weapon – Violet Club/Green Grass – was a fission weapon. See also J. Baylis, 'The development of Britain's thermonuclear capacity, 1954–1961: myth or reality?', *Contemporary Record* 8 (1994), 159–74; K. Pyne, 'Art or article: the need for and nature of the British hydrogen bomb, 1954–1958', *Contemporary Record* 9 (1995), 562–85; Royal Aeronautical Society/DERA, *The history of the UK strategic deterrent: proceedings of a Conference March 1999* (London: Royal Aeronautical Society, 1999).

[22] Lorna Arnold, *Britain and the H-bomb* (London: Palgrave, 2001), p. 220.

[23] Ian Clark, *Nuclear diplomacy and the special relationship: Britain's deterrent and America, 1957–1962* (Oxford: Clarendon Press, 1994), p. 92.

[24] Paper presented by Richard Moore at the 2003 ICBH Summer Conference.

[25] Arnold, *Britain and the H-bomb*, p. 209; Richard Moore paper.

arrangement, US Thor missiles with thermonuclear warheads.[26] From the late 1950s some Valiant and Canberra bombers carried US tactical nuclear weapons, under similar arrangements.[27]

The year 1958 was thus quite crucial to British independent warfighting capacity. But in public terms the key change came with the cancellation of the Blue Streak missile in 1960, which led to a decision to replace it with a US stand-off missile called Skybolt, which was itself cancelled and replaced with an order for submarine-launched Polaris missiles from the USA. Curiously enough this radical atlanticisation of military technology went along with a europeanisation first of big civil projects. The treaties to build Concorde and to develop a European space launcher via the European Space Vehicle Launcher Development Organisation (ELDO) date from the early 1960s.[28] In the late 1960s Harold Wilson proposed the creation of a European Technological Community. From the mid-1960s, there were also many European collaborations in military aviation, including a short-lived Anglo-French variable geometry aircraft, the Jaguar fighter bomber and the pan-European Tornado project, started in the late 1960s. These crucial changes betokened, hardly surprisingly, a reassessment of British techno-nationalism.

The reassessment of national technology

The test explosion of a British H-bomb in 1957 had led to the creation of a huge anti-nuclear movement and the end of consensus over Britain's key weapon. CND was concerned primarily with a moralistic critique of nuclear weapons, pressing for Britain to lead the world to nuclear disarmament. There was no sustained critique or examination of the British military-industrial-scientific complex in this period. The Aldermaston marches took their participants to the moral high ground, not the heart of the nuclear beast.[29] However, the cancellation of the Blue Streak missile in 1960 was a crucial moment in bringing about a change in

[26] See Wing Commander Colin Cummings, 'Thor', *Royal Air Force Historical Society Journal* no. 26 (2001), 22–34.
[27] Humphrey Wynn, 'The RAF nuclear decades', *Royal Air Force Historical Society Journal* no. 26 (2001), 116.
[28] Michelangelo de Maria and John Krige, 'Early European attempts in launcher technology: original sins in ELDO's sad parable', *History and Technology* 9 (1992), 109–37; Lewis Johnman and Frances M. B. Lynch, 'The road to Concorde: Franco-British relations and the supersonic project', *Contemporary European History* 11 (2002), 229–52; Susanna Schrafstetter and Stephen Twigge, 'Spinning into Europe: Britain, West Germany and the Netherlands – uranium enrichment and the development of the gas centrifuge 1964–1970', *Contemporary European History* 11 (2002), 253–72.
[29] See ch. 7.

attitude to the British military-technological complex. The Labour politician Richard Crossman claimed that 'We have now learnt by bitter and wasteful experience that we are not and never can become an independent nuclear power.'[30] Labour opposition's economic spokesman, Harold Wilson, claimed that the then Prime Minister, Harold Macmillan,

> like so many other rather pathetic individuals whose sense of social prestige outruns their purse ... is left in the situation at the end of the day of the man who dare not admit that he cannot afford a television set ... and who just puts up the aerial instead. That is our situation, because without an independent means of delivery, the independent nuclear deterrent, the right hon. Gentleman's cheap, short cut to national greatness, is an empty illusion.[31]

In his speech Wilson repeatedly alluded to a comparison with the groundnuts scheme – a failed Labour programme (under Minister of Food John Strachey) to grow peanuts in Africa in the 1940s which Conservatives constantly taunted Labour with as an example of failed government enterprise.[32] A particular idea about British technology policy, that it had over-emphasised 'prestige' projects, became central to Labour's arguments and to those of later analysts. Within the Treasury R. W. B. Clarke, later to be the permanent secretary at Mintech, was already by 1960 condemning 'prestige projects' which in fact brought no prestige, as they tended to be in areas in which Britain could not compete with the USA and the USSR.[33] By 1964 the Labour line was that the Polaris 'independent British deterrent' would 'not be independent and it will not be British and it will not deter', though it promised only to 'propose the re-negotiation of the Nassau agreement' and to stress 'strengthening our conventional regular forces'.[34]

A crucial element of the debate over British national technology in the late 1950s and early 1960s was that effort should be directed into new areas. In a speech in the constituency of Bristol South East, supporting the candidature of Anthony Wedgwood Benn in a famous by-election in 1961, Patrick Blackett attacked the 'fuddy duddies' in charge of British institutions. Referring to industry he noted that outside aircraft and nuclear power, and a few other industries where government also intervened strongly,

---

[30] R. H. S. Crossman, 'Defence after Blue Streak', *New Statesman*, 14 May 1960, p. 701. Crossman was well informed about defence, see for example his 'The nuclear obsession', *Encounter* 11(4) (1958), 3–10. P. M. S. Blackett was a regular contributor to the *New Statesman* in the late 1950s on the subject of defence.

[31] House of Commons, 27 April 1960 (Blue Streak debate), in *Purpose in politics*, pp. 167, 178, 172.

[32] House of Commons, 27 April 1960 (Blue Streak debate), in *Purpose in politics*.

[33] R. W. B. Clarke to Mr Bell, 'Blue Streak: D (60) 17', 5 April 1960. Clarke Papers, CLRK 1/3, Churchill Archives Centre.

[34] *Let's Go with Labour for the New Britain* (London: Labour party 1964).

government relies on a most rigid interpretation of laissez-faire ... this fundamental schizophrenic attitude of the government, lavish expenditure and some
sort of planning in a few fields related to defence, and complete inactivity elsewhere, is a high point of modern fuddy duddyism.

If the Tories could radically restructure the aircraft industry, as they had
done in the late 1950s, why could the same not be done to civil industry,
he asked?[35] This kind of argument was taken up very strongly by Harold
Wilson as leader of the Labour party from 1963. Wilson attacked a Britain
that did not use its scientific and technical resources effectively. Britain,
said Wilson in early 1963, had

a reservoir of unused and underused talent, of skill and craftsmanship, of inventiveness, and ingenuity, of administrative ability and scientific creativeness which
if mobilised will, within a measurable period of time enable us to become – not the
workshop of the world; that is no longer our role – but the pilot plant, the toolroom
of the world. Our scientists are among the finest in the world. The tragedy is we
don't produce enough of them, and those we do produce we do not use intel-
ligently ... the key to our plan to redynamise Britain's economy, is our plan to
mobilise the talents of our scientists and technicians, redeployed from missile and
warheads, on research and development contracts, civil research and development to produce the new instruments and tools of economic advance both
for Britain and for the war on poverty in under-developed areas of the
Commonwealth and elsewhere.[36]

The 'mobilisation' and 'redeployment', significantly military metaphors,
of the nation's key resources using military means was the key policy.[37]
These were key elements of his famous 1963 'white heat' speech, his first
conference speech as leader of the Labour party. Wilson was critical not
only of 'purely prestige projects that never left the drawing board', which
were conflated with military projects, but also of projects which would not
'increase Britain's productive power' but that led to 'some new gimmick or
additive to some consumer product'.[38] Instead of 'misdirected research

[35] P. M. S. Blackett, 'Notes for a speech in support of A. W. Benn', Bristol South East,
28 April 1961. Blackett Papers, H89, Royal Society. Spelling corrected.
[36] Harold Wilson, Speech at National Press Club, Washington, 1 April 1963, *Purpose in
politics*, pp. 215–16. In his speech on the eve of the 1963 conference speech, Wilson also
used the pilot-plant image: 'we have reserves of skill, and craftsmanship, of science and
technology, design and creative ability, of organisation and salesmanship, which, if given
full scope, will make Britain what we should be, the pilot-plant, the tool-room of the
world'. 'Eve of conference speech on Foreign Affairs', Scarborough, 1963, in *Purpose in
politics*, p. 12.
[37] Military metaphors were not uncommon at this time. In the late 1950s 'the word "break-
through" – a generation earlier a mainstay of Western Front talk – began to circulate
again' in connection with science and technology (Harry Hopkins, *The new look: a social
history of the forties and fifties in Britain* (London: Secker & Warburg, 1964), p. 386).
[38] 'White heat speech', *Purpose in politics*, p. 22.

and development contracts in the field of defence', Wilson said, '[i]f we were now to use the technique of R and D contracts in civil industry I believe we could within a measurable period of time establish new industries which would make us once again one of the foremost industrial nations of the world.'[39] He also made explicit reference to taking up the skills of the possibly redundant missile and nuclear scientists.[40] He concluded his famous speech with these words:

For those who have studied the formidable Soviet challenge in the education of scientists and technologists, and above all, in the ruthless application of scientific techniques in Soviet industry, know that our future lies not in military strength alone but in the efforts, the sacrifices, and above all the energies which a free people can mobilise for the future greatness of our country.[41]

For Wilson, Britain needed to create and use more scientists and to do so in ways derived from military practice. The specifics were hardly laid out, but in its 1964 manifesto, Labour said that it would create a

A New Britain –
mobilising the resources of technology under a national plan;
harnessing our national wealth in brains, our genius for scientific invention and medical discovery;
reversing the decline of thirteen wasted years;
affording a new opportunity to equal, and if possible, surpass, the roaring progress of other western powers while Tory Britain has moved sideways, backwards, but seldom forward.[42]

Specifically on science and technology Labour would

(i)   Go beyond research and development and establish new industries, either by public enterprise or in partnership with private industry
(ii) Directly stimulate new advances by using, in the field of civil production, the research and development contracts which have hitherto been largely confined to military projects
(iii) Set up a Ministry of Technology to guide and stimulate a national effort to bring advanced technology and new processes into industry.[43]

---

[39] Ibid., p. 23.   [40] Ibid., p. 24.
[41] Ibid., p. 28. In January 1964 Wilson again reiterated the theme of civil, rather than military R&D contracts, and the need to expand civil R&D and make it more purposive. 'Labour's Economic Policy' speech at Swansea, 25 January 1964, in Harold Wilson, *The new Britain* (Harmondsworth: Penguin, 1964), p. 33.
[42] *Let's go with Labour.*
[43] *Let's go with Labour.* For a left critique see John Hughes, 'An economic policy for Labour', *New Left Review*, no. 24 (March/April 1964), 5–32.

And yet at the same time, it was all too easy and too tempting, to play the nationalistic card and support additional domestic military R&D and warlike production. Thus in 1964 Harold Wilson complained that Britain was importing aircraft:

Britain pioneered jet aircraft. Yet our airlines are dependent on foreign planes – only in engines do we still lead – our Navy has to go to the US for the new aircraft it needs. And to the US for Army and Navy helicopters too: a week or two ago we had the Minister of Defence in the House of Commons not even presenting the facts and the figures because he was afraid of having to confess that we had to go cap-in-hand to America for essential military and naval aircraft; whether to import them or to build them here on the basis of foreign know-how on a royalty basis. This is humiliating.[44]

Ideologically it was difficult to admit realities either of technological or military dependence. Nevertheless, as we shall see it was under Wilson that there was a more radical turning to the USA for military technology, as the running down of the British missile and warhead programmes implied. The party of the 'white heat' would be cutting back on many national-technological defence projects; civil development contracts were needed, as Wilson pointed out, 'if measures of world disarmament or even less far-reaching changes in defence production, are not to produce widespread redundancy among scientists and technical workers'.[45]

Labour in office

In looking at the 'white heat' we should therefore start with Labour's policies for the warfare state. Labour was committed to and succeeded in cutting defence spending – Denis Healey, the Secretary of State for Defence, reduced defence expenditure from more than 7 per cent to 5 per cent of GDP. 'When I left office', he claimed, 'for the first time in its history, Britain was spending more on education than on defence.'[46] Defence R&D had been falling slowly in real terms since about 1960; in the mid-1960s it would fall much more rapidly, so that by 1970 it was below 1955 levels.[47] For the first time government civilian R&D was greater than military R&D expenditure.[48] Labour had very quickly cancelled most of the Ministry of Aviation's large development projects: the

---

[44] Harold Wilson, 'A first-class nation', in *The new Britain*, p. 45.
[45] 'Wilson defines British socialism', 15 September 1963, *Purpose in politics*, p. 268.
[46] Denis Healey, *Time of my life* (London: Michael Joseph, 1989), p. 271.
[47] Council for Science and Society, *UK military R&D* (Oxford: Oxford University Press, 1986), table 2.1, p. 8.
[48] Council for Science and Society, *UK military R&D*, table 2.7, p. 14.

P-1154, the HS-681 (an advanced transport), and most importantly of all, the TSR2.[49] The cancellations caused a great parliamentary rumpus: from November 1964, a 'series of four or five major aviation clashes ... had come near to dominating the House of Commons stage'.[50] Labour faced down the 'hysterical clamour of the Tory aviation lobby'.[51] Labour also undertook a major enquiry into the aircraft industry, by a committee chaired by Lord Plowden, formerly chief executive of the MAP.[52] The Plowden Report's central argument was that aircraft projects had to be argued for on economic grounds, that the aircraft industry received government support quite out of line with other industries and that a run-down was desirable.[53]

The key corollary of these cancellations and this argument was that British forces would have to rely on US aircraft. Indeed the government ordered the F-4 (Phantom) fighter for the RAF, in addition to the naval order put in by the Conservatives, and also ordered the C-130 (Hercules) transport and the F-111 swing-wing bomber. All except the F-111, the order for which was cancelled in 1968, were in fact bought and became key RAF aircraft. Never before had foreign aircraft been the mainstays of the RAF for the foreseeable future.[54] Indeed military aircraft R&D was cut, from £202 million in 1964/5 to £120 million in 1970/1.[55] Of course even £120 million was a large sum and there was still obviously a great deal of military-funded development. Among the projects were the Hawker-Siddeley Harrier jump-jet, two big Anglo-French projects (the short-lived Anglo-French variable geometry aircraft (AFVGA), which was intended to replace TRS2/F-111, and the Jaguar), some helicopters and, at the end of our period the beginning of the British/German/Italian Multi-Role Combat Aircraft (MRCA) project, which produced the Tornado.

---

[49] Roy Jenkins, *A life at the centre* (London: Macmillan, 1991), pp. 160–6. For an insider's view of the cancellations see Solly Zuckerman, *Monkeys, men and missiles* (London: Collins, 1988), ch. 21. See also S. Straw and J.W. Young, 'The Wilson government and the demise of the TSR-2 October 1964-April 1965', *Journal of Strategic Studies* 20 (1997), 18–44.

[50] Jenkins, *Life*, p. 173.   [51] 'Why the TSR2 must go', *New Statesman*, 22 January 1965.

[52] Jenkins wanted to establish a three-man committee of inquiry into the aircraft industry headed by Sir Edwin Plowden and, very unusually, with two technocratic MPs, the Labour MP Austen Albu and the Conservative former Minister of Supply Aubrey Jones as the additional members. In fact the committee was to be much larger, and to exclude Albu (Jenkins, *Life*, p. 167).

[53] Ministry of Aviation, *Report of a Committee of Enquiry into the aircraft industry*, Cmd 2853 (1965).

[54] Robert Jackson, 'RAF aircraft procurement 1955–1965: the American involvement', in Miller, *Seeing off the bear*, pp. 91–9.

[55] Data from *Estimates*.

By contrast, on the civil side, R&D expenditures in the aircraft industry increased dramatically. In 1964–6 some £20 milloin was being spent in industry, while for 1968/9 the estimate was up to more than £66 million, of which £49 million was going on the Anglo-French supersonic airliner Concorde. Concorde could be taken as the exemplification of what Wilson wanted – the use of military-style contracts for civil development, taking Britain (and France) into a dazzling technological future. It could thus stand for the white heat, and indeed sometimes does. However, the Labour government had wanted to cancel Concorde. But, by January 1965, because of the objections of the French (who were nevertheless probably keen to cancel) Concorde was reprieved.[56] Concorde, it was hoped, was to be the last such 'prestige' project, an unfortunate, though hugely costly, left-over from a previous regime. This was made clear to the aircraft industry. Anthony Wedgwood Benn, by then the minister responsible for aviation, recorded in his diary the reaction to a speech he gave at a dinner of the SBAC in June 1967:

I was determined to indicate that there was a difference between the Ministry of Technology attitude to aviation and the old Ministries of Aviation in the past. I said in my speech that in the old days Ministers of Aviation could get money as easily as pinching pennies off an old man's drum, but now it was going to be different and we had to justify every penny. Those present were absolutely livid at this speech. They thought it was offensive, and it led to a major row, but it was the turning point. It was a warning that there would be no more Concordes and that we would expect them to take some risks.[57]

Benn's diaries record continuing high feeling on these issues. At a by-election meeting in 1968 he noted 'there were some crusty Tory ladies there with big hats shouting about TSR2'.[58] In September 1968 he recorded of another SBAC dinner: 'I find it offensive meeting these big industrialists who live on government work, who are financed by government, and who are violently, bitterly, anti-government from beginning to end.'[59] In May 1969 Benn saw the chairman of Rolls-Royce on television complaining that 'civil servants were not interested in long-term developments and that when you talked to them or politicians about these things a glazed look came into their faces, as if they were thinking of what they were going to have for

---

[56] Johnman and Lynch, 'The road to Concorde'.

[57] Tony Benn, *Out of the wilderness: diaries 1963–67* (London: Hutchinson, 1987), 28 June 1967, p. 505. Jad Adams, *Tony Benn* (London: Macmillan, 1992), p. 277, gives a some-what different text, but notes that the official version of the speech was toned down (p. 499n5).

[58] Tony Benn, *Office without power: diaries 1968–72* (London: Hutchinson, 1988), 22 March 1968, p. 49.

[59] Benn, *Diaries 1968–72*, 18 September 1968, p. 102.

lunch'. This, Benn felt, was 'so unjust and, in the light of all the help we had given Rolls-Royce, so unfair that I wrote him a stinking letter'.[60]

There was therefore no love lost between aeronautical engineers and the party of the 'white heat'. The Royal Aeronautical Society, their learned society, was the forum for denunciations of the government for its alleged lack of support of the industry. The President of the Society, Sir George Gardner, a former director of Farnborough and Controller, Aircraft, criticised the Plowden Report for not believing in the potential of aviation.[61] In February 1966 the society organised a meeting which attracted nearly 350 people and lasted almost three hours.[62] But by the end of 1967 the mood was more resigned: Sir Roy Fedden argued that government listened too much to scientists and not enough to engineers; meanwhile, the 'industry was too inclined to take things lying down'; a Mr Cleaver of Rolls-Royce complained that no one outside the society seemed to take note of its arguments; F. R. Banks, a senior engine specialist, complained that 'no British government of recent years, whether Conservative or Labour, had *really believed* in aerospace activities'.[63]

The machinery of the white heat

As rearmament came to an end in 1955, the MoS lost responsibility for the engineering industry, and had indeed lost responsibility for atomic energy to the AEA. The ministry was much more focused on military production. In 1959 it lost its army supply responsibilities to the War Office, twenty years after it had been formed to take over these functions from the War Office. At this point the Minister of Supply, Aubrey Jones, a modernising centrist Tory, proposed to turn it into a Ministry of Technology, to 'facilitate the transfer of knowledge from the military to the civil field, and to utilise the expertise developed in the placing of military research and development contracts to put it also at the disposal of civil industry'.[64] Jones's scheme was opposed and he resigned over the issue. What remained was a Ministry of Aviation, which was represented in Cabinet between 1959 and 1962 by a former Minister of Defence (Duncan Sandys) and a former Chancellor (Thorneycroft). It was as if the wartime MoS, which had concerned army supply principally, had ceased to exist, while the MAP remained. It was to exist until 1967.

[60] Ibid., 1 May 1969, p. 164.
[61] Sir George Gardner, *Journal of the Royal Aeronautical Society* 70 (1966), 303.
[62] *Journal of the Royal Aeronautical Society* 70 (1966), 545–52.
[63] Taken from *Journal of the Royal Aeronautical Society* 71 (1967), 810–12.
[64] Aubrey Jones, *Britain's economy: the roots of stagnation* (Cambridge: Cambridge University Press, 1985), pp. 85–6, app. I.

The late 1950s and early 1960s were notable for a debate about British economic performance and also the management of both military and civil R&D by government.[65] The Conservative government had created the National Economic Development Council (1962), and its attached 'little neddies', a new Department of Education *and* Science (1964), a new beefed-up industry ministry (based on the Board of Trade) under the humbly born Edward Heath and a new unified Ministry of Defence (1964).[66] The DSIR had launched civil development contracts.[67] Through the early 1960s Aubrey Jones continued to push for more civil development contracts, and for an expanded role for the Ministry of Aviation.[68] In opposition Labour experts and politicians had come up with a whole range of schemes for reforming the state machinery for the support of industry, science and technology.[69] Of particular importance to the Labour programme as a whole was the reduction in the power of the Treasury by the creation of a Department of Economic

[65] See Office for the Minister for Science, *The management and control of research and development* (London: HMSO, 1961). Sir Claud Gibb chaired the committee until his death in 1959, when Sir Solly Zuckerman took over, hence the report is known as Gibb–Zuckerman (Zuckerman, *Monkeys*, pp. 160–4). See also Norman J. Vig, *Science and technology in British politics* (Oxford: Pergamon, 1968) and his 'Policies for science and technology in Great Britain: post-war development and reassessment' in T. Nixon Long and Christopher Wright (eds.), *Science policies of industrial nations* (New York: Praeger, 1975), pp. 62–109.

[66] See for example, Vig, *Science and technology*. Heath was given the title of Secretary of State for Industry, Trade and Regional Development and President of the Board of Trade (John Campbell, *Edward Heath: a biography* (London: Pimlico, 1994), pp. 147–8).

[67] Lord Hailsham, *Science and politics* (London: Faber and Faber, 1963), p. 30.

[68] Vig, *Science and technology*, pp. 74–6.

[69] David Horner, 'Scientists, trade unions and Labour movement policies for science and technology: 1947–1964', 2 vols., unpublished doctoral thesis, Aston University (1986), II, 198, 204. David Horner, 'The road to Scarborough: Wilson and the scientific revolution' in R. Coopey, S. Fielding and N. Tiratsoo (eds.), *The Wilson governments 1964–1970* (London: Pinter 1993), pp. 48–71. On Mintech see Sir Maurice Dean, 'The machinery for economic planning: IV. The Ministry of Technology', *Public Administration* 44 (1966), 43–60; Vig, *Science and technology*; Sir Richard Clarke, 'Mintech in retrospect-I', *Omega* 1 (1973), 25–38; 'Mintech in retrospect-II', *Omega* 1 (1973), 137–63; Vig, 'Policies for science and technology'; F. M. G. Willson, 'Coping with administrative growth: super-departments and the ministerial cadre 1957–77' in David Butler and A. H. Halsey (eds.), *Policy and politics: essays in honour of Norman Chester* (London: Macmillan, 1978), pp. 35–50. See also the papers by Richard Coopey, 'The white heat of scientific revolution', *Contemporary Record* 5 (1991), 115–27; 'Industrial policy in the white heat of the scientific revolution' in Coopey et al., *Wilson governments*; 'Restructuring civil and military science and technology: the Ministry of Technology in the 1960s' in R. Coopey, G. Spinardi and M. Uttley (eds.), *Defence science and technology: adjusting to change* (London: Harwood Academic, 1993), pp. 65–84. Lewis Grundy, 'Technical change, industrial structure and state intervention in the British scientific instrument industry, 1945–1975', unpublished MSc thesis, University of Manchester (1989).

Affairs.[70] One of the ministry's key early functions was the development of the National Plan. On the industrial side there had been much less clarity before 1964, but Labour ended up creating a new industrial and technological ministry which reduced the Board of Trade to a shadow of its former self and took over responsibilities from the Department of Economic Affairs when it was disbanded in 1969. That was certainly not publicly envisaged in the early 1960s.

The new industry ministry had a tortuous history, one in which thinking about the Ministry of Aviation was central. In opposition both Harold Wilson and Richard Crossman wanted to turn the Ministry of Aviation into a Ministry of Technology.[71] Harold Wilson told the journalist Alistair Hetherington in November 1963 – a month after his 'white heat' speech – that 'in considering science and technology, people had overlooked the scientific staff at the Ministry of Aviation' although they had even been used for dealing with the pharmaceutical industry. Wilson thought the scientists 'had to be taken out of the Ministry of Aviation and put into the [new] Ministry of Science and Technology'.[72] Some ten days later he told Hetherington that he had gone further in his thinking and that the 'Ministry of Aviation would become the nucleus of his Ministry of Technology'. The ministry would lose its air transport functions, but would have its civil functions greatly expanded and would take over the NRDC and undertake the development contracts with industry. Wilson recognised that scientists were divided over whether this new ministry should include pure science, but Wilson inclined to the view that it should.[73] Days later he announced, in the House of Commons, plans for a new ministry based on the Ministry of Aviation.[74] When he came into office Wilson gave the job of Minister of Aviation to Roy Jenkins, who was not to be in the Cabinet, telling him the ministry was a mess that would take a year or so to clear up, after which its functions would be dispersed.[75] Meanwhile Wilson created a separate small Ministry of Technology.

---

[70] Christopher Clifford, 'The rise and fall of the Department of Economic Affairs, 1964–1969: British government and indicative planning', *Contemporary British History* 11 (1997), 94–116.

[71] Horner, 'Labour movement policies for science and technology', II, pp. 194, 196.

[72] This ministry was to be completely separate from the Ministry of Education, to include universities, which Wilson made clear in the same interview, he wanted. 'Notes of a meeting with Harold Wilson on November 4, 1963', Hetherington Papers, 5, LSE archives.

[73] 'Notes of a meeting with Harold Wilson on Friday 15 November 1963', Hetherington Papers, 5, LSE archives.

[74] Vig, *Science and technology*, p. 96.

[75] Jenkins, *Life*, p. 157. Jenkins, a journalist, had taken an interest in aviation and had written a couple of articles on civil aviation in July 1964 (pp. 142–3).

This was headed by the trade unionist Frank Cousins, leader of the Transport and General Workers Union.[76] His predecessor, Ernest Bevin, had of course been a key figure in wartime, and indeed Mintech was full of former wartime temporaries.[77] Mintech symbolised new men coming (back) into government, injecting planning, technology, modernity into the languid frame of the aristocratic state.[78] The junior minister in the House of Lords was C. P. Snow, elevated to the peerage for the purpose. Patrick Blackett was its scientific adviser and deputy (to the minister) chairman of the ministry's Advisory Council on Technology.[79] Blackett became, temporarily, an official in the ministry – a 'controller'.[80] Blackett set up 'appraisal groups' – groups of scientists and technologists, which he saw as analogous to wartime operational research teams: 'There is not all that real [a] difference between trying to cope in 1942–43 with submarine losses of 700,000 tons a month and in trying to cope in 1965 with an adverse balance of payments of £700 million a year' he claimed.[81]

[76] Cousins was completely unprepared for the post, according to Solly Zuckerman; see his *Monkeys*, pp. 367–8 and Margaret Stewart, *Frank Cousins: a study* (London: Hutchinson, 1978). Interviews by Christopher Pollitt for his fine book *Manipulating the machine* (London: Allen & Unwin 1984), pp. 56–62, confirm this, and add interesting twists.

[77] As they had been in the immediately preceding period – as in the case of Lionel Robbins and his report, and Sir Claud Gibb and Sir Solly Zuckerman's report on R&D.

[78] Crossman and Blackett, both key figures in science policy discussions, were sons of the old elite (Bar and the City) while figures like Harold Wilson, Denis Healey and Roy Jenkins, all intellectual politicians who studied arts/social sciences in Oxford in the 1930s, had fathers in science, engineering and industry. Harold Wilson's father Herbert was an industrial chemist, without a degree but trained at Manchester Technical College, who had worked in Huddersfield, in Merseyside and spent some time during the war at the Ministry of Supply (Ben Pimlott, *Harold Wilson* (London: HarperCollins, 1992), *passim*). Denis Healey's father studied engineering at Leeds University; he worked at Woolwich Arsenal during the Great War, and in 1922 became principal of Keighley Technical School (Healey, *Time of my life*, pp. 2, 3, 6). Roy Jenkins's father was a miner who went to Ruskin College before the Great War, becoming a miners' union official, local councillor and Labour MP in the interwar years (Jenkins, *Life*, ch. 1).

[79] Former wartime temporaries were everywhere, from Number 10 Downing Street, to the Ministry of Technology, to chairing enquiries of all sorts: Plowden on the aircraft industry, Fulton on the civil service, Franks on the University of Oxford. The principal of Manchester College of Technology, Vivian Bowden, went as a junior minister to the Department of Education and Science. The military correspondent of *The Times* and former soldier Alun Gwynne Jones went, as Lord Chalfont, to the Foreign Office.

[80] The idea had been to have two controllers. Blackett became one. The two posts were merged, and the position was taken over by John Adams of the Culham Laboratory in July 1965. Adams continued to run Culham.

[81] Blackett, 'Comments on the Estimates Committee Report', 22 July 1965, Blackett Papers, E51, Royal Society. One of Blackett's wartime team went to the Board of Trade to set up operational research for industrial purposes. The project was stopped. See Jonathan Rosenhead 'Operational Research at the cross-roads: Cecil Gordon and the development of post-war OR', *Journal of the Operational Research Society* 40 (1989), 3–28;

Table 6.1 *Mintech's research establishments in the late 1960s*

Civil
AEA research group – Harwell, Culham
AEA reactor group – Risley, Winfrith, Dounreay
NPL
Fire Research Station
National Engineering Laboratory
Warren Spring Laboratory
Forest Products Research Laboratory
Hydraulics Research Station
Laboratory of the Government Chemist
Torry Research Station
Water Pollution Research Laboratory
Military
RAE
Aircraft and Armament Experimental Establishment
National Gas Turbine Establishment
Royal Radar Establishment
Signals Research and Development Establishment
Explosives Research and Development Establishment
Rocket Propulsion Establishment
AEA Research Group – Aldermaston

The structure of the new ministry did not correspond with Blackett's plans. Mintech was made up of the same bodies as the Conservative government were going to turn into an Industrial Research and Development Authority.[82] The new ministry was to get the AEA and some of the laboratories of the disbanded DSIR (see table 6.1).[83] It took over the AEA in January 1965; the NRDC in February and its bits of the DSIR in April.[84] Mintech now accounted for only about a third of government civil R&D. In terms of expenditure it was not the beefed-up NRDC Blackett had wanted, but rather a beefed-up AEA: civil atomic energy expenditure amounted to some £50 million, while the rest of

M. W. Kirby, 'Blackett in the 'white heat' of the scientific revolution: industrial moder-nisation under the Labour governments, 1964–1970', *Journal of the Operational Research Society* 50 (1999), pp. 985–93.

[82] Vig, *Science and technology*, p. 101.

[83] The main ones were the NPL, the National Engineering Laboratory and the Warren Spring laboratory. Not all the ex-DSIR applied laboratories went to Mintech: the Road Research Laboratory went to the Ministry of Transport and the Tropical Products Institute to the Ministry of Overseas Development. A number of other DSIR laboratories went to the Science and Engineering Research Council.

[84] Stewart, *Frank Cousins*, p. 121.

Mintech started off by spending only about £12 million.[85] Yet even at the beginning Mintech was not just a ministry for government research and development laboratories: it was also to have an important industrial role. It was given responsibility for the 'sponsorship' of the so-called 'bridgehead industries', a military metaphor used to describe machine tools, computers, electronics and telecommunications.[86]

What followed was radically different not just from Labour's public plans, including Blackett's, but also anything the Tories were proposing. There was a steady process of taking over responsibilities for industry from the traditional industry ministry, the Board of Trade, which was to become essentially a ministry of external trade and the regulator of business rather than a production department. The mechanical and electrical engineering and standards and weights and measures were transferred in 1965, shipbuilding in 1966 and chemicals and textiles in 1969. These transfers were only a beginning of expansion. Mintech took over the bulk of the Ministry of Aviation, which was announced 1966 and put into effect in 1967. From mid-1966 Mintech had a vigorous young Cabinet minister, Anthony Wedgwood Benn, appointed after the resignation of Frank Cousins. Benn felt that he had not merely taken over a ministry but rather been 'given the chance to create a new department that can really change the face of Britain and its prospects for survival'.[87] In 1969 Mintech took over the Industrial Reorganisation Corporation and responsibility for industrial policy from the disbanded Department of Economic Affairs,[88] and the entire Ministry of Fuel and Power. Mintech's second permanent secretary, R. W. B. 'Otto' Clarke, another wartime temporary who it will be recalled scorned C. P. Snow, later thought there had been three Mintechs – the 'Ministry of Technology', the 'Ministry of Engineering' and the 'Ministry of Industry'.[89] The 1964 Mintech may well have had elements of a gimmick about it, but it appears that Wilson

---

[85] The creation of the Ministry of Technology was criticised on two main grounds: that it separated science and technology (which had to some extent been together in the DSIR) between the Department of Education and Science and Mintech; and, that such a Ministry of Technology suggested that technology was an independent economic variable which could be used to stimulate the economy. This last was precisely the objection to it felt by the future economic adviser to the Ministry, Prof Bruce Williams (interview with Richard Coopey, 13/3/91).

[86] Mintech developed the idea of what became the Industrial Reorganisation Corporation, which was passed to the Department of Economic Affairs. One key version of the ideas came from the industrialist Ben Cant, who became Mintech's industrial adviser. Douglas Hague and Geoffrey Wilkinson, *The IRC – an experiment in industrial intervention: a history of the industrial reorganisation corporation* (London: Allen & Unwin, 1983), pp. 8–13.

[87] Benn, *Diaries 1963–67*, 30 June 1966, p. 441.   [88] Hague and Wilkinson, *The IRC*.

[89] Clarke, 'Mintech in retrospect – I', p. 25.

always intended to expand Mintech into an industry ministry.[90] In 1969 Richard Crossman recorded that: 'It looks as if Harold has taken a great deal of care and trouble in the planning of what he really cares about, Benn's new Ministry of Industry, Harold's first love.'[91] After the 1969 mergers Patrick Blackett congratulated Benn on his 'magnificent new ministry'; looking back to the beginning in 1964 he noted that 'In my wildest dreams I had not foreseen the present developments.'[92] Tony Benn made a powerful point when he later called Mintech 'the first techno-economic ministry in the world'.[93]

The most controversial, most agonised over and most important development was the merger with the Ministry of Aviation, which was much larger than Mintech. As we have already seen there were always pressures for returning a supply ministry like aviation to a service ministry. With the merger of the three service departments into the Ministry of Defence in 1964 (under the Conservatives), there was clearly an argument for merging the fourth defence department, Aviation, into it. The Plowden Committee had put two arguments against this: the large scale of the ministry and the need to develop civil aviation, seen as indivisible from military aviation.[94] A former senior official of the MoS suggested that if Aviation was tending towards more military production it should go into the Ministry of Defence; if the civil side was to be favoured it should remain independent or go to Mintech.[95] In June 1966 Wilson announced that while aviation R&D was to be transferred to Mintech, there was to be a review as to whether the aviation procurement functions might go to Defence. In November 1966 he announced that the ministry would be transferred en bloc, but that a minister would be appointed to act as the link to Defence, which would take the lead in international cooperation issues.[96] A split of Aviation into procurement and research would have suited both Mintech and Defence, but could

[90] Harold Wilson, *The Labour government, 1964–1970: a personal record* (London: Weidenfeld and Nicolson, 1971), p. 8.

[91] Richard Crossman, *The diaries of a cabinet minister*, vol. III: *Secretary of State for Social Services, 1968–1970* (London: Hamilton, Cape, 1977), p. 676, entry for Sunday, 12 October, 1969.

[92] Blackett to Benn, 6 October 1969, Blackett Papers, E65, Royal Society. By this stage Blackett was easing out of Mintech.

[93] *Engineering*, 6 November 1970, p. 485.

[94] Ministry of Aviation, *Report of the Committee of Inquiry into the aircraft industry*, Cmnd 2853 (1965), p. 87.

[95] Denis Haviland, contribution to 'Relationships between government and aeronautics – a discussion', *Journal of the Royal Aeronautical Society* 70 (March 1966), 383.

[96] *House of Commons Official Report* (hereafter *Hansard*), 16 June 1966, vol. 729, cols. 1658–9; *Hansard*, 21 November 1966, vol. 736, cols. 939–41.

not be achieved.[97] The merger took place in February 1967. The *New Scientist* reported that 'After some years of hesitation, Mr Wilson is at last having his own way over the Ministry of Aviation.'[98]

The expanded Mintech of 1966/7 to 1970 was in effect a recreation of the MoS as it existed between 1945 and 1955.[99] Both were the largest procurement ministry and R&D ministry, and sponsored the engineering, atomic power and aviation industries. The key differences were that Mintech was not responsible for army R&D and procurement, and that it had responsibility for civil research establishments, more industrial sectors, the energy industries, industrial policy and so on. Thought of in 1945–51 terms it represented most of the MoS, plus the Ministry of Fuel and Power and large parts of the Board of Trade and the DSIR. Mintech was not only broader in scope but came much higher in the ministerial pecking order, and was clearly *the* industry ministry, rather than one of the 'production departments'. Whereas the MoS had been headed by a non-Cabinet minister, by 1969 Mintech was a super-ministry *avant la lettre*, with two Cabinet ministers (Benn and Harold Lever, as Paymaster-General).

Mintech's policy for technology

What would be the policies towards innovation of a ministry so powerful across research and development, industry and procurement? They continued the earlier hostility to large-scale 'prestige' projects, but also went much further into examining the whole issue of the relations of innovation to national economic development. Anthony Wedgwood Benn, as he became minister in 1966, became concerned about the 'big problem which is how we stop ourselves from becoming a party of cancellers, who get the economists in to rule out all the projects advocated by the enthusiastic scientists and technologists'.[100] That concern would become

---

[97] Clarke, 'Mintech in retrospect – I', p. 32. The report of the official committee which had been charged with working out how to split aviation was leaked before Wilson's announcement. See *The Financial Times*, 9 November 1966. For the evidence of the leak and the investigation see George Wigg Papers, 4/107 and 4/87, LSE Archives.

[98] *New Scientist*, 9 February 1967, p. 320. The Ministry of Defence, however, tried to get the Ministry of Aviation away from Mintech (Benn, *Diaries 1968–72*, 13 March 1970, p. 253).

[99] The only contemporary reference to the comparison I have found is in William Plowden, 'Mintech moves on', *New Society*, 12 January 1967: 'Long memories may have recalled Sir Stafford Cripp's post-war Ministry of Supply' which he quotes, was '"to encourage the development of new processes, new products and techniques, and to facilitate the proper development of the various branches of the engineering industry' (p. 51).

[100] Benn, *Diaries 1963–67*, 22 July 1966, p. 459.

a more general one about innovation as a whole. Mintech developed a clear, widely advertised, programme for 'technology'. R&D spending was to shift from defence to civil purposes, from civil aerospace and civil nuclear power to other sectors, and from government laboratories to the private sector.[101] There was also a shift from emphasising innovation as being one of the key problems of British industry to focusing on questions of production, management and industrial structure. Tony Benn wrote after Labour's election defeat in 1970:

Technology is so closely linked in the public mind with Harold Wilson's famous 1963 Scarborough speech that most people have forgotten that a grandiose adherence to technology characterised the Macmillan government's thinking. The Scarborough speech broke away from this romantic attitude: it was an industrial speech, and Labour's Mintech duly evolved into an industrial department ... In Mintech it was quickly recognised that it was not technology that Britain lacked but a strong industrial organisation, good management, real attention to application ...[102]

The last sentence might seem very surprising, given Wilson's rhetoric and subsequent commentary, but Benn's observation was quite accurate. Within Mintech it was soon accepted that Britain was not, and had not been, short of R&D. A powerful implication, at least, of 'two cultures' and 'white heat' rhetoric was rejected.

It was done on the basis of statistical evidence. Overall R&D statistics for a number of countries were prepared from the late 1950s. At the same time comparative economic data were becoming more readily available. The most straightforward inspection of the figures yielded the uncomfortable conclusion that Britain did a great deal of R&D and yet had a relatively low rate of economic growth. Yet this was rarely made clear:

Think how often it is argued in Britain that growth is held down by a failure to spend on research and development as high a percentage of national product as do the Americans. In France (and Germany and Australia) the argument tends to be that growth is held down by a failure to spend as high a percentage as the British,

argued Bruce Williams in 1964.[103] Charles Carter and Bruce Williams, both economists with a particular interest in technical change, pointed out in 1964 that 'It is easy enough to *impede* growth by excessive research, by

---

[101] A. W. Benn, *The government's policy for technology*, Special Lecture given at the Imperial College of Science and Technology, 17 October 1967, (London: Ministry of Technology, 1967) is especially cogent.

[102] Anthony Wedgwood Benn MP, 'Yesterday's men at Mintech', *New Statesman* 24 July 1970, p. 76. A very forthright and interesting article.

[103] B. R. Williams, 'Research and economic growth: what should we expect?', *Minerva* 3 (1964), 57.

having too high a percentage of scientific manpower engaged in adding to the stock of knowledge and too small a percentage engaged in using it. This is the position in Britain.'[104] In the mid-1960s Bruce Williams showed clearly that there was no positive correlation between rates of economic growth and R&D/GDP ratios.[105] Williams was now Mintech's economic adviser, and at the very first meeting that Benn chaired of the Advisory Council on Technology presented these conclusions to his minister.[106] The point was taken up. Indeed Otto Clarke, commenting on statistical work in the ministry, argued for tests 'of popularly held theories which are almost invariably wrong. The recent demonstration for example, that there is no discernible relationship between R&D expenditure and economic growth, has been of first-class importance in getting the Department's thinking on better lines.'[107] Benn and Blackett, the scientific adviser, also accepted this startling result and proclaimed it in public. In 1967 Benn made clear that there was no 'automatic correlation between the amount spent on research and the rate of economic growth', and went on to show there was no correlation at all between civil R&D expenditure and growth.[108] In 1968 Blackett, now also President of the Royal Society, told the House of Commons Select Committee on Science and Technology:

Britain has the highest research and development (R and D) expenditure of any country in Europe ... she also has, and has had for at least a decade or more, one of the lowest economic growth rates. This unpalatable fact is clearly one of the main reasons for the intense national self-questioning now going on about the organisation of the national deployment of R and D, both that paid for by the Government and that paid for by industry.[109]

Also in 1968, the new Central Advisory Council for Science and Technology, chaired by Sir Solly Zuckerman, argued, implicitly but clearly enough, that the British government, and British industry, were spending too much on R&D in absolute and relative terms.[110] It noted that 'a high level of R&D is far from being the main key to successful innovation', and that 'Capital investment in new productive capacity has not ... been

[104] C. Carter and B.R. Williams, 'Government scientific policy and the growth of the British economy', *Manchester School* 32 (1964), 199.
[105] R. Williams, 'Research and economic growth, 57–71.
[106] Benn, *Diaries 1963–67*, 13 July 1966, p. 452.
[107] R.W.B. Clarke to Mr Boreham (ES), 'Statistical work', 15 June 1967, Blackett Papers E 61, Royal Society.
[108] Benn, *The government's policy for technology*, p. 2.
[109] P.M.S. Blackett, 'Understanding technological innovation', *Science of Science Foundation Newsletter* (March 1968).
[110] This body first met in January 1967. It was chaired by the Chief Scientific Adviser to the Cabinet, Sir Solly Zuckerman, and reported to the Prime Minister. On the work of this committee see Zuckerman, *Monkeys*, ch. 34.

matching our outlays on R&D'. The report estimated that in manufacturing industry, excluding aircraft, the investment to R&D ratio was 3:1.[111] The report suggested an optimum ratio in the region of 5:1.[112] Indeed it also noted what it saw as the high proportion, some one-third, of the total number of what were called 'qualified scientists and engineers' who were in R&D.[113] For Zuckerman's committee 'high research-intensiveness is not in itself a good thing. It may represent an uneconomic input of scarce and expensive resources to yield only a small commercial output. As a general goal we should aim at a lower research-intensiveness than at present.'[114] Asked about the question of investment: R&D ratios in May 1969, Benn agreed that

more scientists and engineers should be encouraged to go into production, marketing and management in industry, rather than research and development, to ensure a balanced use of scientific and technological resources over all the stages of the innovation chain. This should produce a better ratio between research and development and capital investment.[115]

The idea became a kind of commonplace among students of the economics of science. For example the Science of Science Foundation, in inviting leading figures to a meeting on 'Technological Innovation and the Growth of the National Economy' noted that:

In the belief that economic development is spurred by scientific research and development, many nations have striven for the magic US expenditure on R and D of 3% of the GNP. To their great disappointment, economic growth has shown little correlation with sharp increases in such funding. The UK provides the most pronounced demonstration of this unexpected result. Although she devotes to R and D a proportion of her wealth second only to that of the US and the USSR, the UK has in recent years achieved one of the lowest economic growth rates of any OECD country.[116]

Similar sentiments were expressed by Sir Willis Jackson, a very senior Imperial College engineer, in a number of speeches in the period 1967–8, including his Presidential Address to the British Association for the Advancement of Science in 1967.[117] Lawrence Pilkington, chairman of Pilkington Brothers, noted the 'fallacy' that 'R&D expressed as a ratio of

---

[111] Central Advisory Council for Science and Technology, *Technological innovation in Britain* (London: HMSO, July 1968), p. 9. This was the only report the committee ever published.

[112] Ibid., p. 7.   [113] Ibid., pp. 10–11.   [114] Ibid., p. 12.

[115] 'The Minister of Technology speaks to Design Engineering', *Design Engineering* May 1969, p. 30.

[116] M. Goldsmith, director Science of Science Foundation to Lord Jackson of Burnley, 24 September 1968. Jackson Papers, FS8, Imperial College Archives.

[117] See Jackson Papers, A/20/3; A/20/6; A/22/1, Imperial College Archives.

turnover', was 'really of fundamental significance', and said: 'I gravely question that British industry needs more R&D.'[118] US analysts also made similar points. The historian David Landes (a noted declinist) observed that in the early 1960s British civil R&D, in absolute terms, was running at four times the level of French civil R&D but that France had the higher growth rate.[119] Merton Peck, using data from the 1950s and early 1960s noted, in the Brookings Report on the British economy published in 1968, that Britain had the highest research intensity in the capitalist world, even though it had only an average quantity of scientists and engineers. Peck noted that Britain spent a lot on military R&D, on basic research, and that it had an industrial sector in which research-intensive industries were especially strong. Furthermore, Britain had a low proportion of scientists and engineers in industry, and a low proportion of engineers to scientists and engineers. Peck proposed cutting back on basic research in government and universities, and cutting back the aircraft industry in order to release resources for industrial R&D in industry, noting also that such an increase would also require an increase in non-R&D technical personnel. Peck was, however, ambiguous as to whether there was a shortage of the right kind of R&D.[120]

Perhaps here is the place to reflect back to that other failed technocratic moment in British politics, the first majority Labour governments of 1945–51. Under Labour, Sir Henry Tizard was recalled to Whitehall as the most senior scientific adviser on both the military and civil sides. In his presidential address to the British Association for the Advancement of Science in Brighton in September 1948, he asked similar questions to those being asked by his successors in the 1960s. In must what be a very early use of the concept of the British decline he asked: 'to what then shall we attribute the relative decline [of Britain as a great power]? Shall we argue that a main cause was that research was on too small a scale, or shall we seek for other reasons?' His preference was clearly for other reasons, he noted for example that Sweden and Switzerland had become success-ful with poor natural resources but no great strength in research, but with strong technology. He went on:

it is not the general expansion of research in this country that is of first importance for the restoration of its industrial health, and certainly not the expansion of

---

[118] The Engineer, 9 April 1970, pp. 14–15.
[119] David Landes, The unbound Prometheus (Cambridge: Cambridge University Press, 1969), pp. 520–1.
[120] Merton J. Peck, 'Science and technology' in Richard E. Caves and associates, Britain's Economic prospects (Washington: Brookings Institution, 1968), pp. 448–83. This paper does not discuss the Labour government's policy.

government research remote from the everyday problems of industry. What is of first importance is to apply what is already known.[121]

As we have seen government research was to have been expanded a great deal, especially in the 1950s, but under Mintech the research corps was to be run down.

Running down the research corps

In 1965 the Atomic Energy Authority won an important victory when the Central Electricity Generating Board and the Ministry of Fuel and Power decided to build its advanced gas-cooled reactors, (AGRs) rather than adopting American light water reactors for Britain's second generation of power reactors. This has subsequently been regarded as a disastrous choice, but was wildly applauded at the time.[122] However, the AEA's R&D budget declined under Labour, even though development of the high temperature reactor, the steam generating heavy water reactor and the fast breeder reactor continued. While Benn praised the AEA and the nuclear industry in 1967, by 1969 his estimation had changed. Benn had, according to the industry's severest critic, Duncan Burn, who was no friend of the left, 'seen part of the light' in complaining about the lack of nuclear exports and in proposing to transfer AEA work and staff to the private nuclear plant industry. Benn called for the integration of R&D and marketing: as Burn put it 'This *was* of course new, in the nuclear industry [original emphasis]'.[123] Mintech wanted to 'profit through technology', it had 'gone commercial'.[124] One journalist reported, clearly echoing Wedgwood Benn, that

it dawned that the answer was not to find fresh grandiose missions to replace those for laboratories like Harwell and Aldermaston had been set up. It was not even true that the scientists themselves only gave of their best when engaged on the great national project, for they have long been disillusioned with the frequency with which big projects ... were abandoned.[125]

---

[121] Sir Henry Tizard, 'The passing world', Presidential Address BAAS, September 1948.

[122] Duncan Burn, *Nuclear power and the energy crisis: politics and the atomic industry* (London: Macmillan, 1978); Roger Williams, *The nuclear power decisions: British policies, 1953–78* (London: Croom Helm, 1980).

[123] Duncan Burn, *The political economy of nuclear energy: an economic study of contrasting organisations in the UK and USA* (London: Institute of Economic Affairs, 1967), p. 174. Burn also noted that Blackett had long believed that a mistake had been made in the 1950s in concentrating reactor development in the public sector (p. 174).

[124] Minister of Technology, 'Address to Press Conference', 15 January 1969, Benn Archive.

[125] David Fishlock, 'Mintech's commercial revolution', *Financial Times*, 30 October 1968, clearly reporting Tony Benn.

The run-down in civil nuclear development work raised the whole question of what to do with the nuclear establishments and the other civil establishments. Already in November 1964 Wilson announced that the AEA was to be encouraged to do non-atomic work, and this became possible with the passing of the Science and Technology Act 1965. Harwell, in particular, did a great deal of work for the private sector.[126] It was a similar story in all the other R&D establishments, for 'in spite of the original expectation, the arguments came to point decisively to redeployment and reduction, rather than expansion, of the numbers in the government-financed establishments'.[127] Mintech later proposed a hiving-off of the laboratories, and the merging of the AEA into a single British Research and Development Corporation, which would be larger than any private R&D organisation. The intention was that this would be funded one-third directly from government, one-third from contracts from government departments and one-third from industry. The strong implication was that one-third of the capacity was surplus to government requirements.[128] The civil establishments were to be taken out of the civil service (as the AEA already was), and given a contractual relation with government departments.[129] This was not to happen, but it was very clear that the great national civil laboratories, whether the NPL or the nuclear centres, would never again be at the heart of great national technological efforts.

In the defence research establishments too there were cutbacks, and attempts to do more civil and industrial work. The Atomic Weapons Research Establishment at Aldermaston began to do a significant amount of non-nuclear civil work.[130] Even before the Aviation transfer (which brought the other main defence laboratories to Mintech) attempts were made to link the military work to civil concerns: Mintech was represented on the Defence Research Committee and links were established between research establishments and Mintech; in March 1966 an industrial systems unit was established at the Royal Radar Establishment at Malvern.[131] In July 1968, when the government announced further cuts in defence

[126] See Philip Gummett, *Scientists in Whitehall* (Manchester: Manchester University Press, 1980), pp. 129–32.
[127] Clarke, 'Mintech in retrospect- III', p. 140.
[128] Benn, *The Engineer*, 9 April 1970, p. 11.
[129] Ministry of Technology, *Industrial research and development in government laboratories: a new organisation for the seventies* (London: HMSO, 1970) (Green Paper).
[130] See Coopey, 'Restructuring', for details of the Aldermaston case. In the 1950s 10 per cent of Aldermaston's budget was for non-military nuclear work, done to attract those physicists concerned to continue publishing (J. Hendry and J. D. Lawson, *Fusion research in the UK 1945–1960* (Harwell: UKAEA, 1993), p. 34).
[131] *Statement on the Defence Estimates 1967*, Cmnd 3203 (February 1967), p. 44.

R&D spending and staffing, it was stated that 'some of those released will be transferred to civil work in the establishments'.[132] Strategies of diversification, and links to industry, of spin-off, were followed in all the military establishments.[133] But the attempt to use the military establishments for civil purposes was not a great success, as Coopey has shown for Aldermaston.[134]

It seems clear though that the research establishments were felt by many to have become too large. The Plowden Report had been very sceptical of Ministry of Aviation suggestions that the aeronautical establishments should retain employment by shifting to civil and non-aeronautical work.[135] R. V. Jones, clearly thought a mistake had been made after the war in holding and then building on research establishments, at the expense of universities and industry; he contrasted the situation in the USA, where wartime R&D expanded in the universities and stayed there after it.[136] The analysis of Sir Robert Cockburn – a former chief scientist at the Ministry of Aviation, and director of Farnborough – was more powerful still: he regretted the 'myth of big science had been born and large research establishments were built up to maintain the momentum of discovery in nuclear energy, aeronautics, electronics, space and in agriculture and medicine'. The wartime achievements in radar, jets, guided weapons, ballistic missiles and the atomic bomb were 'seen as scientific breakthroughs' but 'in fact they were engineering breakthroughs dependent on many years of patient research, culminating at that particular period because of the pressure of military need'.[137]

The run-down in defence R&D and the defence establishments, was, however, not to continue (see table 6.2). In January 1969 Richard Crossman noted:

All our election commitments were to reorientate the whole balance of R&D away from defence to civil affairs. We haven't done it. Instead, Denis [Healey – Minister of Defence] has managed to say that if we are to make major cuts in overseas military commitments we must maintain a predominant position for R&D, and have the best even for our limited, new, European-based defences. If our equipment is reduced it must, he maintains, be of the best and if we are to buy British it means that the R&D can't be cut back in proportion to the cut in our foreign commitments.[138]

---

[132] Supplementary Statement on Defence Policy 1968, Cmnd 3701 (July 1968), p. 12.
[133] The best studied is the Radar Research Establishment. See Coopey, 'Restructuring' and Donald MacKenzie and Graham Spinardi, 'The technological impact of a defence research establishment' in Coopey et al., Defence science and technology.
[134] Coopey, 'Restructuring'.
[135] Ministry of Aviation, Enquiry into the aircraft industry, pp. 88–90.
[136] R. V. Jones, 'Research establishments', in Proceedings of the Royal Society A 342 (1975), 481–90.
[137] Sir Robert Cockburn, commenting on Jones, 'Research establishments', in Proceedings of the Royal Society A 342 (1975), 89.
[138] Crossman, Diaries, III, p. 309.

Table 6.2 *Government funding of defence and civil R&D,*
1960–75, constant 1985 (£ million)

	Defence R&D		Civil
	Total	Intramural	
1960	1748	–	–
1965	1720	689[a]	1543
1970	1325	557	1790
1975	1850	705	2315

Note:
[a] 1966.

Source: David Buck and Keith Hartley, 'The political economy of defence R&D: Burden or Benefit?' in Richard Coopey et al. (eds.), *Defence science and technology: adjusting to change* (Harwood, 1993), pp. 13–44, tables 2.1, 2.3, 2.4.

Crossman was wrong to suggest that nothing had been done since, as we have seen, cuts in defence R&D were very large and proportionally larger than cuts in defence spending overall. But from the very late 1960s two big new projects were started: the MRCA or multi-role combat aircraft (which emerged as the Tornado) and the Chevaline upgrade for the Polaris missile. Chevaline was supposed to penetrate the defences of Moscow and to show the Americans that Britain was continuing with development of nuclear weapons;[139] it was a space project, as well as a nuclear project,[140] involving the 'hardening' of warheads to X-rays and making them steerable in space. According to Solly Zuckerman, who opposed what he saw as a pointless 'modernisation' of the Polaris warhead, the programme was the outcome of a very successful lobby by the Aldermaston scientists and engineers to keep themselves in business.[141] A recent study supports this view, pointing in particular to the role of Sir William Cook and Victor Macklen, another civil service scientist.[142] By the mid-1970s defence R&D had grown very

[139] 'The Ministry of Technology, 1964–1970' (Witness Seminar), *Contemporary Record* 5 (1991), 128–48, esp. 139–42; John Simpson, *The independent nuclear state: the United States, Britain and the military atom* (London: Macmillan, 1986); Zuckerman, *Monkeys*, ch. 32.
[140] Gummett, 'Defence research policy' in M. Goldsmith, *UK science policy* (London: Longman, 1984), p. 64–5.
[141] Zuckerman, *Monkeys*, ch. 32.
[142] Graham Spinardi, 'Aldermaston and British nuclear weapons development: testing the "Zuckerman thesis"', *Social Studies of Science* 27 (1997), 547–82.

considerably and reached levels, in real terms, higher than those of the 1960 peak (see table 6.2). Indeed it would continue to grow into the 1980s.[143]

The defence origins of industrial policy

Mintech's major piece of legislation, the Industrial Expansion Act 1968, was concerned with industrial finance and intervention in industry. The Act, which applied to all ministers, was Mintech's creation, marking Mintech as the key industrial ministry. The Act was essentially an enabling measure, which provided a procedure for selective financing of industrial investment schemes and for the creation of industrial boards through an abbreviated parliamentary procedure.[144] The critical part of the Bill was that it granted general powers of interventions in all sectors of the sort that were restricted to particular industries, or to some aspect only, notably R&D.[145] But these powers would be used, as they already were, in a discriminatory fashion: 'The object of industrial policy, as we see it', said Benn, 'is to pick winners and not to run an undiscriminatory "meals-on-wheels" service for British firms whether they are efficient or inefficient.'[146] The point was not that a new policy of discrimination, or picking winners, was introduced, as the histories of industrial policy focused on the non-discriminating Board of Trade suggest. Government, and particularly the supply ministries, was already discriminating between sectors and indeed between firms. What Labour was doing was extending the scope of discrimination, making it more general. Indeed behind the Bill was a strong sense that highly discriminatory support for certain industries, notably aviation, had gone too far. On the other hand, discriminatory industrial policy was certainly thought to be highly desirable. The sense present in the early 1960s and before that the defence sector provided a model for intervention was clearly still at work in Mintech. For example, in an internal address 1969 Benn noted that the take-over of aviation brought in 'scientists and engineers of exceptional ability' and

an experience of dealing with industry which simply did not exist in any other department in Whitehall. If those who have come with that knowledge of industry

---

[143] Council for Science and Society, *UK Military R&D* (Oxford: Oxford University Press, 1986), table 2.1, p. 8.

[144] The concept of an industrial enabling Act went back to the 1930s, but was usually rejected. Governments preferred the passing of individual Acts of Parliament for particular industrial schemes (e.g. the Cotton Industry Acts). Labour has passed a limited enabling Act for the establishment of industrial boards in 1947. See Tony Benn, *Hansard*, vol. 757, 1 February 1968, cols. 1576–8.

[145] *Hansard*, vol. 757, 1 February 1968, cols. 1576–9.

[146] *Hansard*, vol. 757, 1 February 1968, col. 1584.

into this wider department with its new responsibilities can make that knowledge and information available for more general purposes, then, not for the first time, defence will have pioneered a technology not in hardware but in the relationship between Government and the firms that earn us our living.[147]

In this he echoed not only Cripps's wartime comments but also a comparison the MoS had made between itself and the Board of Trade in 1950: only the former had a great deal of scientific, technical and industrial expertise, as well as close relations with firms.[148] Announcing the further expansion of Mintech in October 1969 Benn argued that 'we have gained very substantially by the merger with the Ministry of Aviation in being able to bring into our work with private industry people who have acquired over the years ... a great deal of knowledge of the defence industries'.[149] The Industrial Expansion Act, symbolically enough, made permanent a slightly amended Ministry of Supply Act 1939.[150]

The Industrial Expansion Act was a major piece of legislation. It was quite widely used for example to finance the setting up of new aluminium smelters (by the Board of Trade) and the production of Concorde. Indeed the debate on the Concorde production clauses in Parliament presents a fascinating glimpse of the politics of technology in the 1960s. By 1968, on the eve of the prototype Concorde's first flight, a decision was needed as to whether the production of Concorde for the airlines should be funded by government. The government decided that it should, and inserted a clause in the Industrial Expansion Bill to allow for loans and the government purchase of special machinery (worth some £30 million) specifically for this purpose. While the Bill was much criticised by Conservatives, they did not oppose the funding of Concorde production. The only open opposition came from two Labour MPs, (Lord) Hugh Jenkins (1908–2004) and Dr Edwin Brooks (1929–), an academic. For their pains they were accused by Conservative MPs of preferring to 'see the Government spending money breeding bigger and better TUC cart horses rather than developing this modern exciting aircraft'.[151] Yet the minister proposing the clauses, Wedgwood Benn, seemed to have more sympathy with the Bill's opponents than its supporters. He defended Hugh Jenkins from the charge of being a member of the anti-Concorde 'lunatic fringe', and said that Jenkins

---

[147] 'Minister's talk to staff', *Mintech Review* (May 1969).
[148] Memorandum, 'Civil Functions of the Ministry of Supply', 20 February 1950, AVIA 49/75, PRO.
[149] *Hansard*, 21 October 1969, col. 1072.
[150] See *Industrial Expansion Act 1968*, 16&17 Eliz 2. Ch 32, para. 13.
[151] *Hansard*, 3 April 1968, col. 521.

might well have argued that if we had spent more money on modernising the railway system, or introducing containerisation earlier or going in for fuel cell development or for the battery electric car, this might have brought a better return in terms of money or human enjoyment.

Indeed, Benn indicated that he wanted to 'tilt the balance a little more in favour of surface transportation and not to allow air transportation to be the only field in which major efforts are made'. Benn had noted 'if ... I am asked what the market for it [Concorde] will be, it is very hard to say'.[152] Hugh Jenkins withdrew his amendment referring to the impossibility of winning against 'blind, touching faith', and the 'evangelical enthusiasm', the 'orgiastic atmosphere' – 'it was impossible to break through this sort of conviction'.[153] Even it seems, for a minister.

That Mintech's attitude to high technology was highly influenced by economic considerations is clear from space policy. The Conservatives had decided to make the Blue Streak rocket, no longer suitable for the military, the basis of a European space launcher. By 1964 the ELDO was established. In the early 1960s the costs of ELDO were comparable with Concorde. Work proceeded slowly and costs overran, as usual, and in early 1966 the Minister of Aviation questioned the whole basis of the project, arguing that the European market was too small and that in any case Europe could not compete with the USA. Britain's European partners rejected these arguments. Nevertheless, Britain continued in ELDO, though paying less. The Conservative opposition, as in the case of Concorde, was supportive of ELDO.[154] But in 1968, after the French vetoed British entry into the Common Market, Tony Benn repeated the earlier arguments and announced that Britain was pulling out of ELDO. At this time, however, Britain announced it would be developing its own smaller-scale programme. While in Britain economic considerations were important, on the continent the desire to build up technological capability took precedence.[155] Mintech was also very cautious indeed in funding more conventional civil aerospace projects. Although the government had co-funded the design study phase of the European Airbus, it pulled out of further development because of the sales prospects; the terms of the agreement proposed (including the lack of commitment to

---

[152] A. W. Benn, *Hansard*, 3 April 1968, cols. 527–8.
[153] Hugh Jenkins, *Hansard*, 3 April 1968, col. 534.
[154] De Maria and Krige, 'ELDO's sad parable', p. 129 note that Conservatives opposed Labour's hostility to ELDO, for example.
[155] De Maria and Krige, 'ELDO's sad parable', 109–37, esp. 125–30. This is not to say that Labour was against European collaboration: as noted above Wilson proposed a European Technological Community, and indeed the Labour government pursued a number of major European ventures in military aircraft.

using Rolls-Royce's RB211 engine); and possible competition from a British aircraft (the BAC 3–11). In the event the British Aircraft Corporation (BAC) asked for support for the 3–11, but did not get it. The only major project launched was the Rolls-Royce RB211 engine. This project led to the bankruptcy of Rolls-Royce and its nationalisation by the Conservative government in 1971. The RB211 has, in many versions, proved to be a very successful engine.[156]

The Conservative Edward Heath, elected as Prime Minister in 1970, regarded Mintech as a gimmick, and had planned to put it into the Board of Trade.[157] Heath, a creator of large 'super-ministries', dismantled one the most important: he put a free-market oriented set of ministers into Mintech, headed by Geoffrey Rippon; a forced reshuffle arising from the death of the Chancellor Ian Macleod later the same year saw the appointment of John Davies, an interventionist businessman. Three months later, Mintech was merged with the remainder of the Board of Trade into the Department of Trade and Industry. Yet in the course of the famous 'U-turn' the new ministry enacted the highly interventionist Industry Act 1972.[158] Under Peter Walker from late 1972, the department 'probably did carry more weight than the Treasury, whose advice Heath was by then disinclined to hear'.[159] However, the crucial procurement functions, and warlike R&D, were put briefly into a Ministry of Aviation Supply (outside the Cabinet) and then into a newly created procurement executive in the Ministry of Defence, where they remain. Heath returned all of procurement to the services, for the first time since 1939.

What then was the 'white heat'?

At some level the 'white heat' was an electoral gimmick of short duration, associated with Harold Wilson's 1964 election campaign, but clearly going back to Labour's reassessment of it position following its defeat in 1959. What was presented to the electorate in terms of policies, as opposed to presentation, was not very different from what the Conservatives were doing, but the presentation mattered a great deal. Yet by 1966 'white heat' had lost its political salience, and in its 1966

---

[156] See Keith Hayward, *Government and British civil aerospace: a case study in post-war technology policy* (Manchester: Manchester University Press, 1983).
[157] Campbell, *Heath*, p. 221.
[158] In subsequent years there would be splits and rejoining of the DTI – separate departments emerged for trade, industry and energy in 1974. Trade and industry were put back together again in 1983.
[159] Campbell, *Heath*, p. 314.

manifesto Labour downplayed science and technology.[160] In 1970 it was hardly an issue either. Yet that is not the whole story for the 'white heat' then and since has been associated with the whole life of the government. One historian says that through to 1970 Mintech was 'incarnating Wilson's faith in the white heat of science-based industries as the motor of expansion'.[161] Of course there is a warrant for this – after all Concorde, and the AGR, and other such investments, were hugely important and very visible. Furthermore Labour was still widely seen as a modernising party committed to science and technology. In 1967 *Private Eye* called Benn, 'the most dangerous man in Britain' because he was a moderniser, keen to replace the old for the sake of novelty, to destroy the city with more cars and so on.[162] In 1969/70 *Monty Python's Flying Circus* made fun of Mintech for its commitment to white elephants. In its second programme it featured obvious references to Concorde in the form of flying sheep, one of which was piloted by one Brian Trubshaw, the then famous British Concorde test pilot. The famous Ministry of Silly Walks sketch alludes very directly to Concorde and to Mintech. The minister with the silly walk meets with an inventor who has a silly walk, and wants 'a Government grant to help me develop it': although not silly enough for the minister, the inventor claims that 'with Government backing I could make it very silly'. The Minister tells him that

the very real problem is one of money. I'm afraid that the Ministry of Silly Walks is no longer getting the kind of support it needs. You see there's Defence, Social Security, Health, Housing, Education, Silly Walks ... they're all supposed to get the same. But last year, the Government spent less on the Ministry of Silly Walks than it did on National Defence. Now we get £348,000,000 a year, which is supposed to be spent on all our available products ... Now the Japanese have a man who can bend his leg back over his head and back again with every single step. While the Israelis ...

However the inventor is lucky: the minister offers him 'a Research Fellowship on the Anglo-French silly walk', which the inventor recognises as 'la marche futile'. The scene then cuts to two stage Frenchmen, one of whom responds 'Merci, mon petit chou-chou Brian Trubshaw'.[163]

These are understandable reactions, but the 'white heat' was, in the framework used above, something different. It was an ending rather than the beginning of an overweening enthusiasm for national technology. Labour ended many large-scale techno-national projects and was hostile

---

[160] Hilary and Steven Rose, 'Where is the scientific revolution?', *Guardian*, 22 March 1966.
[161] P. Hennessy, *Whitehall* (London: Fontana, 1990), p. 431.
[162] *Private Eye*, 4 August 1967.
[163] Taken from www.montypython.net. The flying sheep sketches were broadcast in October 1969; silly walks in September 1970.

to many that survived; it reduced, temporarily, high levels of defence R&D. This was the end of the state research corps as a growing self-confident sector; and the end, for many, of the belief that Britain lacked R&D, at least temporarily. It was highly suggestive that in 1970 – in the *New Statesman* – Benn should have been so keen to argue, over and over again, that Mintech had stopped projects that made no commercial sense.[164] 'No more Concordes' – a line attributed to Mrs Thatcher in the 1980s was, as we have seen, Benn's in the 1960s. The 'white heat' was also the final, and most radical, attempt to use the experience of the military sector for civilian purposes.

Most important of all, there was a great transformation of views about British national science and technology. A key aspect of the technocratic moment ended with a recognition that R&D was not, and had not been, deficient in Britain. Bruce Williams's observation of the non-correlation of R&D spending and economic growth was demonstrated again and again into the early 1970s.[165] By the early 1970s neo-liberal economists were attacking state-led investments in aviation and nuclear power with considerable strength. John Jewkes, long a critic of government intervention, attacked the usual arguments made for government support of 'high' technology with gusto.[166] David Henderson, who had been an economist at the Ministry of Aviation, did a devastating cost–benefit analysis of Concorde and the AGR.[167] Duncan Burn's scathing study of the AGR programme, and of British nuclear policy more generally, attacked the monopoly over nuclear R&D by the AEA and its poor nuclear technology.[168] It is also surely significant that in this period historians produced studies of the history of industrial R&D which were not declinist.[169] As we shall see, however, a new wave of declinist

[164] Benn, 'Yesterday's men at Mintech'.
[165] R. C. O. Matthews, 'The contribution of science and technology to economic development' in B. R. Williams (ed.), *Science and technology in economic growth* (London: Macmillan, 1973), pp. 7–8. See also C. T. Taylor and Z. A. Silberston, *The economic impact of the patent system: a study of the British experience* (Cambridge: Cambridge University Press, 1973); K. Norris and R. Vaisey, *The economics of research and technology* (London: Allen & Unwin, 1973).
[166] John Jewkes, *Government and high technology*, Institute of Economic Affairs Occasional Paper no. 37 (1972).
[167] P. D. Henderson, 'Two British errors: their probable size and some possible lessons', *Oxford Economic Papers* 29 (1977), 186–94. See also his Reith Lectures, published as *Innocence and design* (London: Economist, 1986).
[168] Burn, *Nuclear power and the energy crisis*.
[169] Michael Sanderson, 'Research and the firm in British industry, 1919–1939', *Science Studies* 2 (1972), 107–51; Leslie Hannah, *The rise of the corporate economy* (London: Methuen, 1976); S. B. Saul, 'Research and development in British industry from the end of the nineteenth century to the 1960s' in T. C. Smout (ed.), *The search for wealth and stability* (London: Macmillan, 1979), pp. 135–6.

anti-histories would return, in which the Mintech experience, if it figured at all, was at best a failed attempt to increase R&D and to technologise the British state and industry.

Whatever happened to the arms industry?

After Mintech, British R&D was never the same again. The same was true of the arms industry. The period from the mid-1950s to 1970 saw the last gasp of the traditional armourers. The warship builders suffered with the decline of merchant shipbuilding, and the whole industry became a 'ward of the state', specifically of Mintech, by the end of the 1960s.[170] Fairfield went belly up in 1965 and the government took a 50 per cent stake in the company that took over – Upper Clyde Shipbuilders, which included most of the warship builders on the Clyde.[171] Other groups formed at this time were Scott Lithgow on the Clyde and Swan Hunter (Tyne) (which included the Vickers Tyne yard) leaving Vickers at Barrow, Cammell-Laird on the Clyde and Harland and Wolff in Belfast as warship builders. The Royal Navy's capital ships of the 1960s were the four very large Polaris missile-carrying submarines named after early twentieth-century battleships. *Renown* and *Revenge* were built by Cammell-Laird at Birkenhead, where employment peaked at over 10,000.[172] After this employment was to fall drastically, and in 1970 the government bought 50 per cent of the company. *Resolution* and *Repulse* were built by Vickers at Barrow, which remained a submarine builder. From 1970 onwards, with only a few exceptions, major warship contracts went only to Vosper Thorneycroft, Yarrow, Vickers (Barrow), Cammell-Laird and Swan Hunter.[173] In 1977 the shipbuilding industry was nationalised.[174]

If shipbuilding and traditional naval armaments declined, there was maintenance of employment (but not growth on any scale) in the new core of the arms industry – aircraft and electronics. Table 6.3 gives

---

[170] Owen, *From Empire to Europe*, p. 107.

[171] On the collapse of UCS, and the famous work-in see Willie Thompson and Finlay Hart, *The UCS work-in* (London: Lawrence & Wishart, 1971).

[172] K. Warren, *Steel, ships and men: Cammell Laird, 1824–1993* (Liverpool: Liverpool University Press, 1998), pp. 288–9.

[173] Trevor Taylor and Keith Hayward, *The UK defence industrial base: development and future policy options* (London: Brassey's, 1989), table 2.6.

[174] On the warship builders see Lewis Johnman and Hugh Murphy, 'The rationalisation of warship building in the United Kingdom, 1945–2000', *Journal of Strategic Studies* 24 (2001), 107–27.

Table 6.3 *The largest British arms manufacturers, 1955, by total
employment of the firms*

1955		1965		
AEI	87,000	Hawker-Siddeley	123,000	(merged with De Havilland)
Hawker-Siddeley Group	75,000	AEI	93,000	
Vickers Ltd	70,000	EE	75,000	(lost aviation to BAC)
GEC	60,000	GEC	64,000	
English Electric	39,000	Vickers	56,078	(lost aviation to BAC)
Rolls-Royce	37,500	Rolls-Royce	43,549	
De Havilland	25,990	BAC	42,000	(merger of Bristol and Vickers and EE aviation)
Bristol Aeroplane	21,000			
BSA	18,000			
ESC	16,500			
Mullard	16,000			
Plessey	15,894			
Ferranti	11,378			
Cammell-Laird	10,643			

Source: David Jeremy, 'The hundred largest employers in the United Kingdom in manufacturing and non-manufacturing industries in 1907, 1935 and 1955', *Business History* 33 (1991), 93–111; and *The Times 300* (London: The Times, 1965). Note that GEC, AEI and EE merged under government auspices in the late 1960s to form a new GEC.

employment in the leading arms firms, though not data on what proportion of their workforce was devoted to arms. We know though that the aircraft and aero-engine industries firms were very largely concerned with arms (as they had been in the interwar years), while the electrical firms were much more diversified. In 1955 the names from the interwar years are clearly still present, alongside the major new entrants, the electronic firms, one of which, EE, had also become a major aircraft firm. Within the existing aircraft industry, the greatest changes were brought about by government action in the late 1950s. The industry was forced to merge, producing two airframe and missile makers – Hawker-Siddeley (most Hawker-Siddeley companies and De Havilland), the BAC (EE, Vickers and Bristol); two engine makers, Rolls-Royce, and Bristol-Siddeley (Armstrong-Siddeley and Bristol), and a merger of all helicopter work in Westland.

Rolls-Royce took over the remainder of the jet-engine industry in the late 1960s. The late 1960s also saw the merger, under Mintech/ Industrial Reorganisation Corporation auspices, of the three largest electrical firms – EE, Associated Electrical Industries (AEI) and GEC under the name GEC. By 1970 the arms industry was dominated by BAC, Hawker-Siddeley, Rolls-Royce, GEC and a few other firms including Vickers and Ferranti. From 1970 this private arms industry was nationalised, largely as key firms became potentially or actually bankrupt. Rolls-Royce was rescued by the Conservative government in 1971; Ferranti by the National Enterprise Board in 1975.[175] The aircraft industry, with the shipbuilding industry, was nationalised in 1977. The main private armourer was now GEC, which controlled the bulk of the military electronics industry. The old arms industry was to become a particularly important site for innovative trade union activity, often linked to a new generation of socialist intellectuals. The famous Upper Clyde Shipbuilders work-in of 1970[176] was followed by many discussions, plans, programmes for new forms of state intervention and control of production.[177] The context was the enormously controversial and vigorously resisted policies of the now radical socialist and protectionist Tony Benn at the Department of Industry between 1974 and 1975. One particular focus was the development of 'socially useful production', but interestingly the union-led campaigns for the production of 'socially useful products' made the unstated implication that armaments had no social utility and had not been procured by a social process. Even at this

---

[175] The arms firms were some of the first to be privatised, and indeed old state-created plants were privatised too. The story is long and complex, but Rolls-Royce went back to private ownership; Vickers went back into arms, buying state tanks works at Leeds, it is now part of Rolls-Royce; British Aerospace was privatised and bought the Royal Ordnance factories. VSEL, created as a management buy-out of the old Vickers yards at Barrow was sold to GEC in 1995 (VSEL also included some armaments work at Barrow). GEC already owned Yarrow. In the late 1990s British Aerospace bought GEC's military side, creating BAE Systems, overwhelmingly the largest defence contractor in Britain.

[176] On the collapse of UCS, and the famous work-in see Thompson and Hart, *The UCS Work-in.*

[177] Huw Beynon and Hilary Wainwright, *The workers' report on Vickers* (London: Pluto Press, 1979); Benwell Community Development Project, *The making of the ruling class, final report no. 6* (Newcastle: Benwell CDP, 1979); Coventry, Liverpool, Newcastle, North Tyneside Trades Councils, *State intervention in industry: a workers' enquiry* (London: Spokesman, 1982) (1st edn, 1980); Lucas Aerospace Combine Shop Stewards' Committee, *Lucas: an alternative plan* (Nottingham: Institute for Workers' Control, no date, IWC pamphlet no. 55).

critical moment of reflection on the state and industry by the left and the trade unions, the warfare state was not part of the picture.

The story of British R&D matches the story of armaments. Overall R&D spending, as a proportion of GDP, fell in Britain during the late 1960s. Industrially funded R&D also fell, in absolute and relative terms, for the first time since the early 1930s. Especially noteworthy is the fact that the largest R&D spenders – for example the electrical companies – had been merged with the intervention of the Industrial Reorganisation Corporation and had decreased their R&D spending.[178] By the late 1960s then the hopes so clearly placed after the war in R&D, were waning.

[178] See David Edgerton, 'Research, development and competitiveness' in K. Hughes (ed.), *The future of UK industrial competitiveness and the role of industrial policy* (London: Policy Studies Institute, 1994).

7   The disappearance of the British warfare state

The invisibility of the British warfare state has been longstanding, systematic and deeply entrenched in political commentary and historical writing. We have seen already the way in which many scientific intellectuals downplayed the role of the military in anti-histories of British technocracy. They were far from being alone: British intellectuals in general wrote the warfare state out of their account of Britain and historians followed them. Broadly speaking, up to the Second World War, intellectuals praised Britain for its alleged liberalism and pacifism, its maritime and trading orientation, and such a Britain, it was argued, could obviously not be a warfare state. After the war, however, an emergent militaristic critique attacked exactly those features that earlier intellectuals had celebrated. This militaristic critique, like the technocratic critique, had a significant anti-historical element. The argument was often cast historically; it was assumed the British state was militarily weak and emphasis was placed on examining what were taken to be anti-militaristic liberal traditions in Britain as explanations of the weakness and particular nature of the British armed forces. By contrast, the welfare state loomed large. Social democrats presented a picture of Britain in which war was vitally important for the creation of a welfare state, but ignored the warfare state. After the Second World War then both the left and right underplayed the significance of the military, though for different reasons: one by celebrating the welfare state, the other by condemning liberal anti-militarism. Running through all these arguments was a comparison with something which at first sight was Germany.

Britain is not Germany I: celebrating liberal England

In British accounts of itself a certain image of Germany plays a critical, though often implicit role. From the Great War to the present day, 'Germany' – sometimes just Prussia – has been seen as the model militaristic nation by British intellectuals and propagandists. For many it has also been seen as the model of a scientific nation, in which state and universities promoted new science-based industries. A historical Germany, usually Wilhelmine Germany, served as a model even when contemporary Germany could not.

A standard argument around the Great War was that Germans were scientific and intellectual giants but moral dwarfs corrupted by militaristic doctrines.[1] Less well known is that many saw Germans not simply as militaristic, nor yet merely lacking respect for the rules of international law or war, but as brutal machine-like warriors with a particular predilection for using science and technology for killing. Some few weeks into the Great War, the British Prime Minister, Herbert Asquith, was clear that:

Mankind owes much to Germany, a very great debt for the contributions she has made to philosophy, to science, and to the arts, but that which is specifically German in the movement of the world in the last thirty years has been, on the intellectual side, the development of the doctrine of the supreme and ultimate prerogative in human affairs of material force, and on the practical side the taking of the foremost place in the fabrication and the multiplication of the machinery of destruction.[2]

Two weeks later the Chancellor of the Exchequer, David Lloyd George, dilated on a similar theme. The German peasant, he said,

has been drilled into a false idea of civilisation. It is efficient, it is capable, but it is a hard civilisation; it is a selfish civilisation; it is a material civilisation ... They cannot understand a great Empire pledging its resources, pledging its might, pledging the lives of its children, pledging its very existence, to protect a little nation that seeks to defend itself. God made man in His own image, high of purpose, in the region of the spirit; German civilisation would re-create him in the image of a Diesel machine – precise, accurate, powerful, but with no room for soul to operate.[3]

The Foreign Secretary, Sir Edward Grey, made a particular complaint about German military technology in 1916:

---

[1] See for example, Gilbert Murray, *Thoughts on the war*, Oxford Pamphlets 1914 (London: Oxford University Press, 1914); M. E. Sadler, *Modern Germany and the modern world* (London: Macmillan, 1914). See also Daniel Pick, *War machine: the rationalisation of slaughter in the machine age* (London: Yale University Press, 1993).

[2] H. H. Asquith, speech at the Guildhall, 4 September 1914, in *War speeches by British ministers, 1914–1916* (London: Fisher Unwin, 1917), p. 29.

[3] For Lloyd George, the Kaiser's speeches were 'full of the glitter and bluster of German militarism – "mailed fist" and "shining armour"'. German militarism was the problem, for as Lloyd George explained: 'We are not fighting the German people. The German people are under the heel of this military caste, and it will be the day of rejoicing for the German peasant, artisan and trader when the military caste is broken.' David Lloyd George (Chancellor of the Exchequer), speech at the Queen's Hall, London, 19 September 1914, in *War speeches*, pp. 220–3.

Unless mankind learns from this War to avoid war, the struggle will have been in vain. Furthermore, it seems to me that over humanity will loom the menace of destruction. The Germans have thrown the door wide open to every form of attack on human life. The use of poisonous fumes, or something akin to them, in war, was recommended to our naval or military authorities many years ago, and was rejected by them as too horrible for civilised peoples. The Germans have come with floating mines in the open seas, threatening belligerents and neutrals equally; they have come with the indiscriminating, murderous Zeppelin, which does military damage only by accident; they have come with the submarine, which destroys neutral and belligerent ships in scorn alike of law and of mercy; they have come upon blameless nations with invasion and incendiarism and confiscation; they have come with poisonous gases and liquid fire. All their scientific genius has been dedicated to wiping out human life. They have forced these things into general use in war ... Will the outstanding contribution of Kultur disclosed in this War be such efficiency in slaughter as to lead to wholesale extermination?[4]

While Germany had been the great scientific nation, said Lord Justice Moulton (who was not only scientifically trained, but was also responsible for the supply of explosives) in his 1919 Rede Lectures, 'Yet we find Germany during a period of at least twenty years consciously and deliberately making preparations for a war to be waged upon its neighbours solely for the purpose of self-aggrandizement.' The Germans attacked civilians brutally and 'they introduced the use of asphyxiating gas and all the tortures of so-called chemical warfare ... It is the monster which the Frankenstein of Mary Wollstonecraft created – a human being with his powers magnified to those of a giant but destitute of moral sense.'[5] During the war German science was itself attacked: the chemist Sir William Ramsay claimed that it had not been that good after all[6] and British scientists bearing German names faced calls, even from prominent scientists, for their removal from official posts.[7] Until 1926 German, Austrian, Hungarian and Bulgarian scientists were kept out of international scientific organisations; neutrals faced special restrictions.[8] British scientists were concerned at the association that was made between

[4] Sir Edward Grey, Statement to *Chicago Daily News*, 10 April 1916, in *War speeches*, pp. 197–8.
[5] Quoted in H. Fletcher Moulton, *The life of Lord Moulton* (London: Nisbet, 1922), pp. 177–8.
[6] Lawrence Badash, 'British and American views of the German Menace in World War I', *Notes and Records of the Royal Society of London* 34 (1979), 98–102. Sir William Ramsay claimed that what good science was done in Germany was due to 'Hebrews resident among them' (quoted in J. D. Bernal, *The social function of science* (London: Routledge and Kegan Paul, 1939), p. 183).
[7] Badash, 'British and American views', 93–8.
[8] Just as noteworthy is the fact that the key work on the international relations of British science around the Great War, which demolished the myth of scientific internationalism, was done by non-British scholars. See Brigitte Schroeder-Gudehus, *Les scientifiques et la*

Germany, barbarism and science, for it reflected badly on science in Britain.[9] The application of science to war was now blamed on the Germans.

Some of the Great War descriptions of Germany might seem a quarter of a century too early, so closely do they mirror the British image of the Nazis. There were indeed continuities not only in personnel but in attitudes from one war to the next. In a broadcast in August 1941 Winston Churchill, himself a Cabinet minister before and during the Great War, used images straight out of the previous conflict:

The whole of Europe has been wrecked and trampled down by the mechanical weapons and barbaric fury of the Nazis; the most deadly instruments of war-science have been joined to the extreme refinements of treachery, and thus have formed a combine of aggression the like of which has never been known …[10]

More surprising is the case of J. B. Priestley. His famous *Postscript* broadcasts are known for their image of England but much less so for their contrasted image of Germany.[11] In his first broadcast, Priestley saw the evacuation from Dunkirk as 'typically English' in its 'folly and its grandeur'; 'when apparently all was lost, so much was gloriously retrieved'. He continued:

Out of a black gulf of humiliation and despair, rises a sun of blazing glory. This is not the German way. They don't make such mistakes (a grim fact we should bear in mind) but also – they don't achieve such epics. There is never anything to inspire a man either in their victories or their defeats; boastful when they're winning, quick to whine when threatened with defeat – there is nothing about them that ever catches the world's imagination. That vast machine of theirs can't

---

paix. *La communauté scientifique internationale au cours des années 20* (Montreal: Les Presses de l'Université de Montreal, 1978); Peter Alter, 'The Royal Society and the International Association of Academies 1897–1919', *Notes and Records of the Royal Society of London* 34 (1980), 241–64; D. Kevles, '"Into Hostile Camps"': the reorganisation of international science in World War I', 62 *Isis*(1971), 47–60; Badash, 'British and American views'. The key contribution by a British scholar, a biologist, focused on a few British scientists who campaigned against the exclusion of Germany and its wartime allies (A. G. Cock, 'Chauvinism and internationalism in science: the International Research Council, 1919–1926', *Notes and Records of the Royal Society of London* 37 (1983), 249–88).

[9] Andrew Hull, 'Passports to power: a public rationale for expert influence on central government policy-making: British scientists and economists, c 1900-c1925', unpublished doctoral thesis, University of Glasgow (1994), ch. 3 and, especially, Anna Mayer, 'Roots of the history of science in Britain, 1916–1950', unpublished doctoral thesis, University of Cambridge (2003).

[10] BBC Home Service, 24 August 1941, reprinted in Henning Krabbe (ed.), *Voices from Britain* (London: Allen & Unwin, 1947), p. 111.

[11] Though see Angus Calder, *The myth of the blitz* (London: Cape, 1991), ch. 9 and p. 196 especially. On the connections between Priestley's images and conservative ones see Roger Spalding, 'Popular historiography in the Second World War', *Socialist History* no. 14 (1999), 54–67.

create a glimmer of that poetry of action which distinguishes war from mass murder. It's a machine – and therefore has no soul.

He then went on to celebrate the 'fussy little steamers' involved in the evacuation.[12] In the second broadcast he described a Nazi propaganda film as 'all machines and robot stuff'.[13] This kind of analysis was not confined to the left, as is clear from a military example. General Wavell said the military leader needed 'a background of solid common sense, and a knowledge of humanity, on whose peculiarities, and not those of machines, the whole practice of warfare is ultimately based', 'though we are not, thank heaven, a military nation this tradition of freedom gives to our junior leaders in war a priceless gift of initiative'.[14]

The image of Germans as both militarists and strong innovators and users of high technology in warfare is a still a standard one in popular historical accounts. Television histories of science in war see them as the key linkers of science and war in offensive roles – for example in chemical warfare and in aerial bombing.[15] Television histories of the Second World War routinely show the Germans invading other nations with swarms of Panzers and Stuka dive-bombers. Equally there is a tendency to think that the Priestley image of Britain in some sense reflected or constructed a Britain that was indeed anti-technocratic, even though at some other level we know about British success with weapons of war from battleships to Spitfires. The standard image of the Battle of Britain shows that such projections were also central to our image of that most pure of Anglo-German contests.

Yet there had always been a certain sensitivity about these images of Britain and the defensive responses have themselves been incorporated into our thinking on Englishness. The Great War propaganda image of a military-technological Germany was problematic, given the size and power of that technological marvel, the British fleet. The way this was dealt with has also had an enduring influence on thinking on British militarism. The naval historian Julian Corbett, in a Great War pamphlet called *The spectre of navalism*, suggested that the German idea of British

---

[12] J. B. Priestley, *Postscripts* (London: Heinemann, 1940), pp. 1–4.
[13] Priestley, *Postscripts*, p. 4. Yet again, Priestley echoed a quite standard theme of British thinking about war: the need to create a 'new world order, and this is our real war aim'. This was not possible, 'unless we begin to think differently, and in my own personal view, for what it's worth, is that we must stop thinking in terms of property and power and begin thinking in terms of community and creation' (Priestley, *Postscripts*, pp. 36–7). As we shall see 'community and creation' were to be enduring themes in British historiography.
[14] Sir Archibald Wavell, *Generals and generalship* (Harmondsworth: Penguin, 1941) quoted in Albert Lauterbach, 'Militarism in the western world: a comparative study', *Journal of the History of Ideas* 5 (1944), 470.
[15] See for example, 'Science at war' a six-part BBC series, transmitted in 1998.

'navalism', which he defined as 'the use of naval predominance to deny the world the freedom of the seas and to tamper with national independence' had 'never existed'. In a neat argument he held of 'navalism' that 'We can see it as a reflection cast from their own militarism, but otherwise we cannot see it. Prussia is afraid of her own shadow.' The Germans, like the militarist Napoleon, did not know what the British 'knew and still know' that

in the collective existence of nations there are certain fundamentals on which no man can lay his hand and live. In the statecraft of a maritime people the most sacred of these fundamentals is the freedom of the seas ... the ocean ... [is] a highway along which all men must be free to pass upon their business. That is an irreducible factor in sane world politics.

The British had thrown open the seas of the world and charted them for others; they knew that trade must be free: 'For this reason alone ... British naval supremacy can never become anything that approaches "Navalism".'[16] For Corbett, the only navalist power there had ever been was Imperial Spain.

That Britain and its navy were entirely different from Germany and its army was a commonplace. According to the great Liberal intellectual and statesman, Viscount Bryce, 'England stands for a Pacific as opposed to a Military type of civilisation'.[17] He went on: 'As an industrial people the English desire peace. They have never made military glory their ideal. They have regarded war, not like Treitschke and his school, as wholesome and necessary, but as an evil.' The navy was defensive only, and large only because of the size of the empire; Britain opened its own ports to foreign vessels, it believed in free trade.[18] Indeed the British could even be trusted to exercise naval power scrupulously: the blockade, said the Liberal Prime Minister, Herbert Asquith, was 'carried out with the strictest regard to humanity, and we are not aware of a single instance of a neutral life lost'.[19] The number of German and other co-belligerents'

---

[16] Julian Corbett, *The spectre of navalism* (London: Thomas Nelson, 1917) (first published 1915).

[17] The other four things Britain stood for were liberty; the principle of nationality; the maintenance of treaty obligations; the regulations of the methods of warfare in the interests of humanity.

[18] James Bryce, *The attitude of Great Britain in the present war* (London: Macmillan, 1916), pp. 17, 22. Bryce's commission of enquiry into German atrocities has achieved the distinction of featuring in the *Oxford book of lies*. The theme that the navy guaranteed the freedom of the seas, which could not be entrusted to a militaristic power, was a common one. See A. J. Balfour (First Lord of the Admiralty), *After a Year* (Speech at the London Opera House, 4 August 1915) (London: Darling, 1915).

[19] H. H. Asquith, *What Britain is fighting for: a reply to the German Chancellor* (Speech 10 April 1916) (London: Daily Chronicle, 1916).

civilians was clearly another matter. After the Great War too, this image of the Royal Navy as a global policeman of trade was found, for example in a text for schools:

From the geographical and economic structure of the world, Britain needs the freedom of the seas and consequently the navy is of paramount importance, not merely as a fighting force, but as an international police force, protecting the merchant vessels of all nations against piracy, which, in many parts of the world, is held in check, only by the presence of the Royal Navy. Without the British Navy the shipping of all countries would be seriously handicapped.[20]

The navy was an adjunct of free trade, not primarily a weapon of war and conquest.

In the Second World War too British arms were presented as anything but offensive. The Spitfire and the Hurricane and radar, were defensive technologies. Attacks on Germany were in retaliation. The most aggressive language was often used in the context of Britain acting as a police force for the world extirpating the cancer of fascism. J. M. Spaight, one of the leading British air propagandists, wrote a book called *Bombing vindicated* in 1944 whose flavour is captured by the title of ch. 1: 'The Bomber saves Civilisation'. For Spaight the bomber was 'a murderous weapon. Its only merit is that it can murder war.'[21] Such arguments could be taken to ludicrous lengths. For example, a propaganda book of 1941 claimed that Britain invented essentially defensive weapons; indeed, humour was, 'perhaps, the most potent weapon in the British armoury'.[22] This book, written for foreigners, was prefaced by the Conservative politician Leo Amery, who claimed that the 'The gentle stranger' who read the book would

gather much information that is good for him and also often be left – which is no doubt also good for him – in slightly bewildered uncertainty as to when [the author] is saying what he means, or when he is subtly pulling the innocent foreign leg. But that, no doubt, is the right mood to engender in the minds of the all too logical and clear-cut foreigner when approaching the 'English mistery' [sic].[23]

An English mystery indeed.[24] But it was not just the crass propagandists and the politicians who came out with quite extreme formulations.

[20] T. Chadwick, *Practical citizenship: an introduction to government in the British Empire* (London: Frederick Warne, 1937), p. 157.
[21] J. M. Spaight, *Bombing vindicated* (London: Geoffrey Bles, 1944), p. 152.
[22] Donald Cowie, *The British contribution: some ideas and inventions that have helped humanity* (London: Allen & Unwin, 1941), p. 79. He gave over almost one-third of the chapter on defence to examples! The other chapters were on government, the steam engine, sport, health, empire, exports and Shakespeare.
[23] L. S. Amery, foreword to Cowie, *British contribution*, p. 7.
[24] One should not assume that Amery was ignorant of the world outside Britain; far from it. His mother was Hungarian. Neither he nor his family have been keen to let on that she was Jewish. Amery was pro-Zionist, but one of his sons was executed by the British as a

Also in 1941 the celebrated Conservative historian G. M. Trevelyan added a postscript to his *British history*, covering the years since 1919, in which he described the British people as

Then [in 1940] when at last pleasant theories had given place to harsh facts, and delusions to grim resolve, the tough qualities of our folk were made manifest, symbolized by the leadership of Winston Churchill. The ultra pacifist people, who had chosen to be still half–armed when the fight was forced upon them, were undismayed ... and put up such a fight on sea and air and land that the name of Britain became a banner to rally the forces of freedom all the world over.[25]

The idea that interwar Britain was ultra-pacifist and half-armed became the staples of post-Second World War military history and British history more generally, as we have seen. That is a standard image, but what we need to explain is why it remained so powerful.

Britain is not Germany II: the militaristic critique of Britain

In the Great War David Lloyd George was moved to ridicule Germany by citing a German propagandistic account of Britain:

It has pleased them to believe that we are a decadent and degenerate people. They proclaim to the world through their professors that we are a non-heroic nation skulking behind our mahogany counters, whilst we egg on more gallant races to their destruction. This is the description given of us in Germany – 'a timorous craven nation, trusting to its Fleet'.[26]

But British professors, including history professors, were to make much the same charge *after* the Second World War. The image of Britain as a liberal, non-militaristic, defensive, trading nation, resistant, or rather not beholden, to modern technologies of war, had been taken as a positive image of Britain. During and after the Second World War, something very important changed in British intellectual culture. It came to be argued that Britain really had been like, and was to an extent still like, the propaganda images it had created of itself and that that was the problem. From many perspectives it was argued that Britain should have been less liberal, less naval, more military and militaristic, more committed to the development of weapons of war and science and technology

Nazi. See W. D. Rubinstein, 'The secret of Leopold Amery (an important figure in the British Conservative Party with a concealed Jewish background)', *Historical Research* 73 (2000), 175–96.

[25] G. M. Trevelyan, *British history of the nineteenth century and after: 1782–1919*, 'Postscript 1941' (Harmondsworth: Penguin, 1965), p. 465.

[26] David Lloyd George (Chancellor of the Exchequer), speech at the Queen's Hall, London, 19 September 1914, in *War speeches*, pp. 220–3.

more generally. Lord Hankey argued in 1945 in the familiar way of the interwar years that

Our foreign policy is always and necessarily one of peace, since for a country dependent for its existence on imports of food and raw material, which have to be paid for by exports and invisible exports, peace is the first essential. For centuries there was a tendency to trust to principles of peace, of neutrality and of diplomacy as a substitute for war preparation.[27]

But then came the point: in his view this 'traditional peace policy' was followed by the Liberal government before 1914, and in the interwar years, with nearly disastrous results.[28] Conservative military historians writing contextual histories of Britain and war in the 'war and society' tradition followed this line after the war.

The central theme of their militaristic critique was criticism of the supposed 'British way in warfare' previously held up for admiration, most famously by Captain Basil Liddell Hart. Liddell Hart's 1930s' notion summarised what he took to be a British principle of minimising resources devoted to warfare and of economy in the use of force. The British limited their liability by profiting from the defence given by the English Channel and by using sea power to exert economic pressure. There were two supplementary weapons: subsidies and provisions to allies, and small expeditionary forces.[29] Liddell Hart was a strong supporter of the League of Nations who saw the 'British way in warfare' and collective security as complementary.[30] He claimed that British war aims in 1939 would have to be more than preservation of territory and commerce: 'Our greater object will be to ensure, in the face of an aggressor, the continuance of liberal civilization – those larger ideals which we epitomize when we speak of "England".'[31]

The central theme of the criticism, 'the British way in warfare', was that Britain's maritime strategy had never succeeded alone, that British naval and military strategy was always complementary.[32] The British problem was indeed not seeing that a 'continental commitment' of a British army

---

[27] Lord Hankey, *Government control in war* (Cambridge: Cambridge University Press, 1945) (Lees Knowles Lectures), pp. 19–20.

[28] Ibid., pp. 30, 82–83.

[29] Basil Liddell Hart, *The defence of Britain* (London: Faber and Faber, July 1939), p. 44.

[30] Ibid., pp. 45–6. The 'British way' was contrasted with, in effect, a continental way (pp. 27–8).

[31] Ibid., p. 43.

[32] Hew Strachan, 'The British way in warfare revisited', *Historical Journal* 26 (1983), 447–61.

was required. As Michael Howard wrote in a 1989 preface to a reissuing of his seminal work on the topic:

The experience of 1914–1918 had led an entire generation, whose most articulate spokesman was Liddell Hart, to eschew a 'continental' strategy as an aberration from a historic norm. My own generation's experience of the Second World War and its aftermath indicated the contrary: no continental adversary could be defeated without a military decision on the mainland of Europe and Britain could wield no influence either in war or in peace unless she was prepared to make a major contribution to that decision.[33]

Indeed, the last paragraph of the original 1972 edition was clear enough:

After the Second World War neither the political nor the military leaders of the United Kingdom shrank any longer from a continental commitment. They had learned their lesson; though it was not until 1954, ten years after the Normandy landings, that a final, binding commitment was undertaken to maintain substantial British armed forces on the Continent in time of peace. We are unlikely ever again to have statesmen – or, come to that, strategists – who maintain that the security of the United Kingdom can be considered in isolation from that of our Continental neighbours east as well as west of the Rhine. It is now only rarely that we catch a faint, Curzonian echo from the occasional Prime Minister who maintains that our true frontier still rests on the Himalayas.[34]

The Prime Minister referred to was Harold Wilson. Britain, the USA and the Soviet Union were the only three countries to maintain large forces stationed for very long periods outside their own territory, and most of these were in Europe.

In a particularly powerful formulation of the militaristic critique another military historian, Correlli Barnett, attacked 'the "blue water" myth', as

complementary to the pacifist myth, because it offers a cheap way of winning great wars; it offers victory over powerful opponents without the need for a large field army. As a bonus, it offers commercial plums like sugar islands or oilfields.[35]

For Barnett, the history of the British army 'is of recurrent need rending aside the anti-military illusions of the nation', and the history of the army is central to 'a study of the influence of war on modern British history'.[36] A Peace Pledge Union pamphlet of 1986, which argued that

[33] Michael Howard, *The continental commitment* (London: Ashfield Press, 1989), p. 8 (first published 1972).
[34] Ibid., p. 146.
[35] Correlli Barnett, *Britain and her army: a military, political and social survey* (Harmondsworth: Pelican, 1974), p. xix (first published 1970).
[36] Ibid., p. xx.

'It is the eternal complaint of military historians that Britain has never enjoyed militarism', was far too harsh, yet had a point.[37] One important consequence of these arguments is that military history is equated with the history of British warfare; attitudes to the army were taken as indicative of attitudes to armed forces, a continental-style strategy is seen as essential to success. But in the study of British armed force one cannot ignore the navy and the air force. These were not designed, as so many have argued by way of criticism, for imperial policing, but for use against continental adversaries. It is easy to exaggerate the imperial orientation of Britain's military in the age of high imperialism, and in any case one should not confuse policing an empire and defending it. The key threats to Britain and its empire (other than Japan in the interwar years) were European. Britain was not like Germany but this was not a measure of its backwardness.

Significantly, naval and air history was much less developed, and where it existed it reproduced, as we have seen, the arguments of the military historians about lack of resources for all the services. Clearly a well-founded naval and air history of twentieth-century Britain points to a very different historical account from that of the military historians.

Along with the critique of strategy went a critique of liberalism as pacifist, echoed in university courses in international relations. Britain was dominated by an anti-militaristic liberal ideology, which helped explain the aversion to the army, to a continental commitment, and allegedly weak armaments in the interwar years. British attitudes to war have been described in academic accounts by terms like pacificism, defencism and crusading.[38] For example in an influential political-economic formulation Paul Kennedy saw, as we have seen, Britain following a tradition of appeasement from the 1860s into the 1930s, as a result of its economic position in the world economy, its relative decline, as well as the moralism of its public life and the rise of anti-war sentiment (which he associated with democracy).[39] In Michael Howard's lectures on what he sees as the problematic 'liberal conscience' he defined liberalism very widely to include 'all those thinkers who believe the world to be profoundly other than it should be, and who have faith in the power of human reason and human action so to change it that the inner potential of all human beings can be more fully realised', excluding thereby only hard-line Conservatives and certain 'disciples of Karl Marx and other

---

[37] Peace Pledge Union, *A statement on militarism* (1986), Marx Memorial Library.
[38] Martin Ceadel, *Thinking about war and peace* (Oxford: Oxford University Press, 1989).
[39] Paul Kennedy, 'The tradition of appeasement in British foreign policy, 1865–1939' in *Strategy and diplomacy* (London: Fontana, 1984), pp. 15–39.

determinists'.[40] Howard points out that the liberal conscience in the interwar years put its faith in a League of Nations, in international law, in the punishing of aggressor nations. But Howard notes something very important and too little acknowledged: 'In general ... in the last two years before the war, the liberal conscience was militant rather than appeasing';[41] in 1939 'yet again the liberal conscience endorsed a national struggle as a just war'.[42] And yet, at the end of the book, Howard firmly criticises the liberal tradition for not understanding the international system or war: it was 'often marred by naiveté, by intellectual arrogance, by ignorance, by confused thinking and sometimes, alas, by sheer hypocrisy', but goes on to ask 'how can one fail to share the aspirations of those who carried on this tradition, or deny credit to their achievements?'[43] In his 1989 postscript he argues that the liberal tradition is 'pacific if not actually pacifist'.[44] It is clear that Howard's sympathies are not with the liberal conscience. In a devastating portrait he noted:

The spirit of historical irony will record that it was Mr Attlee and his colleagues, not excepting Sir Stafford Cripps, the men who had voted and spoken so eloquently in the 1930s against power politics and great national armaments, who now took the decision to equip the United Kingdom as a nuclear power; that the Minister of Supply responsible for the construction of the atomic bomb was Mr John Wilmot – the same John Wilmot whose election for the constituency of East Fulham in 1934 [in fact 1933][45] had convinced Stanley Baldwin of the impossibility of persuading the country to accept a major rearmament programme; and that the Secretary of State for Air in 1947, when the Air Ministry began to design the V-bombers which would deliver the bombs, was that most tireless and dedicated advocate of disarmament, Mr Philip Noel-Baker.[46] And in the United States liberals of equally impeccable antecedents, men who had throughout their lives fought against American entanglement in the old world of power politics, now helped to build up an armoury of terrifying strength in order to 'defend the Free World'.

[40] Michael Howard, *War and the liberal conscience* (Oxford: Oxford University Press, 1989) (first published 1978), p. 11.
[41] Ibid., p. 106.   [42] Ibid., p. 108.   [43] Ibid., p. 134.   [44] Ibid., p. 137.
[45] Martin Ceadel points out the getting this date wrong has been very common, the usual dating puts it in 1935. He did not need to point out the significance of this shift. Martin Ceadel, *Semi-detached idealists: the British peace movement and international relations* (Oxford: Oxford University Press, 2000), p. 281. See also p. 384 for evidence of Wilmot's (unsurprising) stand in favour of arms and air defence in May 1939, when he was returned for Kennington (he had lost East Fulham in the 1935 general election to the Conservative William Waldorf Astor).
[46] To be pedantic again, the Air Ministry did not design aircraft; the responsible ministry was the Ministry of Supply, while the design was done in the aircraft industry. The Air Ministry issued the operational requirement.

It is easy enough either to deplore this apparent volte-face as a shameful betrayal of principle, or to sneer at it as a belated acceptance of the facts of life.[47]

There is no denying the ideological power of Howard's account, and of the general mood it reflected. For post-war disarmers, or just plain critics of post-war defence policy, could not endorse the stands taken by their interwar ancestors. Here too not everything is what it seemed to be from the post-war perspective. A. J. P. Taylor is a case of particular significance.[48] Taylor was the son of a Mancunian free-trader who saw Germans as customers, and supposedly revered the memory of the liberal internationalist 'troublemakers'. He was also an important anti-nuclear campaigner in the late 1950s and early 1960s. His fellow campaigner, the Labour politician Michael Foot, who could have been speaking of himself, wrote of Taylor:

> The peace-loving Cobdenite believed it was abundantly right to fight and win the most legitimate war in history, right for the English people he loved, and right for the democratic socialist cause in which he had always set his faith. All the more does he deserve an audience when he tells us that the new weapons transform the scene and that deterrence will not work any more than it did before.[49]

We have here an elision of categories of some significance. Peace-loving anti-nuclear democratic socialist Cobdenism is a strange phenomenon: a Cobdenite could believe that some wars were necessary, perhaps even desirable, but could a Cobdenite believe it would do good for the people who fought it? There were also very similar and equally striking ideological moves in Taylor's own work. Taylor noted that the Tory version of the interwar years was that they would have gone for great armaments had the 'idealists' not stopped them (the argument made by Howard above) but he was himself partial to the argument: 'Their best excuse is that they were carrying out a Dissenting foreign policy twenty years too late' was his comment on the Tory appeasers.[50] Taylor's famous, and for some notorious, *Origins of the Second World War* was not a book obviously liberal internationalist, or democratic socialist in argument or method: it was a diplomatic history, stressing the continuing German tendency to seek

---

[47] Michael Howard, 'Ethics and power in international policy', in Michael Howard, *The causes of wars* (London: Unwin, 1984), pp. 55–6.

[48] The anti-nuclear movement has enjoyed the service of two important historians, A. J. P. Taylor in the 1950s and 1960s and E. P. Thompson in the 1980s. E. P. Thompson, *Protest and survive* (London: Campaign for Nuclear Disarmament, 1980) was directed at a letter Howard had written to *The Times*. See Howard's response, 'Surviving a protest', in *Encounter* November 1980, reprinted in Howard, *Causes of wars*.

[49] Michael Foot, 'Alan Taylor' in Chris Wrigley (ed.), *Warfare, diplomacy and politics: essays in honour of A. J. P. Taylor* (London: Hamish Hamilton, 1986), p. 13.

[50] A. J. P. Taylor, *Troublemakers* (Harmondsworth: Penguin 1985), p. 167.

hegemony in Europe and the importance of errors and accident.[51] It is thus especially surprising that, as Taylor himself put it:

Liking the book becomes a matter of politics. If you're a Left Winger and are against the bomb and the arming of Germany, you may be in sympathy with the thesis; if you're a conservative, a militarist, and for Germany in NATO, you may not be.[52]

Just as surprisingly Taylor was seen as an apologist of appeasement, for his comments on the dissenters are closer to a *mea culpa* than an endorsement:[53]

When I say that Munich was a triumph for all that was best in British life, I mean that the years and years before that, enlightened people, men of the Left – whom perhaps I equate too easily with all that was best – that they had attacked Czechoslovakia, that they had said that the inclusion of the Sudeten Germans in Czechoslovakia was – in the words of one of them, Brailsford – the worst crime of the peace settlement of 1919 ... I mean by that a triumph for all those who had preached enlightenment, international conciliation, revision of treaties, the liberation of nationalities from foreign rule, and so on.[54]

Our image of interwar liberalism and pacifism is that of its critics, even though they sometimes pose as friends.[55] These images of interwar British culture and the British armed forces are still quite standard in the best literature on interwar Britain and the armed forces, for example, the work of Elizabeth Kier.[56]

---

[51] See Gordon Martel 'The revisionist as moralist: A. J. P. Taylor and the lessons of European History' and Edward Ingram 'A patriot for me' in Gordon Martel (ed.), *The origins of the Second World War reconsidered: the A. J. P. Taylor debate after 25 years* (London: Unwin Hyman, 1986). Much of the polemical fire directed at Taylor suggested, absurdly, that he had whitewashed Hitler. For, to the extent that he whitewashed Hitler he blackened Germany. Sisman, Taylor's biographer, argues that by the late 1930s Taylor had rejected the liberal understanding of world affairs of his youth (Adam Sisman, *A. J. P. Taylor: a biography* (London: Mandarin, 1995), p. 117).

[52] Quoted in Ved Mehta, *Fly and the fly-bottle: encounters with British intellectuals* (London: Weidenfeld and Nicolson, 1963), p. 139.

[53] For an analysis of the book and its reception see Sisman, *Taylor*, pp. 288–302.

[54] Quoted in Mehta, *Fly and the fly-bottle*, p. 100. See also A. J. P. Taylor, *The origins of the Second World War* (Harmondsworth: Penguin, 1963), p. 235.

[55] Thus Martin Ceadel argues that in the British case that pacific-ism, born out of liberalism and security, dominated British attitudes before 1939, but cites as evidence the thoughts of notorious anti-liberals, notably Correlli Barnett. See Ceadel, *Thinking about war and peace*, pp. 178–9. Ceadel discusses five variants of attitudes to war which, in order of aggressiveness, are 'pacifism', 'pacific-ism', 'defencism', 'crusading' and 'militarism'. The scheme is useful in that it is not linear – 'militarism' is not the opposite of 'pacifism' – since Ceadel plots his ways of thinking in three dimensions: (1) attitudes to the legitimacy of war in various circumstances, (2) attitudes to the international system, and (3) domestic political ideology.

[56] See Elizabeth Kier, *Imagining war: French and British military doctrines between the wars* (Princeton: Princeton University Press, 1997).

This book has suggested a different sort of interpretation of British liberalism. British liberals were not pacifists, but willing upholders, with force if necessary, of a liberal international order. Interwar liberal internationalism (and the peace movement more generally) was not utopian, pacifist, appeasing, nor was the wider political culture pacifist, nor was Britain disarmed. James Hinton's view that the '"alternative" identity' of Britain put forward by British peace movements 'was not always as removed from the assumptions of Britain's rulers as peace activists liked to think it was', is much closer to the mark.[57] What he had in mind was that they had faith in the British state and the Royal Navy to set the world straight; they were prone to 'imperial grandeur' and shared an 'imperialist pacifism'. One cogent example he gives of this is the emphasis on economic sanctions in the 1930s, both by the peace campaigners and the state.[58] Indeed as we have seen one can strengthen this argument by noting the importance of political-economic core of interwar peace-thinking, both of the older figures still writing – Angell, Hobson and Brailsford, and the younger critics, from John Strachey to E. H. Carr. British peace movements, despite having produced vast amounts of literature focused on arms spending and on the arms trade, did not enquire too much into the nature of the British arms industry, its relations to the state or the actual war fighting strategies of the British state. As Hinton argued these peace movements never really examined the role of the British state in the world system; they were concerned to remove what they saw as the impediments to the British state pursuing its true role; that of peacemaker. Hinton resorted to seeming oxymorons to categorise the position of British peace movements: 'imperialist pacifism' and 'socialist nationalism'.[59]

In recent years new histories of Britain and armed force in the twentieth century of quite different stamp from what had gone before have appeared. Historical work has done much to support this picture of interconnection between political economic understandings of the world and strategic thinking, especially from the Edwardian period.[60]

---

[57] James Hinton, *Protests and visions: peace politics in twentieth century Britain* (London: Radius, 1989), p. viii.

[58] Ibid., pp. viii–ix, 96–7.   [59] Ibid.

[60] A reassessment of the Edwardian period has been critical; see especially Anne Summers, 'Militarism in Britain before the Great War', *History Workshop Journal* 2 (1976), 104–23; David French, *British economic and strategic planning, 1905–1915* (London: Allen & Unwin, 1982); Bernard Semmel, *Liberalism and naval strategy: ideology, interest and seapower during the Pax Britannica* (London: Allen & Unwin, 1986); J. T. Sumida, *In defence of naval supremacy* (London: Unwin Hyman, 1989); Avner Offer, *The First World War: an agrarian interpretation* (Oxford: Clarendon Press, 1989).

Recent synthetic work on twentieth-century British militarism and armed force has presented a startlingly revised account.[61] The term 'militarism' is slowly coming into use in relation to Britain.[62] These are very significant changes given the reluctance with which even very critical historians have avoided the term. Even Michael Sherry, in his brilliant account of the 'militarisation' of the United States from the 1930s, prefers not to use the term 'militarism' because of its political connotations and its implication of stasis.[63] Drawing in part on some of this new work on the Edwardian and interwar periods, I suggested that Britain had a 'liberal militarism'.[64] The term was meant to suggest both British militarism was a particular variant of militarism, that it was related to a particular political formation and indeed that it was not uniquely British. In this account liberal militarism involved something more than an economic approach to warfare; it was also a way of limiting the militarisation of society. I also sought to capture a point made by Hew Strachan, when he commented that the 'maritime' strategies of blockade, and their successors in strategic bombing and nuclear warfare, for 'all their liberal associations' run 'counter to the principles of proportion and non-combatant immunity contained in the ethics of war'.[65]

More recently Hew Strachan notes the high level of public approval of the armed services, high expenditure on them, and that even the army has had a higher profile in the public imagination in the twentieth century 'than the liberal – or perhaps it should be Whig – orthodoxy allows'. Strachan argues that 'militarism' though 'loaded with too many meanings and productive of misunderstanding ... is the only abstract noun that will do the job'.[66] Strachan is particularly concerned here with the political power of the army, and reaches conclusions of great importance for the study of British politics, going well beyond the well-known example of the Curragh mutiny: the military played important roles in the May

---

[61] Strachan, 'The British way in warfare', 447–61; David French, *The British way in warfare 1688–2000* (London, Unwin Hyman, 1990); David Edgerton, 'Liberal militarism and the British state', *New Left Review*, no. 185 (1991), 138–69.

[62] On the origins of the idea of militarism see Nicholas Stargardt, *The German idea of militarism: radical and socialist critics, 1866–1914* (Cambridge: Cambridge University Press, 1994); V. Berghahn, *Militarism: the history of an international debate* (Leamington Spa: Berg, 1981).

[63] Michael Sherry, *In the shadow of war: the United States since the 1930s* (New Haven: Yale University Press, 1995). p. xi.

[64] Edgerton, 'Liberal militarism' and *England and the aeroplane: and essay on a militant and technological nation* (London: Macmillan, 1991).

[65] Strachan, 'British way in warfare', p. 460.

[66] Hew Strachan, *Politics of the British Army* (Oxford: Oxford University Press, 1998), p. 264.

1915 crisis which finished Asquith's purely Liberal government;[67] in the Second World War, the army effectively removed a Secretary of State for War from office.[68]

Of course it is too tempting to be schematic, and to postulate simple historical progression when discussing ideas, and the case of British militarism is no exception. But only when there is clearly something complex and rich for historians to explain will it make sense to look in detail at the many different positions historical actors held about British armed forces in the twentieth century.[69] Still it is important to note the emphasis on liberalism, pacificism and anti-militarism in accounts of the British military and British strategy, and the neglect of the key roles of the navy and air force. The bulk of the armed forces, and the war party, vanished into the a peculiar anti-historical world of the militaristic critique.

Socialism, Labour and war: the rise of the welfare state

Correlli Barnett started his 1970 book on the British army suggesting that

The importance of war and military institutions has been generally neglected in British historical writing, whose tone has been set by the Whig and liberal emphasis on peaceful constitutional progress. In this liberal view war appears as an aberration, and interruption of a 'natural' condition of peace: almost as a form of delinquency unworthy of intellectual attention.[70]

---

[67] Ibid., pp. 127–31.   [68] Ibid., pp. 153–7.

[69] It is also important to note that I have not covered the critics. In the Edwardian years there was certainly opposition to reliance on a high-technology navy for the defence of the realm. Within the navy the 'historical school' favoured a return to Nelsonian principles of heroic command, rather than going down the 'materiel school' road of stressing organisation and technology, and a greater role for engineering officers. See Semmel, *Liberalism and naval strategy*. These differences within the navy were reproduced in the debate between the 'navalists' and the 'nation in arms' lobby. Navalists of all types stressed the economic and military efficiency of navalism – there was no need to have a mass army – advocates of the 'nation in arms' objected to the liberal idea of defence as an insurance policy entrusted to subcontracted sailors and machines: what mattered in war was the martial spirit and patriotic unity of the whole nation. See J. H. Grainger, *Patriotisms: Britain 1900–1939* (London: Routledge, 1986), ch. 14, 'The call to arms'. Both arguments were very public: the first was encapsulated in the battle between Admiral Fisher and Lord Charles Beresford, the second in the campaign for conscription embodied in Lord Roberts' National Service League. See also F. S. Oliver, *Ordeal by battle* (London: Macmillan, 1915) and on Oliver, his friend John Buchan, *Memory-hold-the-door* (London: Hodder & Stoughton, 1940), pp. 208–11. Although Conservative activists pushed for peacetime national service in the late 1930s – and achieved it in 1939 – it was on a very modest basis, aimed at home defence. See N. J. Crowson, *Facing fascism: the Conservative party and the European dictators 1935–1940* (London: Routledge, 1997), ch. 5.

[70] Barnett, *Britain and her army*, p. xvii.

This observation was correct in many ways, but applied to twentieth-century Britain it is highly misleading. British social democratic historians have taken a remarkably rosy view of war, particularly but not only the Second World War, as a powerful motor of peaceful constitutional progress: *The people's war* put us on *The road to 1945* and *The people's peace*.[71] The positive effects of war on twentieth-century British history, in helping the rise of labour and the creation of the welfare state, were the central themes of decades of work on contemporary British history. In the general accounts, the First World War saw a only temporary advance but the initiatives of the Second World War were consolidated, seemingly permanently, after 1945. The underlying argument is the war, total war especially, was a matter of essentially civilian collective effort. War unleashed modernising civilian forces which had been held back by an entrenched liberalism.

A. J. P. Taylor's *English history*, published in 1965, provides some choice examples. Taylor began his *History* with a paragraph which suggested that before 1914 the Englishman was barely touched by the state: he could, for example, 'ignore ... the demands of national defence'.[72] The second paragraph begins: 'All this was changed by the impact of the Great War. The mass of the people became, for the first time, active citizens.'[73] This claim, contradicted by the evidence he then presented of the way the state controlled people's lives, is reaffirmed in the concluding sentence of the paragraph: 'The history of the English state and the English people merged for the first time.'[74] There is no doubt that this is seen positively by Taylor, and that he associates the change with the throwing out of the old liberals, and the coming to power of David Lloyd George. According to Taylor, Prime Minister Herbert Asquith and his supporters 'were men of excessive refinement – almost too fastidious for politics in peacetime' but 'Lloyd George at the ministry of munitions provided the great exception':[75]

Lloyd George's supporters were rougher in origin and in temperament: mostly Radical nonconformists and self-made men in wool or engineering who were doing well out of the war. None was a banker, merchant or financial magnate;

---

[71] Angus Calder, *The people's war* (London: Cape, 1969); Paul Addison, *The road to 1945: British politics and the second world war* (London: Cape, 1975); Kenneth Morgan, *The people's peace: British history 1945–1989* (Oxford: Oxford University Press, 1990).
[72] A. J. P. Taylor, *English history, 1914–1945* (Harmondsworth: Penguin, 1975), p. 25 (first published 1965).
[73] Ibid., p. 26.   [74] Ibid., p. 26.   [75] Ibid., p. 64.

none a Londoner. Theirs was a long-delayed revolt of the provinces against London's political and cultural dominance: a revolt on behalf of the factories and workshops where the war was being won.[76]

There is no sense that the hopes of the 'radical nonconformist' conscience had been destroyed by a world war or that the principal political effect of the war was the entry of Tories into government, indeed that Lloyd George's war Cabinet was dominated by them.[77] It is telling that the conservative historian Lord Blake should have been sensitive to this question in a manner that finds no echo in Taylor:

On almost every issue that came up Conservative tradition and ideology was better suited than Liberal to meet the needs of the hour. Conscription, 'defence of the realm', Ireland, indeed all the necessities of a prolonged war, tended to create doubts and divisions in the Liberals. After all, they were the party of liberty, and liberty is the first casualty of war. They were the party of moral conscience – and that is another casualty of war. They were the party of legalism, parliamentary forms, constitutional propriety – and these were also the casualties of war. Then there was sheer pacifism and its watered down version – belief in the evil of war and of any British government that waged it. True, the pro-Boers had no analogy. There were no Liberal pro-Germans. But the scruples, doubts, misgivings were there. It was the Conservatives who before the war had been anti-German, who had pressed for conscription, for greater armaments, for a tougher foreign policy, for the French and later the Russian alliance.[78]

As I suggested above, Taylor had a deeply ambiguous relationship to liberalism, and indeed socialism.

Taylor's analysis of the Second World War uncannily parallels his account of the First. Chamberlain's War Cabinet was also too fastidious, non-interventionist and respectful of private property. One of his examples has developed a life of its own: the Secretary of State for Air, Sir Kingsley Wood, wrote Taylor, 'met a proposal to set fire to German forests with the agonised cry: "Are you aware it is private property? Why, you will be asking me to bomb Essen next".'[79] As in the case of the Great War, rougher, industrially oriented elements were on hand to save the day. For Taylor the civilian supply ministries were once again critical, precisely because they were civilian, and allowed new men into government. Churchill, while less radical than Lloyd George, did create

---

[76] Ibid., p. 103.
[77] The other members were Bonar Law (Chancellor) Curzon, Henderson, and Milner.
[78] Robert Blake, *The Conservative party from Peel to Thatcher* (London: Fontana, 1985), p. 196. See also John Turner, 'Politics and the war' in John Turner (ed.), *Britain and the First World War* (London: Unwin Hyman, 1988).
[79] Taylor, *English history*, p. 560.

an analogue to the Ministry of Munitions, Lord Beaverbrook's MAP.[80]
Indeed the requirements of war 'produced a revolution in British economic life, until in the end direction and control turned Great Britain into
a country more fully socialist than anything achieved by the conscious
planners of Soviet Russia'. This 'war socialism' was the product of a
shared outlook between businessmen, scientists, intellectuals, trade
unionists, civil servants and ministers.[81] This pulling together created
modern Britain. 'In the second World war the British people came of age.
This was a people's war ... Imperial greatness was on the way out; the
welfare state was on the way in.'[82] Taylor has been hardly alone in his
positive evaluation of the impact of war on British society.Arthur
Marwick, while keen to stress that war, 'is, in its very essence, negative
and destructive; it cannot of itself create anything new',[83] nevertheless
argued that 'War ... without itself creating anything, can be an instrument of social change: the more total the war, the more likely are we to see
all four modes through which war affects society in full play; in a limited
war the destructive, inegalitarian features of war are likely to predomi-
nate.'[84] Of course, war does create new things, but Marwick equates
'creation' with progress. Indeed he claimed that 'Wars are like weddings:
essentially extravagant and unnecessary, but a great stimulant in a con-
vention-bound society.'[85] Writing of the 1960s he said that what was
required was 'the Jamesian "moral equivalent of war": even as a joke,
we dare not now conjure up the vision of another war'. In a footnote to
this he cites A. J. P. Taylor, writing in the *New Statesman* in November
1966: 'If the present government pursue their retrograde policy much
further' wrote Taylor, 'we shall have to have another war in order to
start up social progress (joke)'.[86] But (tasteless) joking apart, the view

---

[80] Ibid., pp. 596–7.   [81] Ibid., pp. 616–17.   [82] Ibid., pp. 726–7.

[83] Arthur Marwick, *Britain in the century of total war: war, peace and social change 1900–1967*
(Harmondsworth: Pelican, 1970) (first published 1968), p. 12.

[84] Marwick, *Century of total war*, p. 15.

[85] Ibid., p. 17.

[I]n destroying the old, the [first world] war helped the rise of the new: out went gold
sovereigns, chaperons, muffin men, and the divine rights of private enterprise; in came
state control, summer time, a new prosperity, and a new self-confidence for families long
submerged below the poverty line, and, in the aftermath, a biting skepticism and challenge to established authorities. The laments for the dead world of 1914 were essentially
products of the sick world of 1921 (Arthur Marwick, *The deluge: British society and the First
World War* (London: Macmillan, 1965), p. 9).

[86] Marwick, *Century of total war*, pp. 462, 463.

that war turned out to be good for Britain has been a historiographical staple since the Second World War. And rightly so, we should at least in part acknowledge.

Central to the account of the Second World War in British histories was, as we have seen, the rise of the 'welfare state'. So much so that while interpretations of the welfare state have changed it has remained the central point of reference. More than this, the welfare state has come to define the British state as a whole even for the most ideologically discerning of historians, including José Harris and Keith Middlemas.[87]The case of Keith Middlemas is especially interesting since his *Politics in industrial society* represented a real break with standard accounts in that it was a uniquely state-centred account of twentieth-century Britain – seeing in the deep policies of the state the origins of policies usually ascribed to civil society and its representatives. The British state created a particularly stable society between the 1920s and the 1960s – it 'discovered how to exercise the arts of public management, extending the state's powers to assess, educate, bargain with, appease or constrain the demands of the electorate'.[88] Parties were, despite appearances, marginal to policy making. His state-centred view may be summarised in his argument that in the twenty years after 1940 'nearly all the deep objectives of the state and of most Governments since the 1920s – in economic planning, social welfare, harmony and the avoidance of crisis seem to have been achieved'.[89] In order to achieve its aims the state encroached on the interests of capital and labour, using their peak organisations to complement its strength. This state-led and sponsored 'corporate bias' resulted in a new system which, 'backward looking in its aims, gradual in method, revisionistic in theory, accommodated itself to change by moving at the least speed commensurate with the interest of each governing institution';[90] one of the results was that 'for all the talk of managing the economy the price ... turned out to be political compromise, industrial featherbedding and low overall growth'.[91] Here Middlemas was on common ground in that he endorsed the view that

---

[87] José Harris, 'Society and the state in twentieth-century Britain' in F. M. L. Thompson (ed.), *Cambridge social history of Britain. III: Social agencies and institutions* (Cambridge: Cambridge University Press, 1990), pp. 63–118; Tom Ling, *The British state since 1945: an introduction* (Cambridge: Polity, 1998); Philip Harling, *The modern British state: an historical introduction* (Cambridge: Polity, 2001); Lawrence Black et al., *Consensus or coercion: the state, the people and social cohesion in post-war Britain* (Cheltenham: New Clarion Press, 2001).

[88] Keith Middlemas, *Politics of industrial society: the experience of the British system since 1911* (London: Deutsch, 1979), p. 18.

[89] Ibid., p. 371.   [90] Ibid., p. 377.   [91] Ibid., p. 230.

the aims of the state were welfarist, and that these aims compromised industrial efficiency.[92]

In these histories the warfare state does not appear to exist, even in wartime. In Taylor's *History* for example the military do not figure, even in passing, in his account of the forces that pulled together to shape modern Britain in the Second World War. If anything they were on their way out with imperial greatness, as the welfare state came in. The great majority of texts on the British state, even in wartime, and even the most recent ones, have little or nothing to say about the military.[93] Very little has been written on British soldiers, sailors and airmen in the Second World War, compared with factory workers, despite the fact that one obvious effect of the war was the conscription of millions for service in Britain as well as abroad.[94] Until very recently we knew more about US forces in Britain[95] in this period than about British forces.[96] So powerful indeed is the civilian-centred welfarist account of British warfare that the new historical sociology of war of the 1980s,[97] which was based on the idea that both liberals and Marxists had great difficulty in conceptualising war,[98] still relied on a conventionally described civilian/British case as

---

[92] Critics took him to task for the lack of evidence of a bottom-up corporatism – e.g. Rodney Lowe, 'Corporate bias: fact or fiction?', *SSRC Newsletter* no. 50 (November 1983), 17–18; Michael Distenfass, 'The politics of producers' co-operation: the TUC–FBI–NCEO talks, 1929–1933' in John Turner (ed.), *Businessmen and politics: studies of business activity in British politics, 1900–1945* (London: Heinemann, 1984), pp. 76–92. See my 'State intervention in British manufacturing industry, 1931–1951: a comparative study of policy for the military aircraft and cotton textile industries', unpublished doctoral thesis, University of London (1986), ch. 1. See also Keith Middlemas, *Power, competition and the state*, 3 vols. (London: Macmillan, 1986–1991), which to my eyes fails to follow through on the novel analysis of *Politics of industrial society*.

[93] José Harris, 'Society and the state in twentieth-century Britain'; Ling, *British state since 1945* and Harling, *Modern British state.*

[94] That is to say, before 1944 the great bulk of all British forces were on British soil, not stationed abroad, and not to be ignored for that reason.

[95] David Reynolds, *Rich relations: the American occupation of Britain, 1942–1945* (London: HarperCollins, 1996), p. xxiii. For an unusual 'other ranks' memoir see Anthony Burgess, *Little Wilson and big God: being the first part of the confessions of Anthony Burgess* (London: Heinemann, 1987).

[96] David French, *Raising Churchill's army: the British army and the war against Germany 1919–1945* (Oxford: Oxford University Press, 2000), see also his 'Colonel Blimp and the British Army: British divisional commanders in the war against Germany, 1939–1945', *English Historical Review* 111 (1996), 1182–1201.

[97] Perry Anderson, 'A culture in contraflow–I', *New Left Review* no. 180 (1990), 41–80.

[98] Martin Shaw (ed.), *War, state and society* (London: Macmillan, 1984); Anthony Giddens, *The nation state and violence* (Cambridge: Polity, 1985); Randall Collins, *Weberian sociological theory* (Cambridge: Cambridge University Press, 1986); Colin Creighton and Martin Shaw (eds.), *The sociology of war and peace* (London: Macmillan 1987); Martin Shaw, *Dialectics of war: an essay in the social theory of total war and peace* (London: Pluto Press, 1988); Michael Mann, *States, war and capitalism* (Oxford: Blackwell, 1988); Bruce D. Porter, *War and the rise of the state: the military foundations of modern politics* (New York:

central to twentieth-century war. For example Michael Mann in his general treatment of militarism labelled the first half of the twentieth century as a period of 'citizen warfare', from which citizens gained major benefits.[99] Martin Shaw correctly criticises this view as Anglocentric but argues for the centrality of the 'military-democratic state' in Britain; welfarism went with a particular form of mass warfare.[100]

Taking the warfare state even out of wartime Britain was an amazing ideological feat, so successful that it still works. That it is still potent is clear from the jarring effect that contemporary dissident views still have today. During the Second World War the anarchist magazine *War Commentary* acidly noted that socialists were putting forward the 'the idea that the war itself and the economic changes which it necessitates are driving England toward socialism' – the result of a 'strange intellectual and labourite mentality, which is very widespread among social democrats and the reformist trade union movement' – without recognising that most such changes were common to all war economies, including Hitler's. 'Being obstinate people', continued *War Commentary*,

we refuse to believe that there is the slightest trace of emancipation in the fact of working at maximum output, consuming as little as possible, and leaving the daily lives of millions of people in the hands of a state power over which they have no control whatever. Propaganda is certainly an industry which has reached a high degree of perfection ... but there are some things which are really too much to swallow.[101]

From the right the economist Joseph Schumpeter thought that a likely outcome of the war was Anglo-American control of most of the world, a kind of 'ethical imperialism', which would require a social organisation he called 'militarist socialism'. He twisted the knife particularly viciously:

there is little reason to believe that this socialism [in Schumpeter's sense] will mean the advent of the civilisation of which orthodox socialists dream. It is much

Free Press, 1994); John M. Hobson, *The wealth of states: a comparative sociology of international economic and political change* (Cambridge: Cambridge University Press, 1997).

[99] Michael Mann, 'The roots and contradictions of modern militarism', in Shaw, *War, state and society*. See also Giddens, *Nation state and violence* for a similar account of the British case.

[100] Shaw, 'The rise and fall of the military-democratic state', in Creighton and Shaw, *Sociology of war and peace*, pp. 143–58, and Shaw, *Dialectics of war*, pp. 73–100.

[101] 'Revolutionary aspects of war', from *War Commentary* (mid-January 1942), reprinted in *The left and World War II: selections from War Commentary, 1939–1943* (London: Freedom Press, 1989), p. 67.

more likely to present fascist features. That would be a strange answer to Marx's prayer. But history sometimes indulges in jokes of questionable taste.[102]

Indeed.

British socialism and the revival of political economy

And if the warfare state hardly figures in wartime, it is no surprise that it is nearly invisible in the post-war years. In historical accounts of post-war Britain, the military and military institutions hardly figure, despite the historically very high levels of defence expenditure and peacetime conscription. 'Korean war' rearmament expenditure is mentioned, given its political consequences, so too to some extent is conscription, but these matters are hardly central to the conception of the British state. In the 1940s and 1950s only communists pointed to high levels of warlike expenditure, and in many cases pointed to the impact of military spending on British R&D, as we have seen, but even they did not have a clear understanding of structures of the warfare state, as their otherwise pioneering accounts of the state show.[103] Particularly curious is that the strong peace movement of the late 1950s and early 1960s did not generate an account of the British warfare state. One reason was the virtual disappearance in Britain of the political economic approach to these questions. In academic international relations, political economy, along with 'idealism', was left behind. In critical commentary on defence policy the political-economic language became rarer, not least because nuclear weapons in the view of many instituted a new era of warfare in which political economy was irrelevant. For example, Commander King-Hall, reflecting on the first atom bombs in what he saw as his 'first News-Letter of the NEW ERA', dated 16 August 1945, argued that the services, and the whole economic infrastructure of war, was now superfluous.[104] Philip Noel-Baker and John Strachey, veterans of the political-economic approach of the 1930s, both wrote books on defence in the late 1950s and early 1960s, which focused on nuclear weapons.[105] This is not to say that political economy was not used, only that it was marginal, restricted

[102] Joseph Schumpeter, *Capitalism, socialism and democracy* (London: Allen & Unwin, 1976), ch. 27, 'A historical sketch of socialist parties from the first to the second world war', pp. 373–75 (First published 1942).
[103] James Harvey and Katherine Hood, *The British state* (London: Lawrence & Wishart, 1958) (pseudonyms for Noreen Branson and Roger Simon) has a section on armed forces under the 'imperial state'; the theme of the book is the classic one of commonality of education, background etc. of all elites.
[104] *National News-Letter* no. 475, 16 August 1945. With thanks to Anne King-Hall.
[105] Philip Noel-Baker, *The arms race* (London: Calder, 1960). John Strachey, *On the prevention of war* (London: Macmillan, 1962) was the third part of a trilogy on democratic socialism.

to figures like Barbara Ward of *The Economist*[106] and elements of the far left, notably the Trotskyite International Socialists with the theory of the permanent arms economy.[107] Another example was the New Left argument for positive neutralism, anti-nuclearism and planned trade with the emerging non-aligned economies.[108] But these were exceptions. The radical opposition to defence policy in the years 1957–63 was informed above all by 'moral imperialism'.[109]

In the 1970s and 1980s there was a great revival in socialist political economic writing on Britain, the British state and on issues of war and peace. Indeed the use of the term 'state' was indicative of a change – traditional political scientists preferred 'government'. Yet this literature too ignored the armed services and the warfare state more generally, concentrating once more on the welfare state.[110] The 1970s also saw a resurgence of British Marxist writing on military expenditure and capitalism, a literature that went beyond the theory of the permanent arms economy.[111] As applied to Britain this literature had at its core the observation that Britain spent considerably more on defence as a proportion of GDP than did most continental European countries and the argument that this defence expenditure negatively affected the economy. Particular attention was paid to the supposed costs of high levels of defence R&D.[112] The 1980s also saw the emergence of mostly declinist

[106] Barbara Ward, *Policy for the West* (Harmondsworth: Penguin, 1951). She later became very well known as a pioneer environmentalist. Sir Leslie Rowan, a retired second secretary at the Treasury, soon to be managing director, and later chairman of Vickers, gave the Lees Knowles lectures in 1960 on *Arms and economics: the changing challenge* (Cambridge: Cambridge University Press, 1960). They are a very undistinguished ramble through the global economic scene.

[107] Richard Taylor, *Against the bomb: the British peace movement 1958–1965* (Oxford: Clarendon Press, 1988), pp. 315–31. See also John Chiddick, 'Neutralism and the British Labour left: the persistence of the idea of the Third Force, 1955–1975', unpublished doctoral thesis, University of London (1998).

[108] Michael Barratt Brown, 'Positive neutralism then and now' in Oxford University Socialist Discussion Group (eds.), *Out of apathy: voices of the New Left 30 Years On* (London: Verso, 1989), pp. 81–7, referring to his own work, and that of John Rex and John Hughes.

[109] Taylor, *Against the bomb*, pp. 305–7.

[110] See for examples, Ralph Miliband, *Capitalist democracy in Britain* (Oxford: Oxford University Press, 1984), Colin Leys, *Politics in Britain* (London: Heinemann, 1983), G. McLennan, D. Held and S. Hall, *State and society in contemporary Britain* (Cambridge: Policy, 1984). Even Tom Nairn's celebrated analysis of the British monarchy ignored the military. See *The enchanted glass* (London: Radius, 1988). Compare with C. Wright Mills, *The power elite* (New York: Oxford University Press, 1956).

[111] Much was published in the *Cambridge Journal of Economics*.

[112] Dan Keohane, *Labour party defence policy since 1945* (Leicester: Leicester University Press, 1993), pp. 49–51. See also *Sense about defence: report of the Labour Party Defence Study Group* (London: Quartet, 1977); Mary Kaldor, Dan Smith and Steve Vines (eds.), *Democratic socialism and the cost of defence* (London: Croom Helm, 1979); S. Aaronovitch

political economies of twentieth-century Britain, which made great play
of the weakness of the British state in matters industrial. The key idea was
that twentieth-century Britain lacked a 'developmental state'.[113] A common argument was the commitment to a strong alliance with the USA,
and high defence spending especially overseas, and sometimes welfarism,
have contributed to a lack of development at home, and hence to the
British economic decline.[114] Long-standing and seemingly unchanged
historical causes were everywhere in these literatures. For example, in
thinking about the Falklands war Anthony Barnett saw in 'Churchillism'
the bringing together of Tory imperialism and labourist social reform,
which characterised post-war Britain.[115] Perry Anderson, in a reprise of
his famous 1960s' article, claimed that the British state

> constructed to contain social conflict at home and police an empire abroad, has
> proved impotent to redress economic decline. The night-watchman state
> acquired traits of the welfare officer, but never of the engineer. Sustained and
> structural intervention in the economy was the one task for which its organic
> liberalism was entirely ill-suited.[116]

Anderson explained this by pointing to the Victorian state, which had
neither a mass army nor a transport infrastructure to develop nor a mass
education system to run (again the implicit comparator is a certain image
of Wilhelmine Germany). Indeed the idea that British policy was

and R. P. Smith, *The political economy of British capitalism: a Marxist analysis*
(Maidenhead: McGraw Hill, 1981); Dan Smith and Ron Smith, *The economics of
militarism* (London: Pluto, 1983); Malcolm Chalmers, *Paying for defence: military spending and the British decline* (London: Pluto, 1985); Ben Fine and Laurence Harris, *The
peculiarities of the British economy* (London: Lawrence & Wishart, 1985).

[113] Andrew Gamble, *Britain in decline* (London: Macmillan, 1981); David Marquand, *The
unprincipled society* (London: Cape, 1988); Scott Newton and Dilwyn Porter,
Modernization frustrated: the politics of industrial decline in Britain since 1900 (London,
Unwin Hyman, 1988); W. R. Garside, 'Industrial policy and the developmental state:
British responses to the competitive environment before and after the 1970s', *Business
and Economic History* 27 (1998), 47–60. For criticism and review of the extensive
literature which insisted on the lack of a 'developmental state' see Simon Lee,
'Industrial policy and British decline' in Andrew Cox, Simon Lee and Joe Sanderson,
The political economy of modern Britain (Cheltenham: Edward Elgar, 1997).

[114] For example, David Morgan and Mary Evans, *The battle for Britain: citizenship and
ideology in the Second World War* (London: Routledge, 1993).

[115] Anthony Barnett, *Iron Britannia* (London: Alison & Busby, 1982).

[116] Perry Anderson, 'The figures of descent', *New Left Review* no. 162 (1987), 75. For
comments and responses see: Michael Barratt Brown, 'Away with all the great arches:
Anderson's history of British capitalism', *New Left Review* no. 167 (1988), 22–51; Alex
Callinicos, 'Exception or symptom: the British Crisis and the world system', *New Left
Review* no. 169 (1988), 97–106, and Edgerton 'Liberal militarism'. See also Colin
Barker and David Nicholls (eds.), *The development of British capitalist society: a Marxist
debate* (Manchester: Northern Marxist Historians Group, 1988).

inexplicable by current political economic conditions became a common theme: thus the political economist Dan Smith could not explain Britain's purchase of the Trident submarine and missile system except

as the reflection of post-imperial inertia, a desire to turn backwards rather than forwards, to see Britain as a great power with the right to appropriate appurtenances of power, an entirely internalised image of power and status, a deep refusal to come to terms with the realities of the late twentieth century. As awesomely destructive as Trident will be, there is nonetheless something deeply ludicrous about Britain's purchase of it: it represents the most archaic tendencies within the British state, and we should have no doubt that these retain a powerful ideological pull.[117]

For others Britain had policed a world liberal order but victory in the Second World War 'postponed the acknowledgement that British world power was finally at an end', with the consequence that Britain continued to defend sterling inappropriately, and maintained high defence expenditure, particularly overseas.[118] In other words the British state was adapted to an older world where it was a great power, and that as such it was incapable as well as unwilling to intervene in industry.

These arguments need to be challenged at many levels. First, the evidence presented in this book shows very clearly that Britain had an interventionist state, led by the supply departments. The literature on the developmental state, and indeed the British state and industry specifically, simply did not 'recognise the extent to which the British state did in fact intervene in industry'.[119] Indeed at a 1980 academic conference on industrial policy and innovation the economist David Henderson, who brilliantly diagnosed the over-investment in high technology of the 1950s and 1960s, noted that most of the policy proposals on offer were not novel, and that the history of even the very recent past was forgotten. Expert analysts wrote as if industrial performance and R&D had not been a central concern of the British government for decades. In particular the whole Ministry of Technology experience was missing. Not surprisingly, he experienced a 'disheartening sense of futility and déjà vu'.[120] Of course

---

[117] Dan Smith, 'The political economy of British defence policy' in Shaw, *War, state and society*, p. 201. For Dan Smith British defence policy has been driven by three incompatible elements: post-imperialism (that is the sort of nostalgic fantasy that led to Trident), atlanticism and europeanism (p. 207).

[118] Gamble, *Britain in decline*, p. 113; Marquand, *Unprincipled society*; Michael Mann, 'The decline of Great Britain' in his *States, war and capitalism: studies in political sociology* (Oxford: Blackwell, 1988), pp. 210–37.

[119] Simon Lee, 'Industrial policy and British decline', p. 109.

[120] David Henderson, 'Comment' in Charles Carter (ed.), *Industrial policy and innovation* (London: Heinneman, 1981), p. 173.

Mintech is extremely well known, but it is known within the terms of the arguments that generated it, not what it did, less still by what it came to understand. Even when Mintech is considered significant its originality and uniqueness is overplayed.[121]

The supply ministries were a great stimulus to British industrial development. For investment in warlike production did positively affect some parts of British manufacturing industry, during and after the Second World War. The concept of war potential did lead to the development of many new industries in Britain that would not otherwise have existed. The great state technological programmes surely also stimulated R&D in other sectors, helping promote a culture celebrating R&D, looking for technological leapfrogs and more generally promoting technological and nationalistic considerations over economic ones. From the point of view of advocates of a 'developmental state' all this could have been seen in a positive light. The negative argument is that the supply ministries had a tendency to generate economically irrational military and civil technologies, but that is not one the left was particularly comfortable with, beyond criticising 'prestige' projects. Indeed, the warfare state, and particularly its scientific and industrial side, generated a culture of secrecy and lack of debate which negatively affected the quality of decision-making in technological and industrial, as well as in other, matters.[122]

If what is to be explained – the supposed lack of a developmental state – is flawed, so are the explanations. First, the relations between policing a world order and high defence spending are not made clear, perhaps not surprisingly since Britain's defence expenditure was lower in its great imperial and free trading years than after the Second World War. In comparative terms pre-1939 Britain was a relatively low spender on defence in terms of proportion of GDP. Indeed Patrick O'Brien argues that low pre-1914 defence spending contributed to the British decline thereafter.[123] The hang-over thesis does not work in another way, since defence expenditure, in absolute terms, was lower in the late 1940s than it was to be in the 1950s and early 1960s. The key ratcheting up of defence

[121] For a review of the historiography of the Labour government's industrial policy with special reference to the treatment of Mintech see Richard Coopey, 'Industrial policy in the white heat of the scientific revolution' in R. Coopey, S. Fielding and N. Tiratsoo (eds.), *The Wilson governments 1964–1970* (London: Pinter, 1993).
[122] David Vincent, *The culture of secrecy: Britain 1832–1998* (Oxford: Oxford University Press, 1998).
[123] Patrick O'Brien, 'The security of the realm and the growth of the economy, 1688–1914' in Peter Clarke and Clive Trebilcock (eds.), *Understanding decline* (Cambridge: Cambridge University Press, 1997), pp. 49–72.

expenditure post-war took place in 1950–4 as a result of rearmament programme focused on Europe. Defence expenditure was also higher in the 1970s than in the late 1960s, that is, after the pull-out from east of Suez. While Britain did engage in imperial wars (Malaya, Kenya, Suez, Cyprus, Aden), the level of involvement was relatively low. What was new, as was noted above, was the maintenance on the continent of Europe of a permanently stationed army, which for many years included conscripts. E. P. Thompson's 1980 manifesto on 'exterminism' rightly criticised the left's political-economic accounts of militarism which centred on imperialism: the cold war's 'logic of exterminism' was centred in Europe and was driven by military-industrial complexes, including the British one.[124]

These political-economic accounts of Britain do not adequately deal with other aspects of Britain's world role.[125] The idea that Britain was free-trading through the twentieth century is obviously not right but nor are the implications of some of the arguments that Britain always wanted free trade. In the middle years of the century Britain was highly protectionist. However, even the commitment to the principle of global free trade went along with a highly interventionist national policy. This national interventionist policy was highly dependent on imperial, rather than global, trade. Britain wanted to open up both the US and the European markets to its trade – hence multilateralism. The movement towards the Common Market in the 1950s represented an abandonment of the hope (not the reality) of such a global trading system, and the willingness to give up many national interventionist powers.[126] The central image of Britain as a global, free-trading nation, pursuing non-interventionist industrial policies, when it should have pursued a European, interventionist policy, is thus very misleading. In the middle of the century, particularly, state intervention increased, import controls increased and military commitment to Europe all increased. There is a broader point to be recalled: that ideologically too Britain was much less liberal that these declinist political-economists contended; indeed the very prevalence of declinist analyses testified to this since declinism usually went along with economic nationalism.[127] Ideologies, policies,

---

[124] E. P. Thompson, 'Notes on exterminism, the last stage of civilisation', *New Left Review* no. 121 (1980), 3–31.

[125] See in particular Lee, 'Industrial policy and British decline'.

[126] Alan S. Milward and George Brennan, *Britain's place in the world: a historical enquiry into import controls, 1945–60* (London: Routledge, 1996); Alan S. Milward, *The rise and fall of a national strategy, 1945–1963*. Vol. I: *The United Kingdom and the European Community* (London: Cass, 2002).

[127] See my review of Clarke and Trebilcock, *Understanding decline* in *The Historical Journal* 42 (1999), 313–14.

practices, possibilities all changed quite radically over the century and were always contested. Historians, among many others, have sometimes been too keen to find deep continuities and long-standing causes to spot the radical reconfigurations that have taken place.

The return of technocratic anti-histories

The erasure of mid-1960s' arguments about the economic benefits to be obtained from R&D provides a particular cogent example of the dangers of doing this, as David Henderson noted. An important and influential example is to be found in the work of Christopher Freeman, founder of the Science Policy Research Unit at Sussex,[128] and a notably historically oriented student of innovation, for whom Wilhelmine Germany was a key model.[129] For Freeman, there was a British paradox – that the amount R&D in industry in the 1950s and 1960s was 'apparently' higher than that of all capitalist countries other than the United States, and yet Britain had a low rate of growth. Freeman resolved this, to his own satisfaction, by pointing to the high proportion spent on government-funded and aeronautical R&D in industry, implying that British industry did less bread-and-butter R&D than Germany or Japan and as a consequence grew less fast.[130] Similar arguments were voiced by others.[131] Unfortunately for Freeman's argument, as was known in Mintech, British industry spent as much (of its own money) in absolute terms as did German or Japanese industry and more in proportion

[128] The others were the Department of Liberal Studies in Science, University of Manchester (which no longer exists in this form) and the Science Studies Unit, University of Edinburgh.

[129] See Christopher Freeman, *Technology policy and economic performance: lessons from Japan* (London: Pinter, 1987) and K. Pavitt (ed.), *Technical innovation and British economic performance* (London: Macmillan, 1980), both of which are largely historical accounts. For a pointed critique of Freeman's naïve Listianism see Lee, 'Industrial policy and British decline'.

[130] Christopher Freeman, 'Technical innovation and British trade performance', in F. T. Blackaby (ed.), *De-industrialisation* (London: Heinneman, 1979). An earlier use of the term and concept of a 'paradox' in this case that there was a peculiarly British problem of lack of correlation between R&D spend and growth – due among other things to too much defence R&D is due to the declinist Michael Shanks, writing in 1970: Michael Shanks, ch. 6, 'Setting the scene five: the United Kingdom' in Maurice Goldsmith (ed.), *Technological innovation and the economy* (London: Wiley Interscience, 1970), pp. 55–61.

[131] Something close to it was first presented by other analysts. For example, (Sir) Ieuan Maddock (1917–1988), FRS 1967 who had been in the MoS from 1940, and had been a key figure in the British bomb project, in Mintech and the Departments of Trade and Industry, wrote 'Science, technology, and industry', *Proceedings of the Royal Society London* A 345 (1975), 295–326. This paper was much referred to, usually very approvingly (see for example, and Pavitt, *Technical innovation*, pp. 9, 322–3). The implication of Maddock's article was that spending *should be* distributed fairly across all industrial sectors, and this would promote growth.

to output.[132] Not only was the thesis refuted before it was written, but it was again refuted in the late 1970s, and again later, with negligible effect.[133] But the core belief, that there should be, and there was for other countries, a link between investment in R&D and the rate of economic growth was a crucial assumption which technocrats could not let go of.[134] There is no warrant for the belief, and a mass of counter-evidence.[135]

Freeman's picture of post-war British R&D was, in one form or another, influential well into the 1990s and this became the standard story about British post-war R&D among the experts.[136] Through the

[132] See David Edgerton, *Science, technology and the British industrial 'decline', 1870–1970* (Cambridge: Cambridge University Press, 1996).

[133] Indeed the economic historian S. B. Saul commented in 1979 that

There are those who have argued that expenditure on R&D has been wrongly directed towards the so-called 'high-technology industries' and that it should have been spread more widely over industries in general. The evidence for this is not very strong.

Saul was pointing in part to the lack of positive correlation between economic growth and R&D expenditure: S. B. Saul, 'Research and development in British industry from the end of the nineteenth century to the 1960s' in T. C. Smout (ed.), *The search for wealth and stability* (London: Macmillan, 1979), pp. 135–6. See also Berrick Saul, 'There's more to growth than R&D', *New Scientist*, 23 September 1976, 633–5.

[134] In the 1980s I often heard it said that Bruce Williams's conclusions about a lack of correlation between R&D and growth could be explained by the fact that his figures included defence R&D. In fact Williams himself thought one reason for the lack of correlation might be that his figures included defence R&D (B. R. Williams, *Investment, technology and growth* (London: Chapman and Hall, 1967)). However, it is clear that even for the 1950s there was no correlation between civil R&D and growth, and the studies above had already shown that the military explanation did not work.

[135] For clear accounts see Terence Kealey, *The economic laws of scientific research* (London: Macmillan, 1994) and Edgerton, *British industrial 'decline'*. The more specialist literature is not clear on this crucial point. The OECD stated in 1992 that 'The proposition that investment in R&D and technological progress are essential to future growth has not yet been conclusively empirically demonstrated': OECD, *Technology and the economy: the key relationships* (Paris: OECD, 1992), p. 184, which is hardly specific enough. Jan Fagerberg, 'Technology and international differences in growth rates', *Journal of Economic Literature* 32 (1994), 1147–75, is especially interesting because despite the title it does not address the issue head on. Here 'technology' generally really means technology gap, misleading measured by GDP per capita differences or what the article sees as a reasonable proxy, the R&D/GDP ratio differences. Thus although the article does not formally address the issue of the relations of the relations of R&D spending and rates of growth, the whole analysis and emphasis of the paper depends on the lack of a positive relationship.

[136] See, for example, K. Smith, *British economic crisis* (Harmondsworth: Penguin, 1982); M. Dintenfass, *The decline of industrial Britain 1870–1980* (London: Routledge, 1992); N. F. R. Crafts, 'Economic growth' and M. W. Kirby, 'Supply side management' both in N. F. R. Crafts and Nicholas Woodward (eds.), *The British economy since 1945* (Oxford: Clarendon Press, 1991); and Robert Millward, 'Industrial and commercial performance since 1950' in R. Floud and D. N. McCloskey, *The economic history of Britain since 1700*, 3 vols., 2nd edn (Cambridge: Cambridge University Press, 1994), III; Maurice Kirby, 'British culture and the development of high technology sectors' in Andrew Godley and Oliver Westfall (eds.), *Business history and business culture*

1970s and 1980s the conviction grew that British industry had been deficient in R&D right through the twentieth century. Keith Pavitt, also of the Science Policy Research Unit, edited a key techno-declinist historically oriented text in 1980, which conveyed that impression very clearly.[137] A US economic historian fashioned the most elaborate anti-history of British industrial research, in which supposedly low levels of industrial R&D were an important cause of British decline.[138] The key conclusions of earlier historians were ignored and it was assumed that lack of growth indicated low R&D.[139] Technocratic anti-histories ran riot, with business historians who wished for more R&D in the businesses they studied, not recording what R&D they did,[140] and historians of the aircraft industry celebrating the potential of cancelled projects while ignoring the millions spent on unsuccessful aircraft.[141] So important were these anti-histories that leading analysts reacted with barely concealed fury to suggestions that the history of British R&D was one of strength not weakness.[142]

Anti-histories became ever more elaborate and influential. In the Thatcher era two works of history stand out as ideologically significant, Martin Wiener's *English culture and the decline of the industrial spirit*[143] and Correlli Barnett's *The audit of war* of 1986.[144] Both were profoundly anti-historical in the sense used in this book. Wiener showed no interest in the actual history of British industry or the industrial spirit; he only chronicled a long-standing anti-industrial spirit. Barnett's anti-histories of state intervention, technical education, research, and much else besides, have had credibility, even when his history has not, as was

(Manchester: Manchester University Press, 1996), pp. 190–221. Here I am only taking examples to make the point that this analysis has been accepted almost universally: many other sources may be cited.

[137] Pavitt, *Technical innovation*.

[138] The most elaborated version of this common argument was that of David Mowery, 'Industrial research in Britain, 1900–1950' in B. Elbaum and W. Lazonick (eds.), *The decline of the British economy* (Oxford: Clarendon Press, 1986).

[139] In particular that of Michael Sanderson, S. B. Saul and Leslie Hannah. For details see D. E. H. Edgerton and S. M. Horrocks, 'British industrial research and development before 1945', *Economic History Review* 47 (1994), 213–38.

[140] See D. E. H. Edgerton, 'Science and technology in British business history', *Business History* 29 (1987), 84–103.

[141] Derek Wood, *Project cancelled a searching criticism of the abandonment of Britain's advanced aircraft projects* revised edition (London: Jane's, 1986) (first published 1975).

[142] See for example the debate between myself, John Van Reenen and Keith Pavitt in the *Guardian* 30 August 1993 and 27 September 1993 and 25 October 1993.

[143] *English culture and the decline of the industrial spirit, 1850–1980* (Cambridge: Cambridge University Press, 1981).

[144] *The audit of war: the illusion and reality of Britain as a great nation* (London: Macmillan, 1986). This had been preceded by *The collapse of British power* (London: Eyre Methuen, 1972), and was followed by *The lost victory* (London: Macmillan, 1995).

evident in the responses, from left and right, to *Audit of war*.[145] Attacked for its treatment of the 'welfare state' many of Barnett's academic critics shared with him key assumptions of the technocratic and militaristic critiques about Britain, its elite, its armed forces, the history of its industry, science and technology, and the relations of all three in Britain and elsewhere.[146] Indeed Barnett combined particularly clearly the technocratic critique and the militaristic critiques of Britain, so long present in more narrowly focused literature. In Barnett, and in much literature on Britain, British science, technology and the British modernising state disappeared once more into historical explanations of their weakness, explanations which were the characteristic creations of British technocrats. It is significant too that key elements of Barnett's right-wing techno-nationalism were endorsed from the left, notably by Perry Anderson and John Saville.[147] It is perhaps not surprising that in Barnett's arguments, implicit and explicit historical comparator is, surprisingly often, Germany.[148] For Barnett, the supposed contrasts between Wilhelmine Germany and late Victorian and Edwardian

---

[145] For critical essay reviews of *Audit of war* see José Harris, 'Enterprise and welfare states: a comparative perspective', *Transactions of the Royal Historical Society* 40 (1990), 175–95; David Edgerton, 'The prophet militant and industrial: the peculiarities of Correlli Barnett', *Twentieth Century British History* 2 (1991), 360–79; A. D. Harvey, *Collision of empires: Britain in three world wars, 1793–1945* (London: Phoenix, 1994), pp. 592–3, 560–63; Sebastian Ritchie, 'A new audit of war: the productivity of Britain's wartime aircraft industry reconsidered', *War and Society* 12 (1994), 125–47. For *Lost victory* see Martin Chick in *Twentieth Century British History* 7 (1996) 399–403; David Edgerton, 'Declinism', *London Review of Books*, 7 March 1996; Jim Tomlinson, 'Welfare and the economy: the economic impact of the welfare state, 1945–1951', *Twentieth Century British History* 6 (1995), 194–219. The political impact of Barnett's work has been remarkable. *Audit of war* was reputedly read by the Thatcher Cabinet, at the instigation of Sir Keith Joseph. Michael Heseltine notes in his memoir that when he became Deputy Prime Minister in 1995 he presented each member of John Major's Cabinet with a copy of *Lost victory* (Michael Heseltine, *Life in the jungle: my autobiography* (London: Hodder & Stoughton, 2000), p. 493).
[146] Edgerton, 'Prophet militant and industrial', analyses other reviews.
[147] Perry Anderson, 'The figures of descent', *New Left Review* no. 162 (1987), 20–77. See Edgerton 'Prophet militant and industrial', Edgerton 'Liberal militarism' (for the critique of Anderson). See John Saville, *The politics of continuity: British foreign policy and the Labour Government, 1945–6* (London: Verso, 1993), ch. 4, pp. 149–75.
[148] A key example specifically concerned with technology is Christopher Freeman, *Technology policy and economic performance: lessons from Japan* (London: Pinter, 1987). Here Japan is very much the Prussia of the east, and it is this and Wilhelmine Germany which provided the contrast to the British case. See Lee, 'Industrial policy and British decline' and 'British culture and economic decline', in Cox, *Political economy of modern Britain*. See Edgerton, *British industrial 'decline'*, for a detailed critique of the use of poor international comparisons (especially with Germany) in describing British science and technology in the twentieth century.

Britain are central, not just to his account of the Second World War, but history since then too.

Julian Corbett, we may recall, claimed that Germany was 'afraid of her own shadow'. Yet it can reasonably be argued that British analysts projected on to Germany British practices, concerns and beliefs. Before 1914 Britain was mainly concerned with German naval power. The German army, always much larger, was much less worrying. In the 1930s a Britain committed to the bomber saw German air power as particularly threatening and innovative. Britain, so very vulnerable to blockade, thought Germany would collapse through economic sanctions.[149] More generally, British commentators have again and again attributed German economic success to R&D, reflecting their own beliefs, rather than an understanding of German beliefs or practices. Thus many British arguments about Germany tell us more about Britain than about Germany. The nature of the arguments made point to the significance in Britain of militarists and technocrats, particularly after the Second World War.

Certainly the standard British views of Germany are not compatible with the findings of comparative history. For example the usual implied stories of German productivity or R&D funding compared to British hardly stand up. The usual images of the German war machine do little better. We know that the German forces, especially in the Second World War, were much less equipment intensive than the British; we also know that it was the British who centred their air force on the idea of strategic bombing and not the Germans. Most remarkably, Stephen Bungay concludes in a recent study of the Battle of Britain that the RAF, not the Luftwaffe, was run by hard-bitten professionals, that the British were the better prepared and the better users of technology, that the British fought with discipline and control while the Germans relied on individual élan, that the British were team players and the Germans individualistic cultivators of the culture of the hunt, and that the British were ruthless and determined while the Germans were the jousting knights of the air.[150] An English mystery, indeed, but one we have had to come to grips with in order to understand the history of the British warfare state and the role of expertise within it.

There were many, interrelated reasons why the warfare state could not be made visible by intellectuals. For the British warfare state would have undermined many vitally important narratives about twentieth-century

---

[149] Jeffrey L. Hughes, 'The origins of World War II in Europe: British deterrence failure and German expansionism', *Journal of Interdisciplinary History* 18 (1988), 851–92.

[150] Stephen Bungay, *The most dangerous enemy: a history of the Battle of Britain* (London: Aurum Press, 2000), p. 395.

Britain. Before the Second World War recognition of the warfare state would have undermined the image of the benevolent imperialist and world policeman so beloved of intellectuals. After the war it would have undermined the anti-histories of British militarism, and the anti-histories of technocracy and state intervention that were central to the militaristic and technocratic critiques which shaped so much thinking about the state. It also, in a different way, would have undermined welfarist accounts. None could co-exist with an account of the scope, role and nature of the warfare state. Thus the term 'warfare state' as applied to Britain has seemed far-fetched, even ridiculous.[151] Yet its very implausibility is a measure of the significance of putting it in to the history of twentieth-century Britain.

---

[151] People often hear, 'welfare state', and politely say 'how interesting'! It is sometimes read that way: in 1998 I wrote an article for the *New Left Review* on 'Tony Blair's warfare state', *New Left Review* no. 230 (1998), 123–30. The title is correct at the head of the article and on the cover, but the contents page gives it as 'Tony Blair's welfare state'.

8   Rethinking the relations of science, technology, industry and war

The account given by British intellectuals of British history and of Britain at war has been a profoundly civilian one: civilian forces led to success in war, shaped strategy, deprived the forces of weapons. It is little wonder that many historians have noted the emergence of a specifically 'civilian militarism' and indeed 'liberal militarism' in the twentieth century, at least in Britain, the United States and France.[1] In the standard accounts of science, technology industry and war, science, technology and industry appear as civilian agencies, of fundamental importance for the transformation of war in the nineteenth and twentieth centuries. These accounts are very partial for they leave the military out of their accounts. The extent to which this has happened needs spelling out to demonstrate the need for a general new account of the production of arms in peace and war. Such an account will change the history of large parts of industry, technology and science, making the military one of the creators of the research enterprise.

Like military intelligence (which in Aldous Huxley's joke was differentiated from both intelligence, animal, and intelligence, human in the encyclopaedias), military science (except in the sense of the art of war) and more surprisingly, military technology, are close to oxymoronic. Again and again, for example, the romanticism of the military is contrasted with enlightened science, technology and industry; militarism and modernity are incompatible, even if they have in practice come together many times in the twentieth century. Given this it is not surprising that Ernest Gellner has claimed that 'civil societies' have vanquished 'militarist romantic' nations in war.[2] But might it not be that 'civil societies' have

---

[1] Michael Sherry, *In the shadow of war: the United States since the 1930s* (New Haven: Yale University Press, 1995); David Edgerton, 'Liberal militarism and the British state', *New Left Review* no. 185 (1991), 138–69.

[2] Ernest Gellner, *Conditions of liberty: civil society and its rivals* (London: Penguin 1996), p. 200. See also p. 33 and 179.

triumphed because of the power and innovativeness of their military as much as of their civil institutions? It seems hardly possible, for even to ask the question we need a reconceptualised account of twentieth-century science, technology and industry and their relationship to the military.

In order to understand the depth and power of the conventional argument, and just how radically different it is from the account developed of the British case in this book, we need to take a close look not just at the academic literature, but also at other writings on science, technology, industry and war. Here we will discover core arguments more clearly revealed. For example, we will find that definitions of armaments and military technology have routinely excluded even warships and aeroplanes; that aeroplanes have been thought of as essentially a civilian transport technology rather than as weapons of war; and that science, technology and industry in general are essentially civilian. Furthermore, we will find the meaning of 'science' commonly narrowed down to scientific research, to civilian scientific research or government-funded civilian scientific research, to pure civil academic scientific research and surprisingly often, plain academic physics. Only as we see these moves at work will it become clear how partial the conventional stories are.

Histories of technology and war

It was not until the 1980s that there was academic interest in the relations of science, technology, industry and the military.[3] The key early works on the relations of technology and war show remarkable similarities in approach, despite the different backgrounds of the authors.[4] There was a central, unexamined assumption in this literature: that civilian science, technology and industry has radically transformed war, by civilianising

---

[3] Mary Kaldor, *The baroque arsenal* (London: Deutsch, 1982); Maurice Pearton, *The knowledgeable state: diplomacy, war and technology since 1830* (London: Burnett, 1983); W. H. McNeill, *The pursuit of power: technology, armed force, and society since AD 1000* (Chicago: University of Chicago Press, 1982); Martin van Creveld, *Technology and war: from 2000 BC to the present* (London: Brassey's, 1991); Robert L. O'Connell, *Of arms and men: a history of war, weapons, and aggression* (New York: Oxford University Press, 1989).

[4] The two British authors Mary Kaldor and Maurice Pearton show clear influence of political economy in their thinking. Pearton is described on the flyleaf as having taken his doctorate at LSE 'on political economy'. We might note alternative accounts – philosophical rather than political economic, and equally abstract, developing the theme of speed and communications in relation to war and to the history of war: Paul Virilio, *Speed and politics* (New York: Semiotext(e), 1986) (original French edition 1977); Manuel de Landa, *War in the age of intelligent machines* (New York: Swerve Editions, 1991). They are not so different in substance.

and industrialising it.[5] For example, William McNeill dealt with the nineteenth- and twentieth-century parts of his story explicitly in terms of the industrialisation of war, and the need for a command economy in order to fight war in the twentieth century. The whole process is driven by civilian innovation, produced above all by private industrial firms which turned their attention to arms in the late nineteenth century. All the key works relied on a notion of difference between the civilian and the military worlds, which merge on civilian terms.[6]

Where the military had the upper hand the result was inadequate military technology. A particular interesting argument along these lines was put forward by Mary Kaldor.[7] She saw technical innovation coming from the civil side, specifically competitive private industry, but she put the military themselves in the picture, though only as conservative consumers. The military wanted more powerful existing types of weapons, not to shift to new ones. The result was a 'baroque arsenal', a phrase which neatly invoked Kaldor's central idea. This was that the over-elaboration of existing technologies of war leads to rapidly diminishing returns, indeed to negative returns. 'Baroque' also captures a historical conjuncture which replicates the implicit model of an ancient military and modern technology. Peacetime military technology had a grotesque, distorted quality. Moreover, in Kaldor's view the industry producing baroque weapons acted as a drag on the development of the economy as a whole. In war, according to Kaldor, crisis conditions result in the overthrow of military conservatism and the adoption of radical new technologies and ways of fighting war, of civilian origin. These new forms themselves become baroque in the ensuing peace.[8]

The obverse of the idea of the creative civilian is the conservative soldier, sailor and airman. This idea is indeed often explicitly stated, as in Kaldor. McNeill writing of the 1880s claimed that 'The ritual routine of army and navy life as developed across centuries discouraged innovation of any kind. Only when civilian techniques had advanced ... did it

---

[5] For an exhaustive survey of this literature in its academic and non-academic versions see Barton C. Hacker, 'Military institutions, weapons, and social change: toward a new history of military technology', *Technology and Culture* 35 (1994), 768–834.

[6] Van Creveld for example is clear that there are differences: 'since technology and war operate on a logic which is not only different but actually opposed, the conceptual framework that is useful even vital for dealing with the one should not be allowed to interfere with the other' (Van Creveld, *Technology and war*, p. 320).

[7] Kaldor, *Baroque arsenal*.

[8] Ibid. For an investigation as to whether, as Kaldor suggested, state arsenals were concerned with the production efficiency, but were very conservative in terms of product development see Colin Duff, 'British armoury practice: technical change and small arms manufacture, 1850–1939', unpublished MSc thesis, University of Manchester (1990).

become possible to overcome official inertia and conservatism.'[9] In more specialised work the contrast between progressive civil technology with its own logic, up against a conservative and indeed blinkered military which surrenders only under the pressure of war, remains very powerful.[10] Although the excesses in this picture are corrected in more recent work, it is clear, for example, that Tim Travers's account of Great War technology relies also on the idea of a technologically determined form of war which – necessarily – took time to adapt to.[11] Jon Sumida's account of naval fire control technology before 1914 also sticks to the model of a technologically reactionary navy (the British navy before the Great War!) facing down a civilian inventor of genius.[12]

The above accounts are by scholars interested in the history of war, not the history of technology. Had they looked to histories of technology they would have found their accounts confirmed. Specifically military technology hardly existed in these histories. For example, the two twentieth-century volumes of a well-known *History of technology* have only one chapter with an explicitly military connection, and that is on atomic weapons.[13] The condensed version of these volumes has a chapter, not in the original, on 'military technology'. This is taken to be guns, tanks, flamethrowers, but not aircraft, radar and so on. These and other technologies, while recognised as critical to war, are buried in civilian-oriented chapters, as they were in the original version.[14] Similarly, science and industry museums do not display tanks or guns; these are left to military museums. And yet in science museums war is taken to be transformed by what are taken as civilian technologies.

Had our authors looked to the key British military writers on technology, Captain Basil Liddell Hart and Major-General J. F. C. Fuller, their

---

[9] McNeill, *Pursuit of power*, p. 224.

[10] John Ellis, *The social history of the machine gun* (London: Croom Helm, 1975), is a particularly clear example of an unthinking invocation of military conservatism.

[11] Tim Travers, *The killing ground: the British army, the western front and the emergence of modern warfare, 1900–1918* (London: Unwin Hyman, 1987); G. Phillips, 'The obsolescence of the arme blanche and technological determinism in British military history', *War in History* 9 (2002), 39–59.

[12] J. T. Sumida, *In defence of naval supremacy* (London: Unwin Hyman, 1989). Sumida's account of naval fire control has been comprehensively challenged by John Brooks, 'Fire control for British Dreadnoughts: choices in technology and supply', unpublished doctoral thesis, University of London (2001).

[13] Charles Singer, A. J. Holmyard, A. R. Hall and T. I. Williams (eds.), *A history of technology*, 7 vols. (London: Oxford University Press, 1954–1984), VII: *The twentieth century, c. 1900 – c. 1950*, parts I and II (Oxford: Oxford University Press, 1978).

[14] T. I. Williams, *A short history of twentieth century technology, c. 1900–c. 1950* (Oxford: Oxford University Press, 1982).

assumptions would have been confirmed again. They too made much of the conservatism of soldiers and the creativity of the civilians. According to Captain Basil Liddell Hart, 'The progress of weapons, has outstripped the progress of the mind – especially in the class who wield weapons. Each successive war of modern times has revealed the lag due to the slow pace of mental adaptation.'[15] Even the fascist–sympathising Major-General Fuller, in his pioneering account *Armament and history* published in 1946, warned that 'civil progress is so intense that there is not only a danger but a certainty that no army in peacetime can in the full sense be kept up to date'.[16] For example although the internal combustion engine and radio were to be central to war, in the interwar years, 'divorced from civil progress, soldiers could not see this'.[17] As it happens Fuller was an admirer of Lewis Mumford who had put the point graphically: 'Fortunately for mankind, the army has usually been the refuge of third-rate minds ... Hence the paradox in modern technics: war stimulates invention, but the army resists it!'[18] The histories of the 1980s were thus drawing on an intellectual commonplace.

Intellectuals, science, technology, industry and war

In order to make even clearer just how dominant this position has been we can look at the pre-academic arguments where the arguments are very explicit. I will look at two closely interconnected and influential groups of commentators on these issues, the political economists and the scientific intellectuals. Taking the British case, I will concentrate on the early part of the century.

For the political economists, even before the Great War, war was being shaped by new industry, science and technology. The 'frail and spectacled British official', claimed Norman Angell, was the master of

teeming thousands of Sudanese; the relatively unwarlike Briton is doing the same thing all over Asia, and he is doing it by the simple virtue of superior brain and character, more thought, more rationalism, more steady and controlled hard

---

[15] Basil Liddell Hart, 'War and peace', *English Review* 54 (April 1932), p. 408, quoted in John J. Mearsheimer, *Liddell Hart and the weight of history* (Ithaca, NY: Cornell University Press, 1988), p. 103.

[16] J. F. C. Fuller, *Armament and history* (New York: Scribners, 1945), p. 20. See also Brian Holden-Reid, *J. F. C. Fuller: military thinker* (Basingstoke: Macmillan, 1987) and Patrick Wright, *Tank: the progress of a monstrous war machine* (London: Faber, 2000).

[17] Fuller, *Armament and history*, p. 135.

[18] Lewis Mumford, *Technics and civilisation* (London: Routledge and Kegan Paul, 1955), p. 95 (first published 1934).

work. It may be said that it is superior armament which does it. But what is the superior armament but the result of superior thought and work?[19]

Generally, he argued, war was no longer a matter for the traditional heroic approach: 'war is becoming as hopelessly intellectual and scientific as any other form of work: officers are scientists, the men are workmen, the army is a machine, battles are "tactical operations", the charge is becoming out of date; a little while and war will become the least romantic of all professions'.[20] During the Great War such arguments acquired greater force: J. T. Walton Newbold, soon to be Britain's first communist Member of Parliament, suggested that 'Never before was the soldier or the sailor a mechanic. Only today is he becoming a machine-minder, an operative.'[21] For F. W. Hirst, the editor of *The Economist*, and author of *The political economy of war*, war had become, through the division of labour, a specialist profession, to 'produce not beauty or utility, but security'. He went on:

Success came to depend more and more upon drill, training, engineering, mechanical skill, equipment, and strategy. Modern battles are won in foundries, machine shops, and laboratories. Unseen agencies kill or maim men by the thousand. The very minister who preached a holy war in the autumn of 1914 was forced after ten months to describe it as a War of Munitions.[22]

War 'has lost much of its romantic glamour, as success has come to depend less and less upon soldierly prowess, and more and more upon the skill of chemists and mechanics'.[23] This way of thinking about war was to continue to dominate political economic writing, as we have seen. Indeed it influenced Britain's way of waging war too.

But it was in the writing of scientific intellectuals that, naturally enough, science and technology got most attention. I will take two intellectuals writing in the 1930s and two key works, H. G. Wells's *The shape of things to come* and J. D. Bernal's *Social function of science* of 1939, to look in more detail at the particular ways in which science, technology and war

[19] Norman Angell, *The great illusion: a study of the relation of military power in nations to their economic and social advantage* (London: Heinemann, 1911), pp. 232–3. See J. D. B. Miller, *Norman Angell and the futility of war: peace and the public mind* (London: Hamilton, 1986).

[20] Angell, *Great illusion*, pp. 234–5.

[21] J. T. Walton Newbold, *How Europe armed for war, 1871–1914* (London: Blackfriars Press, 1916), p. iii. Speaking of himself the author, highly critical of the arms firms noted: 'So long as he lives he will remember the thrill of admiration and something akin to pride that he experienced when he viewed the Grand Fleet at Spithead in July 1914. It was a mighty monument to the science and craftsmanship of Britain' (p. 76). His profound admiration for Fisher and for the navy is also evident (pp. 75–6). Newbold was MP for Motherwell, 1922–3; he resigned from the party in 1924.

[22] F. W. Hirst, *The political economy of war* (London: Dent, 1915), pp. 3–4.

[23] Hirst, *Political economy*, p. 11.

issues were dealt with. Both writers are particularly useful because they, unusually, recognised the importance of military institutions to interwar science, and dwelt on it.

H. G. Wells's the *Shape of things to come*, subtitled *The ultimate revolution* and published in 1933, was the story of how aviators saved the world, but was also an elaborate meditation of the relations of science, technology and war.[24] While a proponent of the standard 'cultural lag' analysis of the these relations, whereby war takes place because mankind has failed to keep up with science and technology, Wells acknowledges the extent of interaction. He also emphasised a fundamental contradiction between the military and science and technology.[25] His story goes like this: in 1914 despite having new weapons at their disposal, the 'professional soldiers were clinging to the idea that nothing fundamental has happened to the methods of their ancient and honoured profession'.[26] The war produced some soldiers who were determined to modernise, and they came to power in the interwar years. As he put it:

A phase of extreme innovation succeeded the conservatism of the older generation. Everywhere War offices stirred with novel conceptions of strange inventions, secret novelties and furtive systematic research. Everywhere obscure reports of spies and informants, carefully fostered by the armament dealers affected, stimulated this forced inventiveness.[27]

Soldiers set themselves 'to overtake the march of invention, to master engineering and engineers, chemistry and chemists, war correspondents and newspaper editors, biology, medicine, and even finance, in their efforts to keep that ancient war idea, the idea of the battling sovereign state, alive'.[28] But the new experts employed were mediocrities, and did not work out the true nature of the new warfare. Secrecy, immunity from criticism and bureaucratic skills, led to a 'certain lumbering quality' in the devices they created.[29] During the wars of the 1930s the military began to distinguish between the subversive and the loyal experts but the

---

[24] This was the work Blackett was referring to in the quotation given on p. 214 in ch. 5.

[25] H. G. Wells, *The shape of things to come* (London: J. M. Dent/Everyman, 1993) (first published 1933). For Wells, the Great War 'arose naturally and necessarily from that irregular and disproportionate growth of human appliances as compared with the extension of political and social intelligence' (p. 55). Indeed, the horrors of the Great War resulted from the disproportion between the capabilities of modern technologies, and 'small and antiquated disputes' they were used to settle (p. 56). More generally, 'biological and especially social invention were lagging far behind the practical advances of the exacter, simpler sciences' (p. 36) an argument which Wells, for some reason, saw as something beyond the nineteenth-century 'formula' that the '"spiritual" ... had not kept up with "material" advance' (p. 37).

[26] Wells, *Shape of things to come*, p. 148.   [27] Ibid., p. 149   [28] Ibid., p. 151.

[29] Ibid., p. 154.

subversive ones were also the creative ones.[30] The total quantity of scientific research fell, but it lived on: 'It shifted from the patronage of the millionaire to the patronage of the war lord; it took refuge in Russia, Spain and South America; it betook itself to the aeroplane hangars, to rise again in due time to its present world-predominance.'[31] The world was devastated by war.[32] Transport became difficult, especially on land, but also at sea. From the air, however, 'the sword of a new order reappeared'. From Basra [Iraq] a 'Transport Union' brought together surviving aeroplane and sea transport, and used as its language the basic English of the aviators, and as its currency the Air Dollar. A Modern State Society, made up of qualified fellows, owned the Air and Sea Control, and the Police of the Air and Seaways. In 1978 they decided to put down the re-emerging national government's opposition with a new gas called Pacificin.[33] *Things to Come*, the 1936 film of the book, brings out the themes particularly clearly: here the Airmen's 'Brotherhood of Efficiency' and 'Freemasonry of Science' was called 'Wings over the World' – they had 'an objection to private aeroplanes' and did not 'approve of indepen-dent sovereign states'. They believed in 'Law and Sanity', 'Order and Trade' and 'World Communication'. This was a very British imperial vision of power through trade and transportation, where the aeroplane was a civilian transportation technology.

J. D. Bernal's *Social function of science*, published in 1939, was a brilliant product both of what has been called 'Anglo-Marxism' and the social relations of science movement. It is best known as a manifesto for planned research in a planned economy. It was also a pioneering statistical investi-gation into research activity, and a rich account of modern science, particularly in its British forms. As we have seen (ch. 3, p. 122) Bernal emphasised 'war research' to convince scientists that socialism was the only solution to the problem of war, and through that convince them of the need for socialism. As Bernal put it: 'More than anything else the question of science and war has made scientists look beyond the field of their own enquiries and discoveries to the social uses to which these discoveries are put'.[34] The history of military research was there as an argument for socialism, not as an example of the utility of science for warfare, or indeed of the power of science. For Bernal this awakening of the scientist's awareness was new in the 1930s. While the mobilisation of

---

[30] Ibid., p. 260   [31] Ibid., p. 132
[32] Ibid. See E. M. Earle, 'H. G. Wells, British patriot in search of a world state', in E. M. Earle (ed.), *Nations and nationalism* (New York: Columbia University Press, 1950), pp. 79–121.
[33] Ibid., pp. 147, 271, 279, 281
[34] J. D. Bernal, *The social function of science* (London: Routledge and Kegan Paul, 1939), p. 186.

science in the rearmament of the late 1930s seemed 'new and sinister developments', he maintained that the 'connection of science and war is by no means a new phenomenon; the novelty is in the general recognition that this is not the proper function of science'.[35] Bernal did not see the military (or indeed private business) as enlightened or creative patrons. He condemned the military for not using scientists properly in the Great War, claiming that research had been done wastefully and inefficiently.[36] In *The social function* he complained of the 'traditional stupidity and conservatism of the military authorities' which imposed a 'check on the development of new weapons' and condemned war research for its 'rush, waste, secrecy and overlapping'.[37] On the other hand he argued that modern wars were industrial and technological and thus that the mobilisation of science was essential. However, Bernal had very particular ideas about the most significant linkages. He claimed that Germany had been successful in the Great War not only because 'their scientists were more numerous' but because 'they were in much closer contact with *industry* than were those in the Allied countries' [my emphasis], rather than as one might expect, with their military.[38] Bernal went on to argue that 'the War, and only the War, could bring home to Governments the critical importance of scientific research in the modern *economy*. This was recognised in Britain by the formation of the Department of Scientific and Industrial Research [added emphasis]'.[39] The DSIR was of course primarily concerned with civil and industrial research; Bernal ignored the huge Great War military R&D organisations, the Ministry of Munitions and the Admiralty. In short, what mattered for modern war was for Bernal, as for so many others, was civilian industry, science and technology.

Modulations

Spelt out as above, the arguments of Wells and Bernal will doubtless appear naïve and perhaps irrelevant. And yet their arguments and assumptions were common ones, and they have continued to be important, even in the most specialist historical academic literature on aviation and on the relations of science and war. For example, ideas of world

---

[35] Ibid., p. 165.
[36] Ibid., pp. 171–2, 182. Writing in 1935, he had argued civilian scientists drafted from the outside made the major contributions; the 'military mind is naturally averse to innovations which make war so much nastier for all concerned', he wrote. J. D. Bernal, 'Science and Industry', in Sir Daniel Hall et al., *The frustration of science* (London: Allen and Unwin, 1935), pp. 45–8, 48.
[37] Bernal, *Social function*, p. 182.   [38] Ibid., p. 30.   [39] Ibid., p. 172.

states, and the need to circumscribe national sovereignty, were staples of international relations thinking in the interwar years, and were closely linked to new technologies, particularly the aeroplane.[40] The idea of an international air police was taken up by Philip Noel-Baker and the Next Five Years group, confirming its centrality in liberal internationalist thinking (see ch. 2).[41] It survived into the Second World War with a very particular emphasis on the need for an Anglo-American international air force.[42] After the war the basic argument was transferred from aviation to other technologies, the atomic bomb in particular, where 'international control' was a key theme of discussion. Similarly a whole brand of European integrationist literature demanded supranational organisation to deal with what were taken as international or supranational technologies – nuclear, aviation and space in particular. Indeed,

---

[40] I. F. Clarke, *The tale of the future from the beginning to the present day* (London: Library Association, 1961), is an invaluable list of works published in Britain from which the following titles and comments are taken. B. Newman, *Armoured doves* (1931) 'An international league of scientists uses secret weapons to put an end to war'; M. Arlen, *Man's mortality* (1933) 'Revolt against the world authority in the days when International Aircraft and Airways is the only government'; G. S. Vierck and P. Eldridge, *Prince pax* (1933) 'Capital cities bombed encourage peace'; F. Stuart, *Glory* (1933) 'Love and adventure in the days when Trans-Continental Aero-Routes control the skies of the world'; J. Gloag, *Winter's youth* (1934) 'By 1960 the power of modern weapons has forced peace on the world'; H. Edmonds, *The professor's last experiment* (1935) 'An inventor is able to stop a war'; B. Tunstall, *Eagles restrained* (1936) 'How the International Air Police put an end to a war between Germany and Poland'. Wells even castigates some of the early 1930s' schemes for an air police as insufficiently radical or naïve. *Shape of things to come*, pp. 271–2.

[41] Philip Noel-Baker, 'The international air police', in Philip Noel-Baker et al., *Challenge to death* (London: Constable, 1934), pp. 206–39.

[42] In 1941, and thus before the US entered the war, Stephen King-Hall wanted a joint Anglo-American fleet and air force, a 'Peace Force' as he called it. The fleet would be three times larger than any other, and twice as strong as three other fleets; the air force would be four times larger than any other, and twice as large as two others combined. Stephen King-Hall, *Total victory* (London: Faber and Faber, 1941), p. 217. The idea was that the League had not been able to agree on measures of collective security: 'Unilateral aggression was opposed by collective talk, threats and hesitations and discords. It is essential that unilateral aggression be crushed instantly by unilateral counter-aggression' (p. 219). Bernard Davy wanted a post-war international air force after the war, which while at first Anglo-American, would 'lead the way ultimately to a World Federation of the Air by securing the inclusion of all nations, large and small. As such, it would be the guarantor of a cooperative international system.' Davy, *Air power*, p. 196. In 1948 Spaight looked forward to a world where the air fleets of the United Nations could, alone, defeat aggression. If not the UN, then 'Great armadas of American and British aircraft could do again what they did then [in WWII] and reduce the aggressor to impotence. They would not need the atom bomb to spoil this adventure' (J. M. Spaight, *Air power can disarm* (London: Air League of the British Empire, 1948), p. 168). Spaight believed that atomic warfare should and would be banned; his view was that 'we have seen the first and the last of the atomic bomb' (p. 160). See also p. 163. See also Sir William Beveridge, *The price of peace* (London: Pilot Press, 1945), p. 54.

many such were set up from Euratom to the Centre Européen pour la Recherche Nucléaire (CERN), to ELDO and ESRO: new civilian technology, it was argued, meant the end of the nation state and the end of war too. In some areas of thinking about international relations, like European integration, the liberal political economic language of peace, free trade and efficiency were staples of propaganda and academic comment. As Alan Milward mordantly put it: 'Moribund in European national politics, liberalism was left to explain all in supranational politics'.[43]

That the aeroplane was fundamentally a civilian transportation technology was also a commonplace which would echo down the decades. As Bernard Davy, the London Science Museum's curator and historian of aviation wrote in 1941: 'Transport is, of course, the true function of the aeroplane.'[44] There was a general reluctance to deal with military aviation within the context of studies of aviation in general. A children's book called *Flight to-day* of the mid-1930s had a chapter on the uses of aircraft which discussed mapping, exploration, taking prospectors to outlying areas, the carriage of luxury items, perishable goods and animals, crop dusting, air medical services and aerial archaeology, with only a few references to military use.[45] The British historical drama documentary *The conquest of the air*, which appeared in 1940, also saw the history of aviation as largely civil, and the true function of the aeroplane as a peaceful one. But these were not just stories for impressionable youngsters.[46] The centrality of the civilian aeroplane is confirmed by the common treatment of the military aeroplane as a corrupted, distorted version of the true aeroplane in liberal and leftist discussions of the 1930s.[47] It was

---

[43] Alan Milward, 'Approaching reality: euro-money and the left', *New Left Review* no. 216 (1996), 57
[44] M. J. B. Davy, *Air power and civilization* (London: HMSO, 1941), p. 161.
[45] J. L. Nayler and E. Ower, *Flight to-day* (London: Oxford University Press, 1936), p. 147.
[46] Of course, literature for boys was highly militaristic right through the interwar years, including much literature on aviation. See Michael Paris, *Warrior nation: images of war in British popular culture, 1850–2000* (London: Reaktion Books, 2000). On cultural continuities at a higher level see Jay Winter, *Sites of memory, sites of mourning: the Great War in European cultural history* (Cambridge: Cambridge University Press, 1995).
[47] J. G. Crowther, 'Aviation' in Hall, *Frustration of science*, pp. 40–1. See also M. J. B. Davy, *Interpretive history of flight*, 2nd edn (London: Science Museum, 1948), pp. 130–1 (first published, 1937). The review of the first edition in the *Aeroplane* noted Davy's concern about the aeroplane's destructive potential, but noted, 'it was written before Air Transport brought the Statesmen of Europe together for peace a few weeks ago' (2 November 1938, p. 536). The reviewer was referring to the Munich agreement: it should be noted that the *Aeroplane*, the leading aeronautical journal in Britain, was strongly pro-German, indeed pro-fascist. On this see Edgerton, *England and the aeroplane*. Davy had been in the Royal Flying Corps, and joined the Science Museum in 1920, later becoming deputy director.

questioned, for example, whether the Great War had 'furthered the utility of flight or, by creating an abnormal background, [had] hindered its true development'.[48] Remarkably after the Second World War standard reference sources on the history of twentieth-century technology still treated, and treat, aviation under transportation, and military aviation within the larger context of civilian aviation. Standard histories of the development of aircraft technology remained centred on the development of civil aviation.[49] Histories of industry in general usually treat the aircraft industry as a largely civilian industry, and histories of the aircraft industry see it primarily as a civilian industry.[50] It is hardly surprising then that the official historians of British war production saw the aircraft industry as civilian.[51]

The many studies of aviation and culture in the interwar years produced in recent years by cultural historians also point to the continued influence of the standard interwar model. For these studies have not been interested in, or perhaps even noticed, the significance of the liberal internationalist account of aviation found in Wells and so many other places.[52]

---

[48] Davy, *History of flight*, p. 139.

[49] Charles Gibbs-Smith, *The aeroplane: an historical survey of its origins and development*, (London: HMSO/Science Museum 1960) developed into *Aviation: an historical survey from its origins to the end of World War II* (London: HMSO/Science Museum, 1970), second edition, 1985. Gibbs-Smith worked not at the Science Museum but at the Victoria and Albert. R. Miller and D. Sawers, *The technical development of modern aviation* (London: Routledge, 1968), pp. 58, 257.

[50] See the work of Peter Fearon, for example 'The British airframe industry and the state, 1918–35', *Economic History Review* 27 (1974), 236–51; Correlli Barnett, The *audit of war* (London: Macmillan, 1986); Peter King, *Knights of the air* (London: Constable, 1989) and Keith Hayward, *The British aircraft industry* (Manchester: Manchester University Press, 1989). Much the same has happened in the case of the US aircraft industry. See as an example, Roger Bilstein, *Flight in America 1900–1983: from the Wrights to the astronauts* (Baltimore: Johns Hopkins University Press, 1984).

[51] W. Hornby, *Factories and plant* (London: HMSO, 1958), pp. 30–1.

[52] George L. Mosse, 'War and the appropriation of nature' in V. R. Berghahn and Martin Kitchen (eds.), *Germany in the age of total war: essays in honour of Francis Carsten* (London: Croom Helm, 1981); Robert Wohl, 'Par la voie des airs. L'entrée de l'aviation dans le monde des lettres françaises, 1909–1939', *Le Mouvement Social* no. 145 (1988), 41–64; K. E. Bailes, 'Technology and legitimacy: society, aviation and Stalinism in the 1930s', *Technology and Culture* 17 (1976), 55–81; Valentine Cunningham, *British writers of the thirties* (Oxford: Oxford University Press, 1988), pp. 155–210; Modris Eksteins, *Rites of spring: the Great War and the birth of the modern age* (London: Bantam, 1989), ch. 8; Peter Fritzsche, A *nation of flyers: German aviation and the popular imagination* (Cambridge, MA: Harvard University Press, 1992). Neufeld has pointed out that the German space-flight fad of the late 1920s was not connected to the prevalence of right-wing idealism, but to Weimar nationalism, combined with a general belief in technical progress and the influence of American consumerism. Michael J. Neufeld, 'Weimar culture and futuristic technology: the rocketry and spaceflight fad in Germany, 1923–1933', *Technology and Culture* 31 (1990), 725–52. Studies of aeronautical enthusiasm in the USA also miss the importance of liberal arguments. Joseph Corn sees naive technological messianism

This is perhaps not surprising: historians have been interested in what they (and Wells) take to be deviant ideologies, and not what is taken as the more benign British and US response to the aeroplane.[53] Most such studies thus associate enthusiasm for the aeroplane with anti-liberal streams of thought, with mysticism, heroism, irrationality, nationalism and fascism. The existence of such images is explained partly by the nature of the aeroplane, especially in relation to images of speed and going up and looking down, to nationalistic ideologies, and to a general crisis of modernity, and of particular nations.[54] And yet it is clear from histories of military aviation that is was the British and the Americans that pioneered, and were most committed to, independent air warfare in the interwar years, not the continental enthusiasts for aviation.[55] This has proved a very difficult point to grasp precisely because (as I have suggested above in discussion of Wells), the liberal internationalist world view did incorporate a powerful commitment to using technology to create new world orders. The bombing aeroplane was very strongly associated, in Britain and the USA, with liberal internationalist thinking about world order and trade. Paradoxically, let us note, these accounts

coming out of Protestantism as the typical manifestation of American aeronautical enthusiasm: Joseph Corn, *The winged gospel: America's romance with aviation, 1900–1950* (New York: Oxford University Press, 1983).

[53] The older literature on responses to aviation in interwar Britain stresses a *fear* of air attack as the most important British reaction to the aeroplane, even in the 1920s even though no comparative evidence for this was adduced. See Uri Bialer, *The shadow of the bomber: the fear of air attack and British politics 1932–1939* (London: Royal Historical Society, 1980) and Barry D. Powers, *Strategy without slide-rule: British air strategy, 1914–1939* (London: Croom Helm, 1976). Powers argued that such views were particularly strong there because Britain had long been invulnerable to attack and because Britain, a compact industrial nation, was particularly vulnerable (pp. 155–7, 109). Bialer also suggests that the peculiar British fear was due to a tradition of worrying about technological threats to insularity (*Fear*, pp. 151–11). For a different view see Edgerton, *England and the aeroplane*.

[54] Kern and Cunningham are both explicit in seeing the airplane in terms of looking up and looking down. Stephen Kern, *The culture of time and space, 1880–1918* (Cambridge, MA: Harvard University Press, 1983), pp. 241–7; Cunningham, *British writers of the thirties*, p. 197.

[55] Lewis Mumford saw in strategic bombing a Nazi creator; it was a Nazi idea and a Nazi creation, which infected the United States, creating the post-war military-industrial mega-machine. Lewis Mumford, *The pentagon of power* (New York: Harcourt Brace Jovanonich, 1970), pp. 251–2. But the British bombers of the Second World War, for all their association with the bombing of civilians are not seen in a negative light. There is no British Vonnegut. See Kurt Vonnegut, *Slaughterhouse-five, or the children's crusade* (first published 1966). The very perceptive reader might recall what Freeman Dyson was quoted as saying about Bomber Command in ch. 5. Such analyses are extremely rare. In any case, there is a direct connection to Vonnegut, as explained in the Dyson essay. But see the case of Peter George (1924–1966), a British CND activist who in 1958 published *Red Alert* (under the name Peter Bryant, the book was also known as *Two hours to doom*). This was the basis of the film *Dr Strangelove*. George later published a novelisation of the screenplay, under the title of the film.

denied the military a central role in technical development and industry, even in the case of aviation.

Bernal's and Wells's view of science and technology as essentially civilian was also a commonplace in the interwar years and later. The military, as we have noted, identified science, though not technology, with the civilian world. But the idea that what really mattered in war was not science applied to weapons, but science applied to civilian problems, as suggested by Bernal, was widely shared on the left. Two weeks after the Munich agreement *Nature* published an editorial written by Bernal entitled 'Science and National Service' which argued that the mobilisation of science for war would not be successful 'unless its ultimate aim – the utilisation of science for human welfare in times of peace – is kept steadily in view'; indeed, '[p]reparation ... for war requires not only a much more thorough organisation of science, but also a much closer integration between scientific research and other activities of the community, particularly those of industrial production, agriculture and health.'[56] These themes were fully endorsed in a well-known, anonymously produced, Penguin Special called *Science in war*, which was written and published in a few weeks in 1940 by a group of progressive scientists, including Bernal. Its central argument was for a greatly expanded use of science by the British state and industry. Again attention was firmly fixed on the civil questions: protection of the civil population, care of the wounded and the rational organisation of the armed forces, economy and society. In a book of 144 pages only 12 were devoted to warlike technologies (aeroplanes, tanks and magnetic mines), compared with 38 pages dealing just with food.[57] Even in war science was a fundamentally civil and progressive activity; war was something which science could abolish. All this betokens a profound ambivalence about the military even at a time of national emergency.

[56] Quoted in P. G. Werskey, 'The perennial dilemma of science policy', *Nature* 233 (1971), 532. Werskey established that Bernal was indeed the author of this (as usual) anonymous editorial. Some doctors confronted helping the military much more directly, but with strong reservations: thus a 1938 text reproduced the classic sentiments: 'Medicine, whether as an art or a science ... admits of no national barriers' (p. 101); 'War introduces nationalism into medicine' (p. 102). The problem was that they were 'witnessing today the emergence of a type of nationalism that is more complete and systematic than any the world had yet seen. This type of nationalism is exemplified particularly in Germany ... appears to deny that there is in effect any universal or international truth' (p. 102). H. Joules (ed.), *The doctors' view of war* (London: Allen & Unwin, 1938).

[57] Anon, *Science in War* (Harmondsworth: Penguin, 1940), p. 14. See also letter by W. A. Wooster of the Association of Scientific Workers to the *Manchester Guardian*, 12 January 1939.

Interestingly enough there were few critics of the standard sorts of accounts of science, technology, industry and war. From the interwar years we can pluck out some interesting cases. For example, the reactionary submariner Bernard Acworth disputed the importance of aviation and challenged the propaganda in its favour.[58] Christopher Caudwell, the Marxist theorist who made his living from writing about aviation, dubbed Wells's vision as one of the 'bourgeois dream-Utopias'.[59] But it was perhaps George Orwell who dissected progressivist thinking most clearly. He memorably noted the key oppositions running through Wells's work: 'On the one side science, order, progress, internationalism, aeroplanes, steel, concrete, hygiene: on the other side war, nationalism, religion, monarchy, peasants, Greek professors, poets, horses.'[60] Orwell, by contrast, saw science and technology marching in tune with the barbarisation of the world, rather than being antithetical to these trends. Modern technology increased nationalism and autarchy, modern means of war were inherently tyrannical, he claimed.[61]

Science, war and British society

Just as post-war accounts of aviation followed interwar models so too did accounts, including historical ones, of the relations of science and war. The academic historical literature on British science in the twentieth century in peace and war is also concerned, without this always being obvious, with civil science, even in wartime.[62] It is also overwhelmingly

---

[58] Bernard Acworth, *This bondage* (London: Eyre & Spottiswoode, 1929), p. 215. Acworth makes reference to 'Neon', *The great delusion: a study of aircraft in peace and war* (London: Ernest Benn, 1927). 'Neon' was the pseudonym of a British writer, Marion Witeford Acworth, and the unusual spelling of her name suggests that they are related. See also Acworth's *The navies of today and tomorrow: a study of the naval crisis from within* (London: Eyre & Spottiswoode, 1930).

[59] Christopher Caudwell, *Studies in a dying culture* (London: John Lane, 1938), pp. 88–9.

[60] George Orwell, 'Wells, Hitler and the world state', *Horizon*, August 1941, reprinted in *The collected essays, journalism and letters of George Orwell*, edited by Sonia Orwell and Ian Angus, 4 vols. (Harmondsworth: Penguin, 1970), II, p. 169.

[61] George Orwell, 'As I please', *Tribune* 12 May 1944, reprinted in Orwell, *Collected essays*, III, p. 173. George Orwell, 'You and the atom bomb', *Tribune*, 19 October 1945, in Orwell, *Collected essays*, IV, p. 24. See also Lewis Mumford, 'Authoritarian and democratic technics', *Technology and Culture* 5 (1964), 1–8.

[62] See for example, Peter Alter, *The reluctant patron: science and the state in Britain 1850–1920* (Oxford: Berg, 1987); William McGucken, 'The central organisation of scientific and technical advice in the United Kingdom during the Second world War', *Minerva* 17 (1979), 33–69; William McGucken, *Scientists, society and the state* (Columbus, OH: Ohio State University Press, 1984); P. G. Gummett, *Scientists in Whitehall* (Manchester: Manchester University Press, 1980); J. F. O. MacAllister 'Civil science policy in British industrial reconstruction, 1942–1951', unpublished doctoral thesis, University of Oxford

concerned with the entry of academic civilian scientists into government in war. It has over-emphasised the role of scientists in advisory positions. The support of the armed services for research, especially before 1939, is systematically downplayed.[63] Hilary and Steven Rose's widely read *Science and society*, published in 1969, deserves some attention because of the clarity with which it summed up arguments and evidence current in the post-war years. The chapter on the 'The chemists' war' argued that in 1914, due to its neglect of science by government and industry, Britain was short of key materials. Government belatedly responded, especially through the creation of the DSIR. The rest of the chapter is devoted to the industrial research associations, the DSIR laboratories, the Medical Research Council and the scientists' trade union, the AScW. There is but a fleeting mention of defence research. The chapter on 'The physicists' war' centred on the Second World War, but has some discussion of the history of defence research, which, before 1914, was 'not of a level which could really be dignified by so grandiose a title'.[64] They mention the development of poison gas and the scientific work of the Admiralty in 1914–18, but they say that by the early 1920s, 'the innate conservatism of the military and the genuine hopes of disarmament ... certainly helped inhibit active war research in Britain'.[65] In the 1930s, however, war research picked up, notably in radar. Research in wartime is discussed in terms of operational research, atomic power, the mobilisation of civil scientists and the higher organisation of the scientific effort, with emphasis on the most senior advisory committees. Thus, not only is military research downplayed, but the impact of science on war is dealt with primarily in relation to the recruitment and use of civilian academic scientists an approach taken by most of the literature.[66]

Work on science in the Second World War is particularly dependent on accounts by *some* scientists' and *some* scientific organisations. We have

---

(1986); Tom Wilkie, *British science and politics since 1945* (Cambridge: Basil Blackwell, 1991) and Jon Agar, *Science and spectacle: the work of Jodrell Bank in post-war British culture* (Amsterdam: Harwood Academic Press, 1998).

[63] There was a large literature on science in the navy and army in the Great War published in the early 1970s, which was all concerned with the work of civilian academic scientists in the forces. The impression given was that before the war the support given to science by the forces was negligible. See for example R. M. MacLeod and E. K. Andrews, 'Scientific advice in the war at sea, 1915–1917: the Board of Invention and Research', *Journal of Contemporary History* 6 (1971), 3–40; M. Pattison, 'Scientists, inventors and the military in Britain, 1915–19: the Munitions Invention Department', *Social Studies of Science* 13 (1983), 521–68.

[64] H. Rose and S. Rose, *Science and society* (Harmondsworth: Penguin, 1969), p. 59.

[65] Ibid., p. 60.

[66] Ronald Clark's work concentrated on radar, radio, and operational research, with emphasis given to the work of academic scientists. R. W. Clark, *The rise of the boffins* (London: Phoenix House, 1962).

many biographies of, and memoirs by, academic scientists who contributed to the war effort. Among the most prolific writers and the most written about figures were P. M. S. Blackett, J. D. Bernal, Solly Zuckerman, Henry Tizard and Frederick Lindemasnn.[67] For example, Angus Calder told the story of wartime science in *The people's war* almost entirely in terms of the scientific left (Bernal, Zuckerman, Blackett), all associates of his father, the science journalist Ritchie Calder.[68] All, as we have seen, were essentially in advisory positions usually attached to the armed services themselves, and many were on the left. Indeed, the most investigated issues in twentieth-century British science have been those in which the left took an interest: the scientific left itself, the planning of science and the central organisation of (civil) science, scientific organisations and trade unions, as well as operational research.[69] There has been a particular left-wing argument which has drawn on the history of the scientific

---

[67] On Blackett see, Sir Bernard Lovell, 'Patrick Maynard Stuart Blackett', *Biographical memoirs of Fellows of the Royal Society* (1975); on Bernal see Werskey, *Visible College* and Maurice Goldsmith, *Sage: a life of J. D. Bernal* (London: Hutchinson 1980), Brenda Swann and Felix Aprahamian (eds.), *J. D. Bernal: a life in science and politics* (London: Verso, 1999) on Zuckerman, his own memoirs *From apes to warlords* (London: Collins, 1988) and John Peyton, *Solly Zuckerman: a scientist out of the ordinary* (London: John Murray, 2001). On Tizard and Lindemann see R. W. Clark, *Tizard* (London: Methuen, 1965); Thomas Wilson, *Churchill and the Prof* (London: Cassell, 1995); Earl of Birkenhead, *The Prof in two worlds* (London: Collins, 1961). *Proceedings of the Royal Society* A 342 (1975) – a special issue on the effect of two world wars on British science, written mostly by veterans of the Second World War, is generally a disappointing rehash of well-known stories, but has one or two flashes of insight and/or serious personal reflection. There is, however, a vast, essentially ephemeral literature of short memoirs, obituaries and so on; it was already huge by the late 1960s. For a comprehensive survey of the largely ephemeral literature available in 1967 see Ronald W. Clark, 'Science and technology, 1919–1945' in R. Higham (ed.), *British military history: a guide to sources* (London: Routledge and Kegan Paul, 1972).

[68] Angus Calder, *The people's war* (London: Cape, 1969), ch. 8. In 1945 Ritchie Calder noted 'it is commonly estimated that our total muster of "scientists" is 45,000 ... Of the scientists whose contributions saved us in the war, the elite corps consisted of a few hundreds.' The only names he gave were Bernal, Blackett, Zuckerman and Sir Henry Dale. Ritchie Calder, 'Science and the state', *New Statesman and Nation* 8 October 1945, p. 384.

[69] The key work is Werskey, *Visible college*. See also David Horner, 'Scientists, trade unions and Labour movement policies for science and technology: 1947–1964', 2 vols., unpublished doctoral thesis, Aston University (1986); Greta Jones, *Science, politics and the cold war* (London: Routledge, 1988); Paul Crook, 'Science and war: radical scientists and the Tizard–Cherwell area bombing debate in Britain', *War and Society* 12 (1994), 69–101; Erik P. Rau, 'Technological systems, expertise and policy making: the British origins of operational research' in Michael Allen and Gabrielle Hecht (eds.), *Technologies of power: essays in honor of Thomas Parke Hughes and Agatha Chipley Hughes* (Cambridge, MA: MIT Press, 2001), pp. 215–52, both pieces particularly focusing on the role of the left. See also the ongoing work by Maurice Kirby, *Operational research in war and peace* (London: Imperial College Press, 2003).

left to make general points about science, planning and the state. This sees the left scientists as the driving force for the planning of science in peace and in war, overestimating their position in the highest councils of the state and the military, and seeing their advanced plans for the post-war period rebuffed by the state.[70] The idea that science was planned in the Second World War, as in part at least a consequence of the plans of the left scientists, or that such planning justified their arguments, is very persistent and is exactly analogous to the arguments linking pre-war theories of economic planning with war planning.

More generally it is notable that the historiography of twentieth-century British science has concentrated on the history of national civilian bodies with *science* in their title. Thus we know a great deal about the Department of *Scientific* and Industrial Research.[71] Often overlapping with this is a literature on national cross-disciplinary organizations of scientists, especially the British Science Guild, the National Union of *Scientific* Workers, the Association of *Scientific* Workers, the British Association for the Advancement of *Science*, and on central government committees with science in the title, like the *Scientific* Advisory Council to the War Cabinet, or Advisory Council on *Scientific* Policy. Indeed much of the literature concerned with the above is a history and pre-history of national 'science policy', which means civil science policy.[72] Such bodies, however, were not at all representative of science and technology. Institutions without 'science' in their titles, from armament ministries to universities, have been much more important for science, in peace and in war, than those with it.[73] As a reflection of this the most important accounts of British science are given in books and articles without science in the title.[74] There is one important exception, which

---

[70] Fred Steward and David Wield, 'Science, planning and the state' in Gregor McLennan, David Held and Stuart Hall (eds.), *State and society in contemporary Britain* (Cambridge: Polity, 1984), pp. 176–203.

[71] See Gummett, *Scientists in Whitehall* and Alter, *Reluctant patron* for detailed references to this literature.

[72] See Gummett, *Scientists in Whitehall* for references.

[73] Imperial College of Science and Technology (and now Medicine) has always been part of London University; UMIST, UWIST and the Royal College of Science and Technology (Glasgow) have been part of larger universities.

[74] Thus Michael Sanderson, *The universities and British industry* (London: Routledge and Kegan Paul, 1972) is by far the best general treatment of British university science there is. Two official histories of the 1939–45 war give the best overall account of defence R&D: R. Hughes and J. D. Scott *The administration of war production* (London: HMSO, 1956) and M. M. Postan, D. Hay and J. D. Scott, *The design and development of weapons* (London: HMSO, 1964). Margaret Gowing's official histories on atomic energy are an essential supplement – Margaret Gowing, *Britain and atomic energy, 1939–1945* (London: Macmillan, 1964); *Independence and deterrence: Britain and atomic*

the historians have neglected: the *scientific* civil service, the research corps, as I have called it.

Yet if interwar military R&D has been ignored, accounts of post-war British science have often made the point that British defence R&D was high, and that this was bad for science and for the economy. As we have seen this was a standard argument. However, there was little if any interest in the relations between British science and the military. A renewed radical science movement in the 1970s was only occasionally interested in the military.[75] When it was it examined US rather than British examples.[76]

energy 1945–1952: Vol. I: *Policy making*; vol. II: *Policy execution* (London: Macmillan, 1974). Other works on defence R&D are R. Bud and Philip Gummett (eds.), *Cold War, hot science: applied research in Britain's defence laboratories, 1945–1990* (Amsterdam: Harwood Academic, 1999) and Brian Balmer, *Britain and biological warfare: expert advice and science policy, 1930–1965* (London: Palgrave, 2001). The significance of the military is now noted: see Soraya de Chadarevian, *Designs for life molecular biology after World War II* (Cambridge: Cambridge University Press, 2002). There is now much interesting new work on the Great War: Roy MacLeod, 'The "Arsenal" in the Strand: Australian chemists and the British munitions effort, 1916–19', *Annals of Science* 46 (1989), 45–67; 'The chemists go to war: the mobilisation of civilian chemists and the British war effort, 1914–1918', *Annals of Science* 50 (1993), 455–81; 'Sight and sound on the Western Front: surveyors, scientists and the "battlefield laboratory", 1915–1918', *War and Society* 18 (2000), 23–46 and Andrew Hull, 'Passports to power: a public rationale for expert influence on central government policy-making: British scientists and economists, c 1900–c1925', unpublished doctoral thesis, University of Glasgow (1994); 'Food for thought? The relations between the Royal Society food committees and government, 1915–1919', *Annals of Science* 59 (2002), 263–98.

[75] On the more academic side the emphasis was remarkably biological, with attention concentrated on such issues as IQ, race, class and gender. The military, and specifically the British military, were virtually absent. For example, David Albury and Joseph Schwartz, *Partial progress: the politics of science and technology* (London: Pluto, 1982) a critical textbook on the politics of science and technology barely mentioned the military. See the very interesting essay review by Bill Schwarz, 'Cooling the white heat', *Capital and Class* no. 23 (1983), 168–80. See also Hilary Rose and Steven Rose (eds.), *The radicalisation of science* (London: Macmillan, 1976); Carol Ackroyd, Karen Margolis, Jonathan Rosenhead and Tim Shallice, *The technology of political control* (Harmondsworth: Penguin, 1977); Mike Hales, *Science or society: the politics of the work of scientists* (London: Pan, 1982); David Dickson, *Alternative technology and the politics of technical change* (London: Fontana, 1974); Les Levidow and Bob Young (eds.), *Science, technology and the labour process: Marxist studies*, 2 vols. (London: Conference of Socialist Economists, 1982); Jon Turney (ed.), *Sci-tech report: current issues in science and technology* (London: Pluto, 1984). See also the *Radical Science Journal* and *Science as Culture*.

[76] The British science writer Robin Clarke's *The science of war and peace* (London: Cape, 1971), deals overwhelmingly with US material, but it does note 'two widespread myths about British defence research' – that it is mainly the responsibility of the Ministry of Defence, and that most was done in government laboratories (pp. 180–1). See also Robin Clarke, *We all fall down: the prospect of biological and chemical warfare* (Harmondsworth: Pelican, 1968). Academic writers followed. See Stuart Blume, *Towards a political sociology of science* (New York: Free Press, 1974) which also has lots of US cases on warlike research and few British; Brian Easlea, *Liberation and the aims of science* (Edinburgh: Scottish Academic Press, 1980); chs., 7, 10, 11, deal with the relations of

The US military-scientific complex

It might be thought that the writing out of the military of the story of science and war is a peculiarity of the British literature, but it is not. For the USA, the traditional story is very similar, though much more richly developed. In the last fifteen to twenty years there has been an explosion of excellent work on science and war and on science and the military, focusing on the Second World War and the early cold war. An important aim of this work has been to uncover the role of the military in the post-war reconfiguration of research in the form of 'big science' and the creation of hybrid military-civilian institutions. This work, led by the classic contribution by Paul Forman, has been revelatory, showing that military agencies were overwhelmingly the most important funders of cold war physical sciences and engineering research, and the consequences this had in changing the nature of physics. And yet we need to attend carefully to what these recent works, as well as the earlier ones, take science to be, or at least what science it is they focus attention on. Once one looks it is very clear: it is, once again, academic research; the interest is in what war and the cold war did on campus. This is true of Paul Forman's key article of 1987, which was explicitly concerned with the 5 per cent of the military R&D budget spent in universities, and how this changed academic physics. Similarly the important collection edited by Everett Mendelsohn and others in 1988,[77] and the work of Michael Dennis, and of Bill Leslie, also centres on campus, not the whole military-scientific complex.[78] In the USA the university was much more

science and the military in the United States as does his *Fathering the unthinkable: masculinity, scientists and the arms race* (London: Pluto, 1983). More recently, Donald MacKenzie, *Inventing accuracy: a historical sociology of nuclear missile guidance* (Cambridge, MA: MIT Press, 1990) looks to the USA as well.

[77] The key work on the cold war is P. Forman, 'Behind the quantum electronics: national security as a basis for physical research in the United States, 1940–1960', *Historical Studies in the Physical and Biological Sciences* 18 (1987), 149–229. See also E. Mendelsohn, M. R. Smith and P. Weingart (eds.), *Science, technology and the military*, 2 vols. (Dordrecht: Kluwer, 1988), the journal *Historical Studies in the Physical and Biological Sciences* for the 1990s in particular, and the special issue on science in the cold war, of *Social Studies of Science* 31 (2001), 163–297.

[78] Stuart W. Leslie, *The cold war and American science: the military-industrial-academic complex at MIT and Stanford* (New York: Columbia University Press, 1993), which recognises in the first few pages that most R&D was not academic; Michael Aaron Dennis, '"Our first line of defence": two university laboratories in the postwar American state', *Isis* 85 (1994), 427–55; Larry Owens, 'The counterproductive management of science in the Second World War: Vannevar Bush and the Office of Scientific Research and Development', *Business History Review* 68 (1994), 515–76; Peter Galison, *Image and logic: a material culture of microphysics* (Chicago: Chicago University Press, 1997), ch. 4.

important in military research than in Britain, but it was nevertheless only a small part of the military research effort. Furthermore, it is significant that the emphasis is very much on science rather than the military, which hardly figure in these accounts except as external funders. Only when we understand the centrality of the academic research scientist to these accounts, can we understand why Everett Mendelsohn in a recent survey of 'science, scientists and the military in the twentieth century', which was not restricted to the United States, had to write an account which focused on the wars, including the cold war, on the contribution of academic science, and wrote of the interwar period that 'Not one of the major military powers developed a clear policy for the role of science and technology in the military during either peace or wars of the future. This meant the re-invention on the eve of World War II of most of the agencies linking science and the military.'[79] And we can understand why Andrew Pickering in an article in which he lays out a general argument for 'cyborg history' centred on the transformation wrought by the Second World War, had to say of the interwar USA, and by implication at least of Britain too, that science and the military were 'more or less decoupled'. Quoting the historian Daniel Kevles, his source, he claims that the service 'technical bureaus' were circumscribed by small budgets, inter-service rivalry and 'limited contacts with civilian science'.[80] Here too the military have disappeared. These are not criticisms of Mendelsohn or Pickering, for in reviewing the most recent literature, they accurately reflect its content.

The generality of the emphasis on the civilian is confirmed if we consider the recent historiography of medicine and war. An underlying argument in some recent studies is the rise of a new kind of rationalised society, with medicine as a key agent of rationalisation, a project pushed forward by war.[81] The story of wartime medicine (for example

---

[79] Everett Mendelsohn, 'Science, scientists and the military' in J. Krige and D. Pestre (eds.), *Science in the twentieth century* (London: Harwood Academic, 1997), p. 185.

[80] Andrew Pickering, 'Cyborg history and the World War II regime', *Perspectives on Science* 3 (1995), 8–9.

[81] See R. Cooter, *Surgery and society in peace and war: orthopaedics and the organisation of modern medicine* (London: Macmillan, 1993); R. Cooter, 'War and modern medicine' in W. F. Bynum and R. Porter (eds.), *Companion encyclopaedia of the history of medicine* (London: Routledge, 1994), pp. 1536–73; R. Cooter, S. Sturdy and M. Harrison (eds.), *War, medicine and modernity* (Stroud: Sutton, 1998); M. Harrison, 'The medicalisation of war, the militarisation of medicine', *Social History of Medicine* 9 (1996), 267–76; R. Cooter and S. Sturdy, 'Science, scientific management and the transformation of medicine in Britain, c.1870–1950', *History of Science* 36 (1998), 421–66; M. Harrison, 'Medicine and the management of modern warfare', *History of Science* 34 (1996), 379–410. I am indebted to Nick Webber's MSc thesis 'Battling for the future: a critique of the current historiography relations to war, medicine and modernity', unpublished, University of London (2000).

dealing with civilians, or soldiers far from the front line) is demilitar-
ised, with an emphasis on what is taken to be the key to modern war, the
home, civilian, front. Here too though there is a replication of the emphasis on creative civilians. Again what we have is not the history of military
medicine, but civil medicine at war, and the impact on the civilian world
post-war, written from the perspective of the civilian doctor.

So powerful are these civilian-centred stories that they also profoundly
shape what is written about technology in the international relations
literature. Thus a recent study linking changes in world power to allegedly
significant 'long waves' in innovative and economic activity, takes them to
be defined by civilian technologies of global scope.[82] The new historical
sociology of war, despite being based on a general critique of liberal and
Marxist accounts of war and international relations, has not generated an
analogous critique of the literature on science, technology, industry and
war. With perhaps one exception it has itself continued to rely on older
civilian-oriented accounts of science, technology and industry in modern
war, despite their liberal and Marxist heritage.[83] The exception is Randall
Collins who argues for the state-centredness of at least early modern
technology, pointing to the key role of the state in the generation of
technologies.[84]

---

[82] One such study takes as an index of a recent long wave, the production of civil aircraft, for
example William R. Thompson, *The emergence of global political economy* (London:
Routledge, 2000). See also George Modelski and William R. Thompson, *Leading sectors
and world powers: the co-evolution of global politics and economics* (Columbia, SC: University
of South Carolina Press, 1996).

[83] For example Michael Mann sees three phases of modern militarism: limited war,
1648–1914; citizen warfare, 1914–45; and since 1945, the nuclear age. In the nuclear
age he distinguishes between capitalist and socialist militarism: one is 'spectator sport
militarism' the other 'militarised socialism', but elites share a 'deterrence-science militarism' (Michael Mann, 'The roots and contradictions of modern militarism', *New Left
Review* no. 162 (1987), 35–50). In Martin Shaw's more refined argument we see political
distinctions between types of militarism (Nazi and Soviet) and also different national
experiences. There is also change over time, not least in that there were great technological differences between the two world wars, which affected their character (*Dialectics
of war* (London: Pluto, 1988)).

[84] He has also disputed whether twentieth-century sea power or air power – which as we have
seen promised to transform the nature of war – have in practice abolished geopolitics.
Randall Collins, *Weberian sociological theory* (Cambridge: Cambridge University Press,
1986), ch. 7. See also Van Creveld, *Technology and war*, pp. 312–19; Ralph Schroeder,
'Disenchantment and its discontents: Weberian perspectives on science and technology',
Sociological Review 43 (1995), 227–50 and Archer Jones, *The art of war in the western world*
(Oxford: Oxford University Press, 1989) which focuses very much on a basic continuity in
war, and in types of weapon system, though these are often transformed in power.

Putting the military in

Putting the military into the history of science, technology and industry has proved to be remarkably difficult. There is, however, a literature, largely by US historians of technology, and on the USA which in very particular ways does put the military in to the history of some technology. Its intellectual context is studies of technology, not technology and the military. Indeed it is primarily concerned with military influence on civil technologies, and particularly technologies of production, communication and control. Lewis Mumford, for example, long ago put the military among his 'agents of mechanisation'.[85] Merritt Roe-Smith turned the conventional view of the 'American system of manufactures' of the nineteenth century on its head finding its origins not in civilian Yankee ingenuity applied to arms, but in 'armory practice', a creation of military institutions which demanded interchangeability of parts for military reasons. David Noble has shown that after the Second World War the US military again played a critical role in the development of production technology, in particular in numerically controlled machine tools, but also in such cases as containerisation.[86] Most recently Ken Alder has looked at artillery officers and their schemes for interchangeability in ancient regime and revolutionary France.[87] And one could add other names and other technologies.[88] In recent years it has become common, when studying a military technologies, to take it as a case of technology-in-general. Thus Donald MacKenzie in his study of a key 'technology of power', the gyrocompass, wishes to address general questions around technology by looking at a military one.[89] But what is missing, partly as a result of lack of engagement with the standard arguments about technology and war, is a reconsideration of the question of the military origins of military technology, the issue of what is to be regarded as a military technology, and of the general role of the military in the development of military and civil technologies.

Yet from a different perspective historians of technology have implicitly made a major contribution to putting the military back in by challenging

---

[85] The title of ch. 2 of Mumford, *Technics and Civilisation*.
[86] Merritt Roe Smith (ed.), *Military enterprise and technological change: perspectives on the American experience* (Cambridge, MA: MIT Press, 1985); David Noble, *Forces of production* (New York: Oxford University Press, 1985).
[87] Ken Alder, *Engineering the revolution: arms and enlightenment in France, 1763–1815* (Princeton: Princeton University Press, 1997).
[88] Paul Edwards, *The closed world: computers and the politics of discourse in Cold War America* (Cambridge, MA: MIT Press, 1996); Janet Abbate, *Inventing the internet* (Cambridge, MA: MIT Press, 1999).
[89] MacKenzie, *Inventing accuracy*.

academic-science-centred accounts of military technology. For example, in contrast to the usual academic physics-based accounts of the atomic bomb, Thomas Hughes examines the military and industrial agencies which were central to the project and had long experience of large-scale work.[90] The military engineer Brigadier-General Groves, not the academic physicist Robert Oppenheimer, ran the project, let us recall. The bomb is, as we have noted, the key example of a new technology of war derived from the civilian academic world. Yet it is usefully seen as taking an academic idea into an existing industrial and military structure. The British case is even clearer in this respect. The post-war British atomic bomb was designed from within a well-established arms laboratory, the old Woolwich research department, by a team led by a mathematician (William Penney), and depended to an extraordinary degree on pre-war scientific civil servants and wartime recruits without an academic career behind them.[91] This is less remarkable than it seems, in that the design of atomic bombs was not primarily a matter of atomic physics, but rather of highly complex fluid mechanics.[92] Indeed the theoretical physicists at Los Alamos were not working on particle physics, but on fluid mechanical problems.[93] Fluid dynamics was of huge importance in the state sciences and technologies of the first half of the century, and one of its most important domains of application was aeronautics. Crucially, aircraft were a brilliant example of a specialised arms technology, produced by what was in many ways the most specialised arms business of all. This is not the only case. The 'pre-history' of computing, control and related cybernetic areas points clearly to the vital importance of means of controlling naval gunfire (fire control in naval terminology) to this whole area, which only subsequently became academic and civilian.[94]

---

[90] Thomas Parke Hughes, *American genesis: a century of invention and technological enthusiasm* (New York: Viking, 1989), pp. 381–427 provide an engineer- and industry-centred account of the Manhattan project, which suitably contextualises the particular role of academic scientists.

[91] Notably John Corner, D. T. Lewis, and Monty Finniston. None was a physicist. See Gowing, *Independence and deterrence*, II, pp. 30–1.

[92] And of course the whole project, in Britain as in the USA, was not, as scientists and historians of science, often implied, in writing about the rise of 'big science' without precedent. Hughes, *American genesis*, correctly points out that the project had plenty of industrial precedents, p. 383.

[93] Thus the practice of giving potted pre-histories of the bomb project in terms of the history of particle physics, or quantum theory, or worse, relativity ($E = mc^2$), is very unhelpful in understanding the scientific and technical resources needed for the project.

[94] David A. Mindell, *Between human and machine: feedback, control and computing before cybernetics* (Baltimore: Johns Hopkins University Press, 2002); John Brooks, 'Fire control for British Dreadnoughts: choices in technology and supply', unpublished doctoral thesis, university of London (2001); Sébastien Soubiran, 'De l'utilisation contingente des scientifiques dans les systèmes d'innovations des Marines française et britannique

There are many other areas in which the military dominated, for example radio, which was also profoundly linked to the armed forces and national power, before, during and after the Great War.[95] To these we should add poison gas, meteorology and much else.

Another straw in the wind is a critique, in various forms, of the idea that mass production has been central to war-fighting capacity. Lurking behind the industrialisation and civilianisation of war thesis is a particular account of modern production which stresses the centrality of mass production. In Kaldor's work, and in much of the literature, modern industry is seen as mass production industry. This general account has been challenged for industry as a whole, but also and specifically for the production of armaments.[96] Not surprisingly one historian, Erik Lund, calls not for a 'production' history of strategy, but what he calls an 'industrial' one which takes into account qualitative aspects like design, including fitness for particular purpose, but also the whole infrastructure of training, maintenance and operation of armed forces.[97] Some studies looking at military medicine have taken a very different view of the military.[98]

This suggests not only that we should retain a sense of the specificity of military institutions, of the specificities of warfare and of the specificities of military technology and science. We need to look at, as this book has done, at the development by states and the military of specialised armed services, military knowledges, sciences, technologies and armament industries. Putting the military back in requires an appreciation that specialist sciences and technology and industrial capacity remained central to warfare. It was with good reason that the military maintained such sciences and technologies and industries in peacetime by making special provision for them. In order to develop these technologies of war the forces developed specialised non-academic research and development which employed civilian scientists and engineers. The early formation and scale of these institutions are enough to suggest that it is

entre les deux guerres mondiales. Deux exemples: la conduite du tir des navires et la télémécanique', 3 vols. unpublished doctoral thesis, université de Paris VII– Denis Diderot (2002),

[95] Daniel Headrick, The invisible weapon: telecommunications and international politics, 1851–1945 (New York: Oxford University Press, 1991).

[96] Jonathan Zeitlin, 'Flexibility and mass production at war: aircraft manufacturing in Britain, the United States, and Germany, 1939–1945', Technology and Culture 36 (1995), 46–79.

[97] Erik Lund, 'The industrial history of strategy: reevaluating the wartime record of the British aviation industry in comparative perspective, 1919–1945', Journal of Military History 62 (1998), 75–99.

[98] Ben Shephard, War of nerves (London: Cape, 2000); Emily Mayhew, The reconstruction of warriors: Archibald McIndoe, the Royal Air Force and the Guinea Pig Club (London: Greenhill, 2004).

misleading to see then as derivative of civilian models, let alone academic ones. The armed forces were co-creators of research-centred science and technology, alongside industry and the academy. It could rightly be argued that these suggest that the overall traditional accounts are correct, that is to say that the military increasingly relied on civilian scientists and engineers, and on private industry for innovation, as the model suggests. As we have seen, the military themselves often thought in exactly these terms. But I want to suggest that it is vital to distinguish between the general case of civilian industry, and science and technology, with the employment of civilians in military institutions, and the maintenance by the military of specialised, civilian arms industries. It is the long-standing military-civilian mixed warfare state out of which the key new weapons of war emerged, like radar, the jet-engine, and to some extent, the atomic bomb. Specialist state experts, researchers and specialised industries were critical, and these have been the ones most ignored. The coming together of militarism and technocracy was a complex process, irreducible either to the militarisation of technology, or the technologisation of the military.

Putting the military in is not the same as adding the military to our existing accounts of science and technology and industry, since it will, to a surprising degree, mean restructuring those accounts. To get anything like a reasonable map of the research enterprise we need to go way beyond the civilian-academic world. We need to shed the assumption, surprisingly common among academics, that it is the civilian academic world which produces most of the significant innovations and novelties. Academic research has always been a small part of a much larger research enterprise. In that research enterprise the military have long been very important. Remember that between a third and a half of British 'scientific research' in the interwar years was war research, despite the period being the least militarised epoch in twentieth-century British history. But it is not just a question of bulk of activity. As we have seen there is good evidence to support the view that most significant innovations of the Second World War came out of the warfare state, not the academy.

Accounts of twentieth-century science which say nothing about industrial (and academic) chemistry, and (military) aeronautics and medical research, are never going to address the key historical questions we might have about the relations of science, technology and society. At best they might tell us about something very different – the university and society. But looking at the research enterprise as whole will also force us to rethink our standard image of academic research in the twentieth century. This is centred on a few branches of physics (quantum physics and particle physics) together with a few branches of biology (evolutionary biology and molecular biology). Academic research was obviously much more broadly based and had much closer relations with industry and the military than the classical cases.

The idea of state sciences and technologies is more significant than might appear at first sight. The state dimension matters because states chose to make it matter, through funding and the control of frontiers. It was not a left-over from previous eras, but the result of choices, which led to attempts not merely to take part in but to control technical development, to win in competition with others. States funded large-scale research projects beyond the pockets of individuals or companies not because they could or felt they should for economic reasons, but for the particular purposes of the state. And here of course armaments research was critical. Furthermore there clearly is a connection between, anachronistically speaking, trade policy and research policy.[99] To put it clearly autarky and militarism (both understood as national) have been profoundly important to the research enterprise in the twentieth century, and not just in the supposedly deviant cases of the interwar years – the USSR, Nazi Germany, Italy and Japan. In other words, the very specific role of the state, and the specific nature of its competition with other states has given states particular roles in the promotion of particular sciences and technologies. States funded research before the standard welfare-economic argument for such funding was invented, and for different purposes. Indeed, in a world of competing states the classical welfare-economic argument suggests not state funding but supranational funding.

Many of the most important technologies of the twentieth century, and earlier periods, are the product of a particular state system (and not just say, capitalism, industrialism, imperialism, or even militarism or the 'cold war') – aviation and nuclear power are central cases. The national dimension is critical, even for those technologies often seen as quintessentially international and internationalising technologies like aviation and telecommunications.[100]

I am not arguing here that we should take a national view of twentieth-century science and technology, only that there are vitally important national dimensions. This is not to say that we should accept the vulgar techno-nationalism of so many studies, for example those which focus on

[99] See Lisbet Koerner, *Linnaeus: nature and nation* (Cambridge, MA: Harvard University Press, 1999).
[100] As recent work makes clear the award of Nobel prizes in physics and chemistry before 1950 was powerfully and systematically shaped by local Swedish politics of science and Sweden's international relations. Robert Marc Friedman, *The politics of excellence: behind the Nobel Prize in science* (New York, Times Books, 2001).

'national systems of innovation'. There are important reasons why we should not be nationalistic: scientific researchers have been part and seen themselves as part of a transnational elite, and have been highly concentrated in particular cities, regions and institutions, which do not necessarily bear 'national' qualities. It could be argued too that national and international agencies chose to standardise on a global basis, enforcing uniform ways of doing things; that the value of research scientists to a particularly military, or a particular state, lies in their being part of a global scientific world (as we saw, the civil service scientists expressed this view). Crucially too there is no straightforward relationship between national scientific technological innovation and national economic growth, though this relation is usually treated as a national one, not just for the British case. It does not work at this level because individual states live within a state system and do not make up an isolated universe. As we have seen, even in the case of military technology there was also a good deal of sharing by means fair and foul. The shifting boundary of the national-international dimension is obviously a matter for research, and the relation of the nation state to science and technology is clearly a topic crying out for it.

Anti-histories and historiography from below

It is remarkable that the history of the relations of science and war has been so shaped by the conceptions established by civilian academics. After all academic historians of science and technology have long debunked what they take to be general misunderstanding of science and technology which they associate with scientists and engineers and the general public: particular philosophical accounts, 'technological determinism', or 'Whiggism', or 'the linear model' have all been attacked.[101]

---

[101] For example, in his scintillating preface to *Forces of production* Noble attacks 'technological determinism', which he sees as the product of a culture with 'objectifies' technology, and attributes supremacy to things. The words he uses in association with 'technological determinism' reveals his contempt for the doctrine and his evaluation of its importance: 'disarm ... divert ... depoliticise ... myth ... collective fantasy ... slogans ... American's fantasies ... cultural fetishisation ... ignore and forget ... ideological inheritance ... impoverished version of the Enlightenment ... habit of thought ... ideology'. Noble, however, is clear about the political uses of the idea of technological determinism (Noble, *Forces of production*). Donald MacKenzie, *Inventing accuracy* is also directed at 'technological determinism' which he alleges, dominates popular and academic thinking about technology. But what neither of these studies do, even though they are overtly directed at changing the way we think about technology is to enquire into how we actually think about technology. See my 'Tilting at paper tigers', *British Journal for the History of Science* 26 (1993), 67–75; 'From innovation to use: ten (eclectic) theses on the history of technology', *History and Technology* 16 (1999), 1–26;

But alternative accounts have tended to be built on new local and micro-scopic accounts of science.[102] In moving to micro-studies of science and technology there was a loss of concern with macro-politics, economics and nations, with the result that important questions concerning the scale and scope of the research enterprise have been dealt with in terms not so different from accounts by scientists and engineers.[103] In this context even academic accounts of macro–dimensions have tended to follow the arguments of scientists and engineers, or rather academic scientists and engineers. One can too easily take from the research scientists the view that the world was always being revolutionised from the laboratory.[104] The science and war case discussed above is just one example. But attacking Whig history, technological determinism and so on is hardly the basis for building an alternative history of science, technology and war, or the history of twentieth-century British science and technology. For the problems for the historian of twentieth-century British science have been 'inverted Whig' history and the overblown and misspecified cultural determinism of the declinist histories. The task here has been to understand the nature of these anti-histories, and more generally to understand the way in which science–society relations were thought about. Although crude and wrong in many cases the models the political economic and other models of the place of science in the world are much richer than 'Whig history' or 'technological determinism' imply.[105]

and my 'The "linear model" did not exist: reflections on the history and historiography of science and research in industry in the twentieth century' in Karl Grandin and Nina Wormbs (eds.), *The science–industry nexus: history, policy, implications* (New York: Watson, 2004). The critical posture is becoming somewhat redundant: when was the last 'Whig history' of science or technology worth noting? Who is the last 'technological determinist' of significance?

[102] Steven Shapin, 'Discipline and bounding: the history and sociology of science as seen through the externalism-internalism debate', *History of Science* 20 (1992), 333–69.

[103] For example, in his widely read piece on Stephen Shapin, 'History of science and its sociological reconstructions', *History of Science* 20 (1982), 157–211, specifically and explicitly excludes many topics, but Jan Golinski's 'The theory of practice and the practice of theory: sociological approaches in the history of science', 81 *Isis* (1990), 492–505, makes no references whatever to macro-studies of science, or to the subjects which Shapin explicitly excluded. The micro-emphasis in clear in Mario Biagioli (ed.), *The science studies reader* (London: Routledge, 1999). For recent overviews of the twentieth century see John Krige and Dominique Pestre (eds.), *Science in the twentieth century* (London: Harwood, 1997) and Roger Cooter and John Pickstone (eds.), *Medicine in the twentieth century* (London: Harwood, 2000); and Thomas Söderqvist (ed.), *The historiography of contemporary science and technology* (London: Harwood, 1997).

[104] Edgerton, 'Paper tigers'; 'Innovation to use'.

[105] Some historians of technology are clearly recognising the importance of studying engineer's own ideological accounts in studying the history of technology, as is nicely illustrated in the essays by Hecht and Allen, Todd, Allen and Hecht, in Allen and Hecht, *Technologies of power*.

Embodied in these accounts were interesting, though questionable, assumptions about, for example, the nature of modern war, notably the central one considered here.[106]

We should take non-academic ideas (high or low) seriously in our academic practice as historians, and reflect on the significance of these ideas for our own work. Yet while writing 'history from below' is of course a commonplace, studying low historical writing and low assumptions used in historical work is not. We are prepared to take history from below, but we prefer historiography from above. Indeed the lower the subject, often the higher the theory.[107] It is notable that a standard course on historiography will look at great historians, and high ideas about history (from Marxism to postmodernism, say). Similarly most books on 'ideology' are not studies of ordinary ideas but the study of the high study of ideas.[108] We do not think of there being a historiography from below which deserves critical attention.

Historiography is one of those difficult terms like 'science' which can mean both a something, and the study of that something. Historiography from below should be understood similarly. It refers first to vulgar, non-professional historical writing. The historiography from below in this sense gives us accounts of what the academic elite did not, and does not, find of interest. If the warfare state, and military technology, is written out of academic histories it is everywhere in ephemera, obituaries, TV documentaries, children's books, encyclopaedias, museums and the

---

[106] For a discussion of reasons why straw men are particularly important in studies of science and technology see Edgerton, 'Linear model'.

[107] Even 'postmodernism' in history, while concerned with the nature of our historical knowledge, and in theory eclectic and open to the marginal, has in practice been more concerned with illustrating theory. In surely unconscious parodies of modernism, we are enjoined to believe in a new age (determined by new technology), which demands new theory (which has been advancing toward the present) which is exemplified by particular heroic theorists. We are invited to assent to caricatures of past knowledge, a profoundly unreflexive account of our own knowledge, and to a new one best way, in ways which should be familiar. In other words central to many postmodern writings are vulgar, Whiggish, technologically determinist stage theories of history, with a good dose of great men too. As an example see, Mark Poster, *Cultural history + postmodernity: disciplinary readings and challenges* (New York: Columbia University Press, 1997). While this tone is evident in programmatic statements, it is not generally noted that this reflects a profoundly modernist mode of thought. An exception is Richard Evans in his *In defence of history* (London: Granta, 1997), p. 201–2, where he cites William Reddy noting 'postmodernism's replication of the eternally recurring pretension of absolute originality characteristic of intellectual debate since the Enlightenment' (p. 278, n.15).

[108] Jorge Larrain, *The concept of ideology* (London: Hutchinson, 1979) is explicitly a study of the concept, but Terry Eagleton, *Ideology: and introduction* (London: Verso, 1991) has no wider a focus. But see John B. Thompson, *Ideology and modern culture: critical social theory in the era of mass communication* (Cambridge: Polity, 1990).

lovingly detailed works of amateur historians. While operational research was written about by academic participants, and then by academic historians, writings on guns, ships, aeroplanes and explosives are the work of non-academics. Such work is a partial counter to the anti-histories of British militarism and British technocracy.[109]

But it is only partial because much such historiography from below, in the case of Britain in the twentieth century, takes very particular forms. Historiography from below also refers to the study of the nature of these non-professional historical accounts. This book has examined, for example, the enormously significant historical writings of C. P. Snow and Patrick Blackett, J. D. Bernal and H. G. Wells, and to a lesser extent the military intellectuals.[110] In the course of this study it was argued that these were particular forms of history, anti-histories indeed. But they were very important in historical writing by other intellectuals, and indeed historians. Historiography from below also refers to the methods and arguments used in non-professional historical writings, and in this book the assumptions were found to have strong elements from political economy, the form of militaristic and technocratic critique.

Many different kinds of high history of twentieth-century Britain, and of twentieth-century science–war relations, which while different in scope, subject, theoretical approach, incorporate the arguments and assumptions of the low historiography. To put it more concretely, C. P. Snow's unoriginal observations on science and war have turned out to be more historiographically significant than his implicit philosophy of science or of history. For example, in his historical writings on Britain, Perry Anderson owes as much to declinism as to Marxism. C. P. Snow is,

[109] Raphael Samuel was a pioneer not just of 'history from below' but of 'historiography from below', though he did not use the term, in his generous recovery of the contributions of industrial archaeologists and others to our historical understanding. See in particular his 'Unofficial knowledge' in his *Theatres of memory: past and present in contemporary culture* (London: Verso, 1994). There is a literature on non-elite systematic knowledges, and of the role within some of them of 'democratic epistemologies' as Logie Barrow calls it in his *Independent spirits: spiritualism and English plebeians, 1850–1920* (London: Routledge and Kegan Paul, 1986). Of course there were also profoundly non-democratic alternative knowledges, among them that advocated by Aleister Crowley, whose influence on tank warfare via J. F. C. Fuller is one of the subjects of Patrick Wright, *Tank: the progress of a monstrous war machine* (London: Faber, 2000). J. M. Keynes read and kept up correspondence with, economic thinkers usually dismissed by academics as cranks. See his *General theory of employment of employment, interest and money* (London: Macmillan, 1936), ch. 23 and Robert Skidelsky, *John Maynard Keynes: the economist as saviour, 1920–1937* (London: Macmillan, 1992), pp. 417, 569, *passim*.
[110] For a case see Victor Feske, *From Belloc to Churchill: private scholars, public culture and the crisis of British liberalism, 1900–1939* (Chapel Hill, NC: University of North Carolina Press, 1996).

lamentably, one of the most important historians of twentieth-century Britain. Vulgar historiography matters.

There is another sense of the term historiography from below. It suggests the recovery of marginal, lost, historical interpretations, and of interpretations, which while not necessarily historical, will affect our historical understanding. In the historiography of science in particular, the recovery of forgotten adversaries of positions which became dominant has been a vitally important development: a famous case was Shapin and Schaffer's insertion of Thomas Hobbes into the history of the Royal Society, and their conclusion that a Hobbesian analysis of natural philosophy provided better tools for the historian than that of the victorious Robert Boyle.[111] In accounts of science, technology and war, repeating the standard stories has often been the norm, and alternative voices were rare, and often despairing.[112] In this book a number of such critics, most hardly known, have appeared from many different philosophical, historiographical or sociological positions.[113] At particular times, and in particular contexts, diehard liberals like F. M. Hirst, Eli Halevy and Michael Polanyi; Marxists and near Marxists and ex-Marxists like H. N. Brailsford, J. D. Bernal, John Strachey, R. Palme Dutt, Christopher Caudwell, E. H. Carr, or Franz Borkenau, or the Sheffield Peace Council; reactionaries like the submariner Bernard Acworth and Bruce Truscott, the pseudonym of a Franco-supporting professor of Spanish at Liverpool University; the anarchists of *War Commentary*; and less easily classifiable figures like George Orwell or F. R. Leavis or Joseph Schumpeter, all intervened with discordant voices. Appropriately enough, E. P. Thompson enters this story many times as someone who took a quite distinctive view of Britain from that of others on the left, in which science and political economy were central

---

[111]   S. Shapin and S. Schaffer, *Leviathan and the air pump* (Princeton: Princeton University Press, 1985).

[112]   John Mearsheimer makes the point that the lack of critical engagement with works of Basil Liddell Hart from the 1930s onwards needs to be understood if one wants to understand both Liddell Hart and his reputation (John J. Mearsheimer, *Liddell Hart and the weight of history* (Ithaca, NY: Cornell University Press, 1988)).

[113]   Bloor's 'law of mystification' is suggestive: he argues that powerless critics of society, and powerful, complacent but unthreatened upholders of the status quo, will produce naturalistic accounts; those whose power is low, or the powerful who are threatened will produce mystificatory accounts (David Bloor, *Knowledge and social imagery* (London: Routledge, 1976), p. 69). It is also clear that there have been radically shifting affinities between political positions and views on science or history. For example, in the 1950s 'historicism' was clearly an anti-radical position, specifically, anti-marxist, while in more recent years it has been associated with leftist positions. See Peter Novick, *That noble dream: the 'objectivity question' and the American historical profession* (Cambridge: Cambridge University Press, 1988).

to British culture; in which Britain played a key role in a European cold war, in which there was a powerful British military-industrial 'Thing' which was obscured in declinist analyses from left, centre and right.

Thinking with history about our historical understanding is particularly useful when thinking about the relations of the economy, industry, technology, science and war.[114] Historical understanding brings out a critical feature of the literature, its repetitiveness over time. As the wits rightly have it: the future is what it used to be; we go back to the future; we are now shocked by the old; the future is always the same, it is the past that changes. Once the astonishing sameness becomes manifest, the apparent authoritativeness of the futurism which dominated writings (even historical writings) on these matters becomes a time-worn banality; a repeated plagiarism of the out of date becomes apparent.[115] Historical awareness will alert us to a lack of automatic cumulation of knowledge. It is particularly notable that studies of science and technology in the twentieth century have achieved neither the radical cumulativeness of some branches of knowledge nor the informed debate between interesting positions characteristic of others.[116] As we have seen crucial understandings were lost, for example the non-correlation between R&D and national economic growth. Many students of the relations of science and society have lamented this lack of learning, but these laments have not themselves cumulated. This non-learning about even the recent past of science and technology is central to understanding its history and its historiography. More generally, the historical study of historiography from below will alert us to the problem that historians are not just the product of their own time, but of earlier times too.[117] History is not just an interaction between past and present, but also with the interpretations of both past and present developed in the interim.

It has been a key part of this book to show that some of its more radical conclusions are amply prefigured in forgotten and/or marginalised historical, sociological and economic knowledge about twentieth-century warfare, science and technology, which is not in the academic literature. This

---

[114] Carl E. Schorske, *Thinking with history: explorations in the passage to modernism* (Princeton: Princeton University Press, 1998).

[115] As the Uruguayan poet and engineer Lautréamont observed, progress implies plagiarism, but one should add, not all plagiarism is progressive.

[116] Ironically of course only in terms of one standard model of science; in others, science is always rendering its own past useless to itself.

[117] Thus we need beware in thinking about the application of history to policy that we do not apply to policy, via historians, the analyses derived from previous policy disputes.

book is in a sense at least in part an exploration of what we might have known all along, from which it has emerged, I trust, that what is significant might not be what is most original, strictly speaking.[118] At a recent conference I was struck by the comment made by a historian of ethnic cleansing in the western Ukraine in the Second World War who said that in his detailed researches he was finding out what he/we should have known all along.[119] He did not mean that he had missed existing secondary sources or was unfamiliar with the area – rather that given what we know about central Europe even some of the (extraordinary) details were not surprising. I hope that this book will provoke a similar reaction in readers, and that reflecting on why that might be will itself be rewarding.

---

[118] See Gar Alperovitz, *The decision to use the atomic bomb and the architecture of an American myth* (London: Harpercollins, 1995), and Barton J. Bernstein, 'Seizing the contested terrain of early nuclear history: Stimson, Conant, and their allies explain the decision to use the atomic bomb', *Diplomatic History* 17 (1993), 35–72 and 'Understanding the atomic bomb and the Japanese surrender: missed opportunities, little-known near disasters, and modern memory', *Diplomatic History* 19 (1995), 227–73.

[119] Tim Snyder in response to a question on his paper presented at the 2002 Anglo-American conference at the Institute of Historical Research, London, 4 July 2002. Tim Snyder, 'The causes of Ukrainian-Polish ethnic cleansing 1943', *Past and Present* no. 179 (2003), 197–234.

Appendices

APPENDIX 1

Scientists and engineers born after 1880 who joined the service departments and the aeronautics department of the NPL before or in 1938, and worked as researchers whose career, usually all in state service, resulted in a *Who's who* entry. They are listed by laboratory first joined, and by date of birth. The date where given, is the date of joining, where known.

AIR MINISTRY

RAE
1. Major W. F. Vernon (1882–1975), Imperial College, 1925[1]
2. (Sir) John Buchanan, (1883–1966), Royal Technical College, Glasgow
3. Harold Grinsted (1889–1955), Imperial College engineer, 1912
4. (Sir) Ben Lockspeiser (1891–1990), FRS 1949 Cambridge scientist, 1921
5. (Sir) Harry Garner (1891–1977), Cambridge, 1927
6. R. McKinnon Wood (1892–1967), Cambridge 1914[2]
7. Hermann Glauert (1892–1934) FRS 1931, Cambridge mathematician, 1916
8. A. A. Griffith (1893–1963), FRS 1941, Liverpool engineer
9. S. B. Gates (1893–1973), FRS 1950, Cambridge mathematician
10. E. T. Jones (1897–1981), University of Liverpool, 1923
11. William Perring (1898–1951), Chatham Dockyard and the Royal Naval College, 1925

---

[1] Vernon was dismissed in 1937 after he was convicted, in dubious circumstances, under the Official Secrets Act. He was a Labour MP between 1945 and 1951, and worked with Tom Wintringham at the Osterley Park centre for the Home Guard. See J. E. Mortimer and V. Ellis, *A professional union: the evolution of the Institution of Professional Civil Servants*, pp. 102–3. He was a member of the LCC.

[2] McKinnon Wood was head of the aerodynamics department, 1919–1934. He left for 'political work', standing for Labour unsuccessfully in 1935. He wrote a notable pamphlet on nationalisation of the aircraft industry. After working at the MAP in the war, he was an LCC member from 1946 to 1961, serving a term as chairman.

12. N. E. Rowe (1898–1995), Imperial College engineer, 1924
13. W. R. McGaw, (1900–1974), Glasgow, 1924
14. (Lord Kings Norton), Harold Roxbee-Cox (1902–1997), Imperial, 1931
15. (Sir) Alfred Pugsley (1903–1998), FRS 1952, London, 1926 (date of joining Cardington, RAE 1931)
16. (Sir) George Gardner (1903–1975), Queen's Belfast, engineer, 1926
17. W. J. Richards (1903–1976), Manchester engineer, 1925
18. (Professor) C. H. Smith (1903–1984) Manchester, 1926.
19. Haynes Constant (1904–1968), FRS 1948, Cambridge engineer, 1928
20. Stewart Scott Hall (1905–1961), Imperial College, 1927
21. (Sir) Walter Cawood (1907–1967), Leeds chemist, 1938
22. Lewis Boddington (1907–1994), Wales, 1936
23. Basil Dickins (1908–1996), Imperial College, 1932
24. (Sir) Robert Cockburn (1909–94), London, 1937
25. (Professor) J. B. B. Owen (1910–1998), Wales/Oxford, 1936
26. P. A. Hufton (1911–1974), Manchester, 1934
27. R. H. Weir (1912–1985), Glasgow engineer, 1933
28. William Watt (1912–1985), FRS 1976, Heriot Watt College, chemistry, 1936
29. (Sir) Morien Bedford Morgan (1912–1978), Cambridge engineer, 1935
30. W. H. Stevens (1913–2001), Queen's University, Belfast, 1935
31. (Sir) Arnold Hall (1915–1999), FRS 1953, Cambridge engineer, 1938
32. Handel Davies (1912–2003), Wales, 1936.
33. (Sir) Clifford Cornford (1918–1999), Cambridge, 1938

Other Air Ministry
1. (Sir) David Pye (1886–1960), FRS 1937, Cambridge, 1925
2. (Sir) William Farren (1892–1970), FRS 1945, Cambridge, 1937
3. (Sir) Robert Watt (1892–1973), FRS 1941, 1919
4. A. P. Rowe (1898–1976), Royal Dockyard and Imperial College
5. R. V. Jones (1911–1997), Oxford, 1936
6. E. C. Williams (1915–1980), Birmingham, 1936
7. R. Hanbury-Brown (1916–2002), Imperial, 1936

NPL Aerodynamics only
1. (Sir) R. V. Southwell (1888–1970), FRS 1925, a Cambridge engineer, NPL 1920–25 (excluded from summary table because of short service)

2. Ernest Relf (1888–1970), FRS 1936, Royal Dockyard apprentice, Portsmouth, Imperial College
3. Arthur Fage (1890–1977), FRS 1942, Royal Dockyard apprentice, Portsmouth, Imperial College
4. Robert Frazer (1891–1959), FRS 1946, Cambridge mathematician, 1914
5. W. J. Duncan (1894–1960), FRS 1947, University College London engineer, 1926

ADMIRALTY

1. (Sir) Charles Wright (1887–1975), Toronto, Cambridge
2. (Sir) Frederick Brundrett (1894–1974), Cambridge mathematician, 1919
3. John Buckingham (1894–1982), Cambridge, 1917
4. (Professor) John Coales (1907–), FRS 1970, Cambridge, 1929
5. H. F. Willis (1909–1989), Cambridge, 1938

WAR OFFICE

1. (Sir) Edward Paris (1889–1985), London, 1923
2. Herbert Gough (1890–1965), FRS 1933, London, 1938
3. (Sir) Nelson Johnson (1892–1954), Imperial, 1921
4. (Sir) Alwyn Crow (1894–1965), Cambridge, 1917
5. Edward Perren (1900–1978), Imperial, 1922
6. (Sir) Donald C. Bailey (1901–1985), Sheffield civil engineer, 1928
7. Oliver Sutton (1903–1977), FRS 1949, Aberystwyth/ Oxford, 1929
8. W. A. S. Butement (1904–1990), University College London, 1928
9. (Sir) W. R. Cook (1905–1987), FRS 1962, Bristol mathematician, 1928
10. L. T. D. Williams (1905–1976), Imperial, 1925
11. E. W. Chivers (1906–1979), Queen Mary College, 1928
12. F. E. McGinnety (1907–1973), Armstrong College, Durham, 1929
13. E. E. Haddon (1908–1984), Queen Mary College, 1929
14. W. B. Littler (1908–1999), Manchester PhD, 1933
15. T. F. Watkins (1914–), Wales, 1936
16. Frank Pasquill (1914–1994), FRS 1977, Durham physics, 1937
17. Wallace 'John' Challens (1915–2002), Nottingham/London, 1936

APPENDIX 2

Academics elected to the Royal Society by 1950 who served in government during the Second World War in research and development. Listed by department and date of birth.

AIR MINISTRY/MAP

1. Professor (Sir) G. P. Thomson (1892–1975), FRS 1930, head of the physics department at Imperial College went to the RAE as a principal scientific officer; later scientific adviser, Air Ministry
2. Professor Harry Plaskett (1893–1980), FRS 1936, the Canadian Savillian Professor of Astronomy at Oxford (who held the chair between 1932 and 1960), went to RAE, and on to the Aircraft and Armament Experimental Establishment, to work on navigation
3. Professor W. J. Duncan (1894–1960), FRS 1947, Professor of Aeronautical Engineering at Hull, RAE
4. Professor (Lord) Patrick Blackett (1897–1974), FRS 1933, head of physics department, Manchester, worked in RAE on bombsights, then operational research, spending most of the war in the navy
5. Professor Herbert Skinner (1900–1960), FRS 1942, Bristol University, Telecommunications Research Establishment
6. Professor George Temple (1901–1992), FRS 1943, mathematician King's College London, RAE
7. Sydney Goldstein (1903–1989), FRS 1937, lecturer in mathematics at Cambridge, NPL aerodynamics department
8. Professor E. J. Williams (1903–1945), FRS 1939, Professor of Physics at Aberystwyth; to RAE before going on with Blackett to operational research
9. Philip Dee (1904–1983), FRS 1941, went to RAE in summer 1939, and in early 1941 to Telecommunications Research Establishment
10. Wilfrid Lewis (1908–1987), FRS 1945, Cambridge, Telecommunications Research Establishment
11. F. C. Williams (1911–1977), FRS 1950; Assistant Lecturer in Electrotechnics in Manchester, joined Telecommunications Research Establishment in 1939
12. (Sir) Alan Hodgkin (1914–), FRS 1948 joined Telecommunications Research Establishment in 1940 as a junior scientific officer

MOS

1. Professor (Sir) Paul Fildes (1882–1971), FRS 1934 set up and ran the biological warfare unit at Porton, though he was technically in the MRC
2. (Sir) Charles Lovatt Evans (1884–1968), FRS 1925, Professor of Physiology at UCL, was at Porton the whole war
3. Professor William Garner (1889–1960), FRS 1937, of Bristol University, became superintendent of chemical and explosives research; he was later deputy chief and then, briefly, chief superintendent armament research, ARE

4. Professor William Curtis (1889–1969), FRS 1934, from Armstrong College, Newcastle, became superintendent of applied explosives, ARE

5. Samuel Sugden (1892–1950), FRS 1934, Professor of Chemistry at University College London was at Porton 1939–1942, and was superintendent of explosives research 1942–43 at the Armament Research Department

6. Professor (Sir) John Lennard-Jones (1894–1954), FRS 1933, Professor of Theoretical Chemistry at Cambridge, a Manchester-trained applied mathematician, became chief superintendent of armament research, ARE, in 1943

7. (Sir) Basil Schonland (1896–1972), FRS 1938, was briefly Cockcroft's deputy at the Air Defence Research and Development Establishment, served in uniform; later worked in operational research

8. Professor (Sir) John Cockcroft (1897–1967), FRS 1936, who had joined the MoS as assistant director of scientific research on the outbreak of war, was made chief superintendent of the renamed Air Defence Research and Development Establishment, becoming the army's radar establishment; later bomb project

9. Professor Douglas Hartree (1897–1958), FRS 1932, of Manchester was attached to the Ministry for the whole war

10. Professor John Gulland (1898–1947), FRS 1945, of Nottingham, was an assistant director in chemical research and development 1943–4

11. Professor (Sir) Patrick Linstead (1902–1966), FRS 1940, an Imperial trained organic chemist, left his chair in Harvard to become a deputy director of scientific research in 1942

12. Professor (Sir) Nevill Mott (1905–1996), FRS 1936, of Bristol, who had been in operational research for the army, became superintendent of mathematical research in armaments, ARE

13. (Sir) Charles Sykes (1905–1982), FRS 1943, formerly of Metropolitan-Vickers combined the jobs of superintendent of technical ballistics, ARE with superintendent of metallurgy at NPL (not an academic, but included here because he transferred)

14. Professor Louis Rosenhead (1906–84), FRS 1946, an applied mathematician from Leeds was from 1940 superintendent of the projectile development establishment, Aberporth

15. Professor (Sir) Harry Melville (1908–2000), FRS 1941, Professor of Chemistry at Aberdeen, was at the Radar Research Station 1943–45, having previously been an adviser to Porton

16. Leslie Howarth (1911–2001), FRS 1950, lecturer in mathematics at Cambridge, joined the External Ballistics Department of the Ordnance Board, 1939–42, and was at ARE 1942–5

THE ADMIRALTY

1. Professor Richard Whiddington (1885–1970), FRS 1925, of Liverpool, was DSR's department 1940–42; later went to the MoS
2. Edward Guggenheim (1901–70), FRS 1946, Reader in Chemical Engineering at Imperial. Mine Design Department, later nuclear project in Canada
3. Professor (Sir) Charles Goodeve (1904–1980), FRS 1940, Deparment of Chemistry, University College London; Mine Design Department, Miscellaneous Weapons Development and Assistant (later Deputy) Controller (R&D)
4. (Sir) E. C. Bullard (1907–1980), FRS 1941, Cambridge geophysicist; Mine Design Department, later naval operational research
5. Professor (Sir) Harrie Massey (1908–1983), FRS 1940, of University College London; Admiralty Research Laboratory, then Mine Design Department, later nuclear project

BOMB PROJECT 1940

1. Professor (Sir) James Chadwick (1891–1974), FRS 1927
2. (Sir) Francis Simon (1893–1956), FRS 1941
3. C. F. Powell (1903–1969), FRS 1949
4. Otto Frisch (1904–1979), FRS 1948
5. Norman Feather (1904–1978), FRS 1945 of Cambridge
6. Professor (Sir) Rudolf Peierls (1907–1995), FRS 1945

APPENDIX 3

A selection of FRS-level scientific advisers, including non-academics.
1. (Sir) William Stanier (1876–1965), FRS 1944, War Cabinet Scientific Advisory Council and Ministry of Production
2. Lord Cadman (1877–1941), FRS 1940, former chairman of BP and former Professor of Mining at Birmingham; Chaired MoS Scientific Advisory Committee
3. Sir Frank Smith (1879–1970), FRS 1918, who on retiring from DSIR had become an adviser to BP; chaired MoS Scientific Advisory Committee
4. Professor F. J. M. Stratton (1881–1960), FRS 1947, commanded the Cambridge University Officer Training Corps until 1928; joined the army and was on various missions concerned with signals
5. Sir Henry Tizard (1885–1960), FRS 1926; chairman Aeronautical Research Committee, scientific adviser to Chief of the Air Staff, scientific adviser MAP, etc.

6. Professor (Lord) Frederick Lindemann (1886–1957), FRS 1920, scientific adviser to Winston Churchill
7. Professor (Sir) Ian Heilbron FRS (1886–1959), FRS 1931, MoS, various, and Ministry of Production
8. Professor (Sir) G. I. Taylor (1886–1975), FRS 1919 was a member of no fewer than fifteen committees and subcommittees of the Aeronautical Research Committee as well as many others for other departments: he was the 'universal defence consultant'
9. (Sir) Charles Darwin (1887–1962), FRS 1922 was the first scientific adviser to the War Office
10. Professor (Sir) Bennett Melvill Jones (1887–1975), FRS 1939, pre-war member of the Aeronautical Research Committee, and its chairman from 1943
11. Professor Neville Andrade (1887–1971), FRS 1935, MoS
12. Professor (Sir) Thomas Merton (1888–1969), FRS 1920, Admiralty and Ministry of Production
13. Professor Sydney Chapman (1888–1970), FRS 1919, Deputy Scientific Adviser at the War Office from 1943
14. Professor (Sir) Ralph Fowler (1889–1944), FRS 1925, Admiralty
15. Professor (Sir) Charles Ellis (1895–1989), FRS 1929, Scientific Adviser War Office from 1943
16. Professor (Lord) Patrick Blackett (1897–1974), FRS 1933, Chief Adviser on Operational Research and from 1944 Director of Naval Operational Research, Admiralty
17. (Sir) Gavin de Beer (1899–1972), FRS 1940 joined the (army) general staff as an intelligence and propaganda officer
18. Professor J. D. Bernal (1901–1973), FRS 1937 Ministry of Home Security then scientific adviser to Combined Operations
19. Professor (Lord) Solly Zuckerman (1904–1993), FRS 1943 Ministry of Home Security then scientific adviser Combined Operations; scientific adviser to the airman Sir Arthur Tedder, as Air Commander in Chief Middle East, and Deputy Supreme Commander under Eisenhower
20. Derek Jackson (1906–1982), FRS 1947; joined RAF in July 1940; he flew operations as a navigator with night fighters, and played an important role in operational development of Window, the radar jamming technique

APPENDIX 4

Who ran R&D programmes during the Second World War and after? In addition to the very senior people mentioned in the main text, there were a number of other senior technical civil servants at high levels.

During the war they included (Sir) Alwyn Crow (1894–1965), the director and controller of projectile development, 1940–5 (at the high salary of £1,800), and J. Davidson Pratt (1891–1978) the controller of chemical defence research (unpaid), who had been in chemical warfare from the Great War until 1928.[3] The wartime British atomic bomb programme, carried out, in contrast to most warlike R&D, in universities (and industry) and formally under the DSIR – was not run by an academic but by (Sir) Wallace Akers (1888–1954), FRS 1952, an ICI director, with the title director of tube alloys from 1941–4.[4] Akers was an Oxford chemist who had been with ICI/Brunner Mond since 1911, and had been in charge of ICI Billingham hydrogenation works in the 1930s. The biological warfare programme reported to Lord Hankey, the team developing offensive capacity was led by (Sir) Paul Fildes, and was paid by the Medical Research Council although the work was done at Porton Down.[5]

The wartime research establishments were generally run by, or at least the chief technical people were, scientific civil servants rather than academics, with a few, but very interesting exceptions. The RAE was run for most of the war by W. S. Farren (£1,700), who had been a Cambridge academic until 1937. The great MAP radar laboratory (known as the Bawdsey Research Station, then the Air Ministry Research Establishment and finally the Telecommunications Research Establishment), was run by A. P. Rowe (1898–1976) (£1,400 by 1942) who had long been an Air Ministry technical civil servant. Farren's deputy at Farnborough was William Perring (1898–1951), a civil servant trained at Greenwich, and Rowe's at the Telecommunications Research Establishment was Wilfrid Lewis (1908–1987) FRS 1945, lecturer in physics at Cambridge, and a signals officer in the Cambridge OTC, who had been seconded to radar work from July 1939 as a senior scientific officer. His salary was in the superintendent (£1050–1,250 range). At the end of the war Lewis briefly took over as Chief Superintendent.[6]

[3] James Davidson Pratt was an Aberdeen chemist. After leaving the War Office he became Director of the Association of British Chemical Manufacturers, and other such jobs. I am indebted to Gerrylyn Roberts' online database of British chemists for this information.

[4] Margaret Gowing, *Britain and atomic energy* (London: Macmillan, 1964), pp. 108–11. The atomic scientists had had no say in who should run it.

[5] Fildes became a very powerful advocate for biological warfare, including the building of anthrax bombs in the USA, an order in fact placed. Brian Balmer, *Britain and biological warfare: expert advice and science policy, 1930–1965* (London: Palgrave, 2001).

[6] He went to Australia soon after the war. Sir Bernard Lovell and D. G. Hurst, 'Wilfred Bennett Lewis', *Biographical Memoirs of Fellows of the Royal Society* 34 (1988). 453–509. One of the most useful such memoirs. J. A. Ratcliffe (1902–1987) FRS 1951 of the Cavendish also appears to have been a deputy to Rowe.

The naval laboratories were headed on the technical side by long-term scientific civil servants, on low rates of pay, but remained under naval control. The continuing exception was the Admiralty Research Laboratory, but this was put into the charge of Colonel A. V. Kerrison, the inventor of the Kerrison predictor for anti-aircraft fire who ran both the Admiralty Research Laboratory and the Admiralty Gunnery Establishment that emerged from it.

Much more dramatic were the changes in the old War Office laboratories. All were headed by military officers at the beginning of the war. (Sir) John Cockcroft (1897–1967), FRS 1936 who had joined the MoS from Cambridge as assistant director of scientific research on the outbreak of war, was made chief superintendent of the army's radar establishment, at £1,400.[7] Gough, the director of scientific research, 'wanted to save the establishment from the military'.[8] At the beginning of the war the chemist and Vice-Chancellor of Leeds, Bernard Mouat Jones (1882–1953) was brought in to run Porton Down (£1,400) briefly. The Research Department and the Design Department were run by brigadiers, though the most senior of Research Department scientist was paid £1,400. Under the Oliver Lucas regime both were civilianised.[9] The new heads would have the status and pay of the director of the NPL or the director of Naval Construction. Two prominent outsiders were brought in. Professor (Sir) John Lennard-Jones (1894–1954) FRS 1933, Professor of Theoretical Chemistry at Cambridge, a Manchester-trained applied mathematician, became chief superintendent of armament research in 1943 at £2,000. (Sir) F. E. Smith (1897–1995) FRS 1957 a Cambridge engineer who had spent most of his career at ICI Billingham where he had been chief engineer since 1932 became chief engineer of armament design, he was unpaid.[10] Just after the war he became technical director and later deputy chairman of ICI. These appointments were linked to important changes in staffing, including the bringing in of senior scientists and engineers into both establishments. According to the official historians,

---

[7] T. E. Allibone and G. Hartcup, *Cockcroft and the atom* (Bristol: Adam Hilger, 1984), p. 104. Cockcroft had been asked to head the Admiralty Research Laboratory in 1939.

[8] Ibid., p. 96

[9] As a result of a critical report by (Sir) H. L. Guy, (1887–1956) FRS 1936 a mechanical engineer, long at Metropolitan-Vickers,

[10] J. D. Scott and R. Hughes, *The administration of war production* (London: HMSO, 1955), pp. 275–81; M. M. Postan, D. Hay and J. D. Scott, *Design and development of weapons* (London: HMSO, 1964), pp. 474–78

when one compares the freedom and authority enjoyed by the civilian scientists and technicians ... in the period 1943–45, with the isolation and subjection of prewar days, the change is among the most striking features of the organisation of British war production, and it would be obscuring the issue not to represent the process as essentially one of liberation.[11]

It is surely significant that the Barlow Committee of 1943, which thought that the scientific civil service failed to get a proper share of the best talent,[12] attributed this partly to pay, but also to secrecy restrictions and to 'the control of civilian scientific staff by officers of the Fighting Services'.[13] The report was fully aware that the extent of military control varied a good deal, and that at MAP there was relatively little. Indeed the radar scientists in MAP, given the strength of their position, were able to operate especially informally.[14] As the Barlow Report had suggested in 1943, and the government stated clearly in 1945, there would be no going back to military control of establishments. Centralised recruitment was brought in for the research corps, together with new pay scales and grades, creating what was called the 'scientific civil service'. It has been claimed that the scientific civil service of the post-war years was 'largely Hankey's work'.[15]

After the Second World War, the chief scientists of the MoS ranked higher than the old DSRs. The first two were Cambridge/RAE men, Sir Ben Lockspeiser and (Sir) H. M. Garner. The third, (Sir) Owen Wansbrough Jones, could count as a partial outsider; he was a Cambridge chemist who stayed after war service. In the Ministry of Aviation the posts were held by two men who had joined the Air Ministry in 1938 from non-Oxbridge backgrounds: (Sir) Robert Cockburn[16] and (Sir) Walter Cawood.[17] In the Ministry of Technology the equivalent post of Controller (Research) was held by (Sir) George MacFarlane (1916–) formerly Director of the Royal Radar Establishment (1962–7) who had been in radar since 1939. At the Admiralty, Sir John Carroll (1899–1974), a Cambridge trained academic astronomer who stayed on after war service, served from 1946 to 1964 as Deputy

---

[11] Scott and Hughes, *Administration*, p. 288
[12] *Report of the Barlow Committee on Scientific Staff* (1943), printed in *The Scientific Civil Service* Cmd. 6679 (1945), para. 5.
[13] Ibid., para. 16.   [14] Scott and Hughes, *Administration*, pp. 327–8
[15] S. Roskill, *Hankey: man of secrets*, III (London: Collins, 1974), p. 601.
[16] See *Guardian*, 5 April 1994.
[17] It is unclear from the *DNB* and *Who's Who* where Cawood was doing his research in the 1930s, though the *DNB* notes that he joined the Air Ministry to work on chemical warfare.

Controller (R&D), the most senior R&D officer. The first two post-war chiefs of the Royal Naval Scientific Service were pre-war civil servants, (Sir) Frederick Brundrett and (Sir) William Cook, and were followed by pre-war and wartime recruits. They were H. F. Willis, a Cambridge physicist who had joined in 1938 from the Shirley Institute (otherwise known as the Cotton Industry Research Association), who served from 1954 to 1962, and R. H. Purcell, 1962–8, formerly an academic at Imperial College.

The post-war heads of great state laboratories also tended to be research corps members. In 1960, the seven main military laboratories, other than Farnborough and Harwell, were in the hands of civil servants: of these seven three were trained at Imperial College, and one each at UMIST, Cambridge, Manchester and Glasgow. In some cases the directors had spend their whole careers in a particular technical branch: up to 1968, all the chief superintendents of Porton Down had been associated with chemical warfare since the interwar years.[18] Most of the post war directors of Farnborough were civil servants, with long service in the Air Ministry: W. Perring from 1946 to 1951; (Sir) George Gardner between 1955 and 1959; Sir Robert Cockburn between 1964 and 1967, and Sir Morien Morgan, between 1969 and 1972. There were exceptions to this rule, particularly in the nuclear field, but also to an extent in aeronautics. William Penney ran ARE, though primarily concerned with nuclear weapons, and then Aldermaston until 1959. (Sir) Samuel Curran (1912–1998), FRS 1953 joined Aldermaston in 1954.[19] Sir John Cockcroft was succeeded at Harwell by academics, (Sir) Basil Schonland and (Sir) Arthur Vick. Farnborough was run by Professor (Sir) Arnold Hall (1915–2000) FRS 1953, between 1951 and 1955, and Professor (Sir) James Lighthill (1924–1998) FRS 1953 between 1959 and 1964. Thereafter the scientific civil servants took over here as well.

---

[18] The chief superintendents and directors of Porton were A. E. Childs (physical chemist; had joined in early 1920s); 1949 Dr H. M. Barrett, biologist; 1951 S. A. Mumford (joined Porton in 1923); 1956 E. A. Perren ('essentially a research chemist of high calibre' had been at Porton from 1922); 1961 E. E. Haddon (had joined the chemical warfare headquarters staff in 1929); 1968 G. N. Gadsby (previously Deputy Chief Scientist (army), no Porton experience); 1972 T. F. Watkins (had joined in 1936). Extracted from G. B. Carter, *Porton Down: 75 years of chemical and biological research* (London: HMSO, 1992), *passim*.

[19] Lorna Arnold, *Britain and the H-bomb* (London; Palgrave, 2001) pp. 79–80. See p. 80 for other high level recruits in the mid-1950s.

APPENDIX 5

CRANKS AND OTHER UNORTHODOX INVENTORS IN THE
SECOND WORLD WAR

The war threw up technological initiatives of many sorts. Many individual inventors, and doubtless many cranks, still believed that individual invention had a place in modern war. As during the Great War, the public flooded the services with inventions.[20] In November 1940 the director of scientific research at MAP claimed that no fewer than 20,000 submissions had been made to his ministry since the beginning of the war.[21] By July 1941 the MoS claimed to have received 50,000 inventions, 4 per cent of them from members of the armed forces, an average of 1,500 per month. In June 1940, however, there were nearly 7,000, 3,750 during the Battle of Britain, and around 2,750 during the Blitz, falling thereafter. The average appears to have been ten times greater than the number of submissions to the War Office in the pre-war period.[22] Individual invention was far from being a matter of cranks only. Thus in aircraft design the government was committed to the view that the spur of competition between separate private design teams and in effect individual designers was essential to success, despite pressure to set up a national aircraft design centre run by the research corps.

Some military officers were responsible for very notable innovations. Frank Whittle, the British jet-engine inventor, was such a man, indeed perhaps the most important. The extraordinary support given him, contrary to legend, is testimony both to the importance attached to new technology and to the individual inventor.[23] But there were other military inventors who found success, and patronage from the highest levels. Others who approached the authorities with various degrees of success were Great War veterans, including the extraordinary Noel Pemberton Billing (1880–1948), Sir Denis Burney (presumably Sir Dennistoun Burney (1888–1968), second baronet, the inventor of the paravane, and the Great War inventor of the interrupter gear, George Constantinesco). In tanks some of the Great War tank designers had their own tank design project, notably Sir Albert Stern (1878–1966) (Eton, Christ Church,

---

[20] They continued to do so. According to Russell Potts who worked with the Defence Research Committee in the 1960s, 'we still had a steady flow . . . I had to deal with them' (personal communication).

[21] News Chronicle, 11 November 1940.

[22] Manchester Guardian and The Times, 25 July 1941.

[23] See the revisionist account in Andrew Nahum, 'World War to Cold War: formative episodes in the development of the British Aircraft Industry, 1943–1965', unpublished doctoral thesis, University of London (2002), ch. 3.

banker) who was leading a project for the design of very heavy tanks.[24]
The extraordinary Stewart Blacker (1887–1964), a pre-Great War army
officer; who was in the Royal Flying Corps in the war and was a member
of the 1933 Everest flight, had his 'Bombard' produced by ICI as an anti-
tank weapon at the beginning of the war. He was involved in the genesis of
another anti-tank weapon produced by ICI, the PIAT anti-tank gun. The
PIAT, and indirectly the Hedgehog, a derivative of the Bombard, were
brought to working condition by two unorthodox service organisations.
The first was called 'MD1' for 'Ministry of Defence 1' a research outfit
under Major, then Colonel (later Major-General Sir), R. Millis Jefferis
(1899–1963) an army engineer. Of Jefferis a colleague recalled that, 'with
a leathery looking face, a barrel-like torso, and arms that reached nearly to
the ground he looked a bit like a gorilla. But it was at once obvious that he
had a brain like lightning.'[25] MD1 was created first under the War Office
and then the MoS, but outside its normal routines. Having a direct line to
Number ten it was dubbed 'Winston Churchill's Toyshop': it came under
Cherwell's control.[26] Churchill himself recorded that in 1940

in order to secure quick action, free from departmental processes, upon any bright
idea or gadget, I decided to keep under my own hand as Minister of Defence the
experimental establishment formed by Major Jefferis at Whitchurch. While
engaged upon the fluvial mines in 1939 I had had useful contacts with this brilliant
officer, whose ingenious, inventive mind proved, as will be seen, fruitful during
the whole war. Lindemann was in close touch with him and me. I used their brains
and my power.[27]

With the end of the war and having lost its essential wartime patrons it
was swallowed up, and destroyed, by the Armament Design Department.
Although MD1 developed the PIAT, Blacker's 'Bombard' was taken
up from MD1 by the navy's own crazy gang, the 'Wheezers and
Dodgers' the 'Department of Miscellaneous Weapons Development'.
They turned it into the successful Hedgehog multiple depth-charge
thrower. The department was created by Professor Charles Goodeve
of University College London who, it will be recalled, was a reserve
naval officer, and included the aircraft maker (and of course novelist)

---

[24] See the Tizard Papers in the Imperial War Museum.
[25] Colonel R. Stuart Macrae, *Winston Churchill's toyshop* (Kineton: the Roundswood Press, 1971), p. 5. Colonel Macrae was a member from beginning to end. After the war Jefferis went to India, and between 1950 and 1953 was chief superintendent of the Military Engineering Experimental Establishment.
[26] Lord Cherwell took personal control. See Lord Birkenhead, *The Prof in two worlds: the official life of F. A. Lindemann, Viscount Cherwell* (London: Collins, 1961), p. 216.
[27] W. S. Churchill, *The Second World War*. Vol. II: *Their finest hour* (London: Cassell, 1949), pp. 148–9.

Nevil Shute.[28] One of its other projects, the 'Great Panjandrum', a giant rocket powered wheel has been immortalised by repeated television showings of the ridiculous progress of the contraption along a wartime beach, and a recreated version was central to an episode of *Dads' Army*.[29] It appears that the only scientists and inventors mentioned by Churchill in his volumes of war memoirs are Lindemann, R. V. Jones (who had been one of Lindemann's students) and Blacker and Jefferis.

[28] His full name was Nevil Shute Norway.
[29] See Gerard Pawle, *The secret war, 1939–45* (London: Harrap, 1956) is a history by a participant of the department.

Index

A. V. Roe (aircraft manufacturer) 79
academic scientists
  desire for 'scientific general staff' 165–6
  image of self-mobilisation of academic
    science 161–2
  importance of distinguishing between
    different roles of academic scientists
    165–6
  many leave research corps at end
    of war 167
  most remain in universities to teach 161
  over-emphasise significance of
    operational research 204–5
  recruitment to advisory positions and
    operational research 163–5
  recruitment of selected academics to
    research corps 162–3
  remain in state service 167
  role in government in Second World War
    160–6
  on science and the military in interwar
    period 122–4
  see also science
Acworth, Captain Bernard 117, 319, 336
administrative class of the civil service
  admiration of scientific advisers for 184–5
  concentration in Whitehall 187
  First Division Association defends 139
  growth after the Second World War 168
  role in policy making 182
  in Second World War 147
  see also civil service and state servants
    and technocratic critique
Admiralty 73, 79
  highest grades in 186
  permanent secretary on role of
    professional civil servants 182
  senior officials of in Second World War
    150–6
Admiralty Research Laboratory 115, 119,
  125, 126, 130, 131
Aeroplane, The 26

Air League 25, 26
aircraft carriers, interwar 30–1, 33
aircraft industry,
  1945–50 101–3
  1950–5 103
  essentially military 42
  no mass production in 43–5
Albu, Austen MP 203
Alder, Ken 327
Amalgamated Engineering Union and arms
  industry 85
Ambler, Eric 196
  on interwar arms engineers 135
Anderson Committee (1923) on
  professional civil servants 138–9
Anderson, Perry 3
  declinism of 225, 295, 302, 335
Anderson, Sir John 71, 109–10, 138, 148,
  149, 155, 169
Angell, Norman 13, 48, 51, 284
  E. H. Carr, relations with 53
  nature of modern war 309–10
  use of force 54–5
anti-history 5, 196, 207, 228, 231,
  299–303, 333
  definition and relation to declinism and
    technocratic critique 191
  examples of 193–4
  significance of 193–4
  C. P. Snow as anti-historian 196, 335–6
appeasement 5, 48–57, 283
Appleton, Sir Edward 216
armament industry, definition of 33, 34, 46,
  306, 316–18
armament industry, after Second World War
  1945–50 101–3
  1955–70 266–9
  increased role of public sector 87–8
  privatisation of arms plants by post war
    Labour government 86–7
armament industry, interwar 33–47
  aircraft and tanks 17–18, 19, 42–5